Introducing Microsoft® Expression® Studio: Using Design, Web, Blend, and Media to Create Professional Digital Content

Greg Holden

Course Technology PTR
A part of Cengage Learning

COURSE TECHNOLOGY
CENGAGE Learning™

Australia • Brazil • Japan • Korea • Mexico • Singapore • Spain • United Kingdom • United States

COURSE TECHNOLOGY
CENGAGE Learning

Introducing Microsoft® Expression® Studio: Using Design, Web, Blend, and Media to Create Professional Digital Content
Greg Holden

Publisher and General Manager, Course Technology PTR: Stacy L. Hiquet

Associate Director of Marketing: Sarah Panella

Manager of Editorial Services: Heather Talbot

Marketing Manager: Mark Hughes

Acquisitions Editor: Megan Belanger

Project Editor: Jenny Davidson

Technical Reviewer: Meryl Evans

PTR Editorial Services Coordinator: Erin Johnson

Copy Editor: Gene Redding

Interior Layout Tech: ICC Macmillan Inc.

Cover Designer: Mike Tanamachi

Indexer: Kevin Broccoli

Proofreader: Sara Gullion

For product information and technology assistance, contact us at
Cengage Learning Customer & Sales Support, 1-800-354-9706

For permission to use material from this text or product, submit all requests online at **cengage.com/permissions**
Further permissions questions can be emailed to
permissionrequest@cengage.com

Microsoft and Expression are registered trademarks of Microsoft Corporation in the United States and/or other countries.

Library of Congress Control Number: 2006904573

ISBN-13: 978-1-59863-156-2

ISBN-10: 1-59863-156-X

Course Technology
25 Thomson Place
Boston, MA 02210
USA

Cengage Learning is a leading provider of customized learning solutions with office locations around the globe, including Singapore, the United Kingdom, Australia, Mexico, Brazil, and Japan. Locate your local office at:
international.cengage.com/region

Cengage Learning products are represented in Canada by Nelson Education, Ltd.

For your lifelong learning solutions, visit **courseptr.com**

Visit our corporate website at **cengage.com**

Printed in the United States of America
2 3 4 5 6 7 11 10 09 08

To my friends at Jewel Heart, for their ongoing support and understanding.

Acknowledgments

The Expression Studio applications are designed to work together to create a good presentation. In the same way, a dedicated group of professionals helped this book to come together. First, I would like to thank my agent at Studio B Productions, Neil Salkind, who worked with Stacy Hiquet at Cengage to get the ball rolling. Jenny Davidson was instrumental in editing and helping to present the content. My assistant Robert Brent contributed much of the content in the section on Expression Media. And thanks to my friend Ann Lindner and my daughters Zosia and Lucy for their ongoing support.

About the Author

Greg Holden has been involved in design and content creation in a wide variety of media. He started out as a reporter for a chain of newspapers based in his hometown near Chicago, where he designed pages and pasted them up the old-fashioned way, with wax and a sharp knife. He helped design recruitment literature and course catalogs for the University of Chicago. He has written books about a variety of computer and Internet-related topics, including the Web design applications Microsoft FrontPage and Macromedia Dreamweaver. He lives in Chicago with his two teenage daughters and assorted birds, fish, and other pets.

Contents

PART II
STANDARDS-BASED DESIGN
WITH EXPRESSION WEB   45

Chapter 3
Formatting Basic Web Site Content   47

Chapter 4
Giving Your Web Site a Look and Feel   83

Chapter 5
Managing Your Site with CSS   127

Chapter 6
Making Your Site Dynamic and Interactive   155

Chapter 7
Publishing and Updating Your Web Site　　　　183

PART III
PROFESSIONAL GRAPHICS WITH
EXPRESSION DESIGN　　　　　　205

Chapter 8
Getting Started with Design　　　　　207

Chapter 9
Creating and Manipulating Images   229

Chapter 10
Working with Text   255

Chapter 11
Gradients, Transformations, and Live Effects   273

Chapter 12
Optimizing Images for Publication   299

PART IV
CREATING USER EXPERIENCES
WITH EXPRESSION BLEND   317

Chapter 13
Introducing Expression Blend   319

Chapter 14
Managing Projects   341

PART V
MANAGING YOUR IMAGE FILES
WITH EXPRESSION MEDIA   429

Chapter 17
Organizing Your Image Files   431

Chapter 18
Editing Images with Expression Media   451

Chapter 19
Creating Presentations with Expression Media   473

PART VI
APPENDICES   491

Appendix A
Other Expression Studio Components   493

Appendix B
Expression Studio Resources on the Web   499

Introduction

The internet is continually becoming more complex in sophistication. To get attention and be credible, your site has to have professional-quality graphics. It needs to be usable and give your visitors an interactive and compelling experience. For professional graphic designers and Web site architects, it's a golden age, because there's so much work to do and the standards are so high.

Those who aren't artists, programmers, or designers are left wondering how to achieve all of those cool effects: how to make our Web sites user-friendly and eye-catching while maintaining Web standards. Microsoft's suite of graphics and design tools, collectively called Expression Studio, provides a terrific option for anyone who wants to create high-quality graphics, Web presentations, or user interfaces.

The Studio applications have been well received in the design and development community because of their adherence to standards that enable presentations to be displayed uniformly across many different browsers, applications, and platforms. These include Cascading Style Sheets (CSS) and Extensible Application Markup Language (XAML).

This book serves as an introduction to using Expression Studio to create Web sites, graphics, and presentations, and to organize and edit media files. You'll learn how to use each program individually, and you'll also learn how easy it is to export files and projects from one application to another. It serves as a starting point for using the complete suite of applications.

How This Book Is Organized

I've written this book so that you can read it from cover to cover, beginning with the application that was released first, Expression Web, and moves from one program to the next. But each application is covered in a separate part of the book, which makes it easy to jump to the program in which you're most interested. For example, if you're primarily interested in creating graphic designs for printed publications, you'll want to jump to Chapters 8–12, which focus on Expression Design.

Part I of the book presents you with an overview of the Expression Studio suite. In Chapter 1, you learn about the origins of the applications and the features that make it exceptional. You learn about features of the interface that are common to the four core applications in Chapter 2.

Part II examines Expression Web in detail. Chapter 3 covers the basics: formatting text, adjusting page properties, and beginning to work with the code for the Web pages you create. The fundamental aspects of your Web site's look and feel are covered in Chapter 4: they include background, default colors, hyperlinks, and layout.

Chapter 5 delves into one of Web's most important aspects, and one that makes it exceptional: the depth of its support for Cascading Style Sheets (CSS). After some introductory information about CSS, you learn how to create style sheets or attach them to the Web pages you're assembling. You also learn about the many reports Expression Web can generate that summarize how your site uses CSS. And the program's options for using CSS to position content with precision are covered as well.

Chapter 6 explores Web's tools for making Web sites interactive. These include forms that gather valuable information from your customers or other Web site visitors. You also get an introduction to making database connections so your Web site content can be as current as possible. Once you have assembled your content, you need to get it online, and Web's ability to streamline the publishing and updating process is the subject of Chapter 7.

Part III delves into Microsoft's professional graphic design tool, Expression Design. Design gives you the ability to work with sophisticated vector graphics and to apply filters that create special effects. Design also lets you assemble sophisticated images in multiple layers so you can edit their component parts more easily.

Chapter 8 introduces Design, examining its ability to work with both bitmap and vector images. In Chapter 9, you learn how to create and manipulate images, and how to divide their contents into multiple layers for easier editing. Chapter 10 focuses on working with type, both for content purposes and as graphic elements in their own right.

Chapters 11 and 12 delve into more advanced topics. In Chapter 11 you begin to apply image filters such as blurs as well as paint and photographic effects, to images. In Chapter 12 you explore Design's tools for creating and editing images and drawings: you learn to manage colors, set resolution, and otherwise optimize your image so they'll look the way you want, whether you want them to appear on the Web or in print.

Part IV of the book introduces Expression Studio's application for creating interactive user interfaces and presentations: Expression Blend.

In Chapters 13 and 14, you are introduced to all the things Blend can do to create content for the Web: you can share projects with other members of a workgroup; you can work with Code; you can edit Visual Studio projects. You learn about the Properties panel, which enables you to edit images, and you learn about Blend's ability to work with XAML code.

In Chapter 15, you begin to assemble the components needed to create a Web presentation: text, graphics, audio, and video.

Chapter 16 examines tools for adding interactivity, such as buttons, scroll bars, list boxes, and other controls.

Part V examines how to organize, manage, and edit your media files with Expression Media. In Chapter 17, you create an image catalog, and you learn how to find files and assign keywords to them. In Chapter 18, you try out Media's tools for editing images and changing the properties of any audio or video files included in your catalogs. In Chapter 19, you create interactive presentations such as slide shows and Web Galleries.

Part VI consists of two appendices that add more to your knowledge of Microsoft Expression and its component applications. Appendix A examines other applications that complement the core Studio programs, such as Media Reader and Expression Encoder. In Appendix B, you explore discussion groups, tutorials, and other training materials available online.

Exploring Microsoft Expression Studio

1 Introducing Microsoft Expression Studio

Every organization, from the largest corporation to the tiniest non-profit, needs a Web site, a set of business cards for its employees, and a graphic identity it can use to portray its image to the public. But graphic identities are not created equal. A simple business card that incorporates one of the stock designs that come with your word processing software isn't going to create the same impression as one you draw and lay out from scratch. Similarly, if you want to create a simple home page, you've got lots of options for doing so. You might not even need a special graphics or Web design application, either: Many Web site and blog hosting services let you create your own content in a matter of minutes using no more than a Web browser.

Digital media, including digital photography, audio, video, and the Web, have become central to business communication. Commercial operations in particular need Web sites and graphic identities that reflect their unique corporate identities. For instance, the Web design tools used to streamline the process of creating Web sites often produce pages that have a similar cookie-cutter design. You've probably seen plenty of them in the course of surfing the Web yourself: There's a logo in the top left corner of the home page, a row of buttons stretching horizontally beneath it, a column of links on the left, and Web page content that appears to the right of these links.

The task of customizing the standard designs produced by many Web editing applications typically falls to graphic designers—the same individuals who are responsible for creating newsletters, brochures, and other printed publications for the company. But those designers typically use programs that aren't compatible with the applications used to create Web pages. The industry standards, Adobe Photoshop, Adobe InDesign, and Quark XPress, have a totally different interface and use different programming languages than the software used to assemble Web pages. Not only that, but Web sites need to present dynamic information in an interactive way. Online sales catalogs need to be up to date, and order forms need to be easy to fill out.

3

Many sites use animation to add graphic interest. Such functionality falls to programmers who frequently have to use several different applications to make Web sites functional. Some will write their code by hand; others take advantage of tools like Visual Studio to add the programming that makes Web pages work. The process of creating the sort of sophisticated Web content that consumers demand is increasingly time consuming and complex, given that three different types of programs, each speaking different languages, are being used by three different groups of professionals. How do you get digital media, Web design, graphic design, and programming to work together to create an integrated user experience? Enter Microsoft Expression Studio.

What Is Expression Studio?

Expression Studio isn't a single application. It's an integrated package containing five integrated applications. At the time this was written, you could purchase some (though not all) of the applications separately if you wished. However, one of the programs (Expression Design) could *only* be purchased as part of the entire package. The Studio suite's applications are described in Table 1.1.

At this writing, the Expression Studio package also included Microsoft Visual Studio, the programming tool commonly used to create Web applications. But Visual Studio is not typically considered part of the Expression Studio package, so it's not included in the table.

Table 1.1 Microsoft Expression Studio Component Applications

Application	Original Code Name	What It Does	Available Separately?
Expression Web	Quartz	Web site design tool and HTML/XML editor	Yes
Expression Design	Acrylic	Raster and vector graphics editor	No
Expression Blend	Sparkle	Visual user interface creation tool	Yes (list price $499.95)
Expression Media	N/A	Digital media file manager	
Expression Media Encoder	N/A	Professional encoding tool for digital media	

What Makes a Suite so Sweet? Unless you work or study at an educational institution and are entitled to buy the Academic Edition of Expression Studio, it's a bit of an investment. (At this writing, the package lists for $599.) Plenty of graphics and Web design applications are available separately for a lower price. What's the advantage of buying all of the applications together rather than getting the ones you need most?

For one thing, you do save some money by purchasing the entire suite. At the time this was written, if you purchased Blend all by itself you'd pay barely $100 less than the suite as a whole. For another thing, as mentioned earlier, some components, such as Design, simply aren't available on their own.

When you buy a set of applications, installation is streamlined if the programs all come on the same CD. Even if they aren't on the same disk, you can be reasonably sure that all the applications share the same system requirements. The most important thing, though, is that they all work with each other: They are designed to communicate and share information because they use compatible programming foundations.

Bringing Consistency to Digital Communication

Microsoft Expression Studio is intended to bring consistency and functionality to the design process. The primary components of the Studio package—Web, Design, and Blend—are intended to provide a coordinated environment that has the same sorts of components and underlying programming languages. As you can see from Figures 1.1, 1.2, and 1.3, their three interfaces look and feel roughly the same; that's because they share the same programming environment. But Expression Web has a much lighter color scheme than Design and Blend, which instead use dark colors.

The Expression Studio applications may not look exactly the same, but the important thing for you as a user is that they are designed to share information; files are intended to be moved from one program to another with ease. By using applications that are designed specifically to share content and "talk" to one another at a programming level, production workers can create content more quickly and easily than ever before. The other components—Expression Media and Visual Studio—help create a complete digital production environment through their media management and programming functions. You don't have to be a professional designer or programmer to use these tools, however. This book will help you get started with

Figure 1.1 Expression Web contains task panes positioned around a central editing area.

Expression Studio and start creating your own Web pages, digital designs, user experiences, and media libraries so you can work smarter and collaborate more effectively.

What's the Concept Behind Expression Studio?

Way back in 1995, when the World Wide Web was in its infancy, I wrote one of the first books about creating Web pages. At the time, the only option was to type the HTML one command at a time. Shortly thereafter, the first Web page editors appeared. They gave budding Web publishers the option of clicking buttons and choosing menu options to create content. That basic function remains at the core of all Web page creation today, right up to Expression Web, one of the products you're going to learn about in this book.

Creating graphics for the Web was, in the early days, a primitive affair. Designers could post images online as long as they were saved in Joint Experts Photographic Group (JPEG) format. Or they could craft some line art and save it as Graphics Interchange Format (GIF) files. They couldn't create Web page layouts using

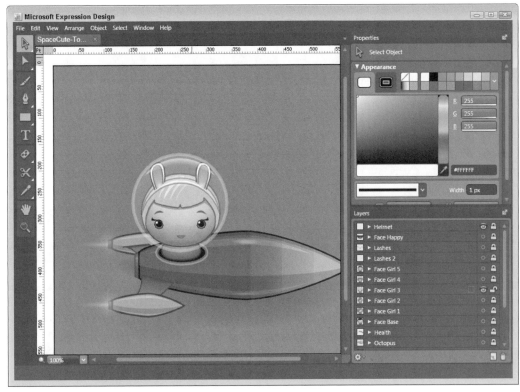

Figure 1.2 Like Web, Expression Design has panels and a workspace, and adds a Toolbox and panels.

sophisticated programs like Quark XPress or complex vector graphics using Adobe Illustrator.

Over the years, programs like Adobe Dreamweaver and Microsoft FrontPage have become increasingly more sophisticated. Web contents grew in complexity and variety as well. Gradually, Web editors were able to handle layout options like tables and frames. In recent years, advanced features like the following have become part of the repertoire of the best Web editors:

> **Layers.** These are containers for text and/or images that can be positioned freely on a Web page and placed partially atop one another for a "layered" effect. You can change the contents of one layer without affecting the other layers.

> **Imagemaps.** These are images containing regions called "hotspots." Hotspots can be rectangular, oval, or round in appearance. Clicking on a hotspot causes the viewer's browser to go to an associated Web page or other object.

Figure 1.3 Expression Blend's work area resembles Design's and adds an Asset Library, among other tools.

Behaviors. These are interactive effects that make Web pages more animated.

Navigation bars. These are rows of clickable buttons that take visitors to various locations, usually within the same Web site.

Forms. All Web editors give designers the capability to create the user input part of a Web page form. FrontPage was virtually unique in that it included small-scale applications called *bots* that processed the form data so it could be read and used.

In recent years, commercial Web sites have sought to present visitors with more than just interactive content and eye-catching layouts. They want to create unique "user experiences" in which the user is drawn in to the site with elements such as animations or clickable objects that cause windows to pop up or design elements to respond in some way. The user is then guided to catalog items or other bits of content with which they are expected to interact. There's been no equivalent of a Web editor for the professional tasked with creating such experiences, however. And the high-quality graphics needed for the top commercial sites can still be created with Adobe Photoshop or other graphics programs, but converting them to a Web page format is a cumbersome process.

Expression Web, the first of the Expression Studio suite, was released in late 2006. Web replaces Microsoft's previous Web editor, Microsoft FrontPage. It's not an upgrade from FrontPage (there will be no upgrades of FrontPage, in fact). Web added support for Cascading Style Sheets and technologies such as XHTML and ASP.NET. The other components in the Expression Studio package are entirely new applications for Microsoft; they aren't based on previous Microsoft products. However, in some cases they are based on other companies' products. For instance, Expression Design is based on a program called Creature House Expression, which Microsoft purchased in 2003.

Note: A Mac OS X version of Expression Design was available early in the product's development cycle, when Design was known as Acrylic. The Mac version was eventually discontinued, and only the version for Windows XP/Windows Vista was available at the time of Expression Studio's release to manufacturing in April 2007.

Considering the Adobe Factor

If you are a Web designer or a graphic designer, you are probably familiar with Adobe Systems' line of products. These include Photoshop, Fireworks, Illustrator, Photoshop Elements, Flash, and much more. Expression Studio is a direct challenge to Adobe's Web design and graphics tools. If you're reading this book, you have either made the decision to purchase Expression Studio already or are thinking about it seriously. I won't go into too much detail as to why Expression Studio is a good choice, other than to say it's perfect if you work in a Windows environment. The following sections will examine features that make Expression Studio unique and that represent a vast improvement over preceding programs, as well as a better choice than competing programs on the market today.

Flash, for instance, is a hugely popular Adobe technology that adds animation and interactivity to Web pages. Flash presentations are becoming more and more common on the Web, and millions of individuals have downloaded Adobe's Flash browser plug-in application so they can view Flash presentations that have been embedded in Web pages. Microsoft hopes to compete directly with Flash through a new technology called Silverlight. Silverlight, which is an integral part of the Expression Studio applications, is Microsoft's way of creating "rich media applications" within Web browsers—in other words, a tool designed to compete directly with Adobe and Flash. One of the most popular applications for Silverlight is the delivery of video over the Web. Silverlight isn't software you download or install; it's technology that's built into Expression Studio applications and that gives you additional functionality. For instance, it can dynamically load content from other applications that support the set of technologies called AJAX.

Note: Silverlight's original code name was Windows Presentation Foundation Everywhere (WPF/E). It's worth making a note of this, as you might see references to WPF in Web pages devoted to Expression Studio or its individual applications.

No Expression Studio User Is an Island When you start using Expression Studio, you have the opportunity to become part of an active user community. Besides the many Web sites Microsoft has published that discuss the Expression line, you can always get useful tips and share your creations with a number of enthusiasts. If you ever need help or want to get feedback on what you've created, you can turn to your fellow users.

Each application has its own set of enthusiasts, and some of the most devoted users have started blogs and Web pages devoted to the topic. Appendix B provides a detailed list of online resources devoted to the Expression Studio applications. Here are just a few examples of the support you can find online:

> **ExpressionBlend.com (http://www.expressionblend.com).** This site contains tutorials, discussions, and XAML code snippets for Blend, among other things.

> **Lynda.com (http://www.lynda.com).** This site, started by well-known designer Lynda Weinman, contains basic instructions on how to use Expression Web, Design, and other Studio components.

> **by-expressions (http://blog.by-expression.com).** An excellent blog that provides news and tips on all components in the Expression suite.

> **Any Expression Designs (http://www.any-expression.com).** A collection of links to tutorials, Web sites, blogs, and other resources that will help you learn Expression Web.

Microsoft, of course, has an extensive set of blogs and sites devoted to Studio and its individual programs. Whether you want to turn to the manufacturer or call on individual users, you'll find lots of support online—and working together with other developers can give you just the inspiration you need to come up with a creative presentation.

Moving Up to Expression Web from FrontPage

Microsoft Expression Web is the only one of the Expression Studio programs to have a direct Microsoft predecessor: Microsoft FrontPage. FrontPage was not universally regarded positively by Web designers. That's because it generated HTML code that no other Web editing application produced and that was not supported by browsers other than Microsoft Internet Explorer. FrontPage used a number of proprietary programming features not supported by all browsers. These included:

FrontPage Server Extensions. These are sets of applications that add functionality to Web pages created with FrontPage, such as forms and discussion groups. In order to make those features work, your Web site needs to be hosted on a server running the extensions.

Web Components. These utilities include news headings and other features that add interactivity to Web pages. Many could only be displayed by Internet Explorer, however. When users tried to view a FrontPage site in Opera, Firefox, or other browsers, pages often appeared blank.

If you are migrating to Expression Web from FrontPage, you'll need to know that both of these features have been deleted. You'll need to re-create the proprietary content using Cascading Style Sheets or other Web standards: languages and applications supported by all browsers. Another big difference is in the way Web page contents are rendered in the editing window before they appear online. FrontPage used Internet Explorer's Trident layout engine. Expression Web, in contrast, uses its own rendering engine, which is able to display CSS and ASP.NET layouts with a high degree of accuracy. And Web generates cleaner code as well.

If you're a former FrontPage user, you'll be happy to know that some visual aspects of the FrontPage interface remain. These include a hierarchical tree showing the folders and files contained in the site that's currently open; a Code pane for viewing HTML or XML code on the current page, a Split pane for viewing code and the design of the current page at the same time, WYSIWYG editing, and features like visual aids, application options, and page editor options. The general look and feel of FrontPage, with task panes grouped around a central editing area, is the same as well.

Note: FrontPage's interface included a Preview tab, which allowed designers to get a quick look at how their page would appear online without actually having to open the file in a Web browser window. The Preview tab is noticeably missing from Expression Web. That's because the built-in rendering engine is so accurate that it's not necessary; what you see displayed in the area is what you'll get online.

Providing Professional Drawing Tools: Expression Design

Microsoft Design is a sophisticated tool for working with the two primary types of computer graphics: raster and vector images. Raster images are made of tiny squares called pixels; each pixel represents a bit of digital information. Vector images are more complex: They consist of segments such as strokes and polygons, each of which has a width and a degree of fill (the degree to which the lines are filled with black or another color). The images you see as you surf Web pages are all raster images. Vectors are primarily used for preparing printed publications, and Design is powerful enough that professional designers can use it to create quality work for print as well as Web graphics.

One of the best features of vector drawing programs is the capability to place text alongside graphics in complex ways with precise positioning. Text can be positioned not just in a straight line but along a curve, around a circle, or in virtually any shape. With a single menu command, you join the text to the path. An example is shown in Figure 1.4.

The premier program in the drawing area is Adobe Illustrator, which has been around since the 1980s. If you are unfamiliar with Illustrator and need a sophisticated vector drawing program that is less expensive than Illustrator, Design represents a good choice. You can't directly compare Illustrator and Design in terms of cost, because Design can't be purchased on its own; it's available only as part of the Expression Studio package. (You'll find out more about Design in Part III of this book.)

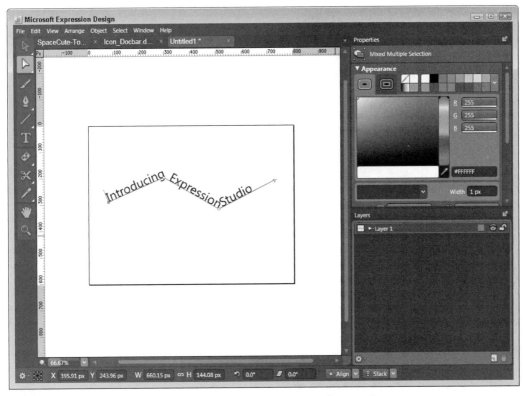

Figure 1.4   Expression Design lets you draw many types of vector images.

Creating Complex Web Experiences: Expression Blend

Blend isn't intended to create simple Web pages or graphics, though it uses both of those elements. Rather, as its name implies, Blend is intended to blend graphics, scripts, and layouts in order to create interactive user experiences. A "user experience" is the entire package of graphic elements, audio or video, and usability elements such as interactive buttons, all of which help you shop, browse, absorb information, or interact with other people.

Think about a Web site you've almost certainly visited at least once: Amazon.com. Amazon has a well-defined and distinctive user experience. It includes the links near the top of the page, the links down the left side of the page, the featured items presented in the center of the page, and video clips that are frequently posted on the home page or other parts of the site. The "1-Click" ordering method used to streamline the purchase process is another part of the user experience. Blend can help you add these sorts of interactive features to your Web presentation, along with professional-quality vector graphics of the sort you create with Expression Design. (You'll find out more about Blend in Part IV of this book.)

Managing Digital Assets: Media and Media Encoder

Media and its accompanying program, Media Encoder, were written using the WPF/ Silverlight language, so they don't really have predecessors as such. They're brand-new products for Microsoft, and they have a different purpose than Web, Design, and Blend. They're not creative tools that let you design content for the Web or print. Rather, they're management tools that are intended to help you keep track of the many different kinds of files a Web site or modern corporation might need for online as well as printed materials.

Media excels at providing the kind of workflow a production office needs: Digital photographs can be imported directly into Media. They can then be cropped, rotated, and edited in Media and exported to other programs in the Expression Studio suite for incorporation into printed or Web-based presentations. Alternatively, Media can present your images itself, through videos, slide shows, and other types of presentations that it can help you assemble.

Streaming audio and video presentations are becoming more widespread in both personal expression and corporate communications. Streaming is the process of continually downloading a file from a Web site so it plays continuously. It's an effective and convenient way of listening to an audio presentation or a song or watching a video clip. Media Encoder enables you to stream audio or video on the Web. It compresses files so they are in an easy-to-handle format, and it lets you produce your own Webcasts as well.

Exploring New Features

Now that you've learned something about what Expression Studio is and how Studio differs from its competitors, to get a really complete overview of the suite you need to learn what's new and what sets it apart from its competitors. Individual chapters in this book will provide you with detailed information about what's new and different in each application; the sections that follow list a few of the more notable features you're likely to use.

Note: Because Expression Studio uses the Silverlight (formerly known as Windows Presentation Foundation) programming environment, it requires .NET Framework 3.0 to run. If you don't have this version of .NET available on your system, you can download it by going to the Microsoft Download Center (http://www.microsoft.com/downloads) and searching for Microsoft .NET Framework 3.0.

Support for Web and Other Standards

As stated earlier, one of the best features of Expression Web is its level of support for Cascading Style Sheets (CSS). CSS allows Web developers to create style sheets that can control the formatting of many Web pages (and Web sites) at once. Because the formatting is contained in a Web document that is separate from the content, it's extremely easy to change the look and feel of an entire Web site and see the changes "ripple" through all the pages in that site. CSS also provides precise control over layout. And because it's a standard—a set of markup instructions that is supported by many Web browsers and other programs—you can be sure that the pages you format with CSS will present a consistent appearance no matter who views it.

Support for other languages extends throughout the Expression Studio suite and distinguishes it from its competitors. Blend, for instance, uses Extensible Application Markup Language (XAML), a set of instructions that designers can use to create Web page designs for developers. There is an exception to this rule: Design does not support a standard computer language called SVG for creating vector graphics. Such standards enable you to create consistent layouts and to transfer files easily from one application to another.

Tip: To find out more about XAML, visit XAML.net, which contains general information about XAML, a How-To page, and links to a wide variety of resources related to it.

Examples of What You Can Do with Studio

The preceding sections described Expression Studio's capabilities and how they can help you and your colleagues work smarter. But such discussions tend to be abstract. Until you get your hands on the product, you don't really know what the process of working with it will be. Not only that, but you don't always know the full extent of what you can accomplish with the software until you have become familiar with it. Subsequent chapters will help familiarize you with Studio. What you do with the product is up to you, but here's a scenario that suggests what you might do with the programs you now have at your disposal.

Suppose you work in a small office—an architectural company with no more than two or three employees. You are responsible for the public image of your company, which involves creating Web pages, managing photos, and getting business cards and brochures printed. Currently, you have a simple Web site that does little more than describe your company and provide visitors with a phone number and e-mail address. You need a better presentation. You install Expression Studio's applications, and you get to work.

Step 1: Assemble and Manage Your Digital Media

You hire a photographer to take photos of your facilities and your special equipment used to create architectural drawings. The photographer also captures some "head shots" of your staff to let prospective customers know more about you. You record an audio greeting on a digital recorder. With your own digital camera, you take a brief video clip showing one of your recent projects; the camera pans from one end of the building to the other to give a complete view of the work.

You now have media sources from three separate input devices: your camera, your tape recorder, and your photographer's equipment. What do you do with all this material? You import it into a digital library that you set up on one of your computers. Using Expression Media, you organize these assets and convert them into file formats you can use either on the Web or in printed publications. For instance, the photos from the photographer might come to you in a format known as TIFF (Tagged Image File Format), which can be used in a variety of publications. The one from your digital recorder is a Windows Media file. The video file from your digital camera is in RAW format. All of these can be converted using Media to formats that can be displayed online, such as JPEG for still images and AVI for video. Finally, you use Media to crop and edit your still images for presentation online.

Step 2: Craft Professional-Quality Graphics

You call in a freelance designer to create the general look and feel of your site using Expression Design. You create a new logo for use on business cards as well as the Web site. You also use Design to select a complementary set of colors you can use online and in your business publications.

Step 3: Create Standards-Compliant Web Sites

You assemble the basic framework of your Web site using Expression Web. You craft the general look and feel of your pages, and you add descriptions of your company and your work as well as biographical sketches of your employees. You import the still images you saved with Expression Media from your digital library. You use

Web's powerful set of Cascading Style Sheet tools to translate your color scheme to your site and give all of your Web pages a consistent graphic identity.

Step 4: Design a User Experience

You put together all of these pieces—images, Web designs, audio, and video—using Expression Blend. Blend enables you to incorporate video and audio into your Web site, turning it into a professional-quality presentation. You are able to show your architectural work using animation, so prospective customers get a detailed look at the quality of your drawings.

Expression Studio is an exciting new addition to the field of design. It encompasses Web design, print design, and interactive user experiences of the sort that are cropping up more and more online. The user communities surrounding Web, Design, Blend, and Media continue to grow. You only need to add your own personal content and give your work your unique twist: Studio has the tools to let you express yourself and enable casual visitors as well as prospective clients and customers to interact. In the next chapter, you'll start exploring the working environments included in the Studio applications so you can learn how to turn your ideas into reality.

2 Working in the Expression Studio Environment

Part of the fun of buying a new car is discovering where everything is and how it works—where you choose the speed of the windshield wipers, tilt the driver's seat to the most comfortable position, and preset the radio buttons so you can flip around among your favorite stations. Suppose you bought a fleet of transport vehicles, each with a slightly different purpose: a pickup truck, a van, a sports car, and a motorcycle. What would be the most logical way to make their acquaintance? You can't learn everything about all four at the same time. You'd probably want to start with an overview of the features that are common to all four vehicles: They all need gas, they all start with a key, they all have a motor and tires that need to be maintained, and so on. Then you can move on to each one's unique features.

Similarly, Expression Studio consists of a group of different applications, each with a slightly different user interface. Although each program has a slightly different look and feel, there are features and basic ways of working that they share. This chapter introduces aspects of the Expression workspace that are common to the four core applications. If you have a general idea of the user interface of all four programs and the main features that are common to them, you'll have an easier time learning the programs. Later chapters will explore fine points of the programs in greater detail.

Exploring Expression Studio's User Interfaces

Web, Blend, Design, and Media all let you work with digital information—computer files of one sort or another. That's the general purpose of the four applications. Within that overarching goal, you have a wealth of features, shortcuts, tools, and tricks for performing specific functions. When discussing the Expression Studio applications as a group, I find it useful to divide them into two categories:

- The three "creative" applications (applications that let you create and edit content): Web, Design, and Blend

- The "organizing" application, Expression Media

The three applications in the first group share features that are at least somewhat similar: They all have a central work area. This work area is surrounded by toolbars, menus, and a variety of other features. In the sections that follow, you'll get a brief overview of how to navigate your way around the four applications individually. Subsequent sections will examine features that are common to the three creative applications. (Expression Media has a more conventional interface and will be described in Chapters 17–19.)

Expression Web

You've probably seen "split screen TV" at one point or another. When you first open up Expression Web and look around the workspace, you'll be reminded of those fancy TV sets. In fact, the screen consists of a central work area surrounded by different containers called *task panes*.

The arrangement in which a central work area is surrounded by separate miniature windows is common to all three of Expression Studio's "creative" applications. In Expression Web, the central area is called either Design View or simply the Editing Window. The task panes, in fact, are only the most obvious supplements to this work area. You also have elements that can help you work with digital files:

- Toolbars at the top of the application. These can be displayed as needed or removed to save space.

- At the very bottom of the window, you have a status bar full of useful information about the Web page you are currently editing.

- Tabs just above Design View that let you switch from one page to another.

- View buttons beneath Design View that let you switch views. Code View lets you see the underlying HTML/XHTML code for a Web page. Split View splits the editing window into two halves: One half shows Design View and the other Code View.

The main features, including a typical selection of task panes, are shown in Figure 2.1.

Note: The term *task pane* is used only in Expression Web. In Blend and Design, the miniature windows grouped around the central artboard are called *panels*, *palettes*, or *property inspectors*.

All of Expression Web's task panes can be relocated onscreen or hidden to give you more space to view the Web page you're assembling. In fact, you don't need to have

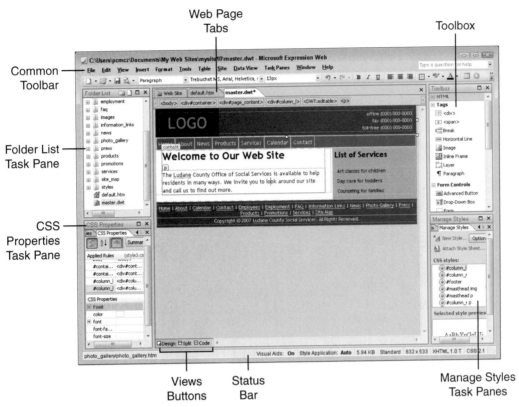

Figure 2.1   Expression Web's central editing area is surrounded by task panes and other tools.

task panes displayed in the application window at all. You can choose to display or hide task panes by selecting or deselecting them from the Task Panes menu. This gives the maximum amount of application window space to the editing window. Figure 2.2 shows the editing window in Split View and without any task panes.

Within the editing window, you have a series of visual aids that help you view specific Web page contents more clearly. You'll get an overview of Web's visual interface elements in the sections that follow and more detailed information in Chapters 3 through 10.

Expression Blend

Expression Blend's interface has been built from the ground up. It isn't really based on any previous application. When you first open the program, you'll immediately notice similarities to Expression Web in terms of the general layout. As you can see

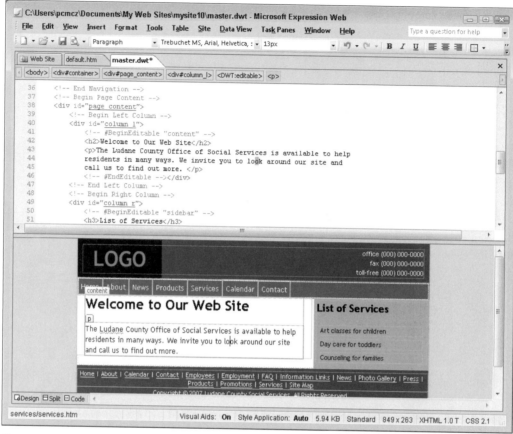

Figure 2.2 Web's application window can be reconfigured so you can work more easily.

from Figure 2.3, the window (which in this case is called the artboard) contains a central editing area, where you do your work. Around it you have two pane regions—one on the left and one on the right—as well as the usual toolbar buttons and menus at the top of the window. What's sure to attract your attention is the sleek and dark color scheme, which is totally different than that of Expression Web.

In Figure 2.3, you'll notice that three of the most important panels (Project, Properties, and Resources) are grouped together in the same space. The separate panels can be brought to the front of the space by clicking on their respective tabs. The ability to group panes or panels into the same space is common to all three creative Expression Studio applications. The palettes in Blend, like the task panes in Web, can also be undocked and moved around the artboard. Click on the icon in the right corner of a palette's title bar to undock it, and click the icon once again to dock it.

Toolbox

Interaction
Panel

Artboard

Project
Panel

Properties
Panel

Resources
Panel

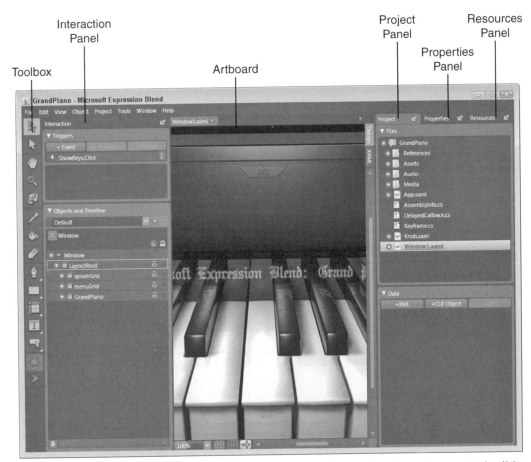

Figure 2.3 Blend's panels and Toolbox help you assemble user interfaces in a central editing area.

Tip: Blend and Design both have darker and sleeker interfaces than Web—at least they do when you first open the program and choose the default interface. Both programs actually give you a choice of two graphic "themes" for the window—Expression Dark and Expression Light. Dark is the default; to switch to a lighter mode, choose Options from the Tools menu, click the Workspace option if necessary, and choose Expression Light from the Theme drop-down list. You can also change the background color behind Blend's artboard: In the Options dialog box, click Artboard, click the Color button under the Background heading, select the radio button next to Color, and choose a color from the selection box that appears.

Expression Design

The Expression Design user interface should be familiar to you if you have used other vector-based graphics programs. Even if you haven't, it should be easy to learn. Like Blend, it has a sleek interface that emphasizes dark colors. And like all the other Studio applications, Design has a central editing area. The area where you draw and edit graphics is referred to in the program's User Guide as either the *artboard* or the *document frame.*

Around the artboard, rulers on the left and the top let you draw with precision; a guide follows your cursor as you move around, indicating exactly where you are in the image (see Figure 2.4). To the right of the artboard, a Properties panel gives you the properties for the current image, and a Layers panel tells you how many layers are contained in the image and lets you switch between them.

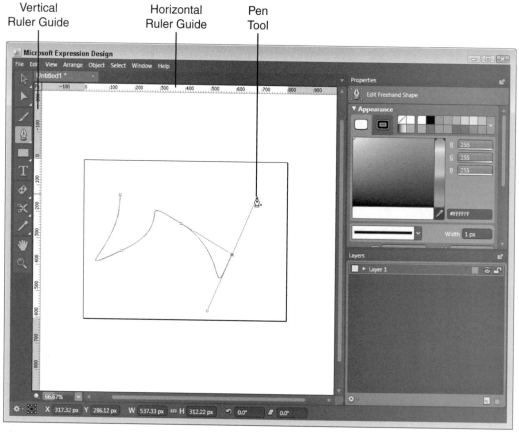

Figure 2.4 Design has a central artboard, a toolbar, and Properties panel.

Each of Design's panels is "docked" by default—in other words, it's located in a specific position in the window that lines up with one or more of the sides. You

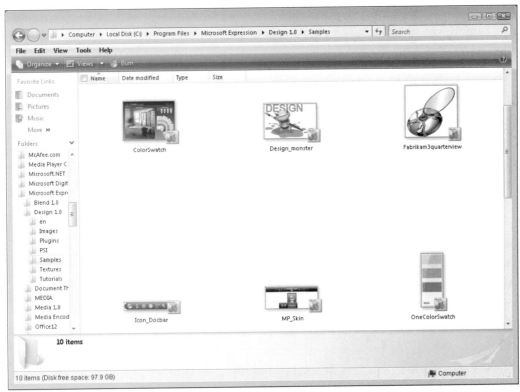

Figure 2.10   You can preview Design's sample images in Windows Explorer to help you choose the one you want.

Figure 2.11   Web lets you change Web page formatting from Tag Properties and other task panes.

(such as onclick and other JavaScript events) that are displayed in Tag Properties can only be accessed in that task pane and not within other parts of the interface, such as the Font dialog box.

Examining Common Elements

Expression Studio's applications are sophisticated, and they let you perform many complex functions. But the tools you use to achieve the effects you want should be familiar to you. They include the menus and toolbars that are common to all applications. Once you learn about these basic, familiar features, you'll be better equipped to delve into the more powerful and complex elements that make the applications special.

Using Toolbars and Menus

At first glance, the Studio applications' menus and toolbars look much the same as you see in every application. Both Blend and Design, for instance, have only a single menu bar, and neither it nor the Toolbox can be moved around the application window.

With Web, however, you gain a level of flexibility that other programs can't match. The menu bar, for instance, can be moved freely around the workspace to match your working style. You can even line it up on the side of the workspace rather than in its conventional position along the top. The single toolbar that appears at the top of the window by default contains only the most common buttons you're likely to use (that's why it's called the Common toolbar, after all). But this is only the tip of the iceberg: Choose Toolbars from the View menu and you are able to choose from no fewer than 11 options. Figure 2.12 shows the menu bar moved to the left side of the workspace, the Common, Formatting, and Standard toolbars stacked at the top, and the Pictures toolbar floating atop the editing window.

Working with Panes, Palettes, and Panels

The terms "task pane," "palette," and "panel" are used in different Studio applications. Expression Web calls them task panes; Blend calls them palettes; Design calls them panels. But they mean virtually the same thing. They are areas within the main application workspace that display specialized information and let you perform specific tasks.

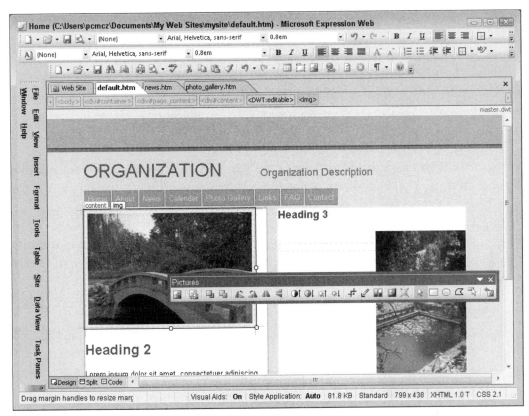

Figure 2.12 Expression Web gives you flexibility in arranging toolbars and the menu bar.

In Design, the panels are grouped to the right of the artboard. By simply pressing the Tab key once, you hide both the panels and the Toolbox and give over the entire application space to the artboard. Press Tab again, and the panels and Toolbox reappear. To undock any one of the panels, click its Dock button in the upper-right corner.

In Blend, the panels appear on either side of the central artboard by default. Click the Dock button to undock any one of the panels to move it around the workspace freely. You can't redock any of the panels in a different part of the window, however. When you click the Dock button on an undocked panel, it snaps back into its previous position.

Web has an extensive selection of task panes, which can be either displayed or hidden by selecting/deselecting them from the Task Panes menu. Each task pane is represented by a tab; you switch from one to another as easily as clicking on its tab. So many task panes are available, in fact, that they can take up more screen real estate than your monitor can provide. To alleviate this problem, Web gives you the ability to combine two or more task panes into a single container.

Choosing the Right Tools

Expression Web has a Toolbox where you can add basic Web page elements like layers and images. The Toolbox is pretty much what you think it would be: a place where you find utilities that let you accomplish common tasks. That sounds dry and boring until you actually add a layer to a Web page or draw a complex line in an image, for instance. With Web, you can interactively drag tools from the Toolbox into Design View (see Figure 2.13). The Toolbox looks and acts like one of Web's task panes, though it isn't formally called by that name.

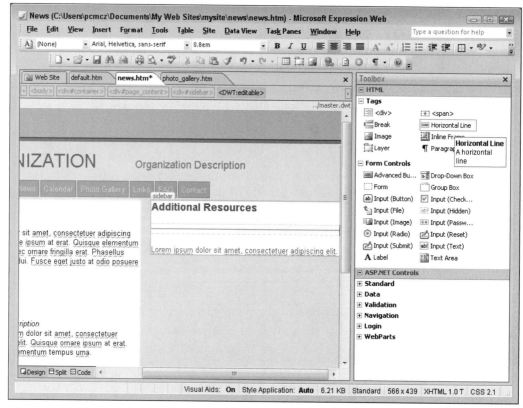

Figure 2.13   You can drag icons from Web's Toolbox into the Web page you're editing.

In Expression Blend, the tools are arranged vertically along the left-hand side of the workspace. From top to bottom, you have:

Selection tools: You have two options. The Selection tool lets you select an object along with its parent container; the Direct Selection tool lets you select only the object, so you can change it without necessarily having to change the container.

Viewing tools: These tools make it easier to inspect what you're working on. You can move your drawing around the artboard with the Pan tool, zoom in with the Zoom tool, or change your point of view with the Camera Orbit tool.

Element creation tools: These are the tools you use to change colors or other aspects of your image: the Eyedropper, the Paint Bucket, and the Brush Transform tool.

Asset creation tools: These are the tools you use to draw shapes and lines as well as other content. They include the Pen and Pencil, the Rectangle, the Grid, the Text Box, and the Button tool.

For the asset creation tools, you are able to right-click and view a submenu of additional tools. At the bottom of the Toolbox you have a special tool: the Asset Library tool. Click it, and a new window pops up that presents you with each of the tools that are part of the Windows Presentation Foundation (see Figure 2.14).

Clicking Show All displays the controls that are currently available on your computer. You can also enter a text string in the search box in the upper-left corner of the dialog box to filter the list down to controls containing that string.

In Design, the set of tools is also arranged on the left side of the window. At the top, you have selection tools; the first lets you select an object, and the second lets you select an individual point on the object so you can manipulate it individually. Tool-tips—small boxes with labels on them—appear when you hover your mouse over any of the tools. That way you won't get an unpleasant surprise when you click on a button (see Figure 2.15).

Other tools in Design's toolbar enable you to draw shapes. The Paintbrush and Pen tools are the most obvious ones. They let you draw basic paths and shapes. Tools that also let you draw or edit paths or shapes include:

- The polygon tool, which allows you to draw polygons.
- The B-Spline tool, which creates smooth panes based on the points you draw.

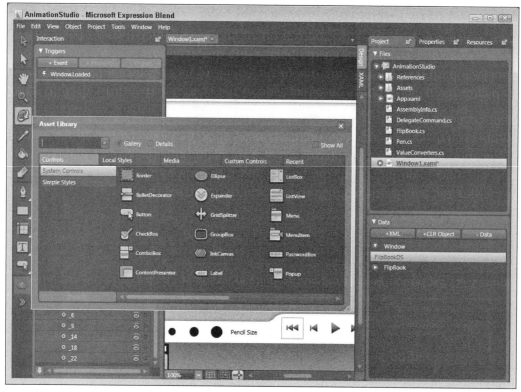

Figure 2.14   The Asset Library helps you add form elements and other contents to a project.

- Shape tools that let you draw rectangles and ellipses; holding down the Shift key lets you constrain them to perfect squares or circles, respectively.

- The Text tool lets you type text strings to accompany your images.

- The Gradient and Fill tools let you control exactly how shapes are filled: They can be filled with gradients that progress in the direction of your choice or fills that consist of solid colors or images.

- The Start Point tool lets you click a point on a stroke so you can designate where a path begins.

- The Scissors tool lets you snip out part of a path, thus splitting it into two separate paths.

- The Eyedropper tool lets you sample a color or fill from an object and copy it to another object.

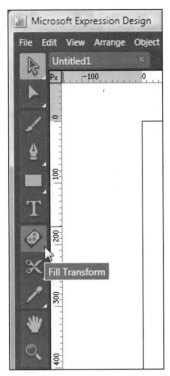

Figure 2.15   Look for Tooltips that tell you what a button's function is before you click it.

Note: Tooltips are available in all of the Expression Studio applications, not just Design. Whenever you're in doubt about a function, hover your mouse pointer over part of the interface, and chances are a Tooltip will pop up with a prompt to let you know its function.

Zooming and Rotating

Blend and Design both have an unusual feature that enables you to zoom in on the workspace itself. In Blend, by choosing Options from the Tools menu and entering a figure greater or less than 100% in the Workspace Zoom box, or by clicking the Zoom menu just beneath the artboard and choosing a value (see Figure 2.16), you can zoom in on the workspace itself. If you zoom out, the task panes actually get bigger so you can see their contents more easily; the artboard shrinks correspondingly. If you zoom in, the task panes shrink, and the artboard grows bigger so you

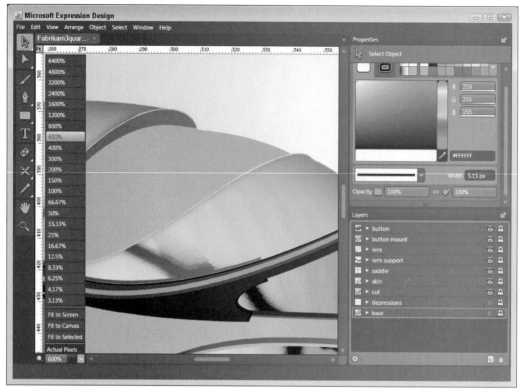

Figure 2.16 You can exert fine-grained control over zooming to view your work more clearly.

can see what you're drawing more clearly. In addition, the pointer turns into a zoom tool so the contents of the artboard become magnified. In Design, you choose Edit > Options > Workspace and enter a figure in Workspace Zoom.

Tip: Blend and Design also provide you with the ability to "pan" or reposition the entire artboard as though it were on a table and you were moving it around with your hand. In Blend, hold down the spacebar; the pointer turns into a hand that you can use to move the entire artboard at once. Hold down the Shift key instead, and you move left and right as you move the pointer. Hold down the Ctrl key, and you zoom in and out. Try it yourself! In Design, click the Pan button (which looks like a Hand icon) in the toolbar, and the mouse pointer turns into the hand icon. You can then use it to move the entire workspace around as much as you want.

In Expression Design, you have a Zoom Index button just beneath the artboard. Click it, and a menu pops up with a wide range of zoom options for the graphic you're editing.

Aligning with the Grid

In most of the Expression applications, you have the ability to snap objects so they align to one another or to a grid that you can either leave invisible or make visible.

In Blend, when you draw two rectangles and drag one close to the other, a line appears to indicate when their edges are in alignment. When you bring one rectangle close to the other, they will snap together so they are close though not actually touching (in fact, they're four pixels apart). There's an enabler key at the bottom of the artboard that turns the "snap to grid" feature on or off. Both this key and the alignment lines are shown in Figure 2.17.

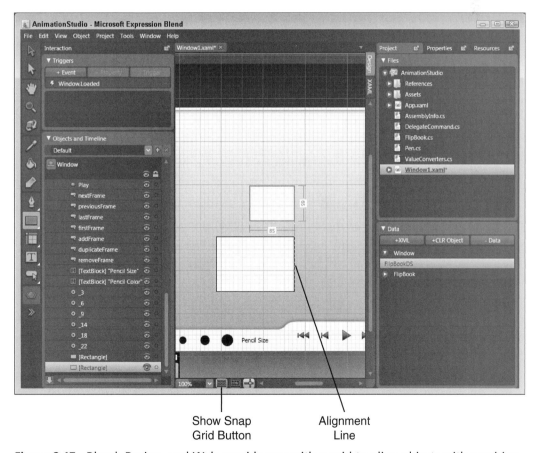

Show Snap
Grid Button

Alignment
Line

Figure 2.17 Blend, Design, and Web provide you with a grid to align objects with precision.

Note: In Blend, the four-pixel distance between objects and other measurements such as an eight-pixel margin between an object and the edge of the artboard are only default values. As you might expect, you can customize them by choosing Tools > Options and indicating different values.

The three creative applications (Web, Blend, and Design) all enable you to display a similar grid so you can align objects and place them with precision.

Working with Objects

The Expression Studio applications are exceptionally interactive when it comes to manipulating, positioning, and grouping objects. Though the exact procedures vary from one program to another, the general procedures are the same. They are described in the sections that follow.

Absolute Positioning

Positioning in Web is extremely easy: You simply drag objects around the screen to position them. As you do so, you generate standards-based CSS. Web lets you overlap elements; you can also specify that an image be exactly 3 pixels from the edge of the page, for instance.

In Blend, you can arrange elements that have been grouped within a container called a Canvas so they conform to absolute x and y coordinates, which are known as Margins.

In Design, the Action Bar enables you to transform a group of objects or a single item. You can specify its x and y values and the width and height as well.

Dragging and Dropping

Blend, Web, and Design all provide you with selection handles for objects so you can manipulate them in different ways. These are handles that appear around the edges and corners of the objects. Exactly what these handles do depends on the application, and the functions will be described in the individual chapters on each program. But it's worth looking into the selection handles in detail; sometimes they let you accomplish sophisticated tasks.

In Blend, for instance, dragging the handles enables you to freely rotate an object you have drawn on the artboard. In Web, dragging some handles lets you enlarge an image; dragging others enables you to add space around it called *padding*.

Grouping and Ungrouping

Grouping is the process of combining two or more objects so they can be handled as a single entity. By grouping, you bring together items that have the same characteristics or that serve the same purpose: a set of links or a series of photos of the same subject, for instance. In Blend, you group objects by placing them in a Layout panel. A Layout panel is a container that helps you arrange and position complex elements on a Web page. Several types of Layout panels are available, such as:

- A viewbox, which lets viewers zoom in on its contents.

- A border, which creates a border or background around another element.

- A ScrollViewer. This type of container has a scroll bar so all of its contents can be viewed.

Layout panels automatically resize to conform to the current window size. They can also be transformed so that you can specify a position where they are to appear in a final layout.

Customizing the Interface

When you're just learning about the interface of different applications for the first time, it might seem a bit premature to talk about customizing them. You have to learn what you've got to work with before you can start thinking about changing it, after all. Suffice it to say that each of the Studio applications gives you ways to create keyboard shortcuts or even (in the case of Blend) add animation to a Toolbox tool.

At this stage, what's most important for you to know is that you are in control when it comes to what appears in the application's workspace. Any one of the Studio applications, and especially the three creative applications, can get very complex. Don't lose sight of the fact that you can press the Tab key to clear away everything except the drawing you're working on (in Design), deselect already selected options in the Task Panes menu or the Toolbars submenu (in Web), or choose Hide Panels from the Window menu (in Blend). That way you can focus on the task at hand.

Standards-Based Design with Expression Web

3 Formatting Basic Web Site Content

With Expression Web, the basic tasks involved in formatting Web site content are simple to use, but they're not really as simple as they seem. For instance, formatting selected text as bold or italic is a matter of clicking the B (bold) button in a toolbar, just as it is in a word processing program. It's just as easy to center a paragraph or choose a new type font. Those tasks are simple to perform. But behind the scenes, some complex functions are being performed that enable your Web page to conform to the latest Web standards.

This chapter focuses on the first tasks you're likely to perform in formatting an individual Web page. Expression Web, like every Web editor, lets you type text, arrange your text in paragraphs, and specify page properties such as titles and background colors. These functions give you a way to understand how Expression Web uses CSS to make your site look the way you want in the widest possible range of browsers, and you'll get a glimpse at how Web generates such code and makes it especially easy for you to view and edit a page's underlying markup instructions.

Working with Web Page Code

The fundamental function performed by any Web editing program is to help you format content without having to work directly with Web page code. You choose menu options and click toolbar buttons, and the program generates the code for you. But these days, many kinds of code go into creating the average Web page. There are lots of advantages to working directly with code; rather than shielding you from having to work with it, a good Web editor should give you a way to view and edit your code correctly.

Expression Web has extensive support for the latest Web development technologies. In the preceding chapter, you learned about its support for Cascading Style Sheets. One of the most important things you need to realize about Expression Web is that, as you create Web pages by typing, formatting, editing images, and specifying page properties, Expression Web generates accurate code for you. The version of code

Expression Web generates is controlled by its doctype and secondary schema settings—settings you are able to specify yourself.

Doctypes and XHTML

Extensible Hypertext Markup Language (XHTML) is a more robust, more flexible, and more rigorous set of markup instructions than the original HTML. It's rigorous in the sense that it requires designers to observe strict requirements for structuring markup commands, which are called *tags*. Multiple versions of XHTML have been released, and each has slightly different instructions than the previous one. The version of XHTML that a particular Web page uses is determined by its doctype declaration (DTD). The DTD appears as the first line of a Web page file, for example:

```
<!DOCTYPE html PUBLIC "-//W3C//DTD XHTML 1.0 Transitional//EN"
     "http://www.w3.org/TR/xhtml1/DTD/xhtml1-transitional.dtd">
<html xmlns="http://www.w3.org/1999/xhtml" dir="ltr">
```

The first line tells a Web browser that this page uses XHTML markup that conforms to version 1.0 Transitional. The second line provides the URL for this version of XHTML on the Web. The third line provides another source for this version of XHTML.

Expression Web is "smart" enough that it automatically inserts a DTD at the beginning of each Web document's code. The declaration isn't visible in the finished page because it is formatted as a comment: Comments, because they are enclosed by the start tag <--< and the end tag -->, are visible only to someone who reads the code for a page; they aren't visible in the page when displayed by a Web browser. The versions of HTML and Cascading Style Sheets that Expression Web generates are specified in the Authoring tab of the Page Editor Options dialog box (see Figure 3.1). You can change the options so that Expression Web will generate the code that corresponds to the version you choose. Your choices also affect how Expression Web implements Code IntelliSense, a feature described later in this chapter.

Note: Expression Web is able to provide you with compatibility reports that tell you if your Web page code conforms to a particular version of HTML or XHTML that your Web site needs to use. Choose Compatibility Reports from Expression Web's Tools menu. When the Compatibility Checker dialog box appears, you can choose the pages you want to check (if you want to run a report on only part of your Web site). You can then choose to run the check based either on the doctype declaration each page is using or on a different doctype or schema.

`mysite.com`, you don't have to enter `www.mysite.com/index.htm` to view your home page. Instead, you simply enter `www.mysite.com`, and the home page appears by default.

Be sure you enter the correct filename extension at the end of a page that doesn't use HTML for its markup. The filename extension is the three- or four-letter extension that comes after the dot at the end of the filename. If the filename is `contact`, and the language being used is HTML, the site that uses pages created with Microsoft's ASP. NET technology needs to have pages that end with the filename extension `.aspx`.

Working with the Folder List Task Pane

The current site's location is given at the top of the Folder List task pane. This task pane provides a hierarchical view of the folders and files in your site. In the Folder List task pane shown in Figure 3.2, the current site's location is `C:\Users\pcmcz\`.

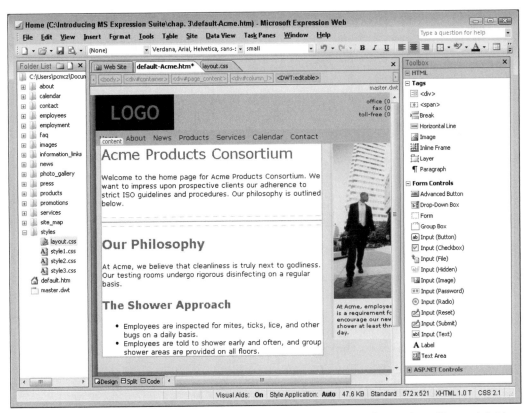

Figure 3.2 The Folder List task pane displays a hierarchical view of your site's files and folders.

Note: The Folder List task pane does more than just provide you with a view of your site's folders. This task pane (like others in Expression Web) has its own miniature toolbar. Click the New Page icon to create a new blank Web page, the New Folder icon to create a new folder, and the Close Window icon to close the Folder List task pane itself.

Viewing and Creating Folders

You can perform many other basic housekeeping tasks with the Folder List task pane. Click a plus sign (+) to expand the contents of a folder, and click the minus sign (−) to contract an already open folder. If you right-click a file's name, a context menu appears that lets you delete or rename it, for instance. If you right-click a folder, a similar context menu appears. Use it to rename the folder. Choose New > Folder to create a new subfolder within the currently selected folder.

Creating a New Page from an Existing One

Suppose you want to create a set of pages, all with a similar layout. You only have to create one from scratch. Once that initial page contains the contents you want to carry forward to other documents on your site, save it to the current site. Then follow these steps:

1. Right-click the page in the Folder List task pane.

2. When the context menu appears, choose New from Existing Page.

3. When the new page with the same content as the original appears in the editing area, click the Save toolbar button.

4. In the Save As dialog box, give your file a new filename and click the Change Title button to change the title.

5. After you change the title, click OK to close the Set Page Title dialog box.

6. When you're done, click Save.

You can also create a template from an existing page and use it as a model for subsequent pages. When you have the content you want on your page, Choose File > Save As. When the Save As dialog box appears, choose Page Template from the Save as Type drop-down list. You'll probably also want to give your page a name that identifies it as a template, such as `catalog_template`.

Pasting Text

One of the best features about Web is its strengthened connection with Word. It's common to copy text created in Word and paste it into a Web page. In the past, this

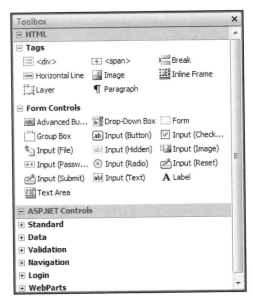

Figure 3.5 Drag the Horizontal Rule icon from the Toolbox into Design View to add it to the current page.

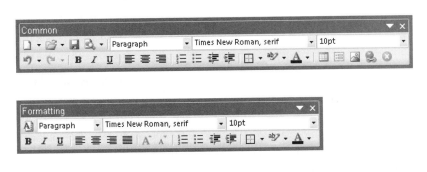

Figure 3.6 You're likely to use these toolbars most often, though Expression Web has eight more for special purposes.

or Publish Site (which are contained on the Formatting toolbar but not the Common toolbar), you need to either choose a menu option or display Formatting instead. In this particular example, you could choose Edit > Find, or File > Publish Site. To display Formatting or any of the other toolbars Expression Web makes available, choose View > Toolbars to display the complete list and then choose Formatting.

You'll notice that, whether you're using the Common or Formatting toolbar, when you click the Font box, the drop-down list of font choices is broken into two sections. The top section contains the fonts that are used on most Web pages: Arial, Helvetica, Courier, and Times. They're the ones supported by nearly all Web browsers. The bottom and much longer section contains all the fonts you have installed on your system. The problem with each of these non–Web-friendly fonts is that they'll only appear if the viewer has the same ones installed on his system. You can choose an interesting and eye-catching font like Bookman Old Style or Franklin Gothic, for instance, but if the font isn't available on the user's system, his browser will substitute the closest match. The font that's substituted will be the one in the same font *family*, and font families are discussed in the next section.

> **Note:** You get a much wider set of font formatting options in the Font dialog box. Choose Format > Font to display it; you'll find checkboxes that enable you to add underlining and strikethrough lines as well as other types of emphasis. You can also adjust character spacing, as described in the next chapter.

Working with Font Families

A family is a group of fonts that shares the same general characteristics. The four characteristics of type fonts are these:

Serif: These are fonts that have curls or straight lines at the tips of their ascenders and descenders. Examples are Times, Bookman, and Garamond.

Sans serif: These fonts have no ornaments at the ends of their ascenders and descenders. They have a cleaner, simpler appearance than serif fonts. Examples include Helvetica, Arial, and Verdana.

Fixed-width: These fonts are made up of characters that all take up the same amount of width. They resemble the characters produced by old-fashioned manual typewriters. The best-known example is Courier.

Proportional: These are fonts in which each character gets only the amount of width it needs. Thin letters such as I are given less width than ones like M, for instance. Sans serif and serif fonts are both proportional fonts; fixed-width fonts are not.

The font families displayed at the top of the Font drop-down list in the Common and Formatting toolbars each have at least one of these characteristics: Arial and Verdana are sans serif, proportional fonts; Times and Times New Roman are serif, proportional fonts; and Courier is a fixed-width font.

Families are useful because they give the browser that displays the page a choice of which one to display. If one font isn't available, the other one is displayed. You can customize the three default families that are displayed in the Font list. You can also create your own font family to serve the same purpose. For instance, you might create a family of three fonts, two of which are nonstandard ones (in other words, not usually found on the Web) contained on your system, and the other that is standard and that virtually everyone has installed on his system.

Suppose you really want your Web pages to be displayed in Palatino, for instance. You can choose Garamond as your first backup font and Times as the standard font that will be displayed if the other two aren't available. Follow these steps to create your own font family:

1. Click the down arrow in the Font box in the Standard or Formatting toolbar and choose Customize Font Family. The Page Editor Options dialog box opens with the Font Families tab in front.

2. Since the option you want (New Font Family) is selected at the top of the Font Families tab by default, you don't need to make any selections from the box in the top half of the dialog box. Move to the box in the bottom half and scroll through the list of fonts. Click a font you want, and its name appears in the Add font box. The Add button also becomes activated.

3. Click Add. The selected font is added to the box in the top half of the dialog box. In Figure 3.7, Palatino Linotype has been added.

4. Choose another font and click Add. The font is added next to your first font.

5. Repeat step 4 until you're done assembling the members of your font family.

6. Click Move Up or Move Down to control where your new font family appears in the list of families.

7. Click OK.

When you're done, go to the Common or Formatting toolbar and click the Font drop-down list box. Your custom font family should appear along with the standard ones. You can use the Font Families tab of Page Editor Options to remove font families if needed or to add fonts to existing font families if you want to.

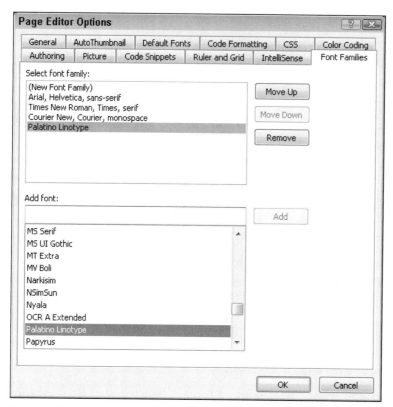

Figure 3.7   Create a custom font family so you can specify the fonts you want as well as backup fonts everyone can see.

Bold, Italic, and Other Attributes

Expression Web, like other applications you're used to working with, has more than one toolbar with buttons you can use to format text and perform many other functions. The toolbars are the most convenient options you have for adding simple types of emphasis such as bold and italic. To make text bold, click the B button in the Common or Formatting toolbar or press Ctrl+B; to make it italic, click I or press Ctrl+I.

To go beyond these two stalwarts of text formatting, choose Format > Font to display the Font dialog box. (Make sure you select the text you want to format before you do so.) The checkboxes let you apply superscript, subscript, underline, or small caps. Sometimes this kind of formatting is distracting; it detracts from and doesn't add to your overall effect.

Some of the checkbox options in the Font dialog box probably seem a bit obscure. They are intended to give browsers the option to format specified text in a generic rather than specific way according to the content of the text. For instance, if you check Emphasis, it tells the browser to give extra emphasis to the text, but whether that means bold or italic (or bold and italic) is up to the browser. The Citation checkbox marks the text as a citation, and the Definition checkbox should be similarly obvious.

Note: You get a far more sophisticated level of control over text formatting by assigning styles to text. By creating styles, you can achieve some effects that aren't available to you in the toolbars and Font dialog box, such as Font Weight and many alignment and spacing options. See Chapter 6 for more.

Changing Type Size

If you are accustomed to designing for printed brochures or other publications, you are used to expressing font size in terms of points or picas. Because of the differences in how Web pages are displayed by browsers and operating systems, font size is best described in relative terms. You *can* specify 24 pt. Verdana for a heading, but it's far more common to choose a relative designation instead such as a Heading 1 or Heading 2 heading, or a "large" or "medium" size. This leaves it up to the user's browser to decide how text should be displayed. Someone who is vision impaired might have his browser set to display type extra large for better readability, for instance.

It's good Web design practice to choose a relative designation for point size. If you really want to, you can get very precise with size and other type settings by choosing Format > New Style, changing settings in the New Style dialog box, and then applying the resulting style to selected text. You can also get an idea of which relative designations correspond to specific point sizes by choosing Format > Font. The Size box in the Font dialog box lets you know that the "x-small" designation corresponds to 10 pt text, "small" to 12 pt, "x-large" to 24 pt, and so on.

Note: You can also read the same point-size and relative designations in the Font Size drop-down list in the Formatting or Common toolbar. You can also click the Increase Font Size or Decrease Font Size button on the Formatting toolbar to change the size of text.

Colorizing Text

By default, the text you type in the Expression Web editing window is black. But there's no reason it needs to be. In fact, if you choose a color for the background of your page that is particularly vivid (such as black), you need to choose a contrasting color so the text will be visible against it. As usual, you have several options for assigning color to text. You can do it by choosing Format > Font and clicking the Color drop-down list in the Font dialog box.

Note: When choosing colors for your text, make sure the colors have strong contrast with the background of the Web page on which they appear. A white page background with yellow type is going to result in practically unreadable content, for instance. Also, try to test your colors on different platforms (Mac and Windows) and different monitors when your site goes online, to make sure everything is reasonable.

Using the Color Selection Box and More Colors

The most convenient way to assign color to text is to select the text and then click the down arrow next to the Font Color button in the Common or Formatting toolbar. When you do, a list box containing 16 colors appears, as shown in Figure 3.8.

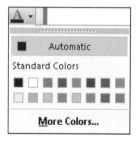

Figure 3.8   Use this box to assign a color to your text.

If one of the 16 initial colors isn't the one you want, click the More Colors link at the bottom of the box. The More Colors dialog box appears, displaying a hexagon that is broken into 135 colors. Click on the one you want, and the color appears in the New part of the box shown in the lower right of More Colors (see Figure 3.9).

"Borrowing" an Existing Color with the Eyedropper

One of the most innovative ways of selecting color is provided by the More Colors dialog box. If you see a color on another Web page—or in a page layout or image

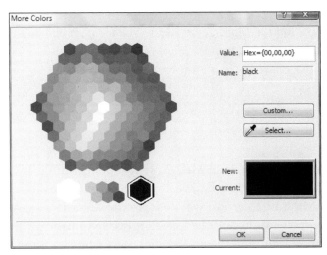

Figure 3.9 The More Colors dialog box contains a wider range of options.

editing application you have open, or any other window open on your computer—you can duplicate it and add it to the Web page you're editing with Expression Web. Follow these steps:

1. Make sure the color you want is displayed on a window that is open somewhere on your computer desktop. It might be a color on someone else's Web page, for instance. Try to position the color so that you can see it onscreen at the same time the Expression Web window is open.

2. Select the text or other object to which you want to assign a color.

3. Open the More Colors dialog box as described in the previous section "Using the Color Selection Box and More Colors."

4. Click the Select button in More Colors. The cursor turns into an eyedropper.

5. Move the eyedropper over the color you have displayed in the other window on your screen. When you are over the color you want, you'll see it displayed in the New area in the More Colors dialog box.

6. Click to select the color.

7. Click OK. The More Colors dialog box closes, and the new color is assigned to text or other item you selected earlier.

Once you assign a color to text on a Web page, you can copy that color from one text segment to another by using the Format Painter.

Note: The 16-color selection box and the More Colors dialog box are common color selection tools that you'll see in other parts of the Expression Web interface. They appear when you attempt to assign color to the background of a Web page, for instance.

Using the Format Painter

You might be familiar with the Format Painter from Microsoft Word. I certainly am: It's one of my favorite tools for copying formatting from one element to another. Suppose you've formatted a paragraph in a certain way: 13 pt type, 20 pt leading, bold, with a half-inch indent on both the right and the left margins. By selecting the formatted text, clicking the Format Painter, and then selecting another block of text, you copy the formatting from the first text segment to the second. You don't change the text itself; you only copy the formatting instructions. Expression Web has the same utility on the Standard toolbar. It works the same way as in Word:

1. Select the text that has the formatting you want to copy.

2. Click the Format Painter button in the Standard toolbar.

3. Select the text you want to format. This can be a word, a sentence, a paragraph, or other text segment. The formatting is carried over.

The Format Painter is a good tool, but it's no substitute for creating a style that has the formatting you want. Once you save the formatting as a style, you can apply it throughout a file as needed.

Adjusting Character Spacing

Kerning is the practice of adjusting the space between characters so that text fits the space available to it. If the space is small, the space is reduced so the letters seem to be "pushed" closer together. On the other hand, sometimes the space between characters needs to be increased to fill out a "loose" line or eliminate an awkward word break. The Font dialog box gives you a way to control just how the spacing is changed:

1. Select the text you want to change.

2. Choose Format, Font.

3. When the Font dialog box opens, click the Character Spacing tab to bring it to the front.

4. Click the Spacing drop-down list and choose either Expanded or Condensed.

5.   In the By box, type the number of pixels by which you want Expression Web to expand or condense the selected text.

6.   Click Apply. A Preview of how the adjusted text will look appears in the bottom section of the Font dialog box. If you need to, change the number of pixels in the By box. When you're satisfied with the result, click OK.

Note: You can adjust the vertical space between regular text and either super-script or subscript text by choosing an option from the Position drop-down list in the Character Spacing tab.

Choosing Paragraph Styles

Every time you press the Enter key while you are typing text, you create a para-graph. Each paragraph on a Web page can be assigned its own designation. You find the available paragraph types by clicking the Paragraph drop-down list in the Common or Formatting toolbar (see Figure 3.10). A heading is considered a para-graph, too. By default, a paragraph is assigned the HTML designation (I hesitate to use the word *style* lest you confuse it with a CSS style). The most common types of paragraphs you're likely to use are listed below (except for lists, which are described in the section "Formatting Lists," later in this chapter).

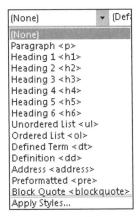

Figure 3.10   Choose paragraph styles from this drop-down list.

Body Text

The default paragraph designation, which is simply called Paragraph, is usually dis-played in Times with left-aligned paragraphs. You can, of course, customize a para-graph by first selecting it and then choosing options from the Common or

Formatting toolbar or the Font dialog box, as described in preceding sections. Besides the Paragraph option, you can choose several paragraph types from the Paragraph drop-down list in the Common or Formatting toolbar:

Address: This designation was used in the early days of the Web to denote the Web page author's e-mail address. It simply formats text in italic and is seldom used. (Yet, it persists as an option in Web editors like Expression Web.)

Preformatted text: When you position your text cursor in a paragraph and choose Preformatted, the text in the paragraph changes to a fixed-width font such as Courier.

Block Quote: When you choose this option, the text in which the cursor is positioned is indented on both the left and right margins to distinguish it from surrounding text.

Headings

Headings are among the most important parts of Web pages. They direct the eye toward important parts of a page, and they divide a page's contents into sections that are easier to digest than a single page-long text block. Headings are divided into six levels: Heading 1 (also known as H1) is the largest size, and Heading 6 (also called H6) is the smallest.

The headings you'll probably use most often are H1 through H4. The logical pattern is to place an H1 heading near the top of the Web page, an H2 below it, an H3 below it, and so on. But you are in control and can arrange headings as you wish. Try it yourself:

1. Open a blank Web page and type `This is an H1 Heading`.

2. Select this text and choose Heading 1 `<h1>` from the Style drop-down list in the Common or Formatting toolbar. The heading is converted to bold and increases in size.

3. Click Split at the bottom of Expression Web's editing area. The HTML code for the heading is displayed in the Code section of the window (see Figure 3.11). In addition, the HTML command `<h1>` appears in the Quick Tag Selector, at the top of the editing area.

Aligning Paragraphs

When you first type or paste text into Expression Web's editing window, it's aligned with the left margin and single spaced. You can change the alignment on the

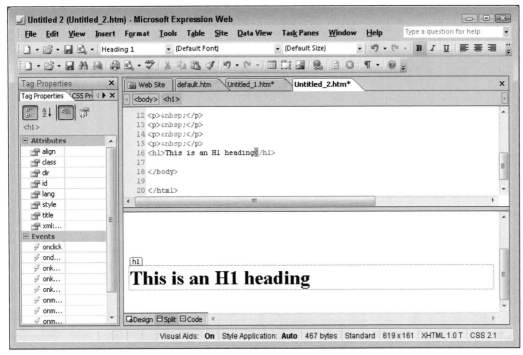

Figure 3.11 An H1 heading is identified in the Quick Tag Selector.

Formatting toolbar: Position the cursor in the paragraph or paragraphs you want to align (you can format multiple paragraphs at once). Click the Align Text Left, Center, Align Text Right, or Justify button.

Note: The Formatting toolbar is the preferred tool for changing alignment because it includes the Justify alignment button. The Common toolbar includes only the Left, Center, and Right alignment buttons.

If you want even more control over aligning paragraphs, choose Format > Paragraph and open the Paragraph dialog box. You can choose the basic alignment options (Left, Center, Right, Justify) from the Alignment drop-down list. Once you select the alignment you want, you can enter the amount of alignment you want in pixels. The Left box lets you indent from the left margin, and the Right box lets you indent from the right margin. The Indent First Line box lets you indent the first line of the paragraph only so you can indent it differently from the rest of the paragraph.

The Spacing section of the Paragraph dialog box lets you change the amount of space before or after the paragraph. By default, you have a single blank space between a paragraph and the others around it. Spacing lets you adjust the gap in pixels. Click the up or down arrow to increase or reduce the space, respectively; you can see the result interactively in the bottom of the dialog box. When you're finished adjusting spacing, click OK. The Paragraph dialog box closes, and you return to the Expression Web window, where the new spacing is in effect.

Adding Borders and Shading

If you've done text formatting with Microsoft Word, you'll be happy to know that a Borders and Shading dialog box that is virtually identical to Word's is included with Expression Web. This feature allows you to enclose a paragraph (including a heading) within a box or to give it a 3 D effect by adding shading.

To add a border, select the paragraph you want to format, and then choose Format > Borders and Shading. When the Borders and Shading dialog box appears, click the kind of border you want to insert in the Setting section. Default is no box at all; Box is a container with four sides; Custom lets you draw your own container. When you click Box, for instance, you are then able to choose a style for the lines that make up the box.

If you want to add a color to your box, click the drop-down Color list. You'll see the Color list box; select a color from it or choose More Colors if you want to select from a wider range. Enter a number (in pixels) that represents the width of the box you want to add. As you make your selections, a preview of your box style appears on the right side of Borders and Shading (see Figure 3.12).

The Padding controls at the bottom of the Borders tab allow you to add space between the text in your paragraph and the border you are adding around it. If you want an additional graphic effect, click the Shading tab and choose a color from the Background Color drop-down list; the color appears behind the text in your paragraph. Choose an option from the Foreground list to "colorize" the text in the paragraph. Be sure to create sufficient contrast between the text color and the background, to keep your text readable. You can also add a background image to a paragraph by clicking the Browse button next to Background Picture and locating the image file on your computer. This usually isn't practical when the image is likely to interfere with your Web page text. Either the image has to be very subtle in nature, or the paragraph has to be virtually empty.

When you're done, click OK to close Borders and Shading and return to the Expression Web window, where your box has been added to the selected paragraph (or paragraphs; you can enclose more than one paragraph in a box, too).

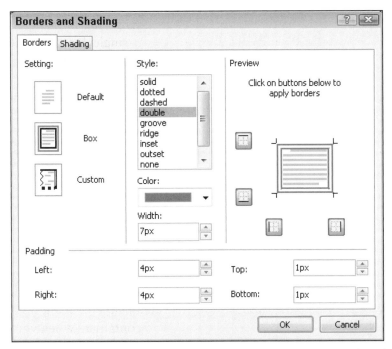

Figure 3.12   A miniature version of your box appears on the right side of Borders and Shading.

Formatting Lists

Expression Web, like other Web editors, makes it easy to arrange text in the form of lists. Lists make text more readable; they also organize your content and make text easy for a reader to scan. You can create three basic kinds of lists:

- Bulleted lists. These are also called unordered lists; they are designated by the HTML tags <UL> and </UL>. They present a set of related items that don't have to be in any particular sequence.

- Numbered lists. These are items presented as a series of steps and are designated by the HTML tags <OL> and </OL> (for ordered list).

- Definition lists. These are a series of terms and definitions. The terms to be defined are flush left with the margin, and the definition is indented beneath it. You don't see definition lists as frequently as numbered or bulleted lists.

(The preceding was a bulleted list, by the way.)

The process of creating all three lists is the same: First you type the items to be contained in the list. You select the list items, and you format them. Here's an example. Type the following in the Expression Web window, pressing the Enter key once after each line to make each a separate paragraph:

Shopping List

Eggs

Bagels

Cream Cheese

To turn this series of paragraphs into a bulleted list, follow these steps:

1. Select the first line (Shopping List) and choose Heading 1 from the Style drop-down list in the Common or Formatting toolbar.

2. Select the next three lines (Eggs, Bagels, Cream Cheese) all together by scrolling across them.

3. When the three lines are highlighted, click the Bullets button in the For-matting toolbar. The three paragraphs are formatted as bulleted list items, each with a dot before it.

The same process is followed for numbered lists: Select the list items and then click the Numbering button in the Formatting toolbar.

You can create a third type of list, a definition list, by choosing two options from the style drop-down list. A definition list consists of pairs of lines. The first line in the pair is the term to be defined; the second is the definition itself. Type the two lines, select the first one, and choose Defined Term <dt> to create the term to be defined. Select the second line and choose Definition <dd> to create the definition.

Once you create a list, you can manipulate it in different ways. For one thing, you can "nest" a list within a list: A series of items is indented as a sublist under a single item in another list. An example is shown in Figure 3.13.

To nest a list, you first create a bulleted or numbered list. Type all the items you need—both the items in the "top-level" list and the items in the one to be nested. Select all the list items and click the Bullets or Numbering button. Then, select only the list items to be nested and click the Increase Indent Position button on the Common or Formatting toolbar. Notice that the indented list items are also assigned a bullet with a slightly different style than the part of the list that is not indented. If you ever need to reformat the list, select the nested items and click the Decrease Indent Position button on the Formatting toolbar to remove the indenting.

You can also create numbered or bulleted lists by first selecting all the items in the list and then choosing Font > Bullets and Numbering. When the Bullets and

Figure 3.13 You can nest a list by selecting its contents and indenting them.

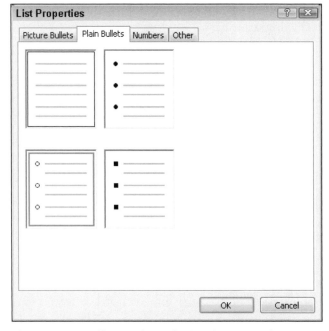

Figure 3.14 Bullets and Numbering lets you select nonstandard list item markers.

Numbering dialog box shown in Figure 3.14 appears, you can choose one of the bullet styles that appear in the Plain Bullets tab (which appears in front by default) for a bulleted list. Click the Picture Bullets tab if you want to use a graphic image as a custom bullet. Click Numbers to create a numbered list. The advantage of using Bullets and Numbering becomes obvious when you click one of these tabs: You are able to assign nonstandard characters, such as letters or Roman numerals, to a numbered list or squares or circles to a bulleted list.

Note: If you position the cursor in a paragraph that has already been formatted as a list item, when you choose Format > Bullets and Numbering, you see an additional tab called Other. This tab lets you format list items as a definition list. The Other tab does not appear if you have the cursor positioned in a paragraph that is not already a list item.

Checking Your Text

All of the credibility and trust you build up when you enter and format text can be undone in a moment if you make spelling errors or grammatical blunders. A single typo in a prominent place can ruin the professional appearance you have tried so hard to achieve. In the rush to get your pages online, it's easy to forget to proofread your work. Expression Web, however, makes it easy by giving you utilities to check your spelling as well as grammar before your work goes online.

Spell-Checking

Expression Web includes a built-in dictionary that it refers to when it checks your spelling. By default, it checks your spelling as you type. Try it: Type a sentence with a typo in it, and you'll notice that the program inserts a red squiggly line under the misspelled word. Right-click the word, and a set of suggested corrections appears (see Figure 3.15); these are words taken from the built-in dictionary.

Sometimes you type a word that the dictionary doesn't recognize but that you know to be correct. In that case, you can right-click the word and choose Add from the context menu to add it to the dictionary. When it's in the dictionary, it will no longer be marked as a mistake when you type it again.

To deactivate the interactive spell-checking, choose Tools > Spelling > Spelling Options. When the Spelling Options dialog box opens, uncheck the box next to Check Spelling as You Type. You can also use this dialog box to adjust the kinds of mistakes the spell-checker flags as mistakes, such as Internet addresses or the paths leading to files.

If you want to check an entire file at once, position the cursor anywhere in the document and choose Tools > Spelling > Spelling or press F7. Expression Web will run a check on the spelling for the entire text file. You can also check a single file in its entirety by selecting the file's name in the Folder List task pane. Selecting more than one file in the Folder List task pane while you have the Spelling window open causes a spell check to be run on those files at the same time—you can check an entire site this way.

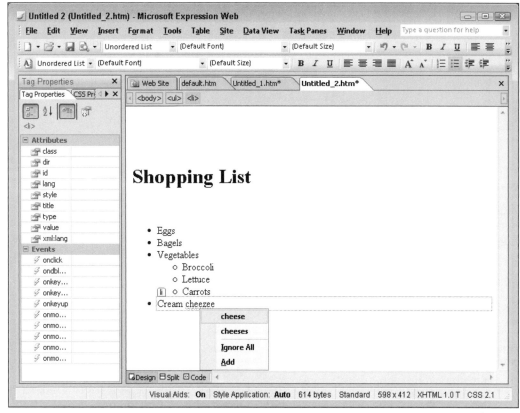

Figure 3.15 Expression Web checks spelling as you type.

Using the Thesaurus

If you're not sure about a particular choice of word, select it and choose Tools > Thesaurus (or press Shift+F7). The Thesaurus dialog box opens with the highlighted word in the box at the top left. If the word is contained in the thesaurus, this box is labeled Looked Up (see Figure 3.16). Definitions are presented beneath it, and synonyms are presented on the right. Select a synonym and click Replace to replace the word currently on your Web page.

If the word you are checking is not in the thesaurus, it is labeled Not Found. Beneath it, an alphabetical list of similarly spelled words or phrases appears. Click one of the words in the list to move it to the right, and click Replace to replace it on your Web page (see Figure 3.17).

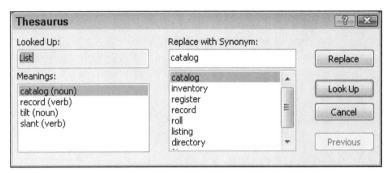

Figure 3.16   For words already in the thesaurus, meanings are presented.

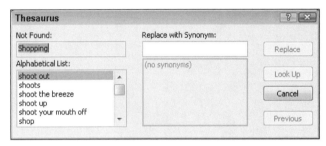

Figure 3.17   For words not in the thesaurus, similar words are presented.

Note: Expression Web also has a well-developed Find and Replace feature that you can use to edit text. Choose Edit > Find or Edit > Replace to find either text in the visible body of your Web page or HTML tags in Code View.

Working with Web Site Code

So far, most of your Web page formatting work has been done in Design View. This, however, is only one of three views available to you. The other two are Code View and Split View.

Before you paste, you might venture a look "behind the curtain" to see what's already part of this seemingly blank page. Although the Web page appears blank in the editing area, if you click Code at the bottom of the editing area you switch to Code View—a way of viewing your Web page that displays the code that underlies your content. As you can see, Expression Web has already generated the following code for you:

```
<!DOCTYPE html PUBLIC "-//W3C//DTD XHTML 1.0 Transitional//EN"
"http://www.w3.org/TR/xhtml1/DTD/xhtml1-transitional.dtd">
```

```
<html xmlns="http://www.w3.org/1999/xhtml">
<head>
<meta http-equiv="Content-Type" content="text/html; charset=utf-8" />
<title>Untitled 1</title>
</head>
<body>
</body>
</html>
```

You already know about the doctype declaration in the code. What does the other code mean? I've highlighted the most important parts for you in Figure 3.18:

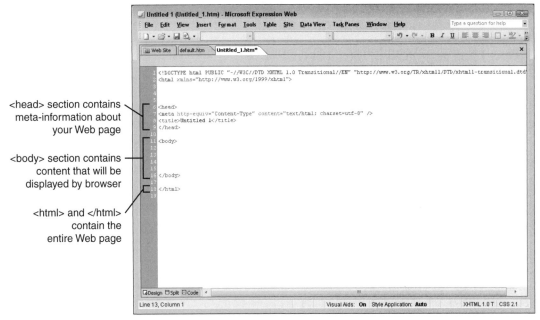

Figure 3.18 A "blank" Web page actually contains this HTML framework.

Working with Code View

Web editors were originally created to give non-programmers a way to edit Web pages without having to work directly with code. The idea is that people who are used to writing their own programs will write Web page code from scratch, and non-programmers like you and me will stick to Web editors like Expression Web and look at the code only when we have to. That division isn't totally true, however. Programmers need full-featured editing programs to verify their code and to implement the increasingly complex code required to make sites interactive and populate them with useful "live" data.

Expression Web's Code View displays the underlying CSS, HTML, XHTML, and other code for the Web pages you edit. Lines are numbered, and code is even color coded so you can scan it more easily. But you can do much more than that in Code View: You can view incorrect code that is automatically highlighted for you, find and replace code, get suggestions for commands you might want to insert, and create and use snippets of code over and over again. Code View is so rich that this short section can only provide an introduction. Subsequent chapters will explore its features in more detail.

Code Shortcuts

Expression Web provides you with a group of tools that streamline the process of working with Web page code. First and foremost, there's the Code View toolbar. Choose View > Toolbars > Code View to display it. Some buttons, like Complete Word, help you finish writing commands. Others, like Find Matching Tag, make it easy for you to find commands. Two other shortcut utilities are described in the sections that follow.

Code Snippets

Suppose you write a bit of code you want to use over and over again on your Web pages. It might be as simple as a comment that identifies you as the author of the code or as complex as a JavaScript program. Rather than having to type such code segments from scratch over and over, you can save them as snippets that you can add quickly whenever you need to. To create a snippet, follow these steps:

1. Choose Tools > Page Editor Options.

2. When the Page Editor Options dialog box appears, click the Code Snippets tab.

3. Click Add to display Add Code Snippet. In the Keyword box, type a word to identify the code snippet when you want to add it later on.

4. Type a description of your snippet in the Description box.

5. Type the actual code for your snippet in the Text Entry box.

6. Click OK to close Add Code Snippet and OK to close Page Editor Options.

When you want to add a code snippet, position your cursor at the spot in your code where you want it to appear. Then press Ctrl+Enter to display a list of snippets. Double-click the name of the snippet you want to insert.

Code IntelliSense

If you write HTML code directly in Code View, you'll notice that Expression Web provides you with helpful suggestions for completing what you write. If you type the less-than symbol and the letter a, for instance, you'll see a menu list pop up with suggestions for tags that begin with the letter a. If you write a start tag, Expression Web will automatically add an end tag for you. These functions are performed by Code IntelliSense, a function within Expression Web that's designed to make sure you write your code correctly and to help you remember code. IntelliSense is the utility that highlights mistakes in your code if you make them accidentally or code elements that don't conform to the version of HTML/XHTML you are using.

If you want to control just how frequently IntelliSense provides you with reminders and suggestions, choose Tools > Page Editor Options. Click the IntelliSense tab and uncheck any of the options you don't want, such as completing HTML, CSS, or ASP.NET statements or automatically inserting tags.

Quick Tag Selector

The Quick Tag Selector, which was mentioned briefly earlier in this chapter, is located at the top of the editing area, just above the content for the Web page you are working on. It gives you a user-friendly way to view and work with the tags that control the item you have currently selected. (Tags are essential parts of HTML commands; most commands consist of both a start tag such as <a> and an end tag such as </s>, though a few like the <img> image command contain only a start tag.)

As you enter and format text, you see the set of HTML tags listed in the Quick Tag Selector grow accordingly. Click anywhere inside a Web page, and you'll see the hierarchy of the tags that affect the object you have selected. Conversely, if you click one of the tags in the Quick Tag Selector, you see the corresponding content highlighted in the editing area. It's a great tool for learning HTML if you don't know it already.

When you hover your mouse pointer over a tag in the Quick Tag Selector, a down arrow appears to the right of it. Click the down arrow, and a list full of options appears that lets you edit the HTML or the contents associated with it:

> **Select Tag:** This selects the start and end tags as well as the contents between them.
>
> **Select Tag Contents:** This selects only the contents, not the start or end tag.

Edit Tag: You can add attributes or values to the tag using the Quick Tag Editor.

Remove Tag: Deletes the start and end tags but leaves the contents alone.

Insert HTML: Lets you add HTML to the page at the spot where the cursor is positioned.

Wrap Tag: Lets you add HTML around the selected tag using the Quick Tag Editor.

Positioning: Lets you specify an absolute, relative, fixed, or static position for the selected item.

Tag Properties: Opens the Properties dialog box for the selected tag.

In Figure 3.19, the heading has been selected, so the corresponding `<h2>` tag is highlighted in the Quick Tag Selector. The down arrow next to the `<h2>` has been clicked to show the menu options listed above.

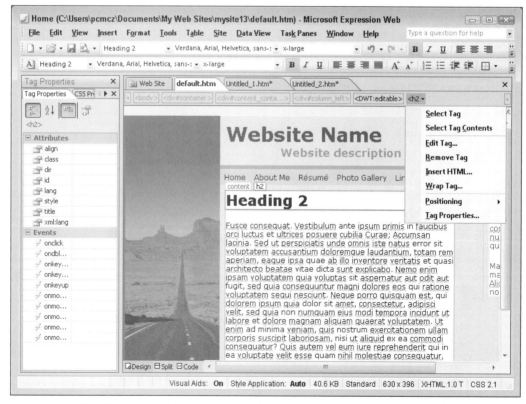

Figure 3.19 The Quick Tag Selector displays the code that controls the selected item.

Quick Tag Editor

If you want to edit code on your Web page, you can use the Quick Tag Editor. You can access the editor either from Design View or Code View. Select the tag you want to edit by highlighting it in Code View and then choosing Edit > Quick Tag Editor or by choosing Edit Tag in the Quick Tag Selector. In either case, the Quick Tag Editor opens with the tag already entered (see Figure 3.20).

Figure 3.20   Edit a tag with the Quick Tag Editor.

You can add HTML to the contents by typing it directly in the box in the Quick Tag Editor. When you're done, check the green checkmark to close the editor and apply the changes. The down arrow on the left side of the Quick Tag Editor lets you wrap a tag around the existing one or insert HTML commands in addition to the current one.

Closing Your Page

When you're done editing your Web page, you can close it in one of several ways:

- To close the page you have currently displayed in the editing area, click the close box (the X in the upper right-hand corner) or choose File > Close.

- To close a page that isn't the currently active one, right-click it in the Folder List task pane and click Close from the context menu. Alternately, you can click the page's tab at the top of the editing area and then click the close box to close it.

- To close all pages in the current Web site, choose File > Close Site or click the close box in the upper-right corner of the Expression Web window.

4 Giving Your Web Site a Look and Feel

In previous chapters, you learned how to create pages and add basic textual content to them. To attract attention and make your site look really professional, you need to give it a graphic look and feel that makes your text and other contents more compelling. You also need to organize your site and ensure that it is easy to navigate. In this chapter you'll learn how to give your site a graphic identity and add the elements that are essential for your visitors to find what they want.

Adding Web Page Must-Haves

Every book has its table of contents, and every magazine has its list of contributors and staff people. Many organizations have style guides that spell out colors, fonts, margins, and other qualities that all printed publications need to have in order to promote the company's identity. Behind the scenes, essential information keeps publications looking the way they should. Expression Web has its own places where you can specify background information about your site so that it looks the way you want and is easy for others to find. Some of the most important examples are described in the following sections.

Adjusting Page Properties

In the preceding chapter, you learned how to assign a title to a Web page when you use the Save As dialog box to assign it a filename. You can also assign a title and provide a substantial amount of important information in the Page Properties dialog box. Choose File > Properties to open it. In the General tab, you can enter a new title or change the current one in the Title box. You can also add the following information, which might help your site be found by search engines such as Google, Yahoo!, or MSN Search:

> **Page Description:** This description will be used by some search engines to describe your site when it appears in a set of search results. Search results are among the most cost-effective and important ways to market a Web site. It's to your advantage to enter the description you want in order to control what

visitors learn about you. It's a way of controlling your "message" and your image that can pay off in positive PR.

Keywords: Some search engines use the keywords you enter here to determine when your site will appear in search results. This doesn't work with all sites (Google, for instance, doesn't use them). But the chance of success with other search utilities is great enough that you should enter as many keywords or phrases as possible. The more relevant terms you enter, the greater your chances that you'll be "found."

The other options on the General tab of Page Properties aren't as critical as these two. On other tabs in Page Properties, you can do some essential formatting that can help your site look the way you want. The Formatting tab lets you specify a background; this is described in the next section. The Advanced tab lets you specify margins for the current Web page, either as a fixed number of pixels or as a percentage of the overall page width. (It's important to realize that these margin settings apply only to the current page; you can set a consistent margin for all the pages in your site by using style sheets.)

The Workgroup tab lets you mark the page contents and its review status, which is helpful if you are preparing your Web site together with other colleagues in your organization. However, another feature called Document Check-in/Check-out lets you track whether the file is being worked on or not.

Document Check-In/Check-Out If you use Expression Web in an office environment, you need to cooperate with the other members of your team. Collaboration can be a challenge when you don't work in the same office but are in far-flung locations and communicate via the Internet. You don't want to double up on one another's efforts: If one person makes a change to the text of a page at the same time someone else is changing the design of the page, it's likely someone's changes either are going to be overlooked or will have to be redone.

Expression Web's document check-in/check-out system is designed for workgroups that need to collaborate on Web sites. First, you need to activate this feature; it's not turned on by default. Choose Site > Site Settings. When the Site Settings dialog box appears, check the box next to Use Document Check-in and Check-out. Leave the box next to Prompt to Check Out File when Opening a Page. Click OK.

Once check-in/check-out has been activated, when you open a file you'll be prompted to check it out before you can start working on it. Click Yes, and the page will open, but they'll be a big green checkmark next to its filename in the Folder List task pane. If someone else tries to open the same file, he'll receive an alert message stating that it's already been checked out. When you're done editing the page, be sure to check it back in: Right-click the file in Folder List and choose Check In from the context menu so your colleagues can work on it.

Changing the Background

As you can see from surfing around the Web, for many sites a clean white page background is adequate for presenting text, images, and animations and putting them in their best light. But the default white page background might not be best for you, especially if you want your site to connect with a young audience, or if your product lends itself to color naturally. If you visit the Web site of Hot Hot Hot (www.hothothot.com), a site that sells many types of hot sauce, you'll notice that it uses a red background and white type—colors that seem ideally suited to its products. The look and feel of your page should complement your content and support your message, in other words. If your page promotes your skydiving business, you might want a sky blue background; if you sell organic products, you might choose light green, and so on.

Choosing Colors

To change the background, you need to be on a page that will permit you to make the change. You then choose File > Properties and click the Background tab or choose Format > Background, which opens the Page Properties dialog box with the Formatting tab in front. If you create a site using one of Web's Dynamic Web Templates (see the section on DWTs later in this chapter) and you have a page open other than the master page, you won't be able to choose Format > Background to make the change. On a DWT site such as the Expression Web templates, you have to open the Master page (which has the filename `master.dwt`). The Format > Background option is then active; when you change the background color on a master page, the change will "ripple" through to all the pages that are attached to it. You'll change the background color on all the pages in the DWT at once, in other words.

Once the Page Properties dialog box is open with the Formatting tab in front, click the Background drop-down list to choose a color. The color box you see is likely to be the same as the one you find in other parts of the Expression Web interface (see Chapter 3 for examples). However, if your site has had colors assigned to it, such as a DWT, you'll have an additional option called Document Colors (see Figure 4.1). This option lets you choose colors that are already part of the color scheme for the site.

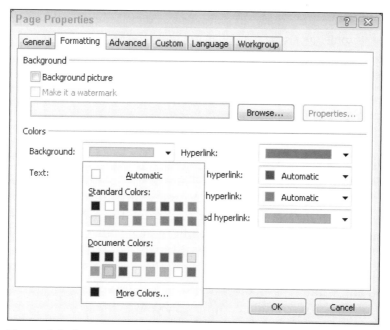

Figure 4.1 Document Colors is available for sites that have colors assigned as part of style sheets.

The important principle to keep in mind when choosing backgrounds is that they must not interfere with the text or other contents on your pages. Make sure they contrast sufficiently with the text: Red text on an orange background just won't work, for instance. Red text on a light cream-colored background will be readable, however.

Choosing Background Images

Instead of a solid background color, you can add an image you can use as the background for your page. The challenge, again, is to choose an image that doesn't clash with the contents of your page and makes the text unreadable. The most successful background images are usually subtle and contain a subtle pattern. The Web browser repeats the image over and over on the page, tiling it so that it fills up the available background. It's the same concept as tiling a wall in your bathroom.

Note: If you create a style and choose a background image as part of customizing that style, you have many more formatting options than are available when you choose Format > Background. You can specify whether the background image repeats only vertically or only horizontally, for instance. See Chapter 6 for more.

To choose an image, select Format > Background as you did before. When the Page Properties dialog box appears, check the Background Picture box on the Formatting tab. You can then browse for an image if you have one saved on your computer. You also have the option of making the image appear as a watermark. A watermark is fixed in place on the page. When the viewer scrolls through the page, the image appears in the same place, and the text seems to "float" above it. If you don't have a background image on your computer, you can "borrow" one from one of Expression Web's templates:

1.   Choose File > New > Web Site.

2.   When the New dialog box opens, click Templates.

3.   Click the template name and scan the thumbnail images that appear on the right side of the dialog box. The site labeled Personal 6 has a wallpaper-like pattern in the left and right columns, for instance. Click OK to create this site.

4.   When the site is created, double-click `master.dwt` to open the master page. The green background appears on the bottom half of the page (see Figure 4.2).

5.   Choose Format > Background and make note of the location of the background image, as specified in the box in the top half of the Formatting tab. (In this example, the location is `images/background_tile.gif`. Also make note of the location of your site. The exact path depends on your file system and where you save your Web site files. The location will probably look like this: `C:\Users\[username]\Documents\My Web Sites\mysite\master.dwt`. The path leading to the background image you want is this: `C:\Users\[username]\Documents\My Web Sites\mysite\images\background_tile.gif`.

6.   Open the Web site that you want to use the background image (or if it is already open, make it the active Web site).

7.   Choose File > Import > File.

8.   When the Import dialog box appears, click Add File.

9.   Navigate to the file where your background image is contained, select the image file (in this case, `background_tile.gif`), and click Open. The file is added to the list in the Import dialog box (see Figure 4.3).

10. Click OK. The image file is added to the Web site files in Folder list.

11. Choose Format > Background.

12. Click Browse.

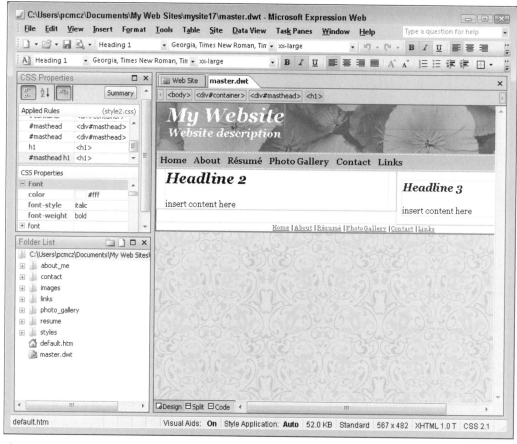

Figure 4.2   You can borrow a background image from one of Web's templates.

13.   Locate the file in the current site and click Open. The file is added to the box in the Background section of the Formatting tab in Page Properties.

14.   Click OK. The image is added to the background of your current Web page.

Note: It's generally a good idea to choose a solid color rather than a photo or drawing as your page background. If you don't choose a solid color, pick an image that has a subtle and non-intrusive design that won't be distracting.

Adjusting Default Colors

If you add a background color or image to your site, or if you just want to give your pages a different graphic appearance, you might want to adjust the default colors. If

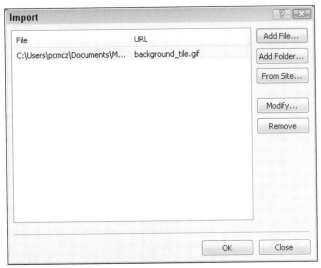

Figure 4.3 You can import an image from another site or location on your computer or network.

you use style sheets to set the graphic look of your site, the colors are specified there. Whether you use style sheets or not, however, you can adjust colors in specific locations such as the Font dialog box. You can also adjust the hyperlink colors for your site in the Page Properties dialog box. The link colors are specified on the same Formatting tab where you specify background colors, under the heading Colors.

By default, hyperlinks on a page that haven't been clicked on are presented in blue. Visited hyperlinks (those that have been clicked on) are purple, hovered hyperlinks (hyperlinks that have the mouse pointer hovering over them) are dark red, and active hyperlinks (those in the process of being clicked) are reddish orange. All these colors make hyperlinks look and feel interactive (which they are). They also give a sense of animation to the page. But they can't clash with the background or be so similar to the background that they aren't visible. Click one of the drop-down lists (Hyperlink, Visited, hyperlink, Active Hyperlink, Hovered Hyperlink) and choose colors from the 16-color drop-down list or the More Colors dialog box to change the link colors on your page.

Note: Unless you are changing hyperlink colors on a master page, the new colors will apply only to the current page, not any others you have linked to it on the current Web site. Change hyperlink colors on a master page to make them apply to the entire site.

Navigational Elements

Every Web site needs to be easy to find, and the pages and resources within it must be accessible through the mouse clicks called hyperlinks, with which you are familiar. Expression Web gives you the capability to create hyperlinks without typing the Web page code that underlies them. You can make links that lead to external Web sites, from one page or another within your own site, or from one part of the current Web page to another.

Hyperlinks

A hyperlink is any object on a Web page that, when clicked by the viewer, takes the browser to another location. A hyperlink can be a word or phrase, a single number or letter, or an image. Some hyperlinks take the viewer from a page on one site to another Web site, while others lead from one location to another within the same site or even on the same page. The destination of the link is determined by the location, or URL, of the object to which the hyperlink points.

Absolute and Relative Links

In order to fully understand hyperlinks, it helps to know something about URLs first. URL (pronounced "Earl") stands for Uniform Resource Locator. It's a standard way of locating a resource on a network by describing the method (or in technical terms, protocol) used to access it and the path to a computer and through directories leading to the object itself. There are two types of URLs:

> **Absolute:** These types of URLs point at the location of an object from the top level of the Web site that contains the object, down through any intervening directories, to the object itself. For example, http://www.mysite.com/family/images/ brother.jpg is an absolute URL.

> **Relative:** A relative URL gives the location of an object relative to another location. For instance, to refer to the previous example, if the page where the hyperlink you want to create is on www.mysite.com in the directory family, and you want to point to the image file brother.jpg, you would simply use the relative URL images/brother.jpg.

Relative URLs are used for internal links—links from one location on a Web site to another—while absolute URLs are used for external links. But internal links can use absolute URLs, while external links cannot use relative URLs. No matter what kind of link (external, internal, or intra-page) you want to make or what kind of URL (absolute or relative) you want to use, the general process is the same and involves two simple steps:

1. Select the text, letter, or image you want to serve as the clickable link. This is the object you want the viewer to click on in order to move to the new location.

2. Identify the destination of the link and associate it with the clickable object.

Inserting Hyperlinks

Expression Web makes both steps easy. First, you select the object on the Web page you are editing. Then, access the Insert Hyperlink dialog box:

1. With the object selected that you want to function as the clickable link, do one of the following:

    ■ Click the Insert Hyperlink button on the Common or Standard toolbar.

    ■ Press Ctrl+K.

    ■ Choose Insert > Hyperlink.

2. When the Insert Hyperlink dialog box shown in Figure 4.4 appears, choose the type of link you want to create in the Link To column on the left. Most of the links you'll create are likely to be to other files or Web pages, so for this example, leave the Existing File or Web Page button selected.

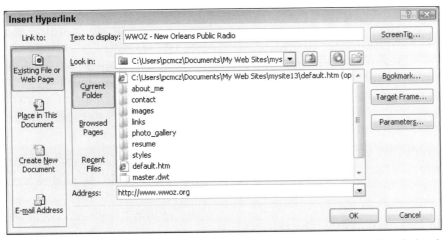

Figure 4.4 Specify the type of hyperlink you want to create using this dialog box.

3. Specify the destination for the link you want to create by doing one of the following:

    ■ If the file you want to link to is contained in the same Web site you are editing, select the file in the Web site's contents displayed in the center of the Insert Hyperlink dialog box.

- If the destination is a file on an external Web site, type the URL in the Address box in the Insert Hyperlink dialog box. Include the http:// prefix, like this: http://www.mysite.com or http://www.mysite.com/images/ pearl.gif.

4. When you're done, click OK. The Insert Hyperlink dialog box closes, and you return to the Web page you are editing, where your hyperlink has been added.

If the link is text based, the text will be underlined and highlighted in a color. (The color depends on the current settings in Page Properties, as described earlier in this chapter.) If the clickable link is an image, you won't see any obvious highlighting to mark that image as clickable. When you preview the page (choose File > Preview in Browser) and pass your mouse pointer over the image, you'll see the destination link displayed in your browser's status bar.

If you switch to Code View or Split View, you can either type the code for your links by hand or get a glimpse at the code Expression Web is generating for your links. The HTML for links uses the anchor tag, which consists of an `<a>` start tag and an `</a>` end tag. An attribute called `href` (which stands for Hypertext Reference) is used with `<a>` to make the link. A link to my own home page looks like this:

```
<a href="http://www.gregholden.com">Greg's Home Page</a>
```

The text between the start and end tags, `Greg's Home Page`, is the clickable link. The URL http://www.gregholden.com is the destination. If the starting point for the link is contained on one page within your site and you are linking to another page, you only have to use a relative URL, like this:

```
<a href="contact.htm"> Contact Us </a>
```

This link assumes that the page that contains the words `Contact Us` and the destination page `contact.htm` are in the same directory. Suppose you are on `index.htm`, which is on the top level of the Web site, and the destination page, `contact.htm`, is located in a directory called `pages`, which is also contained within the top-level directory. The URL would look like this:

```
<a href="pages/contact.htm"> Contact Us </a>
```

Since Expression Web alleviates the need for you to type the code for these links yourself, you can concentrate on what's important: making sure your link text is clear and encourages visitors to click. Avoid using the words "Here" or "Click here" in your links. Instead, focus on giving information about what your visitors will find when they click on the link and visit the destination you want. Give them an incentive to explore. "Discover resources for Web page content" is a far better clickable link than "Click here for resources," for example.

Creating Bookmarks

You've probably visited Web pages that contain a sizeable amount of content and that make the content easier to navigate by including links that lead from one page to the next. You might have a series of links at the top of the page, for instance; clicking on one of the links leads you to a heading farther down on the page. Anything you can do to keep your Web page content easy to digest and use will increase the number of visits and return visits.

Naming Bookmarks. Bookmark hyperlinks make your site easier to navigate, and they keep visitors exploring your site longer. It's easy to make a bookmark link: First you identify the bookmark (the place you want to jump to), and then you make a link to it. Follow these steps:

1. Select the text that you want to convert to a bookmark by highlighting it, or alternatively, position your cursor in the text you want to jump to.

2. Choose Insert > Bookmark to open the Bookmark dialog box (see Figure 4.5).

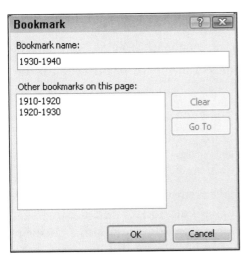

Figure 4.5 Name your bookmarks using this dialog box.

3. If you highlighted a word or phrase for your bookmark, you'll find that text entered in the Bookmark Name box. Otherwise, type a brief name in the Bookmark Name box.

4. Click OK. The Bookmark dialog box closes.

If you highlighted a word or phrase, a dotted line appears underneath it when you view the text in Design View. If you simply positioned your cursor at a point on the page, you see a flag icon at the spot where the bookmark was created. The dotted line and flag aren't visible when someone browses your page. Bookmarks are invisible to your visitors.

Note: You need to have paragraph marks turned on in order to see the flag icon. If you don't see it, select View > Formatting Marks > Show. Make sure the Paragraph Marks option is selected.

Linking to Bookmarks. Once you have marked your bookmarks, you need to make hyperlinks to them. This part is the same as making a conventional hyperlink on a Web page. First you select the clickable link itself—a word, phrase, or image. Then follow these steps:

1. Open the Insert Hyperlink dialog box as described earlier in this chapter (for instance, by clicking the Insert Hyperlink toolbar button).

2. Locate the page that contains the bookmark you want to link to by clicking it in the file list in the center of Insert Hyperlink.

3. Click Place in This Document in the Link To column. The bookmarks you added to the current page are displayed in the list in the center of the Insert Hyperlink dialog box.

4. Click the bookmark you want to link to.

5. Click OK to make the link, and OK to close the Insert Hyperlink dialog box.

If you ever want to delete the bookmark you have created, right-click it and choose Bookmark Properties. When the Bookmark dialog box opens, click Clear. If you have a flag icon rather than dotted text as your bookmark, position the cursor to the right of the bookmark and press Delete.

Linking to an E-Mail Address

One of the most common ways to allow visitors to get in touch with you is to make a link to your e-mail address. This allows users to click on the link and open a message composition window that is preaddressed to you. Because spam e-mailers frequently scrape the contents of Web pages, looking specifically for e-mail addresses to harvest, it's not a good idea to make the clickable link text the same as your e-mail address. In other words, don't make this your clickable link:

`e-mail me at frank@website.com`

Instead, create a clickable link like this:

`Send your questions and comments to our Webmaster`

This clickable phrase can then be linked to your e-mail address. Select the clickable phrase, open the Insert Hyperlink dialog box, and click the E-Mail Address button in the Link To column. Then type the desired e-mail address in the E-Mail Address box in the Insert Hyperlink dialog box. You can also add a subject line in the Subject text box, but this is optional. (Chances are your correspondents will want to add their own subject lines.) When you're done, click OK.

Editing Hyperlinks

Creating hyperlinks is easy, but making sure they actually work and that they continue to work over time is an important and time-consuming task. Right-click the link, whether it's text or an image, and then choose Follow Hyperlink from the context menu. A Web browser opens and displays the destination for the link. If the destination doesn't display what you want, you need to edit the hyperlink. Return to the Expression Web window, right-click the link, and choose Hyperlink Properties from the context menu. When the Hyperlink Properties dialog box appears, you can change the clickable link text, alter the destination URL, or add an additional feature called a ScreenTip.

A ScreenTip is a useful interactive feature your visitors are likely to appreciate. It's a label that opens onscreen when someone passes the mouse pointer over a link. Screen-Tips aren't displayed by older browsers (for instance, versions of Internet Explorer before 4.0). But most newer ones display them, and they give visitors an idea what they'll find when they click on the link. An example is shown in Figure 4.6.

To add a ScreenTip to a link, right-click the link and choose Hyperlink Properties. The Edit Hyperlink dialog box appears. This dialog box looks almost exactly like Insert Hyperlink. Click ScreenTip and enter the text you want to appear in the ScreenTip using the box shown in Figure 4.7.

You can also use Edit Hyperlink to revise other essential aspects of your link. In the Text to Display box, you can change the clickable text shown on your page. If you need to revise the destination of the link, change the relative or absolute URL displayed in the Address box. If you want the hyperlink to open the destination page or content in a new frame, click Target Frame. (The current page has to be part of a set

Figure 4.6 ScreenTips can encourage visitors to click on links.

Figure 4.7 Specify your ScreenTip text in this dialog box.

of frames for this to work; see the section on frames later in this chapter.) If you need to remove the link altogether, click Remove Link. When you're done, click OK.

Verifying Your Hyperlinks with Reports

One of the most important link-related functions you can perform is to verify that the links actually lead where you want them to. Web pages and Web sites change all the time; the constantly evolving nature of the Web is in fact one of its best points. But that means that the URL you provide for a link that's outside of your own control (a link on someone else's Web site) might change from one day to the next. Links on your own Web site can change as well: You might delete the page that a link points to, or you might type the URL incorrectly. A link that goes to a "page not found" page is called a *broken link*, and it can irritate your visitors and discourage them from visiting your site in the future.

To keep people from being turned off by your hyperlinks, you need to verify them. Expression Web is especially well equipped to test your hyperlinks automatically and report which ones are problematic for some reason. To run a hyperlinks report, you need to be connected to the Internet. You also need to save all the open pages on your site by choosing File > Save All. Then choose Site > Reports > Problems > Hyperlinks. The Web Site View in the center of the Expression Web window changes to Reports View and displays a report of any hyperlinks within the current Web site that don't work. If all of your links work, Hyperlinks View won't have anything to display. Any external hyperlinks you may have made aren't displayed yet. To verify them, click the Verifies Hyperlinks in Current Web button in the toolbar at the top of Hyperlinks View (see Figure 4.8). When the Verify Hyperlinks dialog box appears, indicate whether you want to verify all hyperlinks or only those that are unknown. Then click Start.

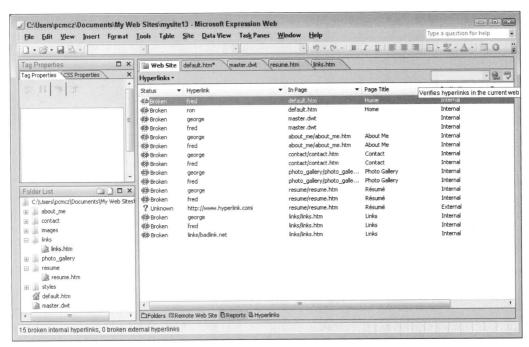

Figure 4.8 Expression Web can run reports that check your hyperlinks for problems.

When you click Start, Expression Web checks any external links you have made. It tries to connect to the URL you have provided and verifies that the link works. A progress bar lets you know the status of the verification process. As each link is checked, a green checkmark appears next to it. When the process is complete, you can read a summary in Expression Web's status bar.

If you encounter a broken hyperlink, double-click the link that is labeled as broken in the Hyperlinks report. The Edit Hyperlink dialog box appears. If you want to change the page that contains the link, click Edit Page. If you want to edit the URL associated with the clickable link (and if the link is broken, you definitely want to edit the URL), click Browse and visit the destination URL. You might have to do some searching around the Web to find the right URL, but when you do, copy it and paste it into the Replace Hyperlink With text box in the Edit Hyperlink dialog box. By default, the link will be changed anywhere it appears in your Web site. Optionally, you can click the radio button next to Change in Selected Pages and click the names of the pages where you want to update the link, which appear in a list in the bottom of the Edit Hyperlink dialog box. Click Replace to make the repairs and close the Edit Hyperlink dialog box.

Note: Since it's so easy to verify links in your Web site, it's a good idea to check them every week or two. That way your site won't contain any incorrect information that will turn visitors away.

Layout Options

Layers, tables, and frames all have a place in many of the Web sites you'll be creating with Expression Web. They help you organize Web page content and gain control over how your pages look and exactly where individual objects are positioned. The three options are very different in appearance, behavior, and the programming that makes them function. Layers and tables are created with Cascading Style Sheets (CSS), while frames use HTML. Layers tend to be more popular among designers who want their Web pages to conform to design standards. Tables, however, are practical and easy to use but some designers consider them more difficult to revise than one that doesn't conform to Web standards. Frames add interactivity to Web pages but are considered outdated because their contents can't be indexed by search engines. In addition, they are not supported by older browsers; as a result, they aren't used very often.

Positioning Content with Layers

Layers give professional designers the capability to design Web pages and overlap images and other content with precision. A *layer*, like a table, is a container that can hold text, images, colors, and other Web page content. In terms of Web page code, a layer is simply a <div> with its position set to relative or absolute. Layers are special because of their dynamic nature: They can be moved around on the page freely, and they can overlap other layers or be nested within larger layers.

For all their flexibility, layers carry one slight limitation: They're not supported by a few of the older browsers. A handful of users who try to view a page that contains layers won't see anything at all—unless you create an alternate version of the page using tables instead of layers.

To add a layer to a Web page, you need to do one of three things:

- Choose Insert > HTML > Layer. This instantly adds a layer to Design View or Code View.

- Drag the Layers icon from the Toolbox into Design View or Code View. This instantly creates a layer.

- Select Task Pane > Layers. This opens the Layers task pane, as shown in Figure 4.9, which is one option in the Expression Web interface for adding or formatting layers. Click the Insert Layer button to add the layer to your page.

Figure 4.9 The Layers task pane lets you create and change the display order of layers on a Web page.

In any case, after you add a layer, you can move it freely around Design View or resize it at will. But first, you need to actually *see* the layer. When you first add a layer to a page, it's empty and not visible. Choose View > Visual Aids > Empty containers to see frames if they're not selected. The borders of the frame will be made visible so you can add content to it.

Note: Another way to add layers is to take advantage of one of Expression Web's predetermined CSS layouts. These don't specifically use the word "layers," but they divide a page into one or more <div> containers, which are essentially layers. Choose New > Page > CSS Layouts and double-click one of the options to create the new page.

Drawing Layers

If you are an artist and comfortable with drawing, you have the option of drawing a layer in the editing area. Choose Task Panes > Layers to display the Layers task pane if needed. Then follow these steps:

1. Click Draw Layer in the Layers task pane.

2. Position the cursor inside Expression Web's editing area; when you do so, the cursor turns into a pen. Click and drag down and to the right to draw the layer. Release the mouse button when the layer is the size you want.

3. If necessary, resize the layer by clicking and dragging one of the resizing handles. (In order to see the resizing handles, click the layer's selection handle.) A layer can also be moved freely by clicking and dragging its selection handle. The handle appears as a label in the upper left-hand corner with the label div#layerx, where x represents the number of the layer on the page (see Figure 4.10).

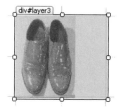

Figure 4.10   A layer can be moved by clicking and dragging its selection handle.

Snapping into Line: the Ruler and Grid   When you're positioning layers, two features of the Expression Web editing window can make your work easier: the ruler and the grid. The ruler gives you both horizontal and vertical measurements. To display the ruler, choose View > Ruler and Grid > Show Ruler. By default, when the ruler appears, the measurements are in pixels. By choosing View > Ruler and Grid > Configure, you can change the unit of measurement to inches, centimeters, or points. You can also change the spacing of the grid at the same time.

Together, the ruler and grid makes creating layouts or tables a snap—literally. Choose View > Ruler and Grid > Show Grid to turn on the grid to draw layers more accurately. If you choose View > Ruler and Grid > Snap to Grid, the table cells or layers you draw "snap" (in other words, jump to) the nearest grid line, which can help you achieve even more precise alignment of layers or other objects.

Ordering Labels

One of the best things about adding layers to a Web page is that they are automatically assigned a "stacking" order (also called *Z-order*). On a page with three layers, for instance, one layer is placed at the top of the stack, the other at the bottom, and the third in the middle. You can adjust the order as needed to control which ones are visible or to change other properties. Layers are assigned a place in their stacking order whether or not they're actually placed atop one another.

You track the order and make changes by choosing Task Panes > Layers to display the Layers task pane. The eye icon at the top of the task pane affects the visibility of all layers at once: Click the eye icon to toggle between hiding and displaying it. If the eye appears open, that means all layers are visible; if the eye appears closed, it means they are invisible. The same applies to the eye icon next to each layer on the page, too. In Figure 4.11, an eye icon appears next to Layer 2.

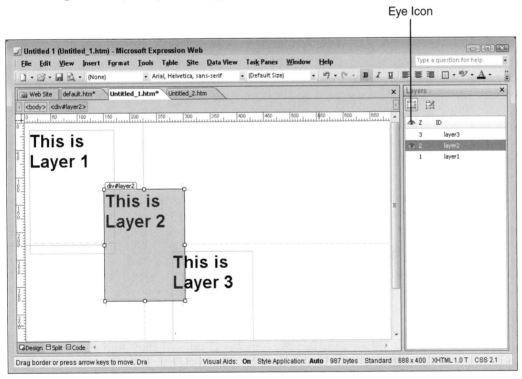

Figure 4.11   Each layer can have an eye icon next to it to indicate that it is visible.

Two other columns in the Layers task pane help you control each layer's attributes:

- **ID:** A default name such as Layer 1 or Layer 2 appears in this column, but you can change the name. A clearer name makes it easier to keep track of objects in the Layers panel or if you're writing scripts for the page.

- Z: This refers to the order of the layer in stacking, and it is used in case the currently selected layer is part of a stack of multiple layers.

Note: You can also position a layer and change its attributes by right-clicking the layer's name in the Layers task pane, and then choosing Positioning from the context menu. You can also create an ID-based style by using a layer's ID name as the style selector, such as `<style> #layer1 {background:aqua} </style>`.

When you first add a layer to a page, not only is it empty, but its borders might not be visible unless it is selected. If layers aren't visible, choose View > Visual Aids > Empty Containers to make them visible even when they are not selected.

In terms of Cascading Style Sheets (CSS), layers play an important role. A layer is a container called a `<div>` that has been placed in a specific position on a page. Many CSS layouts contain `<div>` tags that have not been positioned. Many of the templates contained in the CSS Layouts section of the New dialog box are pages that consist of `<div>` tags that are essentially unpositioned layers. A layer (or positioned `<div>`) can be nested within an unpositioned `<div>`. To add an unpositioned `<div>` to a Web page, choose Insert > HTML > div.

Getting Organized with Tables

Tables are aspects of Web page code that subdivide contents into rows and columns. Tables are often used to present numeric data or any information with headings or categories and multiple types of information beneath them. By default, tables are enclosed within visible borders. The subdivisions within tables also have visible borders by default. But designers have the option of making borders invisible (by changing their width from 1 to 0 pixels, for example). Tables with borders that aren't visible can be used to lay out entire Web pages. This approach isn't encouraged because CSS provides layouts that are more precise and standards-based. However, in case you have special reasons to use tables, the sections below briefly describe how to create simple tables that present small amounts of data and more complex tables that organize Web pages.

Presenting Data in Rows and Columns

The most straightforward type of table is one that organizes data or text in rows and columns. This kind of table is shown in Figure 4.12.

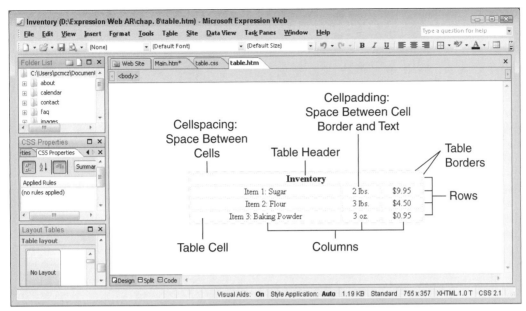

Figure 4.12   A basic Web page table consists of visible rows and columns divided into cells.

The first step in creating such a table is one that doesn't directly involve Expression Web: getting the information together and deciding how you want to present it. You might need to write a list on paper to get an idea of how many columns and rows your table needs. Your initial estimate doesn't need to be perfect; it's easy to add or delete rows and columns after you create a table. You create a table in one of two ways in Expression Web: You draw the table directly in the editing area with a miniature Pencil tool, or you specify the number of rows and tables you need in the Insert Tables dialog box. Choose Table > Insert Table. Open the Insert Table dialog box, and do one of the following:

When the dialog box shown in Figure 4.13 appears, enter data in the appropriate controls to specify the following elements of your table:

- **Rows:** Enter the number of rows the table should have.

- **Columns:** Enter the number of columns the table should have.

- **Width:** The width of a table can be expressed either as a percentage of the width of the page, as displayed in the browser window, or as a fixed number of pixels. Choose Percent or Pixels to switch between the two types of measurement.

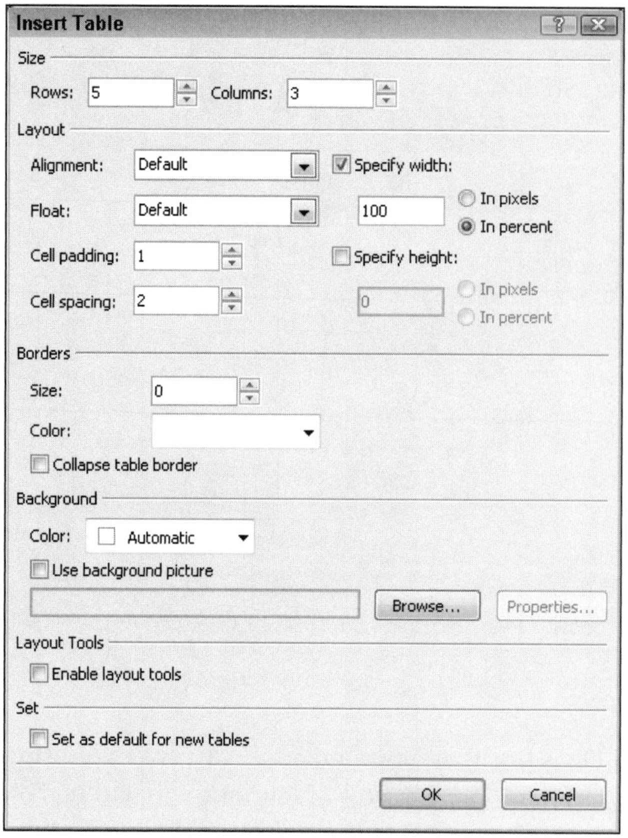

Figure 4.13   The Insert Table dialog box.

- **Border:** Set the border to 0 if you want it to be invisible. (The width shown is in pixels; set the value to 3 if you want a three-pixel-wide border.)

- **Cell Padding:** This is optional; it controls the space (in pixels) between the contents of the cell and the cell border.

- **Cell Spacing:** This is optional; it refers to the space between cells, in pixels.

Note: If you want to use Insert Tables to create a table that is used to design a Web page (rather than Layout Tables, which are described in the following section), you should not only set borders to zero, but you may want to create columns or rows that are empty except for a nonbreaking space. This creates space between columns that contain content.

After you finish specifying values in the Insert Table dialog box, click OK. The table appears in your page. It's worth noting that Expression Web automatically generates CSS to create the table formatting. Some of the table formatting is contained in a style that can be reapplied to other tables you want to create by choosing it from the Apply Styles task pane.

Note: You can also set properties for an existing table in the Tag Properties task pane. Select the part of the table you want to format (such as an individual cell) by positioning the cursor within it or by choosing Table > Select > Table, Column, Row, or Cell. Then click one of the tags in Tag Properties (such as Align). Pass your mouse pointer to the right, click the drop-down arrow that appears, and choose an option from the drop-down list.

Creating Layout Tables

Tables are commonly used to design Web pages for a variety of reasons. They are recognized by virtually all Web browsers, for one thing. They're relatively simple to learn and use, too. They aren't as precise as layers, however. And the W3 consortium, in a page that explains how designers can use CSS for layout rather than tables (http://www.w3.org/2002/03/csslayout-howto), also points out that users who have configured their computers to make contents easier to read due to disabilities might be unable to render some table layouts accurately. A better reason is accuracy: You can position CSS columns more precisely than you can tables. Tables are still perfectly good for most applications where absolute precision is not a critical concern, however.

Choosing a Predesigned Layout Table. Expression Web gives you the Layout Tables feature, which includes a variety of predesigned table layouts. Choose Task Panes > Layout Tables, and you view a set of tables that have been specially designed to arrange the contents of entire Web pages. (You'll probably need to scroll down to the bottom of the task pane to see the layouts.) The most common types of page layouts are contained there, and chances are good that you'll find one layout to meet your needs. Scroll down through the task pane to view the 11 different options, as shown in Figure 4.14. You can use the Layout Table tools for any table, including one you created with the Insert Table dialog box as described earlier. Right-click the table, choose Table Properties from the context menu, and choose Enable Layout Tools. You can also enable the controls by selecting the table and clicking Show Layout Tool in the Layout Tables task pane.

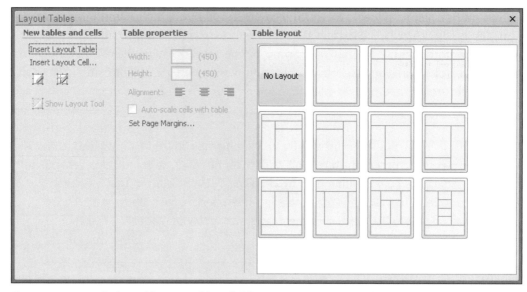

Figure 4.14 Predesigned layout tables divide pages into rows and columns.

Just position the cursor at the spot in the current Web page where you want the table to appear. Then single-click one of the layouts, and it appears in your page complete with corner and size handles showing so that you can adjust it if you need to.

Drawing a Layout Table. If you are an artist or designer and are more comfortable with a pencil in your hand than a computer mouse, you have the option of creating your table by hand. The Draw Table command on the Tables toolbar or in the Layout Tables task pane gives you the opportunity to arrange a page by manually outlining the table itself and the cells within it. To draw a table, follow these steps, which focus on the Tables toolbar:

1. Open the page where you want the table to appear.

2. Select View > Toolbars > Tables. The Tables toolbar appears.

3. Click the Draw Layout Table button in the bottom-right corner. The button is highlighted, as shown in Figure 4.15.

4. Once you have the Draw Table button highlighted, you can start drawing immediately. Click in Design View at the spot where you want the upper-left corner of the table to appear.

5. Press and hold the mouse button, and drag down and to the right. Release the mouse button, and the outer border of the table is created.

Use Pencil to Draw
Table or Table Cells

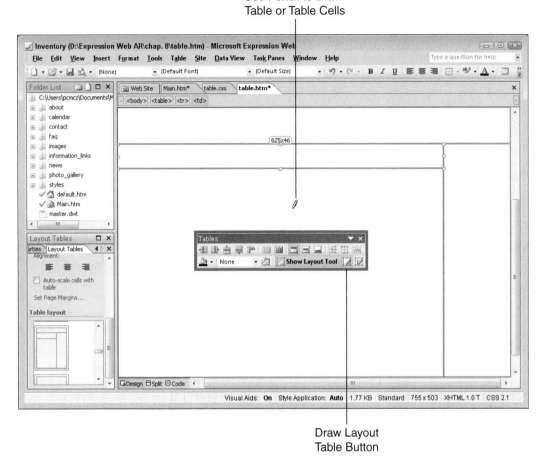

Draw Layout
Table Button

Figure 4.15   The Tables toolbar allows you to draw and edit a table.

6.   Resize the table, if needed, by clicking and dragging one of the four corners.

7.   You can then create a table cell one of two ways:

■ Click inside the table to activate the Tables toolbar buttons. Then click the Column to the Left, Column to the Right, Row Above, or Row Below button on the toolbar to split the table into two rows or columns.

■ Click the Draw Layout Cell button in the Tables toolbar, and draw the cell within the table by clicking and dragging within the table border.

8.   If you don't draw the table cell perfectly the first time, click and drag its corners or on the middle handle at the center of one of the sides to resize the cell.

9. Repeat steps 6 and 7 until the table has the number of rows and columns you need. But keep in mind that you can only resize or move one of the table cells you drew yourself, not other cells that may have been created automatically when you drew a cell.

You can use other buttons in the Tables toolbar, such as Distribute Rows Evenly or Distribute Columns Evenly, to adjust the table. If the Show Layout Tool button is selected in the Tables toolbar, you see handles that describe the exact dimensions of each cell or table border, as shown in Figure 4.16. As you drag a table or cell border, the figures shown in the handles adjust interactively.

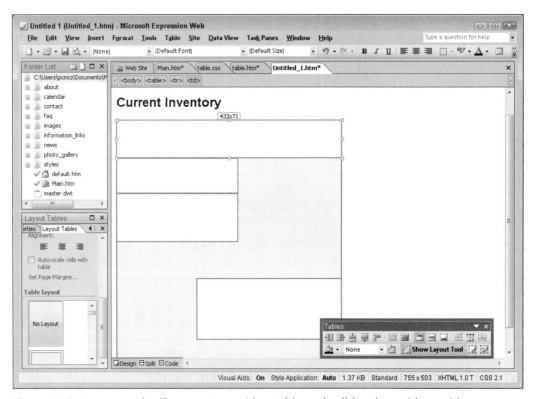

Figure 4.16 Layout tools allow you to position table and cell borders with precision.

Selecting and Editing Tables

Once you have created a table, it's a simple matter to add text or images. Just position the cursor within an individual cell. You can then type and format the text you need, or you can insert a graphic image by choosing Insert > Picture and choosing one of the Picture submenu options.

If you need to select part of a table other than a single cell, you've got a couple of options. First, click to position the cursor within the table. Then select the table by choosing Table > Select > Table. (Or right-click and choose Select > Table from the context menu.) You can format an existing row, cell, or column by clicking it and then choosing Table > Select > Row, Cell, or Column. Selecting the item enables you to delete it if you wish. You also can right-click anywhere within a table and edit by right-clicking and selecting Cell Properties or Table Properties. You can then change the dimensions or add a background color by changing settings in the Properties dialog box that appears.

If you don't want to use the Select submenu options within the Table menu, you can click immediately above a column to select it or just to the left of a row to select it. It takes some practice; move the mouse pointer just above a column until it turns to a down-pointing arrow; click your mouse button, and you select the column. The same approach applies to a row; position the pointer to the left, and when it turns into a right-pointing arrow, click the mouse button to select the row.

When laying out a page on the fly, your initial specifications don't have to be your final ones. As you work with your Web page, you'll probably adjust spacing so its contents are readable. When your table covers most of your Web page and controls the design for most or all of the page, you'll almost certainly need to adjust the spacing between columns so the columns of your page are far enough apart. Maintaining some empty space on a page helps a viewer read the contents more easily and directs the viewer's eye toward the most important contents.

You can make your table easier to read and more visually interesting by assigning background colors to cells or other areas within it. Each cell, row, or column in a table can have its own background color. Select the part of the table you want to format, right-click it, and choose Cell Properties or Table Properties from the context menu. When the Properties dialog box appears, choose a color from the Color drop-down list under the Background heading.

When you choose Task Panes > Layout Tables, the Layout Tables and Cells task pane opens. It gives you a user-friendly, interactive way to edit a table. The New tables and cells section of layout tables lets you draw a table manually. Insert Layout Table lets you draw a table in Design View; Insert Layout Cell lets you draw a cell within a table. Click the Show Layout Tool button if you want to interactively display the size of each table or cell you select by displaying a size handle. The Table Properties section lets you change the overall width and height of the table, or you can change its alignment within the Web page in which it appears. The Auto-Scale Cells with Table option automatically changes the size of the cells within a table as you resize the table; in general, this box should be checked. Otherwise, your table is likely to appear jumbled when the cells remain the same size even as the table changes size.

Formatting Individual Cells

Expression Web gives you a fine-grained level of control over tables through the Cell Properties dialog box. Its controls let you adjust the formatting of each cell within a table. When you right-click a cell and choose Cell Properties, you see three sections that let you control the formatting of a cell:

- **Layout:** This section lets you adjust the width and height of a cell. By default, the measurements are in pixels. (You can change the value to percent using the Cell Properties dialog box.)

- **Borders:** The Borders section lets you control the border around the cell. You can adjust the width of the border, change the color, and even choose one of the five options next to Apply to apply the selected width and color settings to individual sides of the cell border.

- **Background:** The Header cell box identifies the cell as a header. Often, the first row of a table is designated as a header. Alternatively, you can format a header so it appears just above the table and describes the content of the table. And any cell can be designated as a header within the table.

You might create a table to format a catalog of different items. Each cell can describe an individual item. The headers and footers within each cell can provide specific information about the objects depicted. An example is shown in Figure 4.17.

The controls within Cell Header and Footer let you control the height, padding, alignment, background color, and borders of each one of the headers or footers. To activate the options, check the box next to Show Header or Show Footer, or both, depending on which item you want to include within the cell.

Choosing Between Tables and Layers for Layout Tables and layers are both popular options for laying out Web pages, though they have both largely been superseded by CSS. When is it best to choose tables, and when should you use layers instead? It isn't an either/or decision. You can use tables and layers in the same page. You can also use tables for the initial design and convert the tables to layers later on, and vice versa.

Layers aren't supported by a few of the oldest browsers, so you might choose tables when you want to ensure that your page can be viewed by all possible browsers. Tables also let you align page contents in a grid, with rows and columns.

Another consideration that's just as important is your own working style. If you prefer flexibility in overlapping and stacking content, layers are the way to go. Insert and arrange them if you want to overlap some page content. You can then convert the layers to tables to ensure universal visibility.

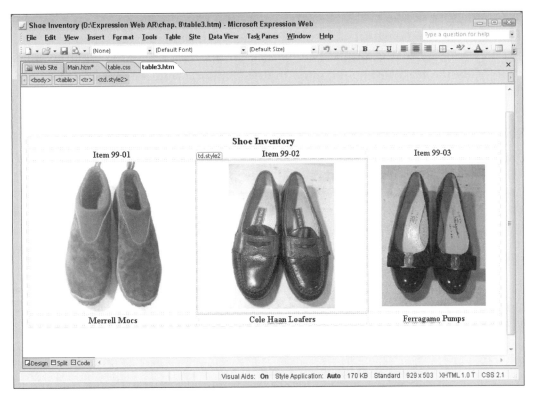

Figure 4.17   Each cell within a table can have its own header and footer.

Dividing a Page into Frames

A frame, like a layer or a table, is a subdivision of a Web page. A frame can contain text, images, links, or a combination of all of these. A frame, in fact, is a Web page within a Web page. A page that has been divided into two or more frames is called a *frameset*: a set of frames. The set includes the original Web page (the page that contains the frames) and the frames pages themselves.

In a typical frameset arrangement, one frame takes the form of a banner across the top of the page. The banner frame might display an advertisement or the name of your company or Web site. Another frame might present the viewer with a set of links along the side of the main page. A third frame might contain the main body text of the page.

Frames enable designers to present a large amount of information in a relatively small space. And they make Web pages interactive: Usually, a link in one frame causes the file associated with the link to appear in an adjacent frame. Frames aren't as popular as they once were on the Web. In fact, you need to be aware that frames are frowned upon by most Web designers, not only because they make pages look overly complex and "clunky," but because they have an old-fashioned look and feel that suggests the designer is behind the times. Not only that, but they interfere with ordinary bookmarking of Web sites, usually hiding the content away from the base URL of a page's master frameset. And they make pages more difficult to find by search engines. You can accomplish the same frames-based effects with layers or JavaScript. Nevertheless, frames are fully supported by Expression Web, which includes a set of frames-based layouts in its Web site templates.

Web pages that have been divided into frames can't be seen by some users. A few of the very oldest browsers don't display frames layouts. A problem that's more likely to occur, however, is with Web-enabled cell phones or handheld devices that don't support frames display. For such users, you need to create an alternate set of content for your page called a *NoFrames layout*. This enables all users to see some content on your site. The alternate content might be something as simple as a message stating that "This page uses frames layout, and you need another Web browser to see it." It's even better to create an alternate layout that uses conventional HTML, and possibly tables, to organize your page's content. The alternate content is contained within the `<noframes>` and `</noframes>` tags in the code for your Web page.

Creating a Frameset

You don't have to write the code for frames from scratch; you choose a common frameset arrangement by choosing New > Page and clicking Frames Pages. Choose one of the frames layouts listed in the box in the center of the New dialog box, and a thumbnail example and brief description appear on the right, as shown in Figure 4.18. Click OK to create the new page, which has been divided into separate frames.

When you first create a frameset, it appears as a new page that has been added to the Web site you are currently editing. The page is divided into frames, each of which contains two buttons: Set Initial Page and New Page. Remember that each frame

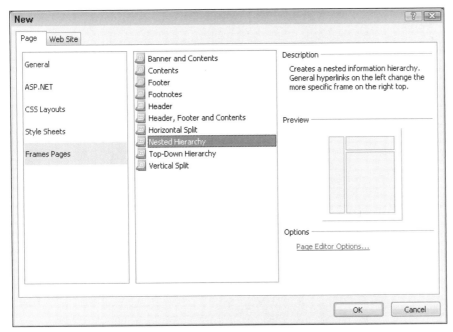

Figure 4.18   You can add one of 10 preconfigured frames layouts to the current Web site.

contains its own Web page. You click one of these two buttons to identify the page that will actually be contained within the frame:

- Click Set Initial Page if you already have a page created that you want to appear in the frame. When you do so, the Insert Hyperlink dialog box opens. Locate the page you want to add in the list in the center, and click OK. The Insert Hyperlink dialog box closes, and the page appears.

- If you don't already have a Web page created that you want to add to the frame, click New Page. This opens a new blank Web page within the frame. You can then begin typing and adding content as needed.

You can adjust one of the templates easily after you insert it. You need only to drag frame borders to resize them. When you save the frameset by choosing File > Save or File > Save All, you are prompted to name and save each of the frames pages in succession. (If you would rather save a single page individually rather than all the pages in the frameset, you can do so by selecting Format > Frames > Save Page or Save Page As. The frameset shown in Figure 4.19, which was created from the template called Nested Hierarchy, actually consists of four pages: the three frames pages and the frameset page, which contains the formatting information for each of the frames.

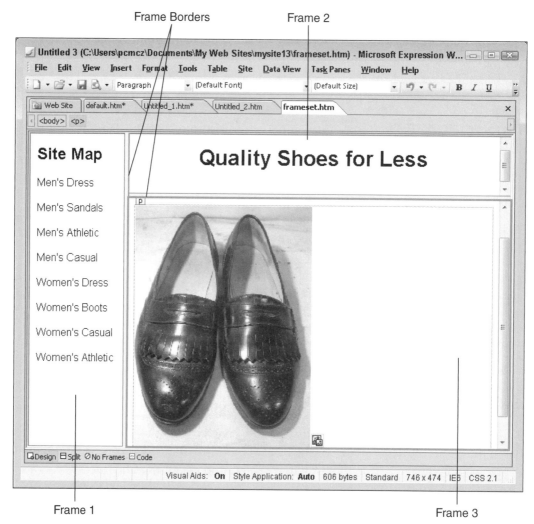

Figure 4.19 This simple frameset consists of four pages, not three.

Note: A particular type of frame called an *inline frame* does not have visible borders. Instead, it is embedded within a Web page. This is in contrast to conventional frames, which have obvious borders. Expression Web enables you to configure both types of frames. Add an inline frame to a Web page either by dragging the inline frame from the Toolbox into Design View or by choosing Insert > HTML > Inline Frame. The advantage of inline frames is that they are Web pages in their own right, embedded within another Web page, but they don't have obvious borders and appear less obtrusive than conventional frames. Viewers don't necessarily know they are looking at a frames layout; they only see the content of the inline frame (unless the inline frame includes scrollbars).

Changing Frame Properties

Each frame in a frameset has its own borders, scrollbars, background colors, and size. Changing these attributes is done by opening the Frame Properties dialog box. Follow these steps:

1. Right-click the frame you want to edit.

2. Choose Frame Properties from the context menu. (Alternately, you could position the cursor within the frame and choose Format > Frames > Properties.)

3. In the Frame Properties dialog box shown in Figure 4.20, change the attributes as described in the next section.

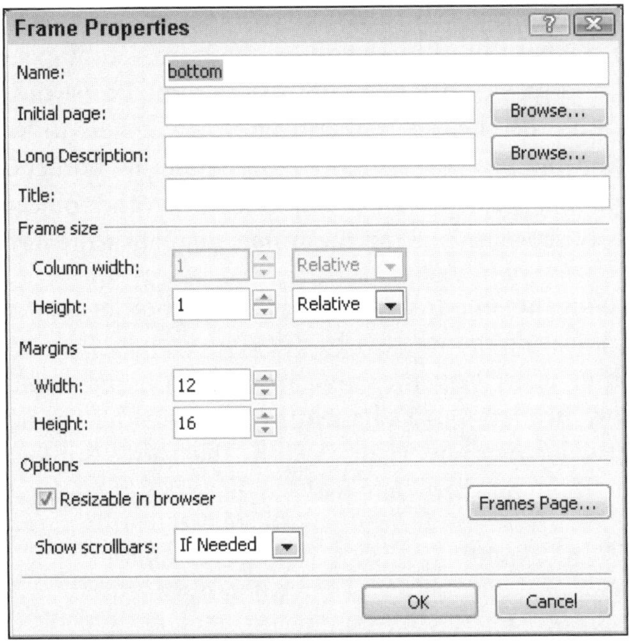

Figure 4.20   Rename a frame or change its characteristics using this dialog box.

Naming and Describing Frames. It's important to give a frame a clear and easy-to-remember name in case you want a link in another frame to point to this frame as a target. To point to a frame, you refer to it by the name contained in Frame Properties. The Initial Page field in Frame Properties gives you the filename for the file that opens when the frame initially appears. Long Description gives you a chance to provide some details about the frame so that viewers whose browsers don't display frames know what's in it. Title is the short descriptive word or phrase that appears in the title bar of the viewer's browser window.

Displaying or Not Displaying Scrollbars. The scrollbar settings in Frame Properties control when or if scrollbars appear in the frame. By default, Expression Web displays a scrollbar when the content of a frame is longer than the frame itself. You may not need a scrollbar at all if the frame contains only a single logo or other image, for instance. In that case you can choose Never from the Show Scrollbars drop-down menu list; this prevents Expression Web from ever displaying scrollbars for that frame. Always means the frame will always display scrollbars, whether or not they are actually needed. If Needed is the default option and means that scrollbars appear only if the frame's content can't be displayed in its entirety in the frame.

Changing Size and Margins. The Frame Size section of Frame Properties allows you to specify the width and height of the selected frame as a fixed number of pixels or as a relative value (relative to other frames that have been given pixel or percentage measurements) or as a percentage (20 percent of the height of the frameset, 50 percent of the width of the frameset, and so on). Another control in Frame Properties, the Resizeable in Browser box, should be checked if you want your viewers to be able to change the frame size within the browser window by dragging its borders. You may want to uncheck this option if your frame contains an ad or other object that you don't want the viewer to obscure by making the frame smaller, however.

Adjusting Borders. By default, each frame in a frameset is assigned a border that is visible and two pixels in width. You can change this by clicking Frames Page in Frame Properties. The Frames tab of Page Properties appears. To make the frame border invisible, uncheck the Show Borders box. Change the value in the Frame Spacing box to make the border wider or thinner. By default, the Show Borders box is checked because frames without borders can make a page look jumbled and confusing.

Targeting Frames

Every link in a frameset needs to have a target: a location where the content of the link will appear. Unless you identify a target where the linked content should appear, the content appears in the same frame in which the link appeared before you clicked on it. In fact, if one of your frames contains a set of links leading to the various important pages on a Web site, chances are good that you want those links to remain onscreen while someone explores your site. If someone clicks one of the links and a new page is launched, that person may have a hard time navigating your site. To target a frame, follow these steps:

1. Create the link you want to target, whether it is text, an image, or other item.

2. Select the link and click Insert Hyperlink in the Common toolbar.

3. In the Address box in the Insert Hyperlink dialog box, enter the URL for the link.

4. Click Target Frame, and choose one of the frames from the list of frames on your page, or type the name of the frame where you want the link content to appear in the Target Setting box.

5. Click OK.

When you divide a page into frames, it's important to use them appropriately. Don't target a link to a page that has itself been divided into frames; having a frames page within a frames page can be bewildering. In general, don't use too many frames, or viewers may easily be confused.

Note: No matter which site layout scheme you use, Expression Web will create special folders with odd-looking names like _vti_cnf and _vti_pvt. These folders contain general configuration information about your site; leave them where they are and don't delete them or their contents.

Working with Images

Expression Web makes images easy to work with; it gives you all the basic controls you need to insert and edit images to your Web pages. There are a few new features, such as IntelliSense, which prompts you to fulfill CSS and XHTML requirements and add an ALT textual description to make your content accessible to visitors with vision problems. And you can perform absolute positioning of images using the ruler and grid as well as dragging images around in Design View. You'll even find some unusual features such as the ability to resample an image in Design View and insert an image from your scanner or camera.

The process of creating graphics for the World Wide Web differs considerably from designing for print or other media. Images have to be captured as digital files, and they have to be saved in a file format that compresses the file so it can be transmitted quickly across the Internet. A compressed file is one in which the data that makes up the graphic—the pixels or the vector objects—is made shorter, usually by means of an algorithm. The algorithm recognizes repeated patterns of binary data and reduces them to "shorthand" data that takes up less room. The three compressed formats are these:

- Graphic Interchange Format (GIF). GIF is commonly used for line art and other images. One of the most important qualities of GIF is that such an image can contain transparency. If the background color is made transparent, the image appears to be "floating" atop the page background. GIF images can also be animated; an animated GIF lets you show a sequence of images, but the sequence is saved as a single file.

- Joint Photographic Experts Group (JPEG). JPEG provides higher compression than GIF because it discards nonessential image information. This makes JPEG better suited for photos and continuous tones of grayscale or color than GIF. JPEG includes the ability to choose between a variety of compression levels when you save an image. The higher the compression, the smaller the file size, but the lower the image quality. Expression Web lets you adjust the compression of a JPEG image according to a scale of 1 to 100.

- Portable Network Graphics (PNG). This image format was created as an improvement over GIF, but this format hasn't caught on widely. PNG does provide excellent compression, combined with excellent image quality, however. There are many varieties of PNG, but Expression Web lets you save images in two forms: PNG-8, an 8-bit version of PNG that is similar to GIF but results in better quality, and PNG-24, a 24-bit version of PNG that is similar to JPEG but provides better image quality than JPEG.

With most Web editors, you need to open and adjust images in a separate graphics program such as Photoshop. You can, however, open a wide variety of digital images within Expression Web and then save them in one of the formats listed above. In fact, if you paste an image that's in a format not supported by Web browsers, such as BMP or WMF, into a Web page and then save the page, Expression Web will automatically try to convert it to GIF or JPEG format. You can also change an image from one format to another manually. You don't have to open the image in a graphics program, edit it, save it, and reopen it in Expression Web. Just follow these steps:

1. Make sure you are in Design View and, with the Web page open that contains the image you want to edit, right-click that image.

2. Choose Change Picture File Type from the context menu. The options shown in Figure 4.21 appear.

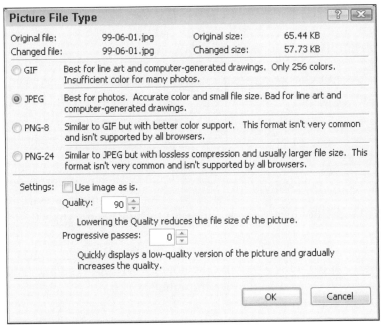

Figure 4.21 You can change file type or control how Expression Web converts image files using these options.

3. If you need to convert the image from one file format to another, choose one of the four options (GIF, JPEG, PNG-8, PNG-24). If you want to choose a different compression level for a JPEG image, uncheck the box labeled Use Image As and choose another Quality setting.

4. Click OK.

You might choose to adjust file compression if your image appears onscreen too slowly; changing it to PNG with its better file compression would make the file smaller. It's not unusual to open a JPEG image that's too big in file size (say, 500K or even 1MB). Such a file will take too long to load in a Web browser, even with a high-speed Internet connection. You can increase the compression in the Picture File Type dialog box to reduce the file size.

You can view or change default settings for a specific type of image file by selecting Tools > Page Editor Options. Click the Picture tab in the Page Editor Options dialog box. The controls on the Picture tab allow you to change default file type settings and default file type conversion procedures.

Adding Images

No matter what format your images are in, it's easy to add them to your Web pages with Expression Web. Begin by doing one of the following:

- Choose Insert > Picture and choose an item from the submenu: From File or From Scanner or Camera.

- Copy an image file from the Folder List task pane or Web Site list in the middle of the Expression Web window by pressing Ctrl+C and paste it into the current Web page by pressing Ctrl+V.

- Drag the image icon from the Toolbox into the editing area.

- Drag an image file from the Folder List task pane into the editing area when you are in Design View.

When you drag the image icon from the Toolbox, the image icon appears where you placed it in your Web page. You need to double-click the icon to open the Picture Properties dialog box. When you choose From File, the Picture Properties dialog box also appears. Click Browse to find the file you want to add; select it and click OK to add it to your page. Before you choose From Scanner or Camera, your digital camera needs to be connected to your computer and needs to be switched on. After you choose this option, a dialog box appears that lets you select the image on your camera that you want to add.

Once you add an image, you might need to resize it. You can crop the image using the Pictures toolbar, which appears when you choose View > Toolbars > Pictures. Click the image to select it, click the Crop button on the toolbar, and draw a box across the part of the image you want to preserve. Of course, you need to see the entire image at once in order to crop it. If you need to resize the image, you need to do one of two things:

- Click the image to select it and scroll through the image until you find the resize handle at the bottom-right corner of the image. Then, hold the Shift key down and drag the corner to resize (drag in toward the center of the image to make it smaller; drag out to make it larger).

- Alternately, because it can be hard to find that resize handle, you can right-click the image and choose Picture Properties from the context menu. You can then change the size by altering the height and width figures on the Appearance tab shown in Figure 4.22. (Make sure the Keep Aspect Ratio checkbox is selected so the image doesn't get distorted.)

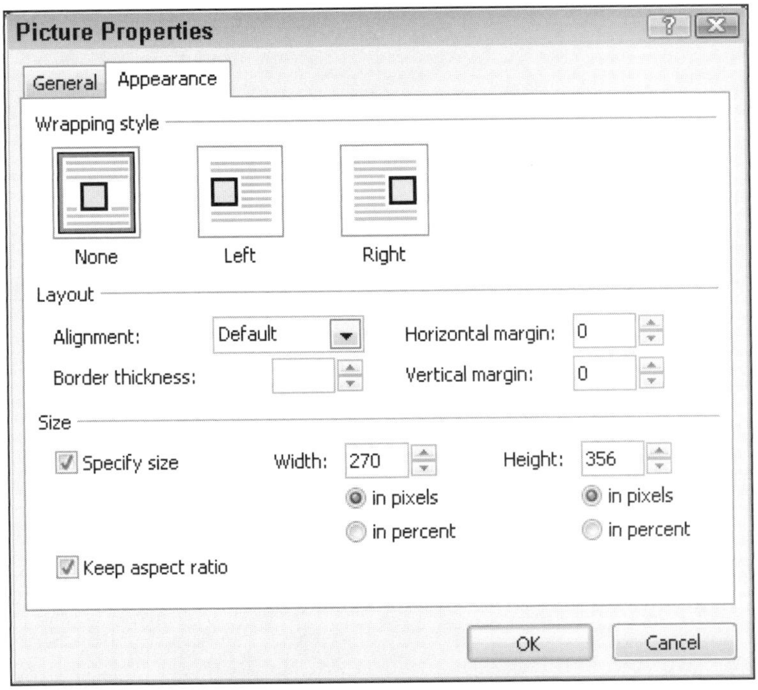

Figure 4.22   You can change the height and width of an image in the Appearance tab.

Note: When you an insert an image, it's important to include an Alt name. The term Alt comes from the HTML tag that identifies this bit of information (`<img alt="name"/>`). An Alt attribute appears when a user passes the mouse arrow over the image and if the browser and version support such messages. Alt attributes serve as alternatives to the image itself. If one of your viewers has image display turned off or images are too slow to load, the Alt attribute appears to describe the image that is supposed to appear. When you insert an image, you are automatically prompted to add the Alt attribute before the image is added to the Web page you're working on.

Adjusting and Positioning Images

When you first add an image, by default virtually no padding (blank space) is inserted between it and the adjacent text. You can add more space by selecting the image and holding Shift down while dragging the edges of the image. The padding appears around the image as blue shading.

Alternately, you can specify a number of pixels for padding in the CSS Properties task pane:

1. Choose Task Panes > CSS Properties if you need to display it.

2. Once CSS Properties appears, make sure the Show Categorized List button is selected.

3. Scroll down the list of headings until you see the heading Padding, which is under the bold Box heading.

4. Click the plus sign next to Padding, and click one of the four options (padding-top, padding-right, padding-left, and padding-bottom).

5. Click the down arrow that appears to the right of the option you want.

6. Click Pick Length to display the Length dialog box, and enter the number of pixels of padding you want in the Length value field.

7. Click OK to close the Length dialog box; the padding is displayed around your image.

As far as positioning images, you have a variety of options. For simple alignment such as making an image flush-left, centered, or flush-right, the simplest option is to select the image and then click one of the alignment options in the Common or Formatting toolbar.

For more precise positioning, you need to take advantage of Expression Web's support for CSS. In order to use CSS for positioning, you first need to make sure the Use Width and Height Attributes for Images Instead of CSS is not selected in the CSS tab of the Page Editor Options dialog box. Then you need to either assign a style to the image or create a new style for it. To create a new style, select the image and follow these steps:

1. Select Format > New Style.

2. When the New Style dialog box appears, click Position under the Category list on the left.

3. Click the drop-down lists on the right side of the dialog box that represent the positioning attributes you want to specify (left, top, and so on).

In each case, choose (value) from the drop-down list and then type a number of pixels.

4. Enter a selector name for the new style, if you wish, in the Selector box near the top of New Style (be sure to precede the name with a dot).

5. Click OK to close New Style.

6. Click the name of the new style that appears in the Apply Styles task pane. The image is repositioned.

You can use the New Style dialog box to resize the image as well as reposition it. The Pictures toolbar contains options for positioning that go well beyond simply aligning an image on the left or the right side of a page. For instance, if you have positioned your image along with other images, you can control where any one of the images appears in the group by clicking the Bring Forward or Send Backward button in the toolbar. Rotate Left and Rotate Right spin the image to change its orientation; Flip Horizontal and Flip Vertical change what appears at the top or left-hand side of the image. There are other Pictures toolbar options, such as Bevel, which adds a three-dimensional border to an image.

You can also wrap text around an image using the Picture Properties dialog box. Right-click the image, choose Picture Properties from the context menu, and choose one of the three alignment options in the Wrapping Style section: Left wraps the text around the left side of the image, Right wraps text around the right side, and None prevents text from wrapping. You can also choose one of the options from the Alignment drop-down list:

Default: This tells Web to use whatever settings are contained in the style sheet that is being used on the page.

Baseline: The baseline of the text (the bottom of letters like e, x, and a, rather than the descenders) is aligned with the bottom of the image.

Sub: The top of the text is just above the top of the image.

Super: The bottom of the image is aligned with the top of the ascender of the adjacent line of text.

Top: This aligns the top of the image with an invisible line just above the top of the text.

Text-Top: This aligns the top of the image with the top of the tallest ascender in the first line of text next to it.

Middle: This aligns the middle of the picture with the bottom of the text next to it.

Bottom: This aligns the bottom of the image with the middle of the line of text adjacent to it.

Text-Bottom: This aligns the bottom of the image with the bottom of the text adjacent to it.

Some of these menu options produce subtle rather than dramatic effects, and you have to try them out yourself to see how they change the position of the image and adjacent text.

Adding Hotspots to Images

Any image that you add to a Web page can be turned into an imagemap: an image that contains one or more clickable *hotspots*. A hotspot is a clickable area; when the user clicks inside the hotspot, his browser goes to a remote location. A classic example is a map of a city, state, or country. Each region within the map is a separate clickable area; when the user clicks the map, the browser jumps to a Web site with more detailed information about the region.

Expression Web's Pictures toolbar makes it easy to draw one or more clickable hotspots on an image and turn those hotspots into hyperlinks. Images that work best are those with well-defined clickable areas and not too complex: You don't want to force visitors to hunt around to figure out where to click. When you are in Design View, select the image. Then choose View > Toolbars > Pictures to display the Pictures toolbar, if necessary. Then follow these steps:

1. Click one of the hotspot buttons on the toolbar: Rectangular, Circular, and Polygonal. They are just to the left of the Highlight Hotspots button shown in Figure 4.23.

Figure 4.23 Draw a shape atop part of an image to turn it into a clickable hotspot.

2. Draw the shape atop the image. When you release the mouse button, the Insert Hyperlink dialog box appears. Use the dialog box's controls to turn the region into a hyperlink. Then click OK to create the link.

3. Click the Highlight Hotspots button to highlight the hotspots in black. This enables you to check whether they are drawn in the locations of the image where they need to appear.

If you have drawn a polygonal hotspot, be sure to double-click when you get to the end of the drawing to tell Expression Web that the shape is complete. If you're not happy with the shape of the hotspot the first time you draw it, click the Highlight Hotspots button and then click and drag its handles to enlarge or move it. You also can highlight the hotspot and click Delete to remove it.

5 Managing Your Site with CSS

O f all Expression Web's innovative and powerful tools, its suite of controls for applying and managing Cascading Style Sheets (CSS) has gained the most attention. CSS is a Web standard—an agreed-upon and official set of instructions that enables sites to be standardized and updated quickly. Standards are recommendations put forth by groups like the W3 Organization (http://www. w3.org), which set rules and technologies that determine how browsers interpret what they encounter on the Web. As more and more Web content appears on laptops, cell phones, handhelds, and other hardware, it becomes increasingly important to separate the content of a Web page from its formatting instructions. By doing so, CSS helps assure that Web sites have a consistent appearance across all Web browsers.

CSS has been closely integrated into the Expression Web program interface. It provides you with separate task panes for applying and managing styles as well as tracking CSS properties. You even have a helpful feature called Code IntelliSense that tells you how to apply styles correctly and reports on how CSS is being used throughout your site. This chapter will help you get started using CSS without having to become an expert at it. As long as you know a little bit about CSS, Expression Web will make sure it's used correctly throughout your site.

Understanding CSS

CSS is a set of instructions that enables you to create sophisticated layouts with columns and layers that are standards based: They can be viewed the same way from one Web site to another. CSS also lets you create style sheets that alleviate the need for formatting words, paragraphs, or other items individually by choosing options like Bold, Center, or Italic from the menu bars. If your Web site contains dozens or even hundreds of separate files, such formatting can consume valuable time. The formatting instructions are included in the style sheet in the form of individual styles. You can define or change the formatting of many Web pages with a single click anywhere in the CSS document.

CSS also gives you a high level of control and precision over Web page content. Style sheets let you handle positioning of Web page elements that conventional HTML doesn't always handle, such as the margins around a Web page, dividing a page into columns, or adjusting the space between columns or other containers. CSS enables you to take design to a new level of precision. You can:

- Specify unusual bullet forms.

- Assign mouseover effects to hyperlinks.

- Create and position layers to contain text, images, and other contents (see Chapter 4).

- Add background colors to individual text blocks.

- Position images or other Web page contents to a precise point or pixel measurement.

- Go beyond straightforward bold, italic, or underlining to specify the degree of bold or italic you want or the kind of underlining you want.

- Make changes globally to some or all of the pages on a site at once by revising the external style sheet that is attached to them.

- Specify the amount of padding or margin space on any of the four sides of any element on the page.

The term "cascading" in the name Cascading Style Sheets comes from the fact that one type of rule cascades into another, creating a virtual style sheet that controls how a Web browser displays a page. An inline style that is added directly to the body of a Web page and that affects a single object on the page has the highest priority. It overrides an internal style sheet—one that is embedded in the <head> section of the HTML document. The internal style sheet, in turn, overrides an external, internal, or inline style sheet, which is a .css file. The style sheet overrides a browser's default settings.

CSS separates the look and presentation of Web pages from their structure. By including formatting commands in a style sheet, you can focus on the structure and content of the pages. You can then update a design easily without having to worry about the content. Once you start using CSS to position page elements precisely, you might never go back to conventional HTML for Web page design. On the other hand, CSS can also coexist with HTML commands and override them; you can use both markup systems together to make your content look just the way you want.

Studying CSS in Code View

CSS instructions can reside in different parts of an HTML document, depending on what they are intended to format. If the CSS styles apply only to the current page, they go in the <head> </head> section of the HTML file. To get a look behind the scenes and learn how CSS files are constructed, follow these steps:

1. Choose New > Page.

2. When the New dialog box appears, click CSS Layouts.

3. Double-click the first layout in the list: Two columns, left fixed. Two files open: Untitled_1.css and Untitled_1.htm.

4. By default, the Untitled_1.htm file appears on top. Click the Code tab at the bottom of the Expression Web editing area to switch to Code view in the currently displayed Web page file. You'll see Web page code that includes the following line:

```
<link rel="stylesheet" type="text/css" href="Untitled_1.css" />
```

This line, which is contained in the <head> section of the HTML file (between the tags <head> and </head>), doesn't contain any formatting instructions of its own. Rather, it refers to the style sheet document Untitled_1.css, which is identified by the filename extension .css. The HTML document contains three divs, which have these IDs:

- left_col

- page_content

- container

Click the tab for the CSS file, Untitled_1.css, and you see the formatting instructions that apply to each of these IDs.

```
#left_col {
    width: 200px;
    position: absolute;
    left: 0px;
    top: 0px;
    }

#page_content {
    margin-left: 200px;
}
```

```
#container {
    position: relative;
    width: 100%;
}
```

This block of CSS contains three rules. Each rule consists of a selector (the HTML element that is being formatted) and the style (or in this case, styles) to be applied to it. The form is as follows:

```
selector { property: value }
```

In the example below, left_col is the first selector. It has a number of properties and values associated with it, such as width: 200px. When multiple properties and values are used, they are listed in series and separated by a semicolon, like this:

```
selector { property1: value1; property2: value2 }
```

In the code above, the properties include `position`, `margin-left`, `width`, and so on. If you have one or more styles that affect multiple pages, they go in their own document—just as they are in this example, with the file `Untitled_1.css`. In other cases, Web pages can have their own internal, embedded style sheets, which are contained in the `<head> </head>` section. And individual elements such as paragraphs or headings can have their own style sheet commands. No matter where they are contained, the CSS formatting commands are the same. Figure 5.1 calls out the formatting instructions (selectors and properties) so you can see them more clearly.

This example presents a series of three rules. Rules are the main building blocks of CSS styles. A single inline rule can affect a single Web page element; a style sheet can contain many rules that affect multiple pages. A rule can declare one or more properties. A property tells a browser how to format a specified element.

The # symbol that precedes certain names identifies them as ID selectors: They each affect a single element within the body of the page, rather than all such elements on the page. A selector is an element that has a declaration associated with it. The declaration consists of a property and its associated value. A value is an attribute associated with a property. For example, in the expression `{ background:yellow }`, `background` is the property, and `yellow` is the value.

There's much more to CSS than this; in fact, style sheets can be quite complicated. But with Expression Web, it doesn't need to become overwhelming. This chapter doesn't tell you how to write CSS all on your own; it takes more work than that. But this section gives you just enough information to get you started and help you understand what you're actually doing when you work with Expression Web's CSS controls, such as the CSS-related task panes.

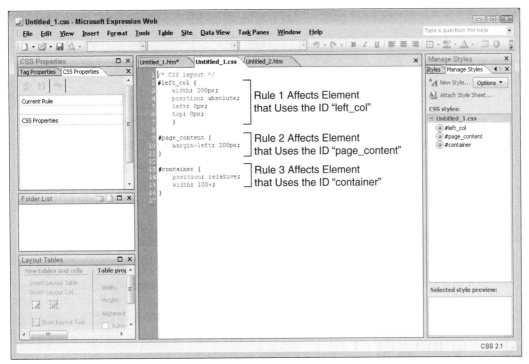

Figure 5.1 You can work directly with CSS in Code view or leave it "behind the scenes" and use the CSS task panes.

Exploring the CSS Task Panes and Toolbars

The primary tools for implementing CSS on your Web site are Expression Web's task panes and toolbars. You need to know about three task panes in particular:

Apply Styles task pane: This is a good place to start when it comes to creating styles. You also use this task pane to modify existing styles, apply styles to parts of your Web pages, or attach an external style sheet. Apply Styles displays each style as it appears in the page so you can quickly locate the one you want. Apply Styles also shows an inline style when the currently selected content uses one.

Manage Styles task pane: Many of the same features in Apply Styles are also in this task pane, which might be confusing, but it means you don't necessarily need both task panes open at the same time. The difference is that you don't get a visual representation of a style in this task pane. You use it to move a style from one style sheet to another. Manage Styles lists all element-based styles in a file. (Apply Styles shows an element-based style only when the currently selected content uses one.)

CSS Properties task pane: This is one of the most useful task panes in the entire Expression Web interface. It allows you to see all the styles used in the current selection. The styles in the CSS Properties task pane appear in their cascading order from highest precedence (lowest in the list) to lowest precedence (highest in the list) according to their effect on the current selection. You also can use CSS Properties to modify styles.

Besides the task panes, you need to know about two toolbars that help you work with CSS. Like Expression Web's other toolbars, you access them by choosing View > Toolbars. The Style toolbar lets you add or remove styles or create and apply new ones. The Style Application toolbar is more advanced. It helps you choose formatting features and tell Expression Web whether to generate a new style or modify an existing style you choose from the Target Rule menu.

Creating a Style Sheet

There's no need to write a style sheet from scratch with Expression Web unless you want to. It's far more practical to start with a style sheet template and modify it or do some formatting on your Web page and create a style from it. Expression Web's Dynamic Web Templates give you another option for accessing style sheets and adds the Master Page feature, which makes it easy to update entire Web sites.

Using a Style Sheet Template

You learned about Expression Web's CSS page layout templates in Chapter 4. Choose New > Page and select CSS Layouts, and you are presented with a selection of CSS arrangements that divide Web pages into multiple rows and columns. But suppose you are primarily interested in finding a combination of colors and type fonts that gives your site just the graphic appearance you want. Maybe you want a modern, space-age feel; maybe you want a restrained, cool look that appeals to a sophisticated audience. If you choose New > Page and click Style Sheets, however, you are presented with a set of style sheet arrangements that have suggestive names. The names suggest the general look and feel of the Web page you create when you apply the style sheet. "Suggest" is the operative word here because you don't see a preview of the finished page. In fact, you don't know exactly what the components of the style sheet are like until you actually open it.

Here's an example. Follow these steps:

1. Double-click the style sheet called Blueprint, and a CSS document opens named Untitled_X.css (X is a number that depends on the number of other documents you have open).

2.   Choose File >Save.

3.   When the Save As dialog box opens, enter the name blueprint.css for the file, and choose CSS Files from the Save as Type drop-down list. Click Save.

4.   Open a new blank Web page file by clicking the New Document button.

5.   Open the Manage Styles panel, if necessary, and click Attach Style Sheet.

6.   When the Attach Style Sheet dialog box opens, click Browse, and locate the blueprint.css file you created earlier. Double-click the file to select it and add its path to the Attach Style Sheet dialog box.

7.   Click OK to close the Attach Style Sheet dialog box and attach the style sheet.

You can see immediately that this style sheet has a bright yellow background. If you type some text, select that text, and then choose the Heading 1 style, you'll see that it also contains dark blue Heading 1 headings in Century Gothic type. These are the attributes of the Blueprint style, and they're shown in Figure 5.2. Also notice that the Manage Styles Task pane presents a list of the styles contained in the CSS file, while

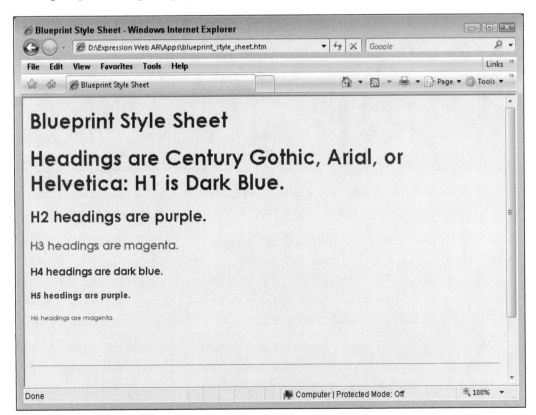

Figure 5.2 Blueprint is one of 13 ready-made style sheet designs.

the Apply Styles Task pane contains previews of the styles as they appear in the HTML file.

In contrast, if you open the style sheet called Neon, you get something very different: neon green text on a black background, with headings that are green, blue, or red: a page that's colorful and high-tech in appearance, in other words (see Figure 5.3).

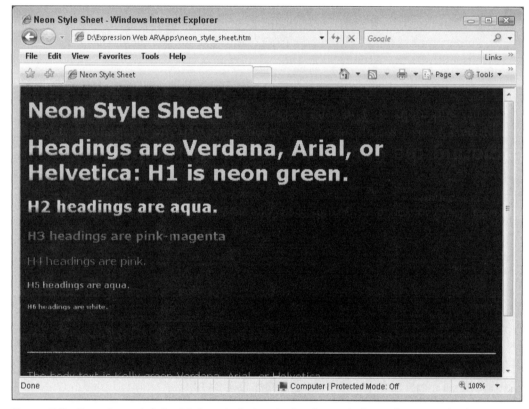

Figure 5.3 Neon has a bright, high-tech feel to it thanks to choices of type and color.

It can be time consuming to open layout after layout to find just the one you want. To help save you some time, Table 5.1 presents the type, color, link, background, and other attributes of all 12 options (the thirteenth option is blank, and this is not included).

Note: The style sheets have more attributes than those shown in the following table. Each one has H2 and H3 colors as well as H1 colors. They also have individual link colors. To keep the table simple, these attributes were omitted.

Table 5.1 Expression Web Style Sheet Templates

Style Sheet	Text Font	Text Color	Heading Font	H1 Heading Color	Background
Arcs	Verdana	Brown	Times	Olive Green	Pale Yellow
Bars	Arial	Dark Gray	Times	Blue-Green	Light Olive Green
Blocks	Bookman	Blue	Bookman	Blue	Light Silver
Blueprint	Century	Blue	Century	Dark Blue	Bright Yellow
Capsules	Arial	Black	Arial	Orange	Light Green
Downtown	Garamond	Yellow	Verdana	Orange	Dark Blue
Expedition	Book Antiqua	Black	Book Antiqua	Brown	Peach
Highway	Verdana	White	Verdana	Orange	Black
Neon	Verdana	Green	Verdana	Green	Black
Poetic	Book Antiqua	Pale Blue	Book Antiqua	Gold	White
Street	Verdana	Navy Blue	Comic Sans MS	Maroon	Light Blue
Sweets	Arial	Purple	Arial Rounded MT Bold	Purple	Pale Yellow

Once you insert one of these templates, you are free to improvise and add or change styles as needed. You can see previews of each style in the Preview area of the Apply Styles task pane to help you determine if the color or type font is the one you want.

Creating Styles from Existing Formatting

Expression Web's style sheet templates work well if you need the application to give you a "starting point"—to suggest the colors, typefaces, and other attributes you want to use to format your content. But many designers want to determine on their own how their Web pages should incorporate styles. They prefer to assemble designs organically by trying out different designs and settling on the ones that look right, and then turning those formatting instructions into styles.

You can try this yourself by opening an HTML document and typing a heading. Choose Heading 1 from the Styles drop-down list in either the Common or Formatting toolbar.

Then apply your own formatting to the heading. For instance:

1. Choose Franklin Gothic Demi from the Font drop-down list.

2. Choose Task Panes > Apply Styles to display the Apply Styles task pane and notice that as you format the heading, a new style called .style1 is highlighted; the style name is displayed in the formatting you add.

3. Highlight the heading and choose Format > Font to display the Font dialog box.

4. Choose Teal from the Color drop-down list.

5. Choose Bold Italic from the Font Style list.

6. Click OK.

7. You have successfully formatted a single heading. But if you want to apply the same formatting to multiple Heading 1 heads, you need to save the formatting as a new style. Rather than using the generic .style1 name you see displayed in Apply Styles, it's better to use a clearly understandable name that you and your co-workers can apply to Heading 1 headings in the future. Pass your mouse pointer over the style name .style1 in Apply Styles.

8. When the drop-down arrow appears to the right of the style name, click the arrow and choose Rename Class ".style1" from the drop-down menu.

9. When the Rename Class dialog box appears, type the new name (such as H1) in the box supplied and click OK. The new style name appears in Apply Styles.

Now, when you are creating Web page content in the current Web site, you only have to type a heading and then click the H1 style in Apply Styles to immediately apply the style you have selected.

The preceding set of steps adds your new style to your Web page's internal style sheet. If you want to apply the style to other Web sites, however, you need to create a new style sheet beforehand and then add the new style to it. To create a new style sheet, choose File > New > CSS. A new blank .css file opens in the Expression Web editing area with the generic filename Untitled_x.css. Choose File > Save and save the document in your site with a clearer name so you and any co-workers can recognize it easily.

Once you have created a new style sheet, you need to attach it to the Web page you're editing, as described in the following section.

Attaching an Existing Style Sheet

Style sheets become more flexible and give you new convenience and power when they can be attached to more than one Web page or even more than one site. You attach an external style sheet in one of two ways:

- If you want to attach the style sheet to more than one page (or if the CSS file you want to attach is not displayed in the Folder list because it is part of another Web site), click Attach Style Sheet.

- If you want to attach the style sheet only to the currently open Web page, drag the CSS document from the Folder list into Design View.

When you click Attach Style Sheet in either the Apply Styles or Manage Styles task pane (or choose Format > CSS Styles > Attach Style Sheet), the dialog box shown in Figure 5.4 appears. A single option in this dialog box is guaranteed to save you hours of work: By choosing All HTML Pages, you tell Expression Web to attach the style sheet to all Web pages in the currently open site, instead of the single page you have displayed onscreen.

Figure 5.4   You can attach a style sheet to a single page or multiple pages.

Choosing Attachment Options

If you want to attach a style sheet to selected Web pages in a site rather than all pages, here's a good option: select the pages to which you want to attach the style sheet by selecting them in the Folder List task pane. (Press Ctrl+C to select files or folders that aren't contiguous.) Then choose Format > CSS > Attach Style Sheet. When the Attach Style Sheet dialog box appears, click Selected Page(s) and then click OK.

The Attach Style Sheet dialog box gives you two different methods for attaching a style sheet: Link or Import. Link is more common and is supported by all browsers. Import is a newer method but not supported by all browsers. Use Import if you want to prevent browsers that don't recognize it from using the styles in the style sheet you have attached using the Import method. Use Link if you want to ensure that the styles are displayed correctly by all browsers. If you want to ensure that the page is displayed correctly by all browsers, you can do both: First link the style sheet, and then import it.

Detaching Style Sheets

Just as you can attach a style sheet, you can also detach it from one or more Web pages. Doing so removes the formatting instructions contained in the style sheet from the attached pages. The steps for detaching are straightforward:

1. If you want to detach the style sheet from an entire site, open the site. If you want to detach the style sheet from selected pages only, select the page(s) in the Folder List task pane.

2. Choose Format > CSS Styles >Manage Style Sheet Links.

3. When the Link Style Sheet dialog box opens, click the name of the style sheet you want to detach.

4. Choose one of the displayed options: Current Page, All Pages, or Selected Page(s). The Selected Page(s) option detaches the style sheet only from pages you have selected. If an additional dialog box called Confirm Format Style Sheet Links appears, click OK to confirm that you want to detach the style sheet.

5. Click Remove.

6. Click OK.

Note: Only style sheets that use the Link method for attachment appear in the dialog box. If you don't see the style sheet listed because it uses the Import method, find it in the Folder List.

Using Code IntelliSense with CSS

Code IntelliSense is an Expression Web feature that presents "hints" for Web page code as you are writing it. IntelliSense can be used to help write many types of Web page content correctly, including CSS. Taking advantage of IntelliSense can help ensure you use the correct syntax when you assign styles to your pages. You can, for instance, stop hyperlinks from being shown as part of references to class-based or

ID-based styles. You can also have IntelliSense prevent the closing curly brace(}) from being added automatically when you make a new CSS declaration.

To access IntelliSense's options for CSS, choose Tools > Page Editor Options. Click the IntelliSense tab of the Page Editor Options dialog box, and select or clear one of the following:

- To control whether or not pop-up lists appear as you work on CSS statements (or other statements), prompting you to automatically insert an item on the list, click the Auto Popup Statement and Parameter Completion items.

- To control whether or not the right curly brace (}) that ends a style declaration block is automatically added after you type the left curly brace, select or clear the Auto Insert item CSS Selector Closing Brace.

- To control whether or not to add an underlined link so you can jump to a class-based style's rule set, select or clear the Code Hyperlinks item.

When you're done, click OK to close the Page Editor Options dialog box. Most of these items are helpful, but you may want to delete them if you want to do things yourself and don't want IntelliSense to interfere with your coding.

Tip: The Page Editor Options dialog box has an Authoring tab that lets you select the particular version of CSS, called a *schema*, that you want to use. Select the version you want from the Schema drop-down list. You can choose the schema version that corresponds to CSS level 1, 2, or 2.1. Or you can choose CSS IE6, which uses only CSS level 1, Internet Explorer 6 extensions to CSS, and CSS level 2 custom cursors. The current CSS schema version you're using is presented in the status bar at the bottom of the Expression Web window. If you double-click the version in the status bar, you automatically open the Page Editor Options dialog box with the Authoring tab in front, so you can change it if you want.

Running CSS Reports

Reports that track down errors or Web site features such as hyperlinks are essential tools for maintaining large-scale Web sites. Expression Web includes a variety of Web site reports, most of which help you track errors or features that don't work right. But the CSS-related reports provide you with substantial data describing how CSS files are used, which style sheets are linked to particular files, and other information.

Using the CSS Reports Task Pane

CSS is all about generating Web site code that is clean and standards compliant. If you have a page that has incorrect markup, styles you don't need, or other commands that aren't used, it's best to either correct it or remove it. Otherwise, your pages will be slow to load. The Web server that hosts your site might also become loaded down with unnecessary material or confused with code that doesn't work right. The CSS Reports task pane is the place to turn when you want to track down such problems.

Before you run a report, however, you have the option of specifying which part of the site you want Expression Web to report on. By default, only the current page in the Web site that is currently active is checked. But you can tell Expression Web to report on selected pages within a site or an entire Web site. To focus the report only on certain pages, select those pages' icons in the Folder list or by clicking the Web Site tab in the central editing area to switch to Web Site View. (You can use Shift +click or Ctrl+click to select multiple files.)

Once the files are selected, choose Task Panes > CSS Reports to open the CSS Reports task pane if needed. Click the CSS Reports button, which appears as a green arrow in the upper left corner of the task pane, if you want further control over how the report is run. Clicking the arrow opens the CSS Reports dialog box in a separate window (Figure 5.5). This dialog box lets you select which criteria you want Expression Web to report on. You can also specify All Pages instead of the Selected Pages option if you wish.

Note: The Selected Pages option in the CSS Reports dialog box is active and "clickable" only when you actually have multiple pages selected in the Folder List task pane or the Web Site view. Similarly, the Open page(s) option is active only if you have more than one page open in the current Web site.

The CSS Reports dialog box is useful if you want to specify which types of errors you want to check or which types of usage problems you want to locate. The Errors tab is there to help you create Web pages that use CSS syntax correctly and are thus standards compliant. The three kinds of errors are all checked by default: Unused Styles, Undefined Classes, and Mismatched Case:

- Unused Styles checks for markup instructions in a style sheet that don't refer to any content in your site.

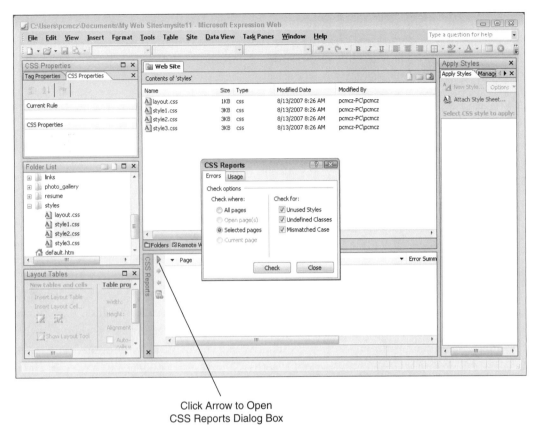

Click Arrow to Open
CSS Reports Dialog Box

Figure 5.5 You can focus a CSS Report on selected pages or an entire site using this task pane.

- Undefined Classes finds styles that are referred to by content in one of your pages but that aren't defined in a style sheet.

- Mismatched Case locates styles that are defined and have the correct references in a Web page but that can't be matched correctly because the reference and the style sheet name use different cases—for example, a style reference is made to "class1," but the style sheet actually lists "CLASS1."

By default, all three options are checked in the Usage tab: Class, ID, and Element selectors. The Usage tab helps you keep track of which style sheets are attached to which pages—a task that can be especially difficult on extensive Web sites with dozens or even hundreds of separate pages.

Uncheck any of the options in either the Errors or Usage tab if you want to focus your report more narrowly. When you're ready, click Check to run the report. (You can also click Close if you want to close the CSS Reports dialog box without running the report.)

Note: You also have the option of generating a third type of report that isn't covered by the CSS Reports dialog box. The Style Sheet Links report provides you with a list of all the pages in your site that include links to an external style sheet. Choose Site > Reports > Shared Content > Style Sheet Links to run a Style Sheet Links report.

Reading CSS Reports

While a report is being generated, the status bar at the bottom of the CSS Reports task pane tells you which page is in the process of being checked. Once you run a report, either in the CSS Reports task pane or the Style Sheet Links submenu of the Site menu, you need to interpret the results and use them. When you create an Errors or Usage CSS Report, the results appear in the CSS Reports task pane. You can click the buttons on the left side of the task pane (see Figure 5.6) to track down individual problems by moving from one item to another or by sorting the results.

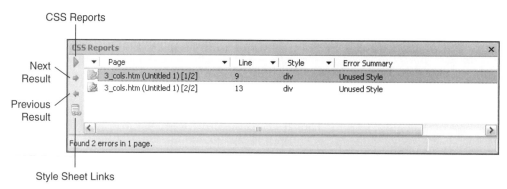

Figure 5.6 Buttons on the left side of the task pane.

If you click Next Result, you not only move to the next result on your list, but you also open the Web page that contains the result so that you can edit it and correct any mistakes right away. Previous Result performs the same function for the previous item. The Style Sheet Links button opens the Style Sheet Links report.

Using Web's Positioning Tools

Expression Web frequently gives you two, three, or even more ways to perform a task, and that includes positioning Web page contents. If you're in a hurry, you can drag-and-drop something on a Web page. Or you can enter values in one of several CSS dialog boxes or task panes. The options all give you a way to place Web page contents with precision while creating layouts that look consistent and use simple, standards-compliant code.

Absolute and Relative Positioning—and More

No matter which of Expression Web's many positioning options you choose, it helps to know something about the general types of positions an object can assume on a Web page. In fact, the control you choose isn't the most important thing. The type of positioning you want to specify is what counts. CSS gives you the capability to exercise control, provided you know what your options are. You can choose from these types of positions:

Absolute. In absolute positioning, an object has a definite position relative to the block that contains it. It's described as being a definite number of pixels or points from the left margin, the top margin, and so on.

Relative. In relative positioning, an object is moved relative to its normal position. For instance, `right:10` moves the object 10 pixels to the left of its previous position.

Layered. Elements are stacked one atop another on the page and can fully or partially overlap one another.

Float. An object is positioned relative to its parent object, and text flows around it.

Static. An object is positioned flush-left in the flow of text. It's like the default positioning for a paragraph of text. It's used only to override an earlier positioning instruction.

Fixed. An object remains where you position it relative to the browser window, and it stays in that relative position whether or not the user scrolls through the page or resizes the window. (This option is not supported by all browsers.)

Inherited. The object's positioning is inherited from another object or from another style sheet.

Fixed and static positioning are difficult to describe. Some Web page advertisements use this type of positioning: The ad appears on the right side of the Web page in the middle of your browser window, for example. Even if you scroll through the page, the ad stays there on the right side in the middle of the browser window. You can't get rid of the ad unless you click a Close button. It's intrusive, to be sure, so use this option sparingly (if at all).

Using the Quick Tag Selector

As its name implies, one of the quickest ways of choosing between different types of positioning is provided by the Quick Tag Selector, which appears at the top of Design View and displays the code elements that apply to the currently selected contents. Once you select the object you want to position, pass your mouse pointer over the tag that applies to it in the Quick Tag Selector. A down arrow appears on the right side of the tag. Click the down arrow, choose Positioning from the context menu that appears (see Figure 5.7), and then choose one of the positioning options from the submenu that appears:

> **Position: Absolute.** The upper-left corner of the Web page or the container (for instance, a layer) that contains the object is considered the zero point.

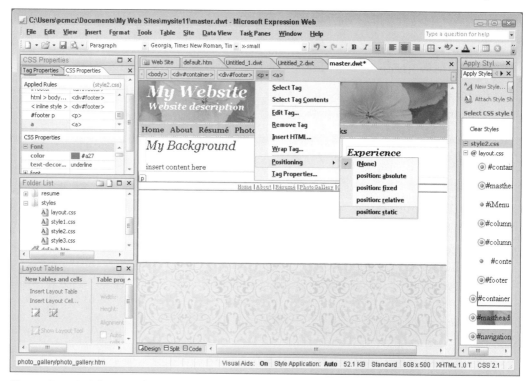

Figure 5.7 Quick Tag Selector lets you specify an object's general positioning scheme.

The actual position is described by the Top and Left coordinates specified in the Position dialog box or in the New Style dialog box.

Position: Fixed. The object's placed where you insert it on the page. Scrolling through the Web page doesn't change the position of the object.

Position: Relative. The object is positioned relative to the point where it is inserted on the page. The insertion point is the zero point. You do the actual positioning in the Position dialog box or the New Style dialog box.

Position: Static. The object is simply flush left and interrupts the flow of text or other content.

Once you have selected the general type of positioning you want, you can get more specific by using the Position dialog box or one of the other tools described in the sections that follow.

Beginning to Work with the Position Dialog Box

When you want precision in your margins or other position settings, you can use the Position dialog box. The advantage of Position rather than the New Style dialog box or another option is that the Position dialog box allows you to change the wrapping style of the object and control the float property if needed. Position your cursor in the object you want to format. Open the Position dialog box by doing one of the following:

- If you are working in Design View, select Format > Position.

- If you are working in the Layers task pane, right-click the item you want to position, and then select Positioning.

After the dialog box opens, as shown in Figure 5.8, click one of the buttons in the Wrapping style to specify how the image will interact with adjacent text:

- Leaving the default option, None, clicked means the image won't interact at all.

- Clicking left means the image will be flush-left and the text will wrap around it to the right.

- Clicking right means the image will be flush-right and the text will wrap around it to the left.

The Positioning Style buttons allow you to specify, in general, where the image will be positioned. Clicking Absolute means that the image will have a specific position, which you specify in the Location and Size section of the Position dialog box. Relative means the image is positioned relative to the text that surrounds it.

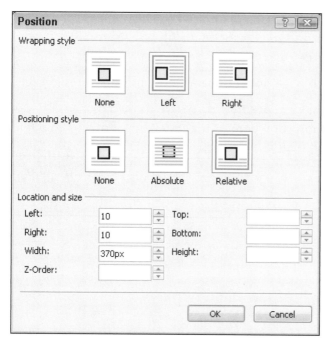

Figure 5.8 Control wrapping and positioning of Web page contents in the Position dialog box.

If you click Absolute in the Positioning style section, the image will be positioned according to the borders of the Web page on which it appears. If you specify a number of pixels in the Top, Left, Right, or Bottom boxes, the image will be positioned that number of pixels from the top, left, right, or bottom borders of the page. If you click Relative, the Top, Left, Right, and Bottom measurements you specify will still be applied, but the image will be positioned relative to any text that also appears on the same page. The z-order box applies if you have more than one layer overlapping on the Web page you are editing, and it enables you to specify whether the layer appears on top of the others and where it appears in relation to the others.

Working with the Positioning Toolbar

The Positioning toolbar contains many of the same positioning controls as in the Quick Tag Selector and Position dialog box. Why go through the effort of selecting View > Toolbars > Positioning to make it visible, instead of using the other controls? The toolbar combines controls from both of the other methods. You can use the toolbar to specify fixed, static, absolute, or relative positioning, just as in the Quick Tag Selector. You can specify height and width as in the Position dialog box. You can also specify the z-order and position relative to any side of the browser window.

Not only that, but you can use the Bring Forward and Send Backward buttons on the far order side of the Positioning toolbar to send a layer backward and forward. These buttons set the z-order number for the selected layer or other object (Figure 5.9).

Figure 5.9   Use the Positioning toolbar to control the placement and z-order of objects on your pages.

Controlling Position with CSS Properties

If you have CSS Properties open onscreen and you need to change the position or other attributes of items on a Web page, you don't need to open the Positioning toolbar, the Position dialog box, or even the New Styles dialog box. Just select the item you want to format and turn to CSS Properties. You can do your formatting right in the task pane because it gives you ready access to all the CSS instructions associated with the item.

One of the advantages of using the CSS Properties task pane is that it presents a visual record of all the styles in use on the object currently selected in the current Web page. You can review the hierarchy of rules that affect a particular object. CSS Properties goes well beyond serving as a reviewing tool, however. You can use it to change the style and formatting of elements displayed in Design View. The feature is interactive; when you make a change in CSS Properties, you see the effect of the adjustment in Design View. When it comes to Web page layout, CSS Properties and its related task pane, Tag Properties, are especially useful tools. They give you the capability to make changes on the fly without breaking the flow of your Web page development.

When you click a property's name in the CSS Properties section, a drop-down arrow button appears that lets you select a specific formatting option, such as Positioning. Sometimes you see three dots instead. The three-dot button is called the Pick button; it often appears as the first option after you click the drop-down arrow button. It lets you select a value such as a number of pixels or a percentage. In either case, a pop-up window appears that lets you make the positioning selection. CSS Properties provides you with more properties you can format than the New Style dialog box.

Working with Dynamic Web Templates

A Dynamic Web Template (DWT) is a ready-made Web site that makes extensive use of Cascading Style Sheets. It isn't a feature or a subset of CSS, but a Web site design tool in its own right. DWTs streamline the process of updating and standardizing Web content, especially when created by a team of editors, writers, designers, and programmers. DWTs contain editable regions to which contributors are allowed to add content, as well as shared content areas contained in Master Pages. Master Page content appears the same from page to page, and contributors cannot edit it. Pages that are attached to DWT Master Pages are like letterheads preprinted on paper: You can add content to the body of the page, but you can't change the letterhead. DWTs, in other words, give you useful examples of CSS in action.

A product catalog is a good example. Each page of the catalog would have a standard layout, with a header and footer and navigation elements that are consistent from page to page. Any editors who contribute to the Web publication by adding descriptions can't change or delete the logo because it is in a restricted area that is available only to users who have access to the DWT file. When you need to redesign the product catalog, you only update a single page—the DWT's Master Page. Save the page, and all the product pages that are attached to the DWT are updated automatically.

Note: In order for Expression Web to automatically update pages that are attached to a DWT, the site needs to have the Manage the Web Site Using Hidden Metadata Files option checked in the Site Settings dialog box. If this option is not active, Expression Web cannot update pages when you update a DWT. Choose Site > Site Settings to open the Site Settings dialog box.

Creating a DWT

The idea behind DWTs is straightforward: You determine where you want the content on all your Web pages to be. For many sites, a border at the top (otherwise known as a header) is the most common convention. It's an area where you can include your logo, an ad, or other content. You might include a narrow column on the left that contains a set of links to all the pages in your site. After designating the regions of the pages where changes are prohibited, you set aside regions where you or others can create or edit content. You then attach the template you have created to new Web pages. When you make a change to the template's Master Pages (the areas that can be edited only by you), the changes are applied to all the attached Web pages at the same time.

To create a DWT, you have three options:

- If you don't want to select a page design and expect to customize your site extensively, choose New > Page and double-click Dynamic Web Template. A set of interconnected Web pages opens—a Master Pages document and the page Untitled_1.dwt that is attached to it.

- If you want to see a thumbnail preview of your site before you create it, choose File > New > Web Site, click Templates, and single-click one of the preconfigured sites listed in the middle of the New dialog box. A thumbnail image of the site appears on the right side of the dialog box. Click OK or double-click the template's name to open the template.

- If you want to attach an existing template to a Web page you are planning to edit, you can choose File > New > Create from Dynamic Web Template. A dialog box opens that enables you to locate the .dwt file (Dynamic Web Template file) you want to attach to the current page. Just make sure you have the page open that you want to attach to the template.

In either case, you edit the DWT by adding your logo or other standard company information to the header or the other non-editable areas contained in the DWT's Master Page, which has the filename master.dwt. You then edit the Web pages supplied with the DWT site or add new pages and then attach the template to the new pages.

You can attach any Web page to a Dynamic Web Template; the page you are editing does not have to be created as part of the template in the first place. This enables you to use the editable regions and restricted areas that have already been applied to the DWT. To attach the template, choose the page(s) you want to attach by clicking them in the Folder List task pane or the Web site window. Then choose Format > Dynamic Web Template > Attach Dynamic Web Template. When the Attach Dynamic Web Template dialog box opens, navigate to the .dwt file you want to open. Double-click it, or click it and click Open. A dialog box appears showing how many files were updated because they are now attached to the template.

When it comes time to redesign your Web site, you might want to detach the old DWT from its pages and possibly reattach a new one. That way, your content stays online, but you gain different formatting that's associated with the new template. To detach pages, select them in the Folder List task pane and choose Format > Dynamic Web Template > Detach from Dynamic Web Template. You can then switch to another template by choosing Format > Dynamic Web Template > Attach Dynamic Web Template. Keep in mind that, if the editable regions in the original template don't match those in the new template one-for-one, the Match Editable Regions dialog box appears to display the names of the regions (see Figure 5.10). The Current Page column lists the editable regions associated with the previous DWT. The Dynamic Web Template column shows editable regions available in the new template.

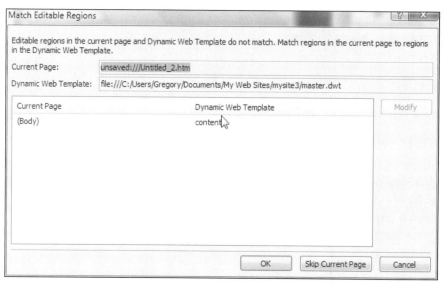

Figure 5.10   Use this dialog box to manage editable regions in a previous DWT that don't match up with a new DWT.

The Match Editable Regions dialog box lets you perform one of the following actions:

- If you want to preserve all the content and structure of the Web page, click Skip Current Page. This prevents the template from being attached to the page.

- To move all the content in the body of the Web page to the default editable region, click OK. If the default editable region contains content, that content is replaced with the content in the page.

- To move the content from an editable region that was specified by the previous template to a specific editable region that is specified by the new template, click the region in the Current Page column and then click Modify. In the list labeled Dynamic Web Template, click the editable region to which you want to move the content. If the editable region in the new template contains content, that content is replaced with the content in the page.

It's important to match editable regions because, if you don't specify any region that will receive the content from an "old" region, the content in the old region will be lost.

Note: If you want to attach more than one file, use Ctrl+click or Shift+click to select them in the Folder List task pane or in Web Site view. If the files to which you are attaching the DWT already contain editable regions, the Choose Editable Regions for Content dialog box appears. (If the file is already attached to a different DWT, you see the Match Editable Regions dialog box.) Use this dialog box to match the editable region names to the editable regions in the new template.

CSS and Dynamic Web Templates

You see the connection between Dynamic Web Templates when you scan the Folder List task pane to view the list of files that make up one of the ready-made Web sites. Double-click the `master.dwt` Master Page for the DWT and you see the reference to the file `styles/styles2.css`. The file also is broken into various divs, with ID names such as `container`, `masthead`, `navigation`, `column_l`, `column_r`, `footer`, and so on. (The number of divs and the filenames depend on the template you're using.) In addition, the ready-made templates you open from the New dialog box make use of a set of CSS files. They are contained in the `styles` directory, and they are assigned the standard names `layout.css`, `style1.css`, `style2.css`, and so on.

Adding or Removing Editable Regions

If you ever want to add, delete, or otherwise manage the editable content regions within a page that has been attached to a DWT, choose View > Toolbars > Dynamic Web Template to open the Dynamic Web Template toolbar. Click the drop-down list in the toolbar to view the names of the current file's editable regions (see Figure 5.11).

If you don't want to open the toolbar, you can also click the Template Region Labels button in the toolbar to display the labels if they aren't already visible.

Suppose you want to add an editable region to a page. You have the option of formatting the template to break the page into columns, table cells, layers, or other "containers" for content. After you have created such areas, you designate them as editable regions by doing one of two things, making sure you don't have an editable region active in the currently open page:

- Show the Dynamic Web Template toolbar, and click the Manage Editable Regions icon.

- Right-click an area in the Dynamic Web Template itself that is not already an editable region, and choose Manage Editable Regions from the pop-up menu.

In either case, the Editable Regions dialog box appears. If you click an editable region, the Rename button appears in this dialog box. If you click a non-editable

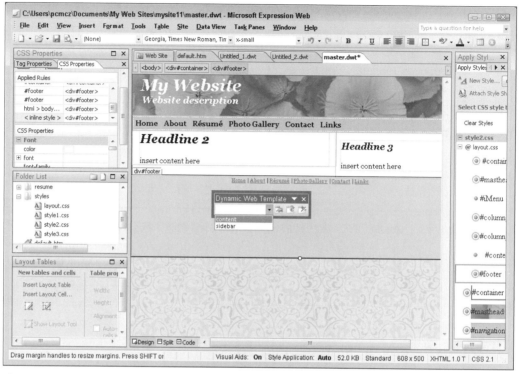

Figure 5.11 You can manage editable regions with the Dynamic Web Template toolbar.

region, the Add button appears. A list of current editable regions is displayed. To add a new editable region, follow these steps:

1. Type the name in the Region Name box. When you type the name, the Add button becomes active, as shown in Figure 5.12.

2. Click Add. The name you have typed for the new editable region is added to the list.

3. If you want to jump immediately to the editable region, click Go To. Otherwise, click Close.

If you need to rename a region, simply select its name in the Editable Regions dialog box. Type the new name in the Region Name box, and click Rename. To remove a region, select its name in the list and click Remove. It's especially important to rename regions if you are switching from one DWT to another and the region names in the DWTs don't match (see "Attaching and Detaching Pages," below, for more).

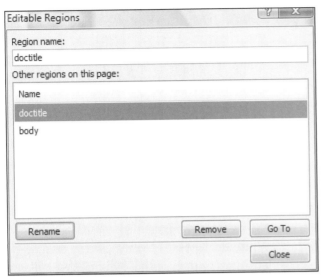

Figure 5.12 You can add, rename, or reorder editable regions using this dialog box.

Note: Before you attach a DWT to a page, it's a good idea to "prep" the page for editable regions first. If the page uses a complex layout, such as a table, to align text and images into multiple columns, you need to eliminate the table and combine the contents into a single text block. Select all the content of one column and paste it into another column. Then copy all the text, delete the table, and paste the text back into the page. You now have a single column of text, and you can attach the template to the Web page. The text should then flow neatly into the editable region of the template.

Attaching and Detaching Pages

Once you have prepped the text in a Web page for a DWT if needed (as described in the preceding Note), it's relatively easy to attach a page to a DWT. Choose the page or pages in the Folder List task pane or in the Web Site window. Then choose Format > Dynamic Web Template > Attach to Dynamic Web Template.

Updating a DWT

One of the best things about working with DWTs is the fact that you can update content on all the pages that are attached to it automatically. You might need to change the address of the company, for instance. If the address appears on the

DWT's Master Pages (`.dwt`) file, open that file, make the editorial change, and then do one of the following:

- Choose Format > Dynamic Web Template > Update Attached Pages. This updates only the pages to which the template has been attached.

- Choose Format > Dynamic Web Template > Update All Pages. This updates all pages that are currently open or listed in the Folder list.

When you save the DWT, you'll be prompted to choose whether or not you want to update pages that are attached to it. If you do, the editorial change will "ripple" throughout the attached pages.

You can also update attached pages manually: select the page or pages in the Folder List task pane or the Web Site list, then choose Format > Dynamic Web Template > Update Selected Page. The Update Attached Pages button in the Dynamic Web Template toolbar will also make the updates. If any pages can't be updated, a dialog box will appear, notifying you of the problem and naming the page in question.

6 Making Your Site Dynamic and Interactive

The most successful Web sites are the ones that don't sit passively, presenting static information, but that get visitors to "talk back" to their creators and interact in some way. Interacting might take the form of clicking on a link and sending an e-mail message. It might also mean filling out a form to subscribe to a newsletter or other bit of information. Or it might mean making a purchase of a tangible good or service.

The best Web sites are also those that present information that is up to date and dynamic rather than static. Static information stays the same until the creator of the Web page on which it appears updates it. Dynamic pages, in contrast, build their content as the viewer loads the page, drawing information from various data sources and compiling it on the fly. Expression Web gives you the capability to create interactive, dynamic pages, and this chapter introduces you to some of the most common strategies: forms, multimedia, using ASP.NET, and working with data sources.

Creating Interactive Forms

What's the most valuable bit of information you'll find on the Web? It isn't a lottery number or activation code. It's a real live human being's contact information: his name, address, phone number, or simply an e-mail address. Once you get such information from someone, you can market your products or services or communicate with him on an ongoing basis.

How do Web page forms work? An individual opens the form in his Web browser. The person submits information back to a Web site by filling out text boxes or clicking check boxes or radio buttons and then pressing a Submit or similarly labeled button to transmit them to a Web server. The data is then processed by a CGI (common gateway interface) script that *parses* or reads the data and presents it (often by e-mailing the data) to the Webmaster of the Web site so that the information can be read easily. The sections that follow focus on the tools Expression Web provides for assembling the data entry part of a form—the check boxes, text boxes, and other controls that visitors fill out with their names, addresses, and other information, and the buttons and check boxes they select. These controls can be used to authenticate users who need to access protected areas of a site.

The part of the form that makes it work is a script that receives the information submitted and processes it in the form of a text file, e-mail message, or database entry so you can work with it. Expression Web won't help you create such a script, however. But chances are you can access a script on a server that hosts your Web site, and you'll learn how to do that later in this chapter so you can receive form results by e-mail and validate them as well.

Note: If you used Microsoft FrontPage's Web Components to process form data on a server that used the FrontPage Server Extensions, Expression Web will let you run those forms on your server. Expression Web supports the use of server extensions.

Creating Forms

Forms are one of the most common tools used to gather feedback on the Web. But it's important to take some time to plan the design of your form before you start using Expression Web to create it. By keeping the design simple and intuitive, you make it easy for users to submit the information you are looking for. It's also a good idea to pay attention to colors, type, and graphics used on your form so the design of the form is compatible with the design of the other Web pages on your site.

The single text box used to enter and submit an e-mail address is perhaps the simplest sort of Web form: one data entry field and one Submit button to send the information to you. Armed with the e-mail address, a savvy marketer can approach a prospective customer with sales promotions, catalogs, newsletters, and other information. When the customer subscribes to any or all of these publications, he can provide more detail. Make a list of just what information you really need and when you need it. You might want to include some of the elements presented in Table 6.1.

Table 6.1 Information Solicited Through Web Page Forms

First Solicitation	Second Solicitation (subscribe to newsletter)	Third Solicitation (premium Web content)
Name, e-mail address	name, address, phone number	name, billing address, credit card number, credit card type, expiration date

By gradually soliciting information, you avoid the danger of overwhelming someone at the beginning. You establish a one-to-one marketing relationship over time. That way, the individual may be less reluctant to send you information after he knows you can be trusted.

Making a List

To get started, you first need to decide what you want to gather. The individual's personal contact information (address, phone, fax number, e-mail address) is only the most obvious type of information you can solicit. You can also use check boxes that enable a user to quickly choose options you present. A set of radio buttons lets your visitor choose from between a set of options. Make a list of the other kinds of information you want your form to solicit:

- Extended comments or questions that can be entered in a text area box

- A password that needs to be entered in the form of dots so passersby can't see the characters being typed

- A drop-down list

It's always a good idea to sketch out your form on a piece of paper and make a list so you have a general idea of how you want it to look and what you want it to contain. Then you can start creating the form. Open the Toolbox by choosing Task Panes > Toolbox if necessary. The longer and more complicated a form is, the greater the chance that someone will find it off-putting and decide not to fill it out at all. If you can identify the information you really want initially, you can create other opportunities to interact in greater detail later on.

Adding the Form Control

The Toolbox contains a complete set of objects you can add to a form to enable a user to do data entry. Click the plus sign (+) next to Form Controls to display all the objects that are available. You need to drag the Form object into the page you are editing, at the location where you want the form to appear. Follow these steps:

1. Position the cursor at the location in the current Web page where you want to add the form.

2. Drag the Form object into the Web page. When the mouse arrow hovers over the page, a plus sign (+) appears to let you know the object can be added.

3. Release the mouse button.

In Figure 6.1, you see that the Form object has been dragged from the Toolbox into the current Web page; a Form container with a label designating the HTML

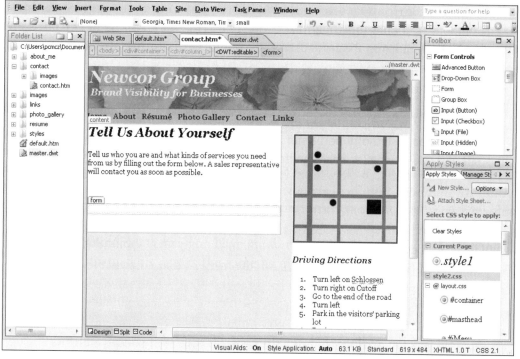

Figure 6.1 The Toolbox lets you drag and drop data entry controls into a form.

command form has been added within the div labeled Content. The Form controls should now be dragged into the Form container. The sections that follow explain each of these objects in detail so you can decide how and where to use them.

Note: Some forms are given their own Web page for simplicity, regardless of whether they are lengthy or not. But as you can see from Figure 6.1, a simple form, such as a search box, can be placed at any location within the body of a Web page that has other contents.

Adding Controls

Perhaps the most important aspect of form design is to map the information you want to the contents of the form. That way you'll make sure you get users to submit what you're looking for. Typical Web page forms include check boxes, drop-down menus, text boxes, radio buttons, and other buttons. The appearance of these items is determined by the HTML commands used to create the page. Expression Web lets you create the basic data entry part of the form without having to work with the HTML directly (unless you want to, of course).

Note: The elements described in the sections that follow can be formatted like other parts of text. They can be aligned or placed on their own lines, and you can move them or remove them by choosing Edit > Cut and Edit > Paste.

Text Boxes

Text boxes are the most common form control you can add (except perhaps for the button labeled Submit or Send). When you drag the Input (Text) box from the Toolbox into Design View, a text field appears. By default, you can enter about 25 characters in this box. To change the default setting and other attributes, double-click the text box itself or double-click `<input>` in the Quick Tag Selector. When the Text Box Properties dialog box shown in Figure 6.2 opens, change one of the following:

> **Name:** It's important to assign a name to each text box or other field in your form so you can interpret the results when you receive them.
>
> **Initial value:** This text initially appears in the text box. The user's input replaces the initial contents.
>
> **Width in characters:** This lets you specify the size of the box in terms of the number of letters and numerals it holds.
>
> **Tab order:** This controls the order in which the user can move through fields by pressing the Tab key repeatedly.
>
> **Password field:** This turns the text box into a password field in which user input appears as dots so passersby can't read characters.

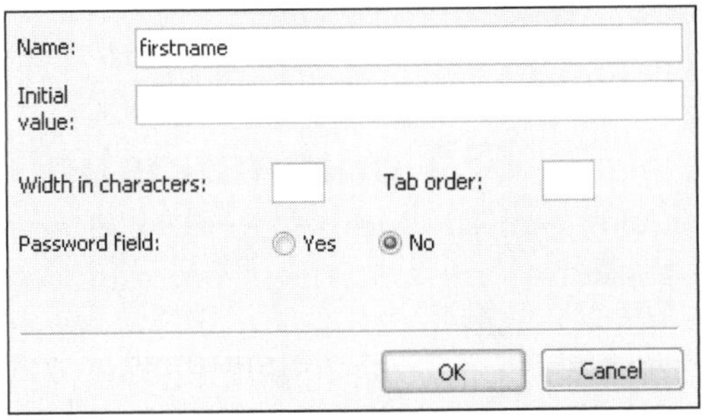

Name:	firstname
Initial value:	
Width in characters:	Tab order:
Password field:	○ Yes ● No
	OK Cancel

Figure 6.2   You can fine-tune text box options using Text Box Properties.

Once you have made the changes, click OK to close Text Box Properties and return to the form you are working on. Besides the Text Box Properties dialog box, you can specify additional formatting options by selecting the text box in the editing area and changing attributes in the Tag Properties task pane such as `maxlength` (the maximum length of the text that can be entered).

Caution: Make sure you give the user enough room to write a full address, for example. You can use the Width in Characters box to specify a size that's either smaller or larger than the default 25 characters. Specifying the width isn't an exact science. Just type an average name, address, or other bit of information and add five to ten extra characters for input that's extra long.

Text Area Boxes

If you want someone to send you a detailed text message, a single-line box isn't enough. You can create a multiline text box by positioning the text cursor within the form and then dragging the Text Area icon into Design View. A box with a scroll bar appears. The text box that appears initially is rather small. You can adjust the width and the number of lines that appear initially by right-clicking the box, choosing Form Field Properties, and changing the settings in the Text Area Properties dialog box. Figure 6.3 shows the default text area box at the top. Beneath it are two boxes that I set to be 25 and 50 characters wide and have more than the default two lines appear initially.

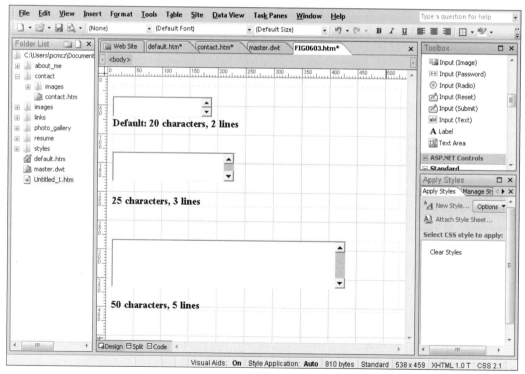

Figure 6.3   A text area box gives visitors room to enter multiline messages.

Note: The Label control in the Toolbox is intended to help you type a text label next to a box, button, or other data entry element in a form. Such labels are essential because they tell your visitor what you want him to do—to type his name or address, to choose his age range, and so on. You can also simply click next to the box or button and type the label onto the form without adding the Label control if you wish.

Password Boxes

If you want visitors to provide a password to enter a protected area of your Web site, you should instruct their Web browser to enter asterisks (****) or dots rather than visible characters as a security measure. You have two options:

- Drag the Input (Password) icon from the Toolbox into Design View.

- Drag the Input (Text) box into Design View, or select an existing text box you want to turn into a password box. Click the Password button in the Text Box Properties dialog box. Press OK to close Text Box Properties and create the password box.

As you can see, a password box is the same as a text box; you can change the size and even enter a default value if you wish, but the input appears as asterisks or dots.

Check Boxes

If you can give users the chance to make choices between two, three, or more options, you save them the few precious seconds required to type an answer in a text box. When the information requested is something they might be reluctant to enter, such as their annual income or their age, giving them buttons or boxes to click so they can make a choice increases the likelihood that you'll get an answer.

Check boxes are especially useful because they give users the chance to select more than one choice from a set. To create a check box, position the text cursor at the appropriate spot in the form and then drag the Input (Checkbox) button from the Toolbox into Design View. The box appears with a highlighted box around it. Either press the spacebar to add one or more non-breaking spaces after the box so you can add some identifying text or insert the Label control from the Toolbox.

Once you add a check box, you need to name it as you would a text box or other element. Double-click the check box to display the Check Box Properties dialog box, and replace the default text in the Name box with a new name, even if it is something as simple as A. The Value box should contain text that clearly identifies what the user has chosen, such as drinks_milk or is_single. You can also use Check Box Properties to specify that the box should appear checked when the form first appears: double-click the box and click the button next to Checked.

Radio Buttons

A radio button is a round button that, when clicked, displays a solid black dot in its center. Radio buttons are displayed in groups, and the user is usually allowed to click only one button in the group. You can use buttons to have viewers answer Yes/No questions or to choose an answer (A, B, or C) from a multiple-choice question. To insert a set of buttons, position the cursor at the appropriate spot in the form and drag the Input(Radio) control from the Toolbox into the form. Then add a number or letter for the box (A, B, C, 1, 2, or 3, and so on) by typing next to it or dragging a Label control into the form next to the button.

Adding more buttons is a matter of inserting a non-breaking space after the first button and pressing the spacebar several times. You can also press Enter after the first button and then insert another button beneath it if you want to position all the buttons vertically (an example is shown in Figure 6.4). To line up the buttons, press the spacebar an equal number of times after each one.

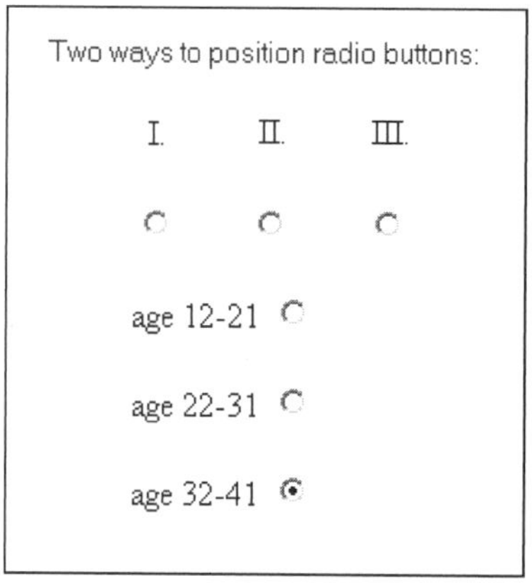

Figure 6.4 You can position a set of radio buttons either vertically or horizontally.

In order for the form to register results if the button is checked, you need to specify two parameters. First, set the name of the button (replace the default name radio1 in the Group Name box in the Option Button Properties dialog box, as shown in Figure 6.5). Then enter a name such as selectionA or something even more specific in the Value box. These names identify the button and its checked value for the CGI script that processes the form. The names should be the same for a group of related radio buttons so the viewer's browser will deselect other buttons in the group after the user clicks one

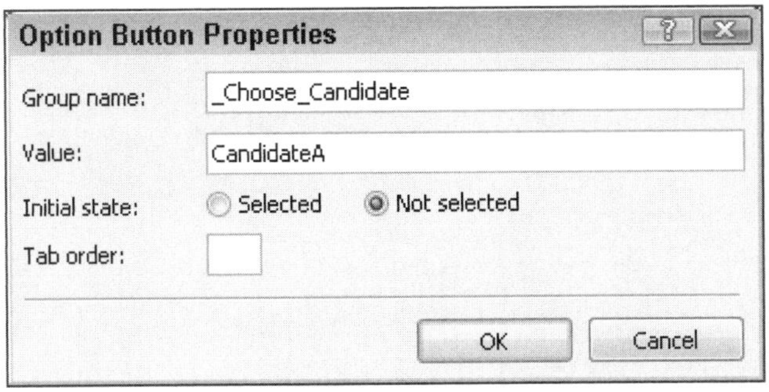

Option Button Properties [?] [X]

Group name: _Choose_Candidate

Value: CandidateA

Initial state: ○ Selected   ● Not selected

Tab order: [   ]

[OK]   [Cancel]

Figure 6.5   Be sure to label buttons clearly so you can process the data submitted to you.

of them. The names you enter must start with the underscore symbol or a character and must not contain blank spaces. If you violate this rule, a dialog box appears telling you the names aren't valid and can't be processed.

If you want a button to appear checked when the form is initially viewed, double-click the button and change the Initial State option to Selected in the Option Button Properties dialog box.

Drop-Down Boxes

A drop-down box (also called a list menu) is a common element in many Web page forms. You click an arrow to the right of the menu, and a set of options drops down. You select one of the options from the list, and the option remains chosen. To add a drop-down list, follow these steps:

1. Position the text cursor at the point in the form where you want the menu to appear.

2. Insert the menu by dragging the Drop-Down Box icon from the Toolbox into Design View. A miniature drop-down menu appears.

3. Right-click the list, and choose Form Field Properties from the pop-up menu. The Drop-Down Box Properties dialog box, shown in Figure 6.6, appears. It allows you to name the series of menu options you want to appear when the user clicks the arrow next to the drop-down list.

4. Type a name for the list as a whole in the Name box, replacing the default text.

5. Click Add. The Add Choice dialog box shown in Figure 6.7 appears.

6. Type the name for the menu item in the Choice box. This is the name that appears in the menu list.

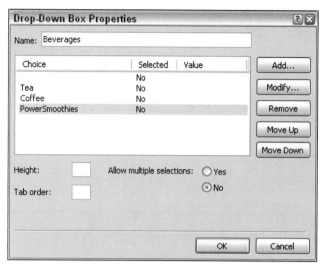

Figure 6.6 Use this dialog box to specify the options to be listed in a drop-down box.

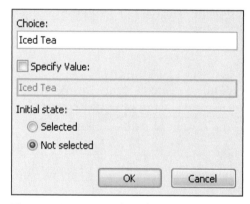

Figure 6.7 Enter values for drop-down box items in this dialog box.

7. Check the box next to Specify Value, and enter a number that you want to represent the value of the list item—the number of the value corresponds to the place in the list where the item appears. If you want the item to appear first, enter 1; if you want it to appear second, enter 2; and so on.

8. Click OK to close Add Choice and return to the Drop-Down Box Properties dialog box.

9. If necessary, select an item, and click Move Up or Move Down to change its position in the list. To delete a list item, click it and then click Remove. When you're finished, press OK to close the Drop-Down Box Properties dialog box and return to the Expression Web window.

10.   Repeat Steps 5 through 9 for each item in the list. When you're finished, click OK.

You don't see the list items actually displayed until you preview the page. If you need to edit the list, double-click it, click a list option, and click Modify to display the Modify Values dialog box, where you can make your changes.

Group Boxes

A group box is a tool for grouping together related Form controls. When you drag the Group Box control from the HTML section of the Toolbox into a form on a Web page, a visible box is added to the form. You can then drag (or cut and paste) multiple Form controls into the box that the user can use for input. Having a group of controls enclosed within a box makes it clearer to the user that the controls are for the same purpose. You might put form elements related to the user's employment history within a box to set it apart from other parts of the form, for instance. Form elements can also be grouped so that they can be cut and pasted all at once when the page is being designed.

Push Buttons

An essential part of any Web page form is a button that tells the user's browser to perform a particular action. That action might be to activate a CGI script on a Web server; it also might be to e-mail the data. The two most common buttons are Submit and Reset.

Choose the type of button you want by choosing its icon in the Toolbox and dragging it into the Form field in Design View. A Submit button sends the data to the CGI script that handles the form. A Reset button clears all form data and returns the form to its original appearance. The button you create does not have to say Submit, Reset, or anything at all. To rename a button, right-click it, choose Form Field Properties, and enter a new name in the Value/Label text box.

Hidden Fields

A hidden form field, as you might expect, doesn't actually appear in the form that the user sees. You can add it to a form to include some reference data to be sent along with the data the user submits. It's data that only you will see, and it tells you something about the data or the form itself. You add hidden fields to the form by dragging the Insert (Hidden) control from the Toolbox into the form. This adds a blank Form field to the form, and you can add a note to yourself in the field.

You also might use a hidden field to include the URL on which the form appears, the version of the form, the author of the form, or other data you would find helpful when reviewing the results. Hidden fields are particularly useful when you have lots of forms and Web pages online and you need to keep track of the results that are submitted. Another common function for a hidden field is to specify the e-mail address where form results are to be sent. Not all scripts require this. However, the `formmail.pl` script described in the sections that follow do require you to use a hidden field for this purpose.

Finding Scripts

Simply giving your visitors the ability to fill out a form and click the Submit button isn't enough. You need to tell the server that hosts your page what to do with the information in the form. You need to post a script on the server that processes the form data in some way. The processing might be as simple as sending the information to an e-mail address you specify. It might mean sorting the data into fields in a database file.

Expression Web doesn't come with such scripts, and it won't help you write them, either. But not to worry: There are plenty of publicly available scripts you can download and install on your server and configure them to work with the forms you create. Some scripts are popular enough that they might come with your hosting package. Ask your Web host before you start looking; you might find that such scripts are already available to you. My own host provides me with one popular script created by Matt Wright and called FormMail. It has the filename `form-mail.pl` and already exists on the Web server on which I rent space from my Web host. Once you have `formmail.pl` or another script, all you need to do is associate your form to recognize it. Follow these steps:

1. Right-click anywhere within the form and choose Form Properties from the pop-up menu. When the Form Properties dialog box appears, choose one of several options.

2. Click Send to Other to use a custom script such as `formmail.pl`.

Tip: Click Send to if your Web server supports the FrontPage Server Extensions. Many Web hosts support the extensions; ask yours to find out. If so, specify the name of a text file you have set up on your file system to store the data, and enter your e-mail address. Click Send to Database if your server supports the FrontPage Server Extensions and you want to save the results in a database file.

---

3. Click Options. When the Options for Custom Form Handler dialog box appears, you enter the script's location in the Action box, such as:
   `cgi-bin/formmail.pl`

4. Next, you need to choose a method that the user's Web browser will use to transmit the data to a remote Web server. Select GET or POST from the Method drop-down menu. Check with your Web host or ISP to see which method is preferred.

5. When you're finished, click OK to close the Options for Custom Form Handler dialog box and return to Form Properties.

6. Optionally, enter a name for your form in the Form Name field. Naming the form can help you distinguish it from others on the same site.

7. Click OK to close the Form Properties dialog box.

Once you have configured your form to work with your script and you have uploaded the script to the correct location on the server if necessary, you need to test the form yourself to make sure everything works right. First, publish the form on your site as described in Chapter 7. Your form might be as simple as the one shown in Figure 6.8.

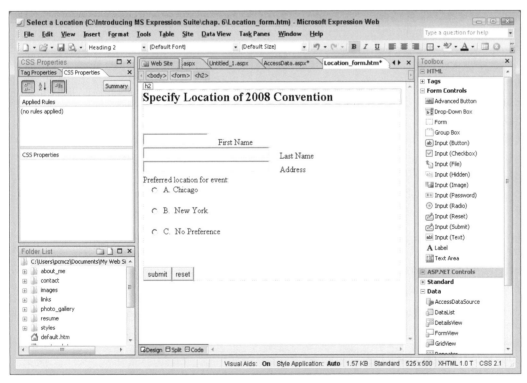

Figure 6.8 Save and test your form yourself before you let visitors try it out.

Then open the form in a Web browser and enter some data yourself. If you use form-mail.pl to e-mail some information to yourself, you'll see the results in an e-mail message with the title WWW Form Submission. An example is shown in Figure 6.9.

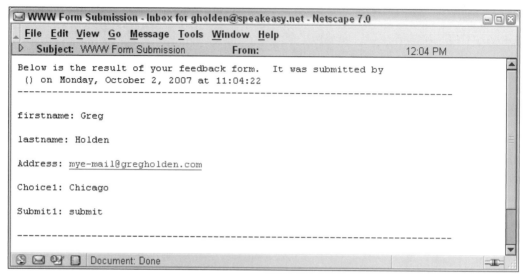

Figure 6.9 You can have form results sent to any e-mail address you specify.

When you create forms, it's important to make sure they conform to Web standards for accessibility. This makes it easier for people with disabilities to read and fill them out. When you begin to design a form, make sure you refer to sites such as The Web Standards Project (http://www.webstandards.org/learn/tutorials/accessible-forms/) beforehand to find out what constitutes accessible layout.

Note: Consult your ISP to make sure it's OK to run CGI scripts on your server. The ISP probably has a location where you can find Perl or another application needed to process the script. You need to make a reference to the program in the script. You'll find free scripts like FormMail at places like Matt's Script Archive (www.scriptarchive.com). Also check out www.bizmailforms.com and www.noviceforms.com.

Adding Behaviors

Expression Web lets you add more than a dozen different behaviors to a Web page. A behavior can be described as a *behavior script* because it is in fact written in Java-Script as part of the code for a Web page. When you create a behavior, you attach an action to an event that occurs on an object or a Web page. The event might be a mouse click or a mouse hover; the action might be a page transition or an image swap (for instance, when you hover your mouse over one image and a new image appears to replace it).

Using the Behaviors Task Pane

With Expression Web, you don't need to write the JavaScript that creates a behavior. Rather, you control and track behaviors through the Behaviors task pane (see Figure 6.10).

Figure 6.10   You can add interactive behaviors to objects using this task pane.

The Insert button lets you choose a behavior. The command next to the Tag heading designates the object on the Web page that the behavior will be associated with—the behavior that will be made interactive, in other words. Behaviors that are attached to the object are listed beneath the Events and Actions headings. Any Web page object can have more than one behavior associated with it. If the user presses a key on the keyboard, one event can occur. Passing a mouse over the same object can cause another event to occur. The up and down arrows on the right side of the task pane control the ordering of the behaviors associated with the currently selected object. You create a behavior by following these steps:

1. Select the object on a Web page that you want to associate with a behavior. You can't attach an event to plain text; rather, you select a link, an image, a layer, or the body of the page.

2. Click Insert and choose from a list of possible actions. The ones available to the selected object are available. When you make a choice, typically a dialog

box appears that lets you specify more about the action. For instance, if you choose Popup Message, a dialog box appears in which you type the text of the message.

3.   When you choose an action, your choice appears beneath the Actions column in the Behaviors task pane. A default event (for instance, `onclick`) appears under Events. Pass your mouse arrow over the default event and click the down arrow that appears to specify a different event the viewer should perform in order for the action to occur.

4.   Choose File > Save to save your changes, and then choose File > Preview in Browser to test the behavior when the page is loaded in a Web browser.

An event is what the user does in order to trigger the specified action. Expression Web provides an extensive list of events from which to choose when you click the Events drop-down arrow. Each event is listed by its JavaScript command. Here are some examples:

onclick: Event occurs when the user clicks the left mouse button.

ondblclick: Event occurs when the user double-clicks an object.

onmouseover: Event occurs when the mouse pointer is hovered over an object.

onmouseup: Event occurs when the user releases the mouse button.

ondrag: Event occurs when the user drags a Web page object.

onresizestart: Event occurs when the user starts resizing an object, such as an image.

oncopy: Event occurs when an object is copied to the Clipboard.

oncut: Event occurs when an object has been cut to the Clipboard.

Tip: The full list of possible events is quite lengthy. You can find more at http://www.w3.org/TR/html4/interact/scripts.html.

You can use the Behaviors task pane to assign more than one action to an event. You also can determine the order in which the actions occur. When you assign an action to an object, you're actually using Expression Web to add JavaScript to your Web page behind the scenes or at the head of the page. If you know JavaScript, you can assign many more actions than those Expression Web supports (provided they are allowed by the doctype you are using). After you create a behavior, you can switch to Code View and see the JavaScript commands that you added. The JavaScript code for a pop-up message behavior appears as follows:

```
<img alt="" src="lp.gif" width="367" height="172" onmouseover="FP_popUpMsg
('Copyright 2008 Amalgamated Products Inc.')" />
```

If you need to change the action or delete the behavior at some point, you do so with the Behaviors task pane. Reopen the Web page that contains the behavior and select the event/action pair in the Behaviors task pane. Press Delete to delete the behavior, or click the drop-down arrow to specify a different event. You can also change the order of a behavior so that it occurs first (for instance, if you want a pop-up message to appear when the page loads). Select the event/action pair and click Move Up or Move Down in the Behaviors task pane.

Adding Multimedia and Other Interactive Content

Some interactive features commonly seen on the Web don't fall easily into a single category. Some are behaviors, some (like page transitions) might be called "special effects," and others (such as audio files) might be called "multimedia." I'm going to avoid labels and simply list some of the compelling content that you can add easily to your pages with Expression Web.

Playing Audio Clips

Sounds that you can add to a Web page fall into "good" and "bad" designations. Background sounds that play when a page loads are almost universally disliked. However, visitors are more open to sounds that play in response to a mouse click or a mouseover. Sounds work especially well if they help illustrate what you do for a living. (An audio clip is ideal for a voiceover actor or actress, for example, or a musical group wanting to provide a sample of its work.) To play a sound, you first need to create a sound clip and save it on your computer in a common format such as .mp3 or .wav. Then follow these steps:

1. Select the text or the image that you want to associate with the sound and click Insert in the Behaviors task pane.

2. Choose Play Sound. The Play Sound dialog box appears.

3. Click Browse, locate the file on your file system, and click OK. The filename is added to the Play Sound box, as shown in Figure 6.11.

4. Click OK. The sound behavior is associated with the object. By default, onclick is specified in the Events column of the Behaviors task pane if you have selected the body of the current Web page.

Figure 6.11 Use this dialog box to link to a sound file you have already saved.

5. Choose File > Save to save your page and then press F12 to preview the page in a browser so you can try out the new behavior.

Adding Page Transition Effects

A page transition is a Web page special effect that takes place when a browser moves from one page to another. Most of the time, nothing special happens: The browser moves from one page to another. But page transitions enable the page to "wipe" or fade in and out as the browser moves from one page to another. Follow these steps to implement them:

1. Open the page that you want to have the transition effect.

2. Choose Format > Page Transition.

3. When the Page Transitions dialog box appears, choose the event you want to occur in order to trigger the transition behavior. You have four options: Page Enter, Page Exit, Site Enter, and Site Exit.

4. Type the number of seconds you want the effect to last in the Duration box.

5. Choose the type of effect that you want in the Transition Effect list on the right side of the dialog box.

6. Click OK.

Page transitions are one of those things that, like background sounds, seem "cool" to you, the Web site designer, but that have the potential to turn away visitors. Most Web surfers are in a hurry and like their Web pages to appear in rapid and predictable fashion. Use page transitions sparingly, if at all.

Introducing ASP.NET

One of Expression Web's most powerful features is its support for ASP.NET, Microsoft's primary technology for building Web pages. The support for ASP.NET is made possible by the built-in ASP.NET development server that installs with the .NET Framework 2.0 Software Development Kit (SDK). This is a lightweight server designed to help developers create ASP.NET pages on versions of Windows. When you preview an ASP.NET page, the development server starts up automatically, and an icon that looks like a gear appears in your browser status bar. When you hover your mouse over the status bar icon, you see which port or virtual information channel the server is using (see Figure 6.12).

ASP.NET Development Server - Port 59082
7:36 PM

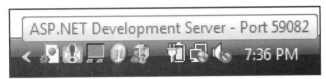

Figure 6.12 The ASP.NET development server icon gives you current port information.

Expression Web helps you implement and test ASP.NET scripts you write for your Web site. For security purposes, the ASP.NET team locked down the ASP.NET development server to only serve pages locally, however. If you double-click the ASP.NET development server icon, you learn the local location of the file being served (see Figure 6.13). This book isn't going to attempt to teach you how to write such scripts. But if you have some available, you will be able to use ASP.NET to make your site more functional and interactive. The sections that follow will describe how.

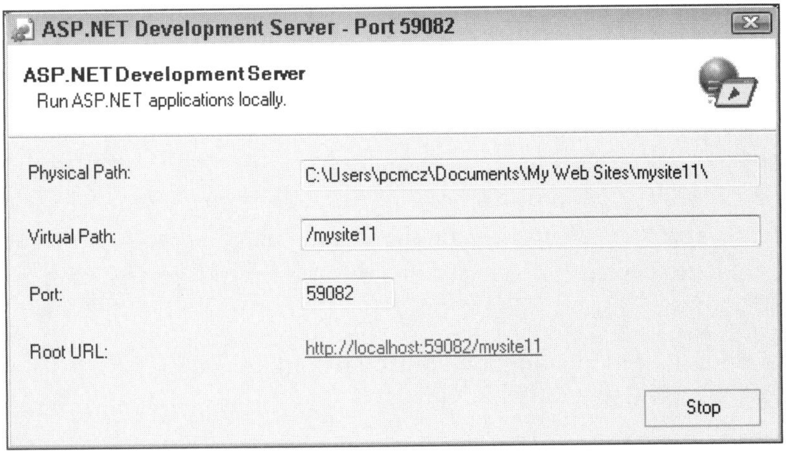
ASP.NET Development Server - Port 59082
ASP.NET Development Server
Run ASP.NET applications locally.
Physical Path:
C:\Users\pcmcz\Documents\My Web Sites\mysite11\
Virtual Path:
/mysite11
Port:
59082
Root URL:
http://localhost:59082/mysite11
Stop

Figure 6.13 ASP.NET enables you to test pages only on your local computer.

Note: You should already have the .NET Framework 2.0 installed on your machine, as you will need it to do any ASP.NET work in Expression Web. If you are going to develop ASP.NET applications, which is the focus of this entire section, it is available for download from the Microsoft download site at http://www.microsoft.com/downloads.

Choosing ASP.NET Instead of HTML Form Controls: Earlier in this chapter, you learned about creating forms using the Form controls contained in the Toolbox. There's a complete set contained under the ASP.NET heading in the Toolbox, however. Which one should you choose, and why?

The ASP.NET controls should be used only if your site is hosted on a server that supports the ASP.NET scripting environment. Use the ASP.NET controls only if you plan on saving the Web page that contains the form with the .aspx file extension.

Use the HTML controls if you are working in an HTML environment rather than ASP.NET. ASP.NET controls are especially powerful when it comes to checking user input to make sure you're getting the information you want and in the form you want. But if you aren't comfortable working with ASP.NET, you can still validate form input using publicly available scripts that process the data for you.

Creating Master Pages

In Chapter 5, you were introduced to Dynamic Web Templates, which allow you to display specified content on every page in your Web site. The same function is performed with a feature of ASP.NET version 2.0: master pages. The big difference between the two is flexibility: DWTs can be used on static sites (HTML only) as well as ASP.NET sites. Master pages require ASP.NET to work.

A master page is another sort of ASP.NET server control, like the Ad Rotator. It contains content that is common to all pages in the site. You link other pages in the site to the master page. That way, you don't have to do coding for menus or other content on every single page; you do it only in the Master Page area. A site that consists of several subdirectories can also contain multiple master pages, each of which works with each subdirectory.

Your own master page will differ, depending on your own content. To create a master page, the general steps are as follows:

1. Create a new directory to contain your Web site.

2. Create folders to contain your content. The exact names of the folders will depend on your own needs, but be sure to include one called `images` for your image file and one called `master` for your master page content. For example:

   - `images`

   - `css`

   - `company`

- `products`
- `contact`
- `master`

3. Copy the logo for your site (a standard item for master pages) and paste it in the `images` folder.

4. Click File > New > Page and then choose Master Page on the General tab. You will name this file `mysite.master` and save it in the `master` directory.

5. Choose Task Panes > Toolbox if necessary. Click the plus sign next to the HTML heading within the Toolbox and then the plus sign next to the Tags subsection. Drag the following controls and other items from the Tags subsection of the Toolbox onto the master page.

   - A div with the ID of `container`. All other divs that follow go inside this div. To create the ID, switch to code view and manually type, inside the <div> tag, id="container", to read <div id="container">. Be sure to add a single blank space between div and id.
   - A div with the ID of `masthead`.
   - A div with the ID `leftcol`.
   - A div with the ID `rightcol`.

6. Inside the div with the ID of `masthead`, add an H1 heading with the text "Acme Products Incorporated" and an H3 heading with the text "Your Source for Products."

7. Add a new page to the site called `default.aspx` by choosing File > New and then choose Create from Master Page. The page might look like the sample below if you use C# for your markup. Save the `default.aspx` file in the root directory (the top-level of the site, the same level as the directories you created earlier).

```
<%@ masterpagefile="file:///C:/mysite/master/mysite.master"
language="C#" title="Untitled 1" %>
```

8. You will now have to type in the content regions for the page, as Expression will not create them for you. The code might look this:

```
<asp:Content ID="Leftcol" ContentPlaceHolderID="Leftcol" runat="Server">
<h3>Heading 3</h3>
</asp:Content>
<asp:Content ID="Rightcol" ContentPlaceHolderID="Rightcol" runat="Server">
<h4>Heading 4</h4>
</asp:Content>
```

Once you have created the content regions, you can preview your page. If you are going to work with master pages in your site, you should also consider choosing View > Toolbars> Master Page to open the Master Page toolbar. It does not have a lot of features, but it will help you work through a rather complex page based on a master. The toolbar contains the following shortcuts.

Regions: This drop-down list displays Content Place Holder regions (master page) or Content regions (pages using the master page) on your page. On a complex page it will move you to the insert point in that region in both Code and Design Views.

Manage Content Regions: This button allows you to easily add, edit, and delete `ContentPlaceHolder` regions on a master page.

Template Region Labels: This button toggles labels on and off to indicate where `ContentPlaceHolder` regions are located on a master page.

On complex page layouts, the Master Pages toolbar can save you considerable time.

Note: Pages created from a master page do not have content regions created automatically. You have to create content regions yourself as described in the preceding set of steps.

Linking to Master Pages

Master pages aren't intended to work by themselves. Once you create the master page itself, you link Content Pages to it. Those Content Pages will contain the standard content you have added to the master page. Content Pages are saved using the .aspx extension, which identifies them as ASP.NET pages. You create content controls such as divs, and you add text and other controls to those controls.

Embedding ASP.NET Controls

The Toolbox contains the ASP.NET controls you can use with Expression Web. You drag controls from it into the editing area as needed. The part of the Toolbox that applies to ASP.NET is shown in Figure 6.14.

Standard Controls

The ASP.NET standard controls are controls that are commonly used in ASP.NET pages. If you move to Visual Studio 2005, you will find many of these controls in the Common section of the Visual Studio Toolbox.

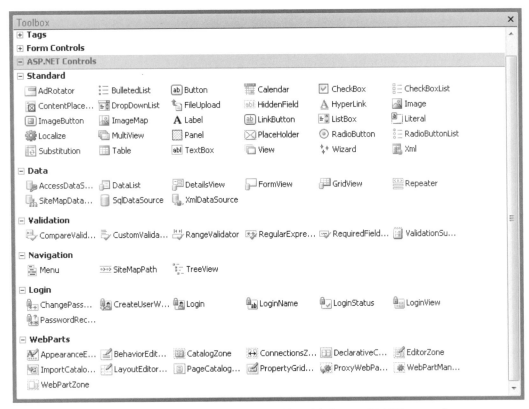

Figure 6.14 The Toolbox task pane lets you quickly add these ASP.NET controls.

AdRotator. The AdRotator control is used to display banner ads in a page. They use an XML file (generally called adverts.xml) to list information about the ads, including the URL for the image, the alternative text (for accessibility), the number of impressions, and a keyword to group together different types of ads.

Data Controls

The Data controls are used to connect data to a form so you can bind it to elements. At the end of this chapter, a set of steps briefly examines using data controls using the AccessDataSource control with a GridView. The data controls included with Expression Web Designer are:

> **AccessDataSource:** This data source control is used to connect to an Access database.

DataList: This presents a list of data items.

DetailsView: This presents a detailed view of a data record, which is normally used in conjunction with a Grid View.

FormView: This is a form view of a data record, which is normally used in conjunction with a GridView.

GridView: This control presents a spreadsheet-style view of data.

Repeater: This presents an easily customizable view of multiple records of data.

SiteMapDataSource: This data source control is used to connect to a web .sitemap file.

SqlDataSource: This data source control is used to connect to a SQL Server database.

XmlDataSource: This data source control is used to connect to an XML file.

Validation Controls

Validation controls are used on forms to validate the data submitted to you using a Web page form. The following controls are available for validation purposes:

CompareValidator: This compares two values, generally from two different controls.

CustomValidator: This lets you use custom JavaScript to validate in the browser.

RangeValidator: This ensures that the values in a control are between a specified range of values.

RegularExpressionValidator: This validator uses regular expressions to validate input in a form control.

RequiredFieldValidator: This ensures that the control is filled in.

ValidationSummary: This provides a summary of all of the controls that fail to validate the data submitted.

Navigation Controls

Navigation controls give you different ways to view the files in a site map:

Menu: Used to display a site menu.

SiteMapPath: Creates a breadcrumb menu for a site. Normally uses a site map file as its data source via a SiteMapPath control.

TreeView: Hierarchical view of data. TreeView controls are often used to display contents of a folder or hierarchical menus.

Login Controls

The Login controls should be called *authentication controls*. This section contains a variety of controls to help you set up secure pages on your site. The controls in the Login section are:

ChangePassword: This control is used to change a user's password.

CreateUserWizard: This control is used to create user accounts.

Login: This control requires the user to enter a username and password to log into a site.

LoginName: This control captures a user's name when he is logged in.

LoginStatus: This control allows a user to log in or out, depending on his current status.

LoginView: This control presents material for logged in users. This allows you to alter content based on a user's status.

PasswordRecovery: This control allows a user to retrieve his password and have it displayed or sent to an e-mail address.

WebParts Controls

Web parts are useful for creating configurable Web sites. You will find these controls most useful if you are interested in creating portals: specialized Web sites that function as a gateway to a corporate Web site or an extensive set of information. Web parts are beyond the scope of this book.

Retrieving Data with ASP.NET

Data access is the central activity of dynamic Web sites. Web sites have to draw on some sort of data source in order to be considered "dynamic." If you use ASP.NET and Expression Web to prepare your pages, it's easy to switch from an Access file to an SQL Server database. This section just gives you a brief introduction to retrieving data using one type of database.

Data access in ASP.NET (and in other .NET applications) is done using 10 *namespaces*. (The term namespace is a term used in programming to denote an abstract container that provides context for terms used in that language.) Most of the data retrieval work you are likely to do makes use of the SystemData namespace. You'll also use one of the namespaces that inherit from System.Data.Common. In most cases, you'll probably use `System.ata.OleDb` or `System.Data.SqlClient`. Since you are using Expression Web, you'll use the data source controls found in the namespace called `System.Web.UI.WebControls`.

Making a Database Connection

Here's a simple example of how to make a database connection using Expression Web's ASP.NET data source controls. For this exercise, you can use the Northwind database, which Microsoft lets you download for learning purposes. It comes in versions for both Access and SQL Server.

1. Create a new Web site for this exercise called `website1`. Make sure the site is located in the default path on your Windows file system where Web sites are located. This path takes the form `C:\Users\<your_username>\Documents\ My Web Sites\<site_name>`. For this example, assume `<site_name>` is `website1`. (It's important to locate the site here so the ASP.NET development server can test your pages.)

2. Within the `website1` folder, create a folder called `Data`.

3. Download the database in Access format from `http://tinyurl.com/ 2zxayb`. Double-click the `.exe` file you download and install the database file (`Nwind.mdb`) in the `Data` folder you just created.

4. Choose File > New > ASPX to create a new `.aspx` page. Name the page `AccessData.aspx` and save it in the `website1` folder.

5. Display the Toolbox task pane, if necessary, and drag a `GridView` control onto this page. `GridView` is located in the Toolbox under the Data section of ASP.NET Controls. The grid shown in Figure 6.15 appears.

6. Click the right-pointing arrow in the upper right corner of the Grid View menu to display a table called Common GridView Tasks. Click AutoFormat and choose Professional. Then, click Choose Data Source and choose New DataSource from the drop-down list that appears. The Data Source Configuration Wizard appears.

7. On page one of the wizard (see Figure 6.16), choose Access Database and change the name to `SampleDataSource`. Click OK to move to the next page of the wizard, which is entitled Choose a Database.

8. On page two of the wizard, click Browse and find the `nwind.mdb` file in the `Data` folder. Double-click the file; the path leading to it appears on the Choose a Database page of the wizard. Click Next to move to the next page.

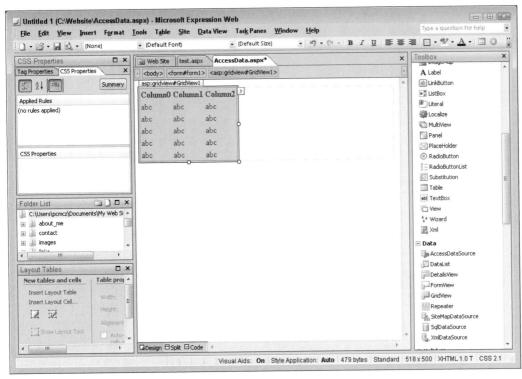

Figure 6.15 Drag a `GridView` into the ASPX page you have created.

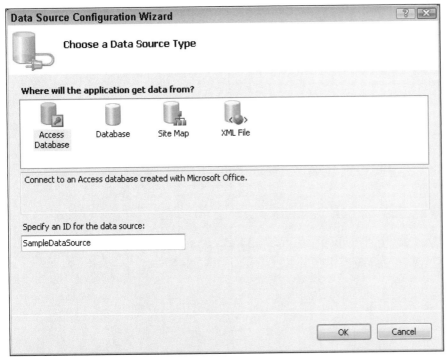

Figure 6.16 The Data Source database lets you connect to a data source.

9. Click the drop-down list beneath the heading Name and choose the asterisk (*) from the list.

10. Click Next. On the next page, click the Test Query button if you want to preview your data. Then click Finish.

The wizard closes, and the database opens in the Expression Web window. The data doesn't appear yet; click File > Save and then File > Preview in Browser to open your page in a browser. The ASP.NET development server retrieves the data (see Figure 6.17).

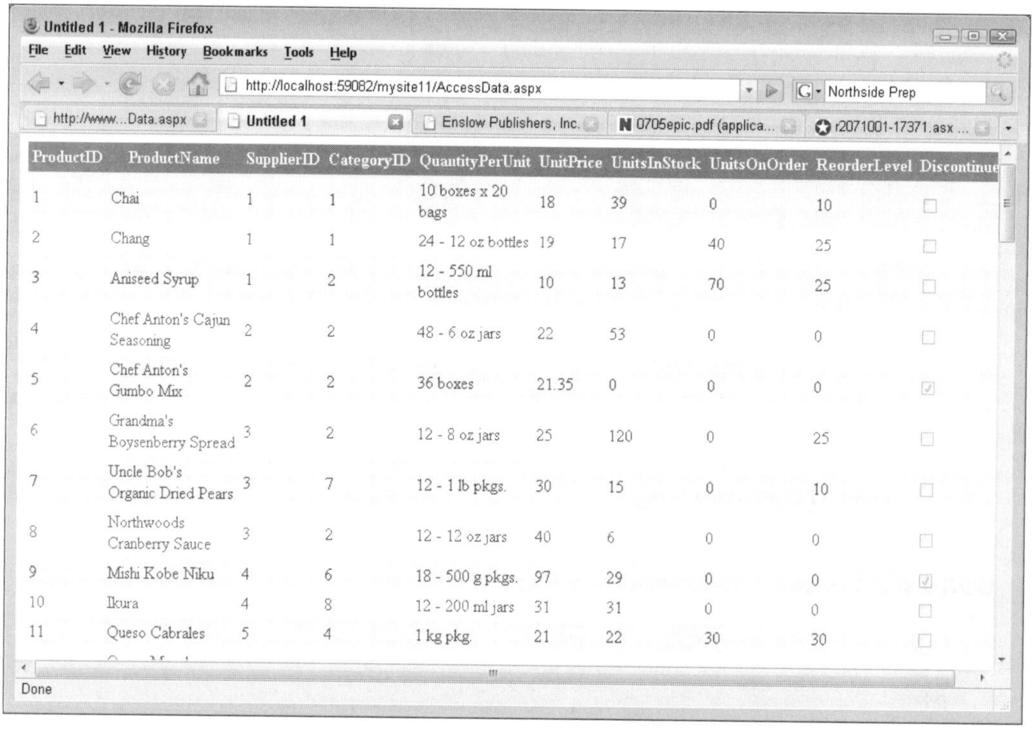

Figure 6.17 The ASP.NET development server lets you preview data on your computer.

Note: If you don't have visual aids for ASP.NET controls turned on, a dialog box will appear advising you to turn them on. Click Yes to activate visual aids so you can see the data.

7 Publishing and Updating Your Web Site

Web sites are effective only if their Webmasters and content creators are able to update and publish them on a regular basis. Luckily for you, Expression Web's built-in publishing and updating tools make it easy to accomplish these essential tasks. Ongoing maintenance keeps your Web site content fresh and up-to-date. Regularly updating and republishing pages, in turn, improves your site's search ranking on Google. (The frequency with which pages are changed is one of several factors Google considers when developing its rankings.)

Expression Web allows you to maintain the two versions of your site you need to maintain once everything is moved from your computer to your Web server: the local version you keep on your computer, and the remote version that resides on your Web server. You'll find it easy to move files from the local to the remote site using the program's built-in file transfer utility. You can also control access so workgroup members don't get confused as they work on files. Finally, you can synchronize files on both sites to keep everything running smoothly.

Finding a Web Host

Before you can even think about publishing a site, you need to have a place for your files to go. In order to make your site visible on the Web, you need to place it in the appropriate directory on a Web server. Web server space is probably provided by your Internet service provider (ISP) as part of your Internet access package. But for commercial Web sites, it's far better to sign up for an account with a full-time Web hosting service. You typically get more space and more features for your site, as well as an easy-to-use control panel that helps you manage files if you need to (though Expression Web can also help you track your files on the remote server, as described later in this chapter).

This chapter won't take a comprehensive look at finding a Web hosting service, because it's a book about Expression Studio rather than setting up a Web site. And there are plenty of books out there that explain how to find a Web hosting service. But there are some features you should consider when looking for a host:

E-mail addresses: Most Web hosts will give you multiple e-mail addresses you can use in addition to Web server space.

Price: This isn't necessarily the most important concern. You don't want to choose a hosting service that is low priced only to find that the service does not provide the bandwidth to support its current clients and you, too.

Storage space: To begin with, shoot for 20MB to 50MB of storage space for your Web page files along with your hosting contract. Most services will let you upgrade your package later on.

Domain name: Most Web hosts will help you obtain an easy-to-remember domain name that takes the form mycompany.com, but they'll charge extra for the name. It's better to register your domain name with a registrar such as GoDaddy.com (http://www.godaddy.com) so you can transfer it easily later on. One service, Microsoft Office Live (officelive.microsoftcom), gives you a domain name for free.

Bandwidth: Bandwidth is defined as the amount of traffic a particular network connection can permit at a given time. You're likely to start out with more bandwidth than you need; you can increase it later on if needed.

SQL Server: If you intend to use your Web site to connect to a data source, you should make sure SQL Server is present on the Web server.

I'm personally aware of hosts such as Pair Networks (www.pair.com), which has hosting options that range from $5.95 to $49.95 per month. Typically, hosting services run from $9.95 to $24.95 per month, though full-featured options can cost more. You can find a Web host on sites such as The List (http://www.thelist.com) or vervehosting.com (http://vervehosting.com).

Previewing Your Pages

On large-scale corporate sites, a single change such as altering a filename can make many links unusable. That's why it's important to preview your pages and try out your pages to make sure your forms, animations, and other interactive content work right. This applies especially to sites that contain hundreds or even thousands of files.

One of the most common complaints against Web editors is the lack of fidelity when it comes to Web page design. But the Preview feature now available in Expression Web gives you control over the environment in which you do the previewing.

In order to preview your pages, you must do one of three things, as discussed in the following sections.

Design View Gives You a Good Preview Even if you don't preview your page in a browser window, you'll still get a good idea of how your page will really look online while you're working on it. Design View can help you preview your page and determine how much of it will be visible to your visitors.

You can even adjust what you see in Design View by choosing from among the most common resolutions—640×480, 800×600, and 1024×768. These resolutions are included in the Expression Web View menu: Choose View > Page Size, and view the common page sizes from the submenu. It's even easier to access them from the status bar, where the Design View page size is listed. Click the page size, and a pop-up menu appears with a selection of other sizes from which to choose.

Whether you use the View menu or the status bar, to select a different size, choose Modify Page Sizes. Then click Add and enter the width and height you want and a description that matches the new size.

Proofreading Your Text

The first step in getting ready to publish is deceptively simple: proofreading your pages. It's always a good idea to get a friend or colleague to look over your work, because a set of fresh eyes can catch mistakes you've overlooked. Expression Web can help, too. Just choose Tools > Spelling or press F7 to check your spelling; the built-in spell-checker zooms through your text. If it finds a word that appears to be misspelled, it presents you with the chance to change it or add it to the Expression Web built-in dictionary. Click Ignore if you want to retain the current spelling. Click Ignore All to keep EW from checking the same word if it appears again. Click Change to change the spelling; you can use EW's suggestion in the Change To box, or you can type your own word. Click Change All to change all instances of the displayed word (see Figure 7.1).

You can specify whether Expression Web should spell-check your entire Web site or a selected page or pages. Display the Web Site window or Folder List task pane, if needed. Then choose Tools > Spelling > Spelling. The dialog box that appears will give you the option to check the whole site or just selected pages.

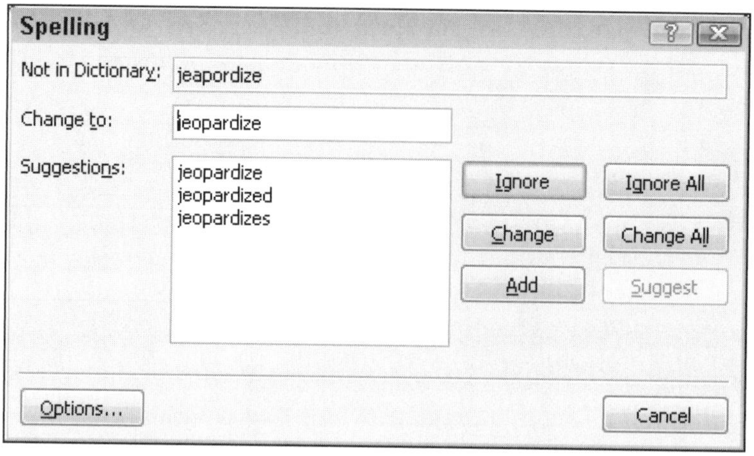

Figure 7.1 Before you publish, first spell-check your pages.

Tip: Expression Web also has a built-in thesaurus. If you need to check your word choice, select a word, and choose Tools > Thesaurus or press Shift+F7. The thesaurus appears with the selected word displayed in the Looked Up box. (If the term you are checking isn't contained in the dictionary, the box is labeled Not Found; make sure you spelled the word correctly in that case.) Scan the definitions in the Meanings box, and select one. A set of synonyms appears in the right-hand column. Double-click one to replace the word you highlighted.

Checking Your Code

Along with checking the text that appears in the body of your Web pages, it's a good idea to check the content behind the scenes as well. Code that contains errors can slow a browser down and possibly prevent some content from appearing. Expression Web has the ability to check your code and even suggest corrections. It can alert you to out-and-out usage errors or code that is incompatible with the version of HTML or XHTML you are using.

One of the fundamental ideas behind eXtensible HTML (XHTML) is that it requires Web designers to use code in well-defined ways. But keeping track of the correct usage can be tricky because there are so many different versions. You can verify the current version being used in the page you are editing, and also see how many versions are available, by opening a page in Design View and scanning the status bar. The current versions of XHTML and CSS appear at the far right. Double-click the XHTML version type to open Page Editor Options with the Authoring tab open. Click the down arrow in the Document Type Declaration drop-down list to view other versions: XHTML 1.0 Strict, XHTML 1.0 Transitional, XHTML 1.1, and so on.

One way to have Expression Web check your code is to automatically display incompatibilities and errors. You do this by choosing Tools > Page Editor Options and clicking the General tab. Make sure the Highlight Invalid HTML and Highlight Incompatible HTML options are checked. If so, you can switch to Code View at any time and scan your code for errors as you edit a page. Code that is incompatible with the doctype version you are using will be highlighted, and commands that are in error will be marked with a red wavy line.

Another option: Optimize your HTML by making sure it doesn't have unnecessary elements (such as comments) that can slow down page loading and "confuse" a Web browser. Choose Tools > Optimize HTML. When the Optimize HTML dialog box shown in Figure 7.2 appears, you can specify the commands you want to identify that are considered improper. By identifying such elements, you instruct Expression Web to strip them out when it cleans up your code.

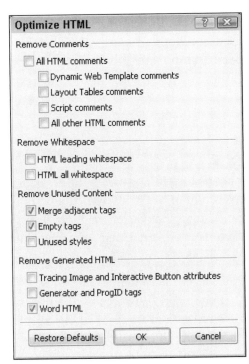

Figure 7.2 Strip out "bad" Web page code by identifying it with this dialog box.

Running Site Reports

You can also check your code by running one of the many other reports that Expression Web can prepare. Reports ensure that your site conforms to accessibility and compatibility guidelines established by the W3 Consortium. They not only ensure that your sites can be viewed by the widest number of Web surfers, but that their content will appear just the way you designed it, too. Table 7.1 lists some of the reports you can run that are geared toward improving your site's code.

Table 7.1 Expression Web Site Report Options

Report	How to Access It	What It Catches
Accessibility Reports	Tools > Accessibility Reports	Makes sure sites are accessible to those with disabilities
Compatibility Reports	Tools > Compatibility Reports	Code that does not conform to the version of XHTML you are using
Problems	Site > Reports > Problems	Unlinked pages, pages slow to load, or hyperlinks that don't work
CSS Errors	Tools > CSS Reports > Errors tab	Errors with your CSS code

Testing with Multiple Browsers

You don't know what kind of Web browsers the visitors to your site will be using. And sometimes Web browsers render Web page content very differently. For that reason, it's a good idea to try out your page by loading it in a variety of Web browsers to make sure it looks good in each one. Expression Web excels at giving you plenty of browsers from which to choose, as well as different screen resolutions for each of those browsers.

To preview the current Web page, choose File > Preview in Browser and then select a browser from the submenu that appears. Initially, several versions of Microsoft Internet Explorer appear, followed by different versions of Mozilla Firefox or any other browsers that are installed on your system. You can edit the list to specify other browsers. The browser launches if it isn't open already, and your page appears in your chosen browser window.

Viewing in Multiple Browsers

Because different browsers can display certain Web content very differently, you should test a Web page in at least two browsers (if not more). To add options to the browser list, select File > Preview in Browser > Preview in Multiple Browsers. When you do so, the page appears in (most likely) Internet Explorer and another browser, such as Firefox, if it is available. When you do this, you may notice some interesting differences. Review the two images shown in Figure 7.3 and determine what's different about them.

The navigation bar shown on the left in Internet Explorer probably doesn't show up due to poorly formed code as browsers interpret code differently. Some are more forgiving of non-standards code than others.

Figure 7.3   Viewing in more than one browser lets you identify content that might not display correctly.

Specifying Additional Browsers

If you want to add more browsers to Expression Web's list, choose File > Preview in Browser > Edit Browser List. When the Edit Browser List dialog box appears, follow these steps:

1.   Click Add to open the Edit Browser List dialog box.

2. Click Browse to open the Add Browser dialog box, from which you can locate a browser to add to the list of those EW uses. Navigate through your computer resources until you locate the icon for the browser you want, and then click Open.

3. The path leading to your additional browser is added to the Command field in the Add Browser dialog box, as shown in Figure 7.4. Click OK to close Add Browser and return to the Edit Browser List dialog box.

4. Check the box next to the name you just assigned to your new browser.

5. Click OK to close the Edit Browser List dialog box.

Figure 7.4 You need to name your new browser before it is added to your list.

Configuring File Transfers

When you're finished editing, proofreading, and testing your pages, you need to publish them by transferring the necessary files from your computer to your space on a remote Web server. Some Web editors require you to use a separate FTP (File Transfer Protocol) application to publish your files. By publishing the files online, you move them from your local file system to a remote Web server. Expression Web has a built-in publishing application that alleviates the need to use a separate FTP program. In addition, it has features such as selective file viewing and synchronization that most FTP programs don't provide.

For example, when you choose File > Publish Site, the Remote Web Site Properties dialog box appears. On the Publishing tab, you are given the option of publishing only those pages in the current site that have changed since the last time you published the site with Expression Web. You also tell Expression Web whether or not to compare the source and destination sites when deciding what pages have changed. It's a high-level function most FTP programs can't perform.

In order to publish and then work with the files on your remote Web site from within the Expression Web interface, you need to tell Web where your site is located and what sort of file transfer technology your server supports. You do that by choosing File > Publish Site. (Alternatively, if you're in the Web Site tab in Design or Code View, click Remote Web Site Properties.) If you have any unsaved changes in the Web pages you have been editing, an alert box appears asking if you want to save your changes. If such a dialog box appears, click Yes. Then, when selecting an option for Remote Web Server Type, these are your options:

FrontPage Server Extensions: Choose this if your Web host supports the FrontPage Server technologies and you plan to use them in your Web site.

WebDAV: Select this if your hosting server supports the Distributed Authoring and Versioning system for keeping track of revisions to files.

FTP: Virtually all Web servers support File Transfer Protocol (FTP), so this is practically a default option. Choose this if you are not using the FrontPage Server Extensions or WebDAV.

File System: Select this option if you're publishing the site locally on your file system so you can test it out before putting it online.

You also need to identify the location of your space on the server—at least, you need to do so if you plan to use Expression Web as your file transfer software. Chances are you received an e-mail message from your hosting service when you first signed up that contains this information. Otherwise, check the hosting service's Web site FAQ. The program has the ability to transfer files from your computer to your Web site for you. You do this by entering the URL of the site in the Remote Web Site Location box, shown in Figure 7.5.

Setting up your file transfer information in advance makes publishing and updating your pages go more quickly in the long run. You frequently need to make small editorial changes to a page, save the changes, upload the updated file to the Web server, and view the results online. If you transfer the files using the same application in which you did the editing (EW), you eliminate the time and effort required to open a separate file transfer program, such as an FTP application, and do the uploading. You don't have to open a separate program, and you free up some computer memory as well.

The View drop-down list in the upper left corner of Remote Web Site Properties gives you different options for viewing the files as they are contained both on your local site and on the remote server. They include:

Folder Contents: This displays all the files in the current folder.

Files to Publish: This displays only the files you want to publish.

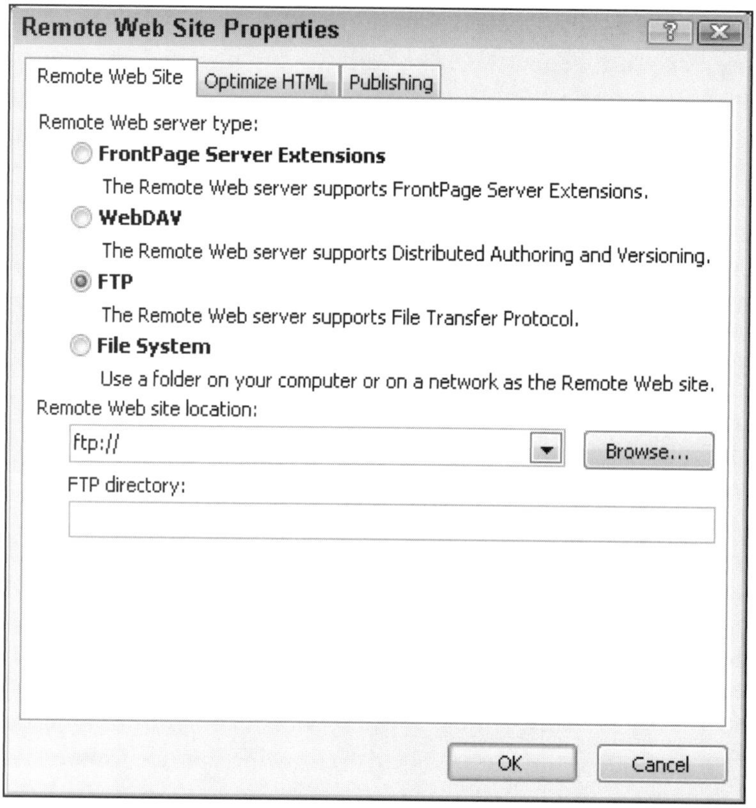

Figure 7.5 Provide Expression Web with information about where you need to publish your site.

Files Not to Publish: This shows any files you have marked as not publishable.

Files in Conflict: This displays files on one site (local or remote) that have the same name but different contents than files on the other site.

When you choose File > Publish Site in the future after you have supplied the location of the remote Web site, Expression Web remembers the publishing location, and you are automatically prompted to log in with your username and password when you want to access the remote location. The Expression Web workspace changes into an FTP program window when you connect to the remote site: The left pane contains the version of the site that is on your local file system, and the right pane contains the remote site, as shown in Figure 7.6.

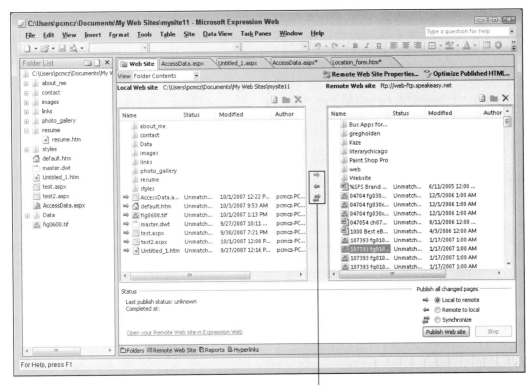

Click here to Move Selected
Files from One Site to Another

Figure 7.6   Expression Web can handle file transfer tasks after you have finished editing.

Synchronizing Local and Remote Sites

It's important to transfer any revisions, deletions, or moves you make on the local version of your Web site to the remote version of the site—the one that appears on the Web and that everyone can see. Instead of requiring you to search and replace files and folders one by one, Expression Web saves you time and effort by enabling you to automatically synchronize the hyperlinks on both sites.

After you have defined the local and remote versions of your sites, you can connect to your remote site as described in the preceding section. To automatically synchronize files, click the Synchronize button at the bottom of the Web Site View and then click the Publish Web Site button. The newer versions of your documents are moved to either the local version or remote version of your site. In addition, any files that are contained on one version of the site but not the other are transferred as well. The end result is that your local and remote sites contain the same versions of the same files. The Status column in both the local and remote sides of the window gives you information about each file listed: Conflict indicates that there is a conflict, and Unmatched indicates that a file on one site is not matched with a file on the other site, for instance.

Controlling Access to Your Web Documents

Few large-scale Web sites are created by a lone operator. It's more common to have many hands involved in revising Web pages. Potential problems involve duplication of editing efforts by several people and pages that need to be edited being overlooked. You need to keep track of two essential areas of workgroup operations:

> **Workflow:** This is the process followed when a team prepares, publishes, and maintains a set of documents, such as a set of Web pages.

> **Access Control:** This enables group members to "check in" or "check out" files and have them labeled as checked out so others cannot access them at the same time.

Expression Web contains a variety of tools for helping members of a workgroup coordinate their efforts efficiently so Web pages can be updated as needed. It also provides designers and editors alike with a Check In/Check Out mechanism that helps everyone track which pages are being edited. Both features are described in the following sections.

Tracking Workgroup Members

In order to use Expression Web to track the activities of a workgroup, you have to have a place where members are identified by name. Expression Web makes it easy to list the names of the workgroup members:

1. Open the site you expect to edit as a group.

2. Make sure you have metadata activated by choosing Site > Site Settings and making sure the box is checked next to Manage the Web Site Using Hidden Metadata Files. (If this option is grayed out, the site is a subweb, part of a "parent" Web site. You need to work with a parent Web site to use this option.)

3. In the Folder list, select the name of any file in the site.

4. Choose File > Properties or right-click any file and choose Properties from the context menu. The properties sheet for the site appears (see Figure 7.7).

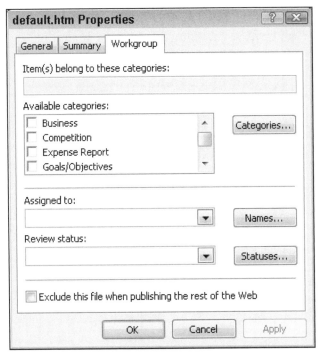

Figure 7.7 You can choose names of workgroup members in this properties sheet.

5.   Check the boxes next to one or more categories that describe your file.

6.   Choose a member's name from the drop-down list. If you haven't yet entered names, click the Names button. The Usernames Master List dialog box appears, as shown in Figure 7.8.

7.   Type a name in the New Username box.

8.   Click Add. The name is added to the list box in the lower half of the Usernames Master List.

9.   When you're finished, click OK to close the Usernames Master List and return to the Properties dialog box.

Once you have added the names of your workgroup members to the properties sheet for this single page, the same names appear in the properties sheet for all other pages on the same site. You can choose the name from the Assigned To drop-down list so you can assign the page you've currently selected to one of your colleagues.

Figure 7.8 Add workgroup member names using this dialog box.

Tracking a Page's Status

The same properties sheet you use to assign pages to workgroup members can be used to identify the status of each page. That way those of your colleagues who have been assigned to edit a page can tell when it has been approved or not. Follow these steps:

1. Right-click the page you want to track in the Folder List task pane and choose Properties from the context menu.

2. Click the Workgroup tab.

3. Choose a name from the Assigned To drop-down list; the names you added earlier appear in the list.

4. Choose an option from the Review status drop-down list to indicate to your fellow workgroup members where the Web page stands. You can choose from the following:

   - Approved
   - Rejected
   - Pending Review

5. When you're finished, click OK to close Properties and return to the Web page you currently have open.

If one of these designations isn't what you're looking for, you can create your own. Click the Statuses button in the Workgroup tab. The Review Status Master List dialog box appears. Type your own status designation in the New Review Status box and click Add. The new status will be added as an option to the list in the Workgroup tab of the properties sheet.

Note: When you have a file open and you choose File > Properties, another dialog box called Page Properties appears. This dialog box lets you specify language settings and other advanced information. But it also contains the same workgroup information as the smaller properties sheet; you can use it to assign pages or track the status of the currently selected page.

The last option in the properties sheet (either the small or the large version) contains an important setting related to publishing your Web pages. If you want to publish only pages that have been approved by the appropriate personnel, check the box next to Exclude This File when Publishing the Rest of This Web Site. You have to check this box for each page that has not yet been approved. The check box applies only to the currently open page.

Running a Workflow Report

Expression Web's error reports were mentioned earlier, but the program also provides a tool for tracking the status of each of the pages in a Web site. When you have a Web site open and you click the Web Site tab at the top of the main editing area rather than the tab that contains the name of an individual page, you can adjust the columns so that they present you with information about workflow. Choose Site > Reports > Workflow, and then choose one of the four available options from the Workflow submenu (the last one is grayed out until Check In/Check Out, which is covered later in this chapter, is activated):

Review Status: Columns appear with headings such as Review Status, Assigned To, Review Date, and Reviewed By, as shown in Figure 7.9. You or your co-workers can record when a page is reviewed or when it needs to be reviewed.

Assigned To: Choose this option, and the columns in the Folder list read Assigned To, Assigned Date, Assigned By, Comments, Type, and In Folder.

Categories: You get two column headings here—Category and Type—in addition to the standard Name, Title, and In Folder.

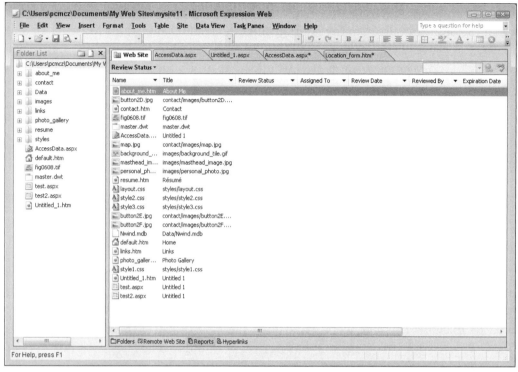

Figure 7.9 You can review status information by running a Workflow report.

Publish Status: You get the categories Publish, Modified Date, Review Status, and Size, in addition to the standard ones.

If you do not have metadata enabled for your site in the General tab of the Site Settings dialog box, you'll get an error message when you choose any of these options.

The Web site's Reports View workflow columns are directly connected with the information entered in the Workflow tab of the Properties dialog box. The category information you record in the properties sheets appears in the Category tab, for instance.

For each of the Workflow submenu options, additional filtering options appear in Reports View above the column headings. For example, if you choose Categories from the Workflow submenu, you can choose an option from the drop-down menu list that appears just above and to the right of the column headings (see Figure 7.10). This option lets you view all files that have been designated as being in the Business category, for example. You also can create your own custom filter by clicking the down arrow next to the heading name and choosing Custom from the context

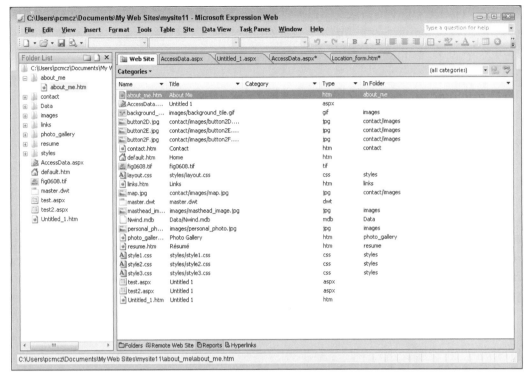

Figure 7.10   You can configure filters to locate exactly the Web page content you want.

menu that appears. Then enter filtering options for the type of information you want to view. For example, if you want to view all files that are JPEG images, choose Custom from the Type drop-down list and type jpg in the Custom AutoFilter dialog box.

Revising Your Web Pages with Check In/Check Out

Even if you create a Web site, you might not be the one who edits it down the road. Chances are many different contributors will be adding and updating your site's pages as needs arise. If you are only one of many editors, you need to keep track of who has edited a file and when each editing task has been completed so your co-workers don't duplicate (or undo) your efforts.

The Check In/Check Out file management system can help members of a workgroup when they first create pages or do long-term editing. This Expression Web feature tracks editors when they're working on files so others don't duplicate their efforts and only one person works on the document at a time. First, you need to enable Check In/Check Out for the site you're working on. Open the file and follow these steps:

1.   Open the site you want to edit and choose Site > Site Settings.

2. When the Site Settings dialog box appears, verify that the box next to Manage the Web Site Using Hidden Metadata Files is checked in the General tab.

3. Check the box next to Use Document Check-In and Check-Out, as shown in Figure 7.11. The options in the bottom half of the General tab, which were grayed out before, become active.

4. Click the button next to Check Out Files from the Local Web Site.

5. You also can check the box next to Prompt to Check Out File when Opening a Page. If you check this box, whenever you open a page in the site (or any type of file), you're prompted to check it out.

6. Click OK.

7. An alert dialog box appears, notifying you that you have changed the source control settings for the site and advising you that recalculating hyperlinks will take a few minutes. Click Yes.

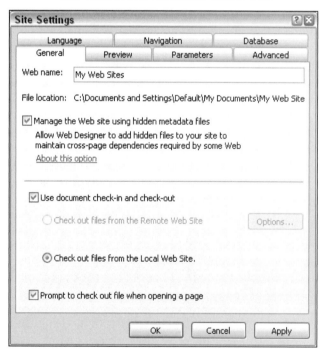

Figure 7.11   Before you can track file use, you need to activate the Check-In/Check-Out system.

Once you have turned on the Check-In/Check-Out system, you can start to work on the file by checking it out yourself. Double-click the file you want to work on. The dialog box shown in Figure 7.12 pops up. Click Yes to check out the file.

Figure 7.12   The Check-In/Check-Out system prompts you to check out a file before you can start editing it.

Tip: If you didn't tell Expression Web to prompt you to check out automatically when you open a file, you need to do so manually. Highlight the name of the file in the Folder list and choose Edit > Check Out or press Ctrl+J. Alternatively, you can right-click the file's name in the Folder list and choose Check Out from the context menu.

Once a file is checked out, a green checkmark appears next to its name in the Folder List task pane. You can review the status of this file as well as others in the same site by choosing Site > Reports > Workflow > Checkout Status. The dialog box shown in Figure 7.13 appears, along with the name of your computer.

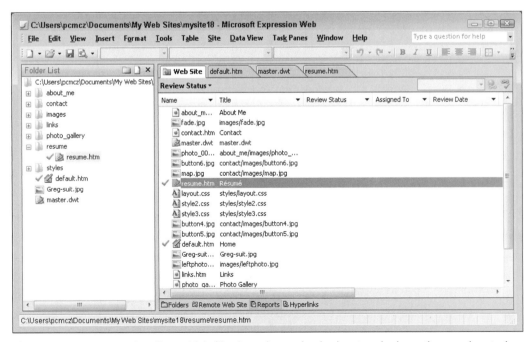

Figure 7.13   Reports View lists which files have been checked out and where they are located.

After you're finished editing the file, you check it in by right-clicking its name in the Folder list and choosing Check In from the context menu or by choosing Edit > Check In or pressing Ctrl+Shift+J.

Analyzing Web Traffic

Once you publish your site, it becomes important to track how many visitors your site receives, where those visitors come from, and which pages attract the most traffic. Your Web host probably provides you with such reports, and the place to start is to call your host's tech support staff or read through the FAQ on its Web site to find out how to access such reports. In case you find the reports inadequate, or if you don't have access to such reports because you're hosting your site on your own Web server, some options for analyzing Web traffic are described below.

Installing a Hit Counter

The hit counter was one of the earliest tools for tracking visits to a Web page. A hit counter is a bit of code that produces a graphical display on a Web page that indicates how many people have viewed that page. Counters are still widely used, and they are relatively primitive in the amount of information they can provide.

You don't have to create your own hit counters, and Expression Web doesn't provide them for you. Rather, you should download and install one of the many free ones you can find online.

Caution: Hit counters have several downsides. They look old-fashioned, and some of the ones that are made available for free actually gather information about people. Basically, a hit counter records the number of visits a Web page receives. It doesn't tell you how many different individuals visited your site or when they visited. If one person visits a page 10 times in a day, the hit counter will register 10 visits, and you won't be able to tell if 10 different people visited or not. It's preferable to use log file analysis tools to track visitors with greater precision.

Analyzing Log Files

The term "log file" sounds pretty technical, and with good reason. A log file is a record of the traffic on a network, and the data retrieved can consist of numbers and code that look like gibberish if you aren't familiar with it. Your Web host should provide you with software that turns the numbers into graphical representations that are easier to determine, however.

If you don't have a tool available or are looking for an alternative to the one you are given, consider applications such as Log Analyzer Lite by Alterwind (www.alterwind. com) or SmarterStats (www.smartertools.com). Both programs are free to download and install. Whether you use an analysis tool provided by your host or one you install yourself, you should look for a package that provides you with basic information such as:

- Hits on your site, broken down to each individual item requested

- Browser types for your users

- Operating systems in use by your users

- Number of hits on a day-by-day basis

- Hits by hour of the day

- Hits by day of the week

- Browser used

- Host IP addresses and possibly host names

- Referring sites

- Errors generated on your site

The more sophisticated tools can show you paths through your site and a decent idea of which users are using your site at the present moment. These types of features are reasons to consider buying a professional tool rather than using a free version. The industry leader, WebTrends (www.webtrends.com) is especially powerful but expensive and designed for corporate Web sites rather than small businesses or individuals.

Professional Graphics with Expression Design

- On a Macintosh, only one of two "forks" of the graphics file is used (the data fork), which makes it compact and simple.

GIF is best suited to type, line art, or images with well-defined edges, in contrast to JPEG, which is optimal for photographs and complex illustrations that need greater compression.

JPEG (pronounced "jay-peg") stands for Joint Photographic Experts Group, the name of the group that originated the format. JPEG is the other widely used graphics format on the Web. Like GIF, JPEG is a means of compressing bitmap images. JPEG works with 24-bit images and provides better compression than GIF because it discards non-essential image information when the file is compressed. It takes advantage of the human eye's ability to perceive small changes in color and brightness. JPEG is better suited for large photos and continuous tones of grayscale or color than GIF.

JPEG compression discards some data in the course of making the file smaller. JPEG compresses bitmaps by first converting them into squares and then applying an algorithm called Discrete Cosine Transformation to convert the data from squares into curves. The smallest curves are discarded in the course of the compression process. As a result, a JPEG graphic cannot be decompressed and reconstructed in its original form. Still, JPEG images are regarded as being of high quality and are highly compressed.

The Promise of PNG

PNG, which stands for Portable Network Graphics, was developed as an alternative to GIF. PNG can achieve compression rates 10 to 30 percent better than GIF. Like GIF, it supports 1, 2, 4, and 8-bit graphics, and like JPEG it can support 24-bit color, but it can support color depths of up to 48 bits per pixel. Other features include:

- Cross-platform control of image brightness

- Two-dimensional interlacing

- Lossless compression

- Support for three main image types: TrueColor (24-bit), grayscale, and palette (8-bit)

PNG, however, is still not widely used on the Web, though it is becoming more common than it used to. If you have the option to use PNG, you should try it because such images gain great compression as well as high quality.

Drawing Vector Graphics

Vector graphics are comprised of lines rather than bitmaps. Instead of displaying the colors or shades of gray that are contained in an image as tiny dots, vectors are made up of objects, each of which is a mathematical definition of a curve, line, or other shape. (Vectors are often called *object-oriented* graphics.) Each object in a vector graphic contains its own color information. PostScript is a computer language that forms the basis of programs like Adobe Illustrator that are commonly used by designers to create vector graphics. One common vector format is Encapsulated PostScript (EPS).

Vector images are especially well suited to high-resolution computer graphics such as computer-aided design (CAD) or 3-D modeling. They also have the ability to print out images at high resolutions such as 600 dpi or 1200 dpi. Each object in a vector graphic can be altered independently without necessarily having to redraw the other component parts. And when you stretch or resize a vector graphic, it doesn't become blurry the way raster images do, because its lines aren't made up of pixels.

Understanding File Compression

File compression is a fundamental concept with respect to viewing digital graphic formats and especially bitmaps. A compressed file is one in which the data that makes up the graphic—the pixels or the vector objects—are made shorter, usually by means of an algorithm. The algorithm recognizes repeated patterns of binary data and reduces them to "shorthand" data that takes up less room. For example, if a graphics file contains several instances of the following data:

10101101011010

the algorithm creates a short version of the same data, like this:

100110

The process is like using the abbreviation U.S.A. instead of writing United States of America many times. Yet enough data is saved during compression so that, when the image is decompressed and displayed by a Web browser or other graphics program, it appears the same, even though it contains less data than it did before. All compression methods represent a trade-off: Image quality is compromised, but in return, the image is rendered visible by different computers and becomes easily transportable across a network such as the Internet.

Two types of compression methods are used to create Web graphics. *Lossy* compression makes bitmap files dramatically smaller; however, some essential color information is lost in the process of changing the binary information associated with each pixel. In contrast, *lossless* compression allows the data in the file to be made smaller without losing essential visual information.

Exploring Paths, Strokes, and Fills

Vector graphics are made up of lines and curves called paths that are defined by mathematical definitions. Paths, in turn, are comprised of points called nodes and line segments in between them. All paths have a start point and an end point. The end point is designated by the arrow at one end of the path.

Design can draw two types of paths: Bezier curves and B-spline curves. Bezier curves use nodes that have control handles. The control handles determine the direction of the path and how it changes at the node. A corner point changes direction very sharply, while a curve point changes only gradually. B-spline paths also use nodes and have start and end points, but the nodes do not have control handles.

Each object in Design, including a path, consists of a stroke and a fill. A stroke is the outline of the object; the fill is the color inside the path or shape. Both the stroke and the fill can have their color set to None, which means they won't be visible. You'll learn more about strokes and fills later in this chapter.

Managing Files

The Design window and its main features were described in Chapter 1, so this chapter will focus on working with documents. When you first open Design, before you have created or opened any files, the main work area (the artboard) is gray. To get started working with Design, you need to open a document so that you can either start drawing or creating graphics or editing preexisting files. Both options are discussed in the sections that follow.

Creating New Blank Documents

Whenever you work with Design, you do so in the context of a document. As stated in Chapter 1, to open a new document in Design you choose File > New or Ctrl+N. When the New Document dialog box shown in Figure 8.3 appears, you can name the file immediately by typing a name in the Name box. You can also choose a preset size for the document frame by making a choice from the Presets drop-down list. When you're done, click OK.

A document opens within a rectangular frame called a *document frame*. The document frame is located on the artboard—the large work area bounded by rulers that takes up most of the Design window and that, by default, is white (see Figure 8.4). The part of the artboard outside the rectangle is sort of a storage area where you can

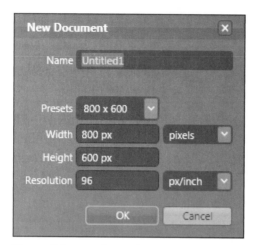

Figure 8.3 You have the option of naming a file before you even open it.

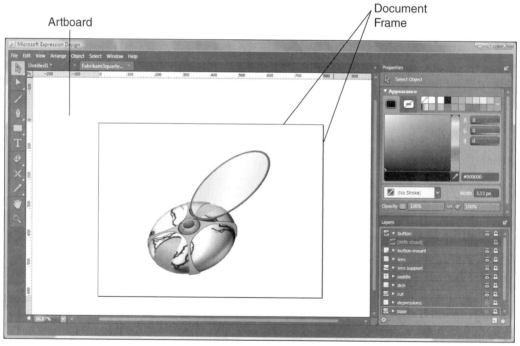

Figure 8.4 The document frame is located on the Expression Design artboard.

place miscellaneous graphics or objects. The part in the document frame is what will be exported to Blend or printed, or that can receive live effects. In other words, you need to keep the graphics you want to save and use inside the document frame rather than outside it.

Adjusting Rulers

If you look closely at the rulers that bound the artboard, you'll notice that they define the boundaries of the document frame. The sides of the frame are mirrored by a light area in the rulers. You can change default units of measurement, as well as other ruler features, by choosing Edit > Options > Units and Grids. When the Options dialog box shown in Figure 8.5 opens, click the down arrow next to Document Units to choose a new unit of measurement, such as pixels or picas.

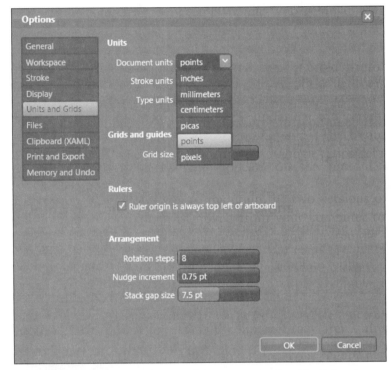

Figure 8.5   Choose a new unit of measurement in this dialog box.

By default, the ruler starts at zero at the upper-left corner of the image depicted on the artboard. If you don't want the "zero point" of the rulers to be in the default position (for instance, if you want to add a feature at a specific location), choose File > Set Document Origin. Then click anywhere inside the artboard, and the ruler origin points adjust to the point where you clicked.

As you move the cursor around the document frame, markers appear in the ruler to indicate its x, y position (see Figure 8.6). When you click somewhere in the frame with the pen tool, the actual x, y position is indicated in the bar just beneath the artboard. The measurements are relative to the zero point of the ruler.

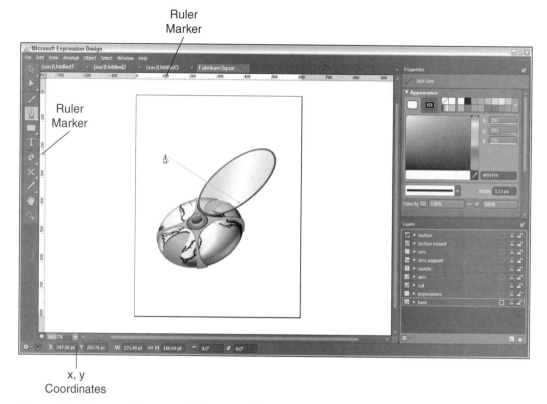

Figure 8.6 You can draw or edit images with precision by using the x, y coordinates.

Editing Existing Files

To open an existing file, you only have to choose File > Open, locate the object in the Open dialog box, and click Open. When you have multiple files open, their filenames are listed in a series of tabs that appear just above the horizontal ruler above the artboard. Files you haven't named yet are designated as Untitled. Those with names will have the filename extension .design, which is Design's native file format. Switch from one file to another by clicking on their respective tabs. If Design can't accommodate all the open files in the space above the artboard, click the down arrow and choose another file from the list that appears (see Figure 8.7).

Figure 8.7 Multiple open files are listed in separate tabs above the artboard.

Tip: You can press Ctrl+Tab to move to the right from one document to another or Ctrl+Shift+Tab to move to the left from one document to another. An asterisk (*) next to a filename indicates that a change has been made to that file but hasn't been saved yet.

Working with Design's Tools

Whether you are drawing your own file or editing an existing document, Design gives you an extensive selection of tools for doing so. The place to start is with the Toolbox. Once you have selected the tool you want, you can then choose more specific options for working with that tool in the Properties panel.

Touring the Toolbox

What would an image editor be without tools? Expression Design provides a virtual palette of tools that rivals and in some cases exceeds those found in other leading image editing programs. In this section, you'll examine the tools within Design, with each toolset grouped by function and featuring examples of where and how they are used.

The Toolbox is the set of buttons along the left side of Expression Design. The first thing you need to know is that the tools you see aren't the only ones available. If you see a white triangle in the lower right corner of a button, it means the tool you're seeing is only one of a tool group. Click and hold down on the visible button, and the other buttons in the group fly out from it. The Pen tool, for example, is part of the largest tool group. The entire tool group—Pen Tool, Add Anchor Point tool, Delete Anchor Point tool, Convert Anchor Point tool, Polyline tool, and B-Spline tool—is shown in Figure 8.8.

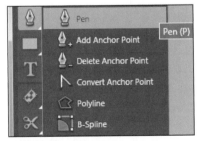

Figure 8.8 Many tools are part of tool groups.

As you can see from Figure 8.8, each tool has a keyboard shortcut that is presented in parentheses. In the case of the Pen tool, typing P will make that tool active.

Drawing Tools

Chapter 9 will focus more fully on actually drawing shapes with Design's tools. But in order to get acquainted with selection, viewing, and other tools, it's helpful to draw a few shapes to begin with. Follow these steps to get started:

1. Choose File > New, choose the 800 × 600 preset size, and click OK to create a new blank document on the artboard.

2. Click the Rectangle tool or press M to make the tool active.

3. Click anywhere in the document frame, hold down the mouse button, and drag down and to the right to draw a rectangle. Release the mouse button when you are done.

4. Click the Pen tool or press P to make it active.

5. Click and hold down anywhere in the document frame and drag to draw a line. Release the mouse button when you are done.

6. Click the Text tool or press T to make the Text tool active. Click anywhere in the document frame and type a few characters.

Now that you have a few graphic objects on the artboard, you can practice using the selection tools.

Selecting Objects

The tool at the top of the Toolbox is simply called the Selection tool. (Its shortcut key is the letter V.) Try it out by clicking each of the objects you drew earlier in succession. When you do so, a selection box appears around the object. The handles around the selection box shown in Figure 8.9 can be dragged in different directions to change the shape of the object.

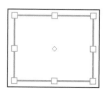

Figure 8.9 Selection handles let you "stretch" and change the shape of an object.

Press Shift+click to select each of the objects in turn. When they are all selected, choose Arrange > Group or press Ctrl+G. This groups the selected objects into a single entity. Click anywhere on the artboard to deselect the grouped objects. Click on any one of them again; now a single selection box appears around the entire group (see Figure 8.10).

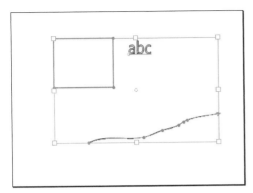

Figure 8.10 When you group multiple objects, you can select and arrange them at the same time.

If you ever need to select a single member of a group of objects, you need to use the tool that's found in the same tool group as the Selection tool. It's called Group Selection, and its shortcut keys are Shift+A. Try it: Click outside the group to deselect it, and then click an individual object to select it all by itself. Press Shift+click to select all the items, and then choose Arrange > Ungroup or press Ctrl+Shift+G. This ungroups the objects so that you can try the other selection tools on them.

The Direct selection tool (shortcut key: A) lets you select individual nodes on a path. Select this tool and click the shape you drew earlier with the Pen. When you click on the line, a series of nodes and their control handles appears. Click on one of the nodes, and it is highlighted in red.

Underneath the Direct selection tool you find the Lasso selection tool. This tool, which is commonly used in other graphics programs, lets you draw a freeform selection shape over an object or just a set of nodes within the object. If you draw the selection shape over a set of nodes, only those nodes are selected. Otherwise, if you draw the selection lasso over an object, the entire object is selected. In Figure 8.11, a selection "lasso" has been drawn around a single node on a path.

You can also use Design's Select menu to select objects. You might not think of using a menu to make selections when the selection tools are so convenient. It's worth exploring the Select menu, however. When you choose Select > Select By, you gain the capability to select objects by their attributes by choosing options in the Select By dialog box (see Figure 8.12). On a complex drawing where you have dozens of separate images grouped in multiple layers, it can be useful to choose every object that has an orange fill or a white stroke color, for instance. When you're done, click OK. You can then change all the selected objects at once—you can change one font to another one or change one fill color or gradient to a different option.

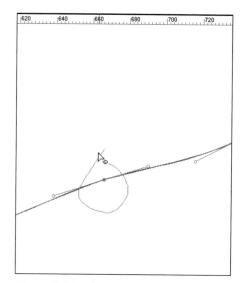

Figure 8.11 The Lasso selection tool lets you draw a freeform selection shape.

Figure 8.12 Use these options to select by attribute.

Another option on the Select menu lets you make group selections and save time. If you already have a set of items selected—all shapes that have a white fill, for instance—choose Select > Invert to select all other objects in the current image at one time.

Viewing and Moving Objects

When you are using the Selection tool, it's easy to move an object by clicking the arrow keys repeatedly. Alternately, to move the object, click and drag one of the sides of the box other than the selection handles.

The Pan tool (shortcut key: H) lets you move the document frame around by clicking and dragging it. When you do so, the objects appear to move as though you're pushing them with a hand. Of course, you can also move vertically or horizontally around the artboard by moving the vertical scrollbar just to the right of it or the horizontal scrollbar just beneath it.

Tip: You can access the Pan tool at any time by pressing and holding down the spacebar. It doesn't matter what tool you're working with at the time; when you do this, the Pan tool becomes active.

The Zoom tool (shortcut key: Z) lets you zoom in on part of an object; press and hold down the Alt key while you click with the Zoom tool in order to zoom out. You can activate the Zoom tool at any time by holding down Ctrl+spacebar for zooming in and Ctrl+Alt+spacebar for zooming out. The View menu, of course, contains several options that let you zoom in and out on your work.

The Arrange menu, for its part, contains some controls for viewing objects in different ways. The Align submenu options beneath the Arrange menu enable you to arrange selected objects in different ways. (Be sure to select one or more objects, or the Align submenu options won't be active.) When you are trying to align multiple objects precisely, choosing one of the options can save you lots of time spent tediously moving objects pixel by pixel and watching the ruler to make sure the position is just right. You can make all objects align by their left or right edge, by their vertical or horizontal center, or by many other attributes. The best way to understand them is to try them yourself with multiple objects you have open on the artboard.

Editing Objects

Many of the tools in the Toolbox are intended to help you adjust, edit, and revise shapes and objects you have already created. Their use probably won't be completely clear until you draw objects with the Pen, B-Spline, or other tools as described in Chapter 9. But here's a quick rundown so you know about all the path editing tools available in the Toolbox:

> **Add or Delete Anchor Point:** Anchor points, also called nodes, are the points that determine the shape of a path. The spacing of the points and the positions of their respective control handles determine the shape of a curve or the direction of a straight segment. By adding points, you can make a curve change shape more gradually. Clicking the Add Anchor Point tool on a path (or pressing the equals sign, =) adds a point. Clicking the Delete Anchor Point tool on an existing node (or pressing the hyphen -) removes a node.

Convert Anchor Point: Anchor points come in three varieties: curves, corners, and cusps. With the Convert Anchor Point tool, you change one type of point to another. See Chapter 9 for more.

Scissors: The scissors lets you split an existing path into two separate paths, each with a start point and an end point.

Reverse Path: Every path has a direction, as indicated by the arrow at one end of the path. Even a closed path, such as a rectangle, has a start and end point and a direction. Clicking anywhere on the path reverses the direction.

Start Point: Since every path has a direction, it follows that every path has a start and end point. Clicking on a path with this tool moves the start point to that spot.

You can use the start point or any of the aforementioned tools with open paths and closed paths. An open path is shown at the top in Figure 8.13. A closed path is shown beneath it.

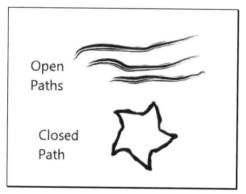

Figure 8.13 Paths you draw and edit with Design can be either closed or open.

Transforming Objects

A fill is a color or a series of gradually changing colors called a gradient that is placed within a set of anchor points on a path. The most obvious fill is applied to the center of a closed path such as an ellipse or rectangle. But curves and other areas of open paths can have fills as well. Once you have specified a fill using the Properties panel, you can then transform the fill if you're not happy with the initial results.

With the Fill Transform tool, you can select an image fill. Then you can perform the same kinds of actions you would with the selection tools—you can stretch the fill or scale it up or down or even rotate it. The same selection box that appears when you use the Selection tool surrounds the object. When you stretch the box's handles or move the box, only the fill is repositioned, not the outer shape, as shown in Figure 8.14.

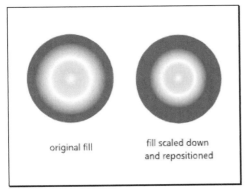

original fill

fill scaled down
and repositioned

Figure 8.14 With the Fill Transform tool, you affect a gradient's size, direction, and other characteristics.

With the Gradient Transform tool, you can change the starting and ending points of a gradient as well as the angle of the fill. To determine the angle at which you want a gradient to travel, click the gradient to select it. Then click with the Gradient Transform tool at the spot where you want the gradient's starting point to be and drag in the direction you want the gradient to move. Hold down the Alt key while dragging with the Gradient Transform tool, and you change the second angle of the gradient—the angle that determines how the gradient is skewed.

The Color Dropper tool gives you another way to "transform" fills and other objects. The transformation occurs when you move a color from one object to another. First, select the Color Dropper. Then, click the fill area of the object that has the color you want to copy. Hold down the mouse button and drag the dropper to the object to which you want to assign the new color. Release the mouse button to copy the color from the first object to the second.

The Attribute Dropper, which is in the same tool group as the Color Dropper, lets you copy attributes such as a stroke pattern or a fill from one object to another. It's a quick and powerful way to save formatting time: Once you have formatted one object with just the color, stroke, fill, and other attributes you want, you can move all of the formatting at once to a second object by clicking the first object with the Attribute Dropper, holding down the mouse and dragging, and then releasing the mouse button over the second object. If you release over the stroke of the second object, the attributes are moved to the stroke; if you release over the fill area of the second object, the attributes are moved to the fill area of the second object.

Using the Properties Panel

The Properties panel is the place where you give life and character to the shapes you create with the Toolbox. Here, you apply fills, gradients, and other attributes to your objects. You also select stroke patterns and widths. In other words, the Toolbox gives you the tools you need to create basic shapes, but the Properties panel is where you turn them into graphic designs. Most of the tools mentioned in the following sections are found in the Appearance section of the Properties panel. Other sections, like Type and Layers, are mentioned in subsequent chapters.

Using Fills

Fills are applied to objects by first selecting the object you want to format and then clicking the Fill button in the Appearance section of the Properties panel. At that point you can choose a fill in one of several ways:

- By clicking one of the color swatches near the top of the Appearance section
- By clicking anywhere in the Color Picker box
- By clicking the More Swatches down arrow and making a selection from the Favorites, Most Recent, or Categories section
- By entering values in the R, G, and B boxes

You already know what happens when you fill a closed shape such as a polygon. When you select an open path such as the one shown in Figure 8.15, fills are still applied to the path's open areas. The path on the top has no fill; beneath it you see the same path with a fill applied.

As you'll see in Chapter 10, you can apply fills and strokes to text as well.

Choosing Different Strokes

Think of the word "stroke" as being short for "brushstroke," and you get a good idea of what this aspect of the Properties panel enables you to do.

When you go to a paint store, you have a wide variety of paint brushes from which to choose. It's a good bet the brushes you find in a brick-and-mortar store aren't as widely varied as the ones you find in the Properties panel. You don't get a full idea of the brush options available to you until you click the Paintbrush tool and then choose one of the patterns from the Basic drop-down list in the Appearance section of the Properties panel. The patterns listed under Categories are only the most obvious ones you can see; scroll down and click on one of the categories at the bottom of the menu (Dry Medium, Graphics, Ink, Oils), and you'll find a seemingly limitless selection of brush patterns. So many options are available that you have to try them out individually. You're sure to find one that suits your needs.

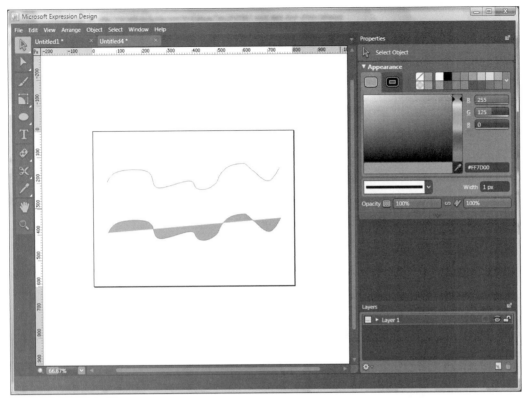

Figure 8.15   Applying a fill to an open path.

Assigning Color to Strokes

Whenever you choose a stroke or a fill, you can assign a solid color or gradient to it. First, click the button (Fill or Stroke) that corresponds to the element you want to "colorize." Then click one of the three buttons immediately to the right of the Stroke button as shown in Figure 8.16: None, Solid Color, or Gradient. (The fourth button, Image, is disabled when you are working with strokes.) Once you have selected either Solid Color or Gradient, you can choose a color using one of the options mentioned earlier: the Color Picker, the color swatches, or the R, G, B boxes.

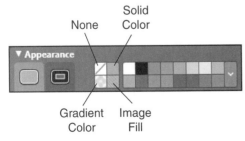

Figure 8.16   Specify the type of color you want to assign before you actually choose a color.

Working with Acquired Images

Expression Design isn't solely a program for creating your own graphics from scratch. You can also import existing images from your digital camera, from an application like Adobe Illustrator, or from other applications. The method you use to bring the image into Design depends on the format in which it was saved.

Understanding Image Formats

Digital images need to be saved in formats that enable them to be processed and displayed by particular software programs. Adobe Photoshop applications are saved in PSD format so they can be displayed in Photoshop. On the other hand, common graphics formats like TIFF can be displayed in Design and a variety of graphics programs.

Table 8.1 lists some of the types of graphics files you are likely to encounter when you work with Design and the filename extensions that are associated with them:

Table 8.1 Graphics Formats and File Extensions

Format	Abbreviation	Extension
Graphics Interchange Format	GIF	.gif
Joint Photographic Experts Group	JPEG	.jpg, .jpeg
Portable Network Graphics	PNG	.png
X Windows or XBM Bitmap	XBM	.xbm
Windows Bitmap	BMP	.bmp
Macintosh PICT	PICT	.pict
Tagged Image File Format	TIFF	.tif, .tiff
Expression Design	N/A	.design
Adobe Acrobat	PDF	.pdf

Importing Images

Expression Design lets you edit images that were created and saved in other programs. In the case of common image formats like TIFF, JPEG, PSD, GIF, and the like, you can simply choose File > Open, navigate to the file in question, and click

Open. If the image opens in the Design workspace, you can start working with it. If it does not open, try one of the other options for bringing image files into Design:

Copy and paste: Copy the image to your operating system's Clipboard in whatever application you use to view it—Mozilla Firefox or another Web browser, for instance. Then make Design the active application and press Ctrl+V or choose Edit > Paste.

Import the image: Choose File > Import or press Ctrl+I. When the Import Document dialog box appears, locate the file on your computer file system or on your network. Select the file and then click Open.

Drag and drop: With both the Design window and the window of the application in which the image appears visible, click the image you want to import, hold down the mouse, and drag the image into the Design window. Release the mouse button.

Design supports PSD files from version 7 or earlier of Photoshop: TIFF, JPEG, GIF, PNG, BMP, Windows Media Photo (WDP, HD Photo, or HDP), or ICO files. In any of these cases, the image should appear on the Design artboard in the current layer of the file that's currently open in the Design window. There is no link between the original image file and the version displayed in Design. If you make any changes to the original, those changes are not made correspondingly in the version that's displayed in the Design window.

Converting Bitmap Images to Paths

The bitmapped images you import into Design don't look as smooth and sharp as those that consist of vector graphics. You can convert the bitmap into a vector image if you wish, though it's not certain what kind of results you'll get. Follow these steps:

1. Select the bitmap on the Design artboard. If you need a sample bitmap to work with, open one contained in the Samples folder in your Office12 folder (or in the folder that contains your current version of Microsoft Office).

2. Choose Object > Image > Auto Trace Image.

3. When the Auto Trace Image dialog box shown in Figure 8.17 appears, specify the number of colors Design should apply in the vector version of the image.

The Pre-filtering setting determines the amount of smoothing to apply to the image before it is converted to paths. The Tightness of Fit setting determines how closely the vector paths should conform to the original bitmapped image. The tighter the fit, the more paths you'll have. The image will be more complex, but you'll retain more

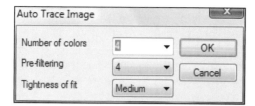

Figure 8.17 Design can automatically trace a bitmap to turn it into vector paths.

information from the bitmapped version. When you're done, click OK. An example of a bitmap image and the traced result is shown in Figure 8.18. As you can see, when a complex image is traced, it can turn out looking quite abstract—though it can be quite a work of art in its own right.

 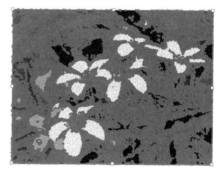

Figure 8.18 A bitmap (left) and the auto-traced vector version (right).

9 Creating and Manipulating Images

As a tool for professional designers and artists, Expression Design provides a full selection of both basic and advanced tools and techniques for using them. The preceding chapter gave you an overview of the available tools, but simply knowing what they're called and what they do isn't enough. With a drawing tool like Design, you need to roll up your sleeves and start actively using the program. This chapter begins with some basic exercises to get you started with your own graphics. After the basics, you learn about more advanced topics such as combining images and working with layers.

Drawing Your Own Graphics

Design isn't primarily an image editing tool. You can use it for editing and modifying images created in other applications. But the program excels in the number of tools and options it gives you for creating images from scratch. This set of exercises will get you started with Design's tools for drawing and editing images—tasks you can tackle even if you don't consider yourself to be a professional artist.

Drawing Shapes

Even if you aren't an artist, you can use Expression Design to do much of the drawing work for you. Like any graphics program, Design provides you with tools for drawing common shapes. By default, the Rectangle tool appears in the Toolbox; click and hold down on the Rectangle tool, and a pop-up menu appears with extra tools for drawing ellipses, polygons, and lines.

Get started with drawing on your own by following these steps:

1. Click File > New.

2. Set your specs for your new file in the New Document dialog box or accept the default settings (which you can change later) and click OK.

3. When the new file opens in the artboard, click the Rectangle tool to select it.

4. Click, hold, and drag down and to the right to draw the rectangle. When you release the mouse button, the rectangle is created.

5. Hold down the Shift key and draw another rectangle. This time, you create a square.

6. Next, create another rectangle, but don't release the mouse button. Press the Ctrl key and continue to draw. When you do so, notice that the rectangle rotates freely.

7. Draw a fourth rectangle and, without releasing the mouse button, hold down both the Shift and Ctrl keys. Notice that this time the rotation is constrained. Instead of rotating freely, the rectangle rotates only to 45-degree and 90-degree positions.

8. Release the mouse button. Your artboard should resemble the one shown in Figure 9.1.

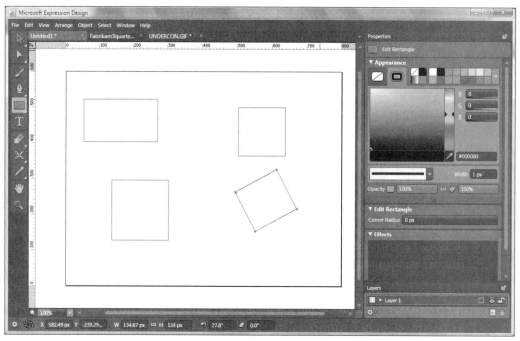

Figure 9.1 The Shift and Ctrl keys let you draw different types of rectangles.

By now, you've probably noticed that each of the rectangles you have drawn has nodes on three of the corners and an arrow on the fourth. These four markers denote that the outline of the rectangle is a single path. The arrow indicates the direction of the path.

By default, the rectangles have 90-degree corners. You can change the degree to which the corners are rounded in the Properties panel. When you have the rectangle tool selected instead of a triangle, the Properties panel has the heading Create Rectangle at the top. Click on the outline of any one of the four rectangles you drew, and this heading changes to Edit Rectangle. You can now change the attributes of the rectangle by adjusting the controls in the Properties panel. You might need to roll down other areas of the Properties panel, such as Layers. When you do so, the Edit Rectangle section of the Properties panel becomes visible. In the box next to Corner Radius, change the default value (0 px) to 10 px. The corners of the rectangle you selected become rounded to a 10-pixel radius (see Figure 9.2).

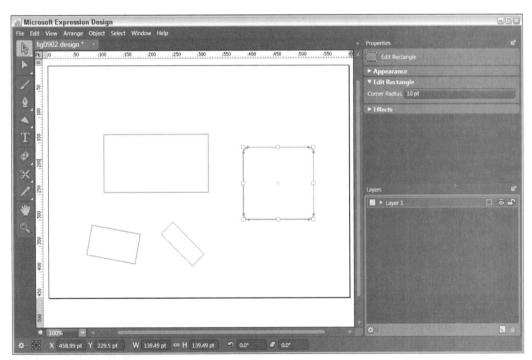

Figure 9.2   You can edit attributes of rectangles or other shapes using the Properties panel.

The basic techniques you have used apply to the Ellipse tool as well. To clear out the rectangles so you can start drawing ellipses on a "clean" artboard, choose Select > All. Then press the Delete key to delete all at once. Click and hold down on the Rectangle tool and select the Ellipse tool from the pop-up menu. Then click in the artboard and drag down and to the right to draw an ellipse. Hold down the Shift key and drag down and to the right to draw a circle.

Choose Select > All to select the ellipses you drew and press Delete to delete them. Then press and hold down the Rectangle button in the Toolbox and choose the Polygon tool.

The Polygon tool takes some getting used to, but the best way to get acquainted with it is simply to start using it. Click near the center of the artboard and drag in any direction. As you can see, it doesn't matter which direction you drag because the sides of the polygon are drawn all at once, moving out from the center point. When you release the mouse button, the polygon is created. Next, draw a polygon and, before you release the mouse button, drag the mouse pointer around to see how the polygon rotates freely.

When you have a polygon selected, the settings in the Edit Polygon section of the Properties panel control its attributes (see Figure 9.3). Change the number next to Points to alter the kind of polygon you create. By default, a three-pointed or triangular polygon is specified. Change Points to 5 to create a pentagon, 6 to create a hexagon, and so on.

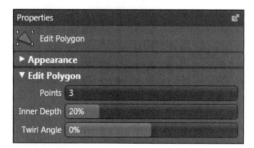

Figure 9.3 Use Edit Polygon to change the shape and other attributes of a polygon.

The Inner Depth and Twirl Angle attributes are hard to describe. It's probably easier to try them out for yourself to see what they do. These two settings in the Edit Polygon section of the Properties panel control the angle and twist of the sides of the polygon. (You might have to scroll down to see this part of the Properties panel.) Figure 9.4 shows examples of how the different settings change the appearance of the sides. Play around with it yourself to get some experience with it.

Along with changing the Inner Depth and Twirl Angle through the Properties panel, you can also edit a shape by selecting and moving nodes. (Make sure you select the Selection tool before doing so.) Once you have a set of polygons drawn on the artboard, leave them open so you can practice selecting them in the section that follows.

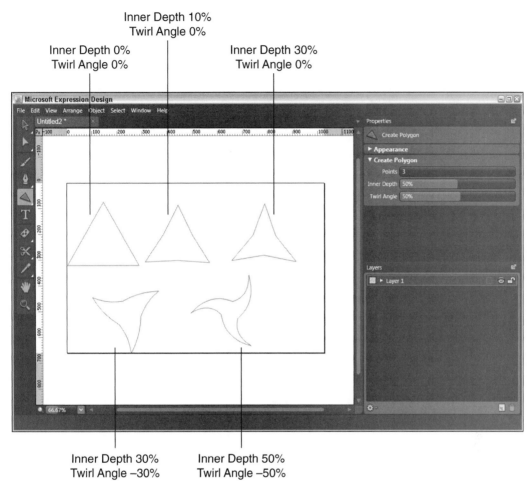

Figure 9.4   Inner Depth and Twirl Angle alter the sides of the polygon you're drawing.

Note: The Line tool, the other drawing tool in the Rectangle-Ellipse-Polygon group, lets you create simple straight paths. Holding down the Shift key constrains the Line tool to 45- or 90-degree angles.

Selecting Objects

The four selection tools at the top of the Toolbox are easy to use and quickly let you select one or more objects or their component parts (such as nodes). The Selection tool lets you select a single object either by clicking on any part of it or by clicking and dragging to draw a selection marquee around it. You only have to draw the marquee around part of an object, and the entire object is selected. Try this now with the set of polygons you have left over from the previous section. (If you don't have a set of images available, draw a few now.) Select one by drawing a marquee over part of it. When you select a polygon, for instance, a rectangle appears around it with eight selection handles around it (see Figure 9.5).

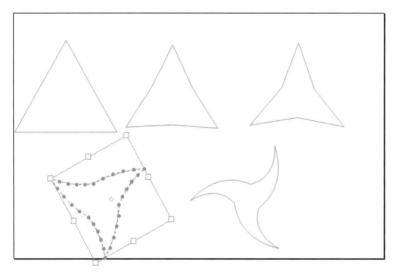

Figure 9.5 When you select a shape, a selection rectangle appears around it.

The selection handles let you manipulate an object in various ways. Click and drag on a handle to stretch or compress the image. Click on the selection box (not the handle) to move the image around the artboard. To select more than one image, hold down Shift and click adjacent ones in turn. When you select two or more images, you'll notice that a selection rectangle is drawn around all of them at once so they can be handled as a single group.

Grouping and Selecting

The Group Select tool's name is potentially misleading. Rather than letting you select a group of objects quickly, its purpose is to help you select items that have already been grouped into a single entity. You then use this tool to choose items within the group. To try out this tool, you first need to create a group of objects. Follow these steps:

1.   Select all of the images in your set of polygons by using the Selection tool to choose each one in turn. Press Shift+click to move from one item to the next, or draw a marquee around the entire set.

2.   Choose Arrange > Group or press Ctrl+G.

3.   Click anywhere outside the selection rectangle to deselect the group.

4.   Click any one of the objects in the group and notice that you immediately select the entire set.

5.   Click and hold down on the Selection tool to access Group Select from the pop-up menu. The Group Select icon looks just like the Selection tool's icon except that it has a plus sign (+) next to it.

6.   With the Group Select tool, click any one of the items in the group or draw a marquee around it. A selection rectangle appears around the single object rather than around the group.

Once you're done with the exercise, draw a selection marquee around the whole group to select them at once (see Figure 9.6) and then choose Arrange > Ungroup to ungroup them again.

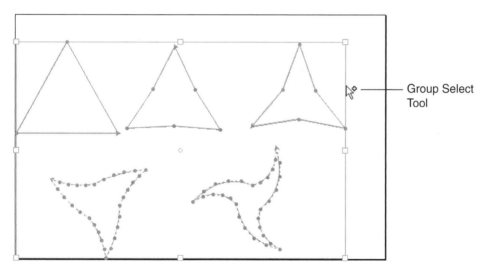

Group Select Tool

Figure 9.6   Group Select lets you select an individual object from within a group you have created.

Selecting Nodes

Two selection tools are especially designed for helping you select nodes within an object. The Direct Selection tool is a good choice when you want to select a single node. When you click the node, only it is selected, not the object as a whole. When you click on an object's path with the Direct Selection tool, the entire path is highlighted, just as it is with the Selection tool. But when you click directly atop a node, only that node is highlighted.

Hold down the Shift key and you can use the Direct Selection tool to highlight more than one node in turn. Pressing Shift lets you select both adjacent nodes and those that are not adjacent (see Figure 9.7).

Figure 9.7   The Direct Selection tool lets you select one or more nodes within an object.

The Lasso selection tool is one you're probably familiar with from other graphics programs. You use it to draw a free-form selection area rather than a rectangle. Because the Lasso tool gives you great freedom, it's particularly easy to select individual nodes or groups of them. Follow these steps to try it out:

1. Click and hold down on the Direct selection tool and choose the Lasso selection tool from the pop-up menu.

2. Choose View > Zoom In (or press Ctrl+=) two or three times to zoom in on one of your polygons.

3. Click next to one of the sections of the polygon and draw a free-form area around that section to select it (see Figure 9.8). When you release the mouse button, a selection rectangle appears around the section.

Once the area has been selected, drag one of the handles around the selection rectangle to change the shape of your image (see Figure 9.9).

The Lasso selection tool can also be used to draw a selection area around individual nodes within an object. You'll probably have to zoom in on the object to select the nodes easily. To zoom out again, choose View > Zoom Out, press Ctrl+-, or choose View > Actual Size or Fit to Screen.

Painting and Drawing

Expression Design is quite flexible when it comes to creating and placing ready-made shapes, and up to now we have worked with rectangles, polygons, and other common shapes that Design draws for you with a click and drag of the mouse. But much of the time, you'll probably want to do free-form drawing. The primary tools for creating your own lines and shapes are the Paintbrush and Pen, and these and related tools are examined in the sections that follow.

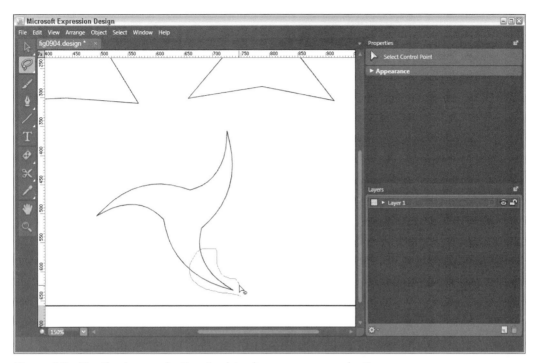

Figure 9.8   Use the Lasso selection tool to draw your own selection area.

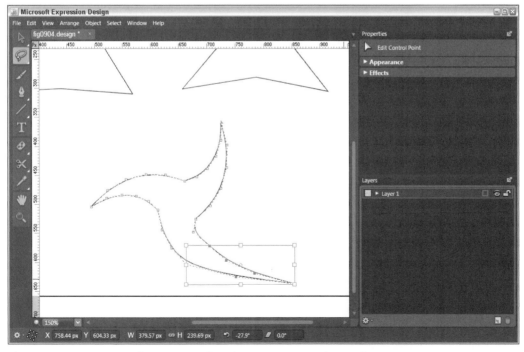

Figure 9.9   Once you select a part of an image, you can change it.

Painting with the Paintbrush

Expression Design's Paintbrush is a versatile and flexible tool that can serve you well in many cases where you have to create original graphics. Even if you don't draw a path just right the first time, you can adjust the many attributes of Paintbrush-drawn lines or move nodes and control handles until you get the path you want. Here, as with other tools, the best way to get acquainted is simply to start using it:

1. Select File > New and click OK in the New Document dialog box to create a new blank artboard space on which to draw.

2. Click the Paintbrush in the Toolbox or press B.

3. Draw a line—any line—on the artboard. The result (see Figure 9.10) probably isn't very inspiring. But with some work it can be whipped into shape.

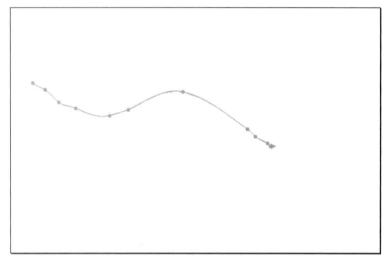

Figure 9.10 You draw a freehand path with the Paintbrush tool.

4. The first thing you can do to edit your path is to stretch out and move the individual nodes. The nodes are highlighted; zoom in and choose the Direct selection tool or the Lasso tool to select the ones you want to move.

5. Click and stretch the nodes to smooth out the path and make it more graceful. Gently move the nodes up and down to smooth out the curves in your line.

6. Turn to the Appearance section of the Properties panel to add some character to your simple path. Right now, this path consists of a simple stroke with no fill. First, change the stroke by clicking the Stroke button and

choosing a color from the swatch shown—choose blue, for instance. When you deselect the path, the new color appears.

7.   Scroll down to the bottom section of the Appearance section by clicking beneath its scrollbar (see Figure 9.11).

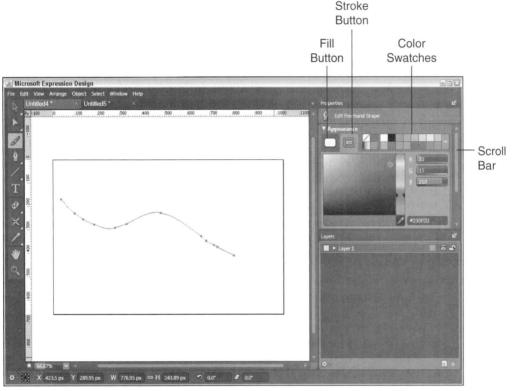

Figure 9.11   Use the Appearance panel to change the attributes of your painted path.

Adjusting Stroke Options

By itself, a path doesn't look like much. There's a good reason why it doesn't look very interesting; it's just an indicator that defines the structure of what you're drawing. You might think of a path as a skeleton; what you need, then, is to put some meat on the bones. You do that by assigning a stroke and a fill to the path. Change to a different stroke shape by choosing an option from the Stroke drop-down list menu. For this example, choose the calligraphic option (it's the option at the bottom of Figure 9.12).

Once you choose a style, you select the width you want by entering it in the Width box—although if you choose the calligraphic style of stroke, a default width of

Figure 9.12 Choose a stroke style from this drop-down list.

53.33 pixels is already entered for you. When you make the stroke choice, the stroke appears in the artboard, and a new default width appears as well. Click Show advanced properties, and you can adjust options for the stroke.

An even more powerful set of options is available to you in the Options dialog box: Click Edit > Options > Stroke to display it. Choose Tight or Very Tight from the Tightness of Fit drop-down list to make the stroke conform to the shape of the path.

Drawing Closed Paths

Drawing a straight-line or curved-line path enables you to adjust the stroke, but you can't do much with the other critical attribute of a vector shape: the fill. Specifying a fill with a path that is open can result in some strange effects: The areas within curves become filled with your color, but nothing else does. Fills make sense when you draw a closed path. To create one, draw a path and bring the cursor close to the starting point of the path. When the cursor is over the starting point, a circle appears next to it to let you know the path is closed (see Figure 9.13). You should release your mouse button at that point.

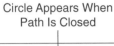
Circle Appears When
Path Is Closed

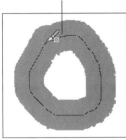

Figure 9.13   A circle appears to let you know when you have closed a path.

Once your path is closed, and while it is selected, you can choose a fill color from the Appearance section of the Properties panel. Click the Fill button and choose a color by either selecting its color swatch, clicking within the color gradient, or entering RGB (red-green-blue) values for the color if you know them. You can also enter a hexadecimal equivalent for the color in the box beneath the RGB values.

Point-Dropping with the Pen

As you learned in Chapter 8, the Pen tool lets you create paths by combining anchor points and control handles. It isn't for drawing lines or curves as you do with a ballpoint pen, in other words—or, for that matter, with the Line tool or Paintbrush tool. The Pen simply lets you drop anchor points from place to place on the artboard so Design can join them together with segments. Each segment of a path is bounded by two nodes or anchor points. Each node/anchor point, in turn, has two control handles. Depending on the type of path you want to create, the nodes on each path can take three different forms:

A **Cusp Point:** A cusp point occurs when a curve meets a straight line segment. A cusp point has either one handle retracted or two visible control handles that operate independently.

A **Smooth Point:** This point exists where the path curves from one direction to another. The Smooth point's control handles determine how gradually or sharply the path curves. You elongate or change the position of the control handles to change the curve.

A **Corner Point:** A corner point causes a path to change direction at a sharp angle rather than a gradual curve. A corner point doesn't seem to have control handles, but it does; the control handles have been retracted.

The three types of points are shown in Figure 9.14.

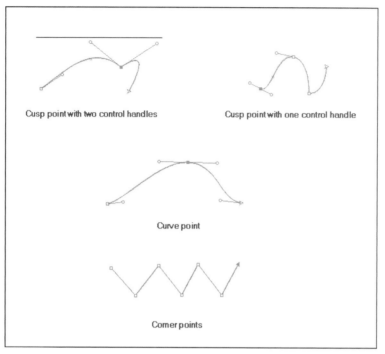

Cusp point with two control handles

Cusp point with one control handle

Curve point

Corner points

Figure 9.14 Two cusp points (top), a smooth point (middle), and corner points (bottom).

Creating Control Points

When you were working with polygons earlier in this chapter and changed the Twirl Angle associated with their sides, you probably noticed that the more "curvy" the sides were, the more anchor points they had. A straight line path needs only two anchor points, one on each side. One that has a complex and graceful curve needs many anchor points so it can change direction in a gradual way.

Drawing Corner Points. The Pen tool is ideal for creating control points. Simply clicking anywhere in the workspace will let you create a corner point. Try it now:

1. Open a new blank document.

2. Single-click anywhere on the artboard. A single anchor point appears. The anchor point appears to have no control handles; it does, but they are retracted completely into the anchor point and not visible.

3. Click the anchor point, hold down, and drag outward in any direction. The two control handles appear.

4. Press Delete to delete the anchor point you created. Click at two separate spots on the artboard. The two anchor points are joined by a straight line path, and the second point has an arrow to indicate the direction of the path.

5. Click once more at a 90-degree angle to the first two points. You now have two segments joined by a sharp corner point (see Figure 9.15).

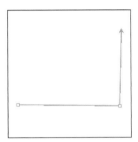

Figure 9.15 Use the Pen tool to draw paths one segment at a time.

Optionally, keep clicking elsewhere on the artboard. As long as you click, the path you started to create keeps extending itself. When you double-click or press Enter, the path stops drawing, and you can create a new one.

Tip: If you double-click on the corner point, it disappears. If you hold down the Alt key and click on a corner point, however, the sharp corner turns into a graceful curve. If you hold down the Alt key and click and drag on any one of the anchor points, control handles appear on all of them. You can manipulate the corner handles to change the sharp corners to curves if you wish. Also, if you hold down the Shift key while clicking or dragging, you constrain either the new anchor point or its handles to 45- or 90-degree angles.

Creating Curves. Drawing a curve is slightly different than drawing straight paths and sharp corner points. With some practice and some trial and error, you'll be able to create curves that look just the way you want. Remember to press Ctrl+Z to undo any work you've done, or press Ctrl+A and then Delete to clear the artboard completely so you can start over. Follow these steps:

1. With the Pen tool, click and drag anywhere on the artboard. An anchor point is created, and as you drag, control handles are created as well.

2. Release the mouse button and move elsewhere on the artboard, at an angle slightly up or down from the previous anchor point. Click and drag again to draw another set of handles.

3. Click and drag elsewhere to create a third point.

4. Press Enter. A set of curves is created.

Practice making other curved paths by varying the distance between anchor points or changing the angle. Also notice how the sharpness of the curve changes when you drag the control handles out to elongate them or when you change their position. Some variations are shown in Figure 9.16. The set of curves at the top has short handles; the curves and the control handles get longer with the middle and bottom examples.

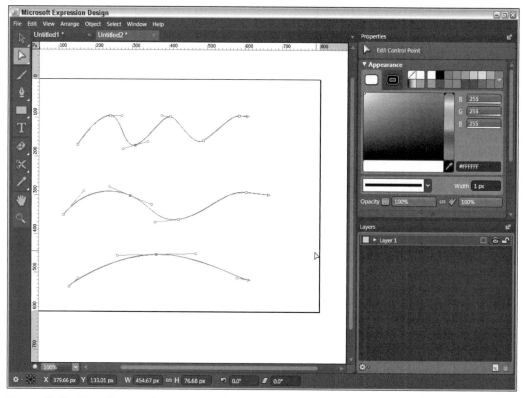

Figure 9.16 The distance between anchor points and control handle length determines the shape of curved paths.

Crafting Cusps. A cusp point can have either one or two control handles. To create the one-handle version, click to create the anchor point and then hold down both the

Ctrl+Alt keys while you drag. As you drag, the control handle is drawn out of the anchor point. Click to stop extending the control handle. Then move the Pen and click elsewhere on the artboard to create the next point on the path. To create the two-handle version, follow these steps:

1. Click and drag to create an anchor point with two control handles.

Note: On an anchor point with two control handles, one handle is the "in" handle and the other is the "out" handle. The difference is in the direction of the path you are creating. The "in" handle leads in to the anchor point from the beginning of the path, and the "out" handle leads out to the end point of the path.

---

2. Go back to the "out" handle and press Alt while dragging the "out" handle. You don't have to drag the handle far or drag it completely back atop the anchor point so it becomes hidden. Just dragging it slightly while holding down Alt makes the two handles operate independently of one another and turns the anchor point from a curve point to a cusp.

3. Release the mouse button and click elsewhere on the artboard to create the next point on the path.

4. Double-click or press Enter to complete the path. The cusp point is joined to the new point. You can move the control handles independently to change the angle of the cusp.

When you need to select a node/anchor point or manipulate the control handles, switch to the Direct selection tool in the Toolbox. If you keep using the Pen, you'll just create new paths as you click.

Adding Anchor Points. Adding anchor points to a path enables you to control the direction and shape of the path with greater precision. To add anchor points, switch to the Add Anchor Point tool by clicking and holding down on the Pen tool. Then click anywhere in the path to add an anchor point. Once you add a point, you can move it to change the shape of the path. (The shape of a Bezier curve doesn't change when you add an anchor point, though it might change when you are adding a point to a B-spline path.)

To delete an anchor point, switch to the Delete Anchor Point tool. Click on any point in a path to delete it. When you use Delete Anchor Point, the path isn't split. (If you use the Scissors tool described below, it is.)

Using the B-Spline Tool

The paths you create with the Pen tool are all Bezier curves, which describe paths by means of nodes and control handles. They aren't the only kinds of paths you can create with Design, however. The B-Spline tool lets you create B-spline paths. With Bezier paths, the nodes lie right in the center of the path. B-spline paths have nodes that lie just outside the path.

Creating B-splines is a little different than assembling a path with the Pen. First, access the B-Spline tool by clicking and holding down on the Pen tool and selecting it from the pop-up menu. Then click anywhere in the artboard to start creating the path. It's easy to draw straight lines with the B-Spline tool—especially if you hold down the Alt key, which creates a sharp corner by default. To create a curve, you have to click in short intervals and build the curve gradually. When you are done, double-click or press Enter to create the path. You can also move the mouse pointer over the start point to create a closed path, just as you would with a Bezier path.

Filling Images

A fill is a color, gradient, or image that you place inside a shape, path, or any object you create with Expression Design. To add a fill, you click the Fill button in the Appearance section of the Properties panel. Then choose a fill color or gradient from the color swatches or other options provided. You learned about filling with solid colors earlier in this chapter. You can also fill an object with a gradient by clicking the Gradient Fill icon in the Appearance section, next to the solid colors. When you click the icon, if you have a closed path drawn on the artboard, it is immediately filled with the gradient.

A gradient can also be assigned to a stroke so that it appears to fade in color from the center outwards. Keep in mind that if the default gradient doesn't suit you, you can click the More Swatches down arrow on the right edge of the Appearance section. Scroll down to the Gradients section of the More Swatches pop-up (see Figure 9.17) and choose the pattern that appeals to you.

The main feature of gradients is the fact that their color changes gradually from one side to another. Where the colors that make up the gradient actually change is something you can control. Beneath the large color box in the Appearance section you see the gradient bar, a slider with different markers above and below it. The gradient nodes—the three markers beneath the gradient bar—control the colors themselves. Click a node and then click a color from a swatch or the color box, and you change one of the colors in the gradient. The gradient nodes let you create a custom color gradient. Instead of having shades of gray or red, for instance, you can click the gradient node on the left and choose blue; you can click the middle gradient node

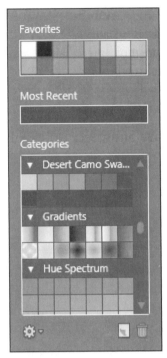

Figure 9.17   You can choose an alternate gradient from the More Swatches dialog box.

and choose purple; you can click the one on the right and choose red. You'll have a gradient that starts out blue, turns to a shade of purple, and turns eventually to red. You might not actually like the look of such a gradient, but it's good to know that you can create one if you want to.

You can also fill an object at any time using the Color Dropper tool. The Color Dropper makes it easy for you to pick up a color from one object and transfer it quickly to another object. Click the color you want to copy in one object and hold down the mouse button. Then drag the Color Dropper to a second object and release the mouse button to apply it to the second object. If you release the mouse button when the dropper is over a fill area, the color is used as a fill. If you release the button when the dropper is over a stroke, the color is applied to the stroke.

Editing Objects

The descriptions to this point have described how to build paths and shapes and apply colors to them or add anchor points. But another essential editing task is splitting the paths or changing their attributes in a fundamental way. The sections that follow describe tools that enable you to edit graphics once you create them.

Splitting Paths. You have two options for splitting paths: You can use the Scissors tool or press the Delete key. To access the Scissors tool, either click its button in the Toolbox or press C. You can split paths created with the Line tool, the Shapes tools, or the B-Spline tool. First, select the object with one of the selection tools or with the Scissors itself by single-clicking it. The first time you click an object with the Scissors, you only select it. You don't immediately split the path. The second time, you can click with the Scissors either on a part of the path or on a node. In either case, clicking splits the path and creates two end points. The path doesn't immediately look like it's been split, but you can select it with the Selection tool and then drag one of the sections away from the other one to show that it's been split.

Alternatively, click the Direct selection tool in the Toolbox to select one or more nodes within the object. Then press the Delete key to delete those nodes and split the path accordingly.

Redirecting Paths. Another fundamental way to edit a path is to reverse its direction. Every path has an arrow. The arrow indicates the end point; the point at the opposite end is the start point. (With a shape like a rectangle, the start point and the end point are in the same place.) The path is important in relation to certain tools like paintbrush types: Some brush strokes appear to fade out or end near the end of the stroke; the stroke follows the path direction.

Tip: If you want to see the direction of a path more clearly, select it, and then choose a pointer from the Pointers section in the Stroke drop-down list of the Properties panel. The Stroke drop-down list is located beneath the Color Picker box in the Appearance section. Click the down arrow, scroll down to the Pointers section of the Categories box, and click the style of pointer you want.

To reverse the direction of a path, click the Reverse Path tool, which is in the same group of tools as the Scissors. You might need to click and hold down on the Scissors to display Reverse Path. With the Reverse Path tool selected, click the path to flip the arrow around so that it moves to the previous start point and points in the opposite direction.

The Start Point tool, which is also part of the Scissors group, changes the location of the path's start point. If you use the Zoom tool to zoom in on the path, you'll see that there are multiple arrow points in it. When you pass over the path with the Start Point tool, it looks like a flag that's drooping down at a 45-degree angle. When you pass over one of the arrow points, the flag pops up to indicate that you can click on the path at that point (see Figure 9.18). When you click on the arrow, it changes direction.

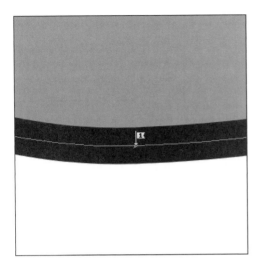

Figure 9.18   Click on an arrow point with the Start Point tool to create a new start point.

Copying Attributes. The Attribute Dropper is a sophisticated copying and pasting tool. While the Color Dropper lets you copy and drag a color from one object to another, the Attribute Dropper gives you a way to copy the fill, stroke, and live effect attributes all at once.

First access the Attribute Dropper tool from beneath the Color Dropper if necessary. Then click either the fill or stroke area of the object that has the attributes you want to copy. Drag the Attribute Dropper over to the object to which you want to assign the attributes. Release the mouse button when the dropper is hovering over the fill or stroke area of the second object or over its path.

Working with Layers

Layers are powerful tools for editing and assembling complex, professional-quality graphics. By dividing a graphic image's contents into layers, you give the image a feeling of depth and complexity. You also gain the ability to make editing changes to individual layers while not affecting the appearance of other layers. They organize image contents and help you keep track of which component objects have been used to create graphics. This section gives you a brief overview of this essential part of the Design interface.

Working with the Layers Panel

Layers aren't something you need to consciously create when you work with objects in Expression Design. Every object you draw is automatically on its own layer; by default, in other words, every image file has a single layer by default. You create, delete, and organize other layers through the Layers panel. To make the Layers panel visible or invisible as needed, choose Window > Layers or press F4.

Usually, when you work on an image, the Layers panel displays Layer 1 under the heading Layers. To create a new layer, click the Layer Options down arrow next to the wheel icon at the bottom of the Layers panel. Three options appear in the top half of the Layer Options menu (see Figure 9.19) that let you perform basic functions:

- Choose New Layer to add a new layer to your image file.

- Choose Duplicate Layer to duplicate the contents of the currently selected layer.

- Choose Delete Layer to delete the currently selected layer.

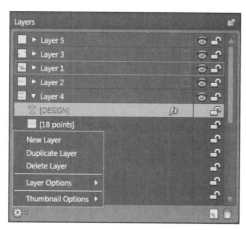

Figure 9.19   The Layer Options menu lets you manage layers in a vector graphic.

To select a layer, single-click its line in the Layers panel. Working with layers becomes clearer if you open an image that already has a variety of layers created, with individual objects contained in each layer. Open one of the sample files provided with Expression Design. They are located in the Samples folder, which is in the Expression Design folder (which is probably named Design 1.0, Design 2.0, or another name, depending on the version you installed). The exact location of the Design folder depends on where you originally installed the program. A likely location is C:\Program Files\Expression Studio\Design 1.0\samples. For this section, double-click the Design_Monster.design file to open it. When the file shown in Figure 9.20 appears, you see five layers listed in the Layers panel. Click the down arrow next to Layer 4, and you get a list of the separate paths and other objects contained within that layer.

10 Working with Text

Expression Design is primarily intended to help you create graphic images. But text can be an essential part of many images, providing headings, slogans, and labels that illustrate what you've labored so hard to draw. Design goes well beyond simply adding labels to your images. Text can be a graphic element in and of itself. It can be made to follow a path or converted to a path; live effects can be applied to text just as they can to graphics. This chapter will examine the ins and outs of working with text in Expression Design.

Creating Text

Whenever you want to create text, whether it's on an image or on a blank artboard, you need to select the Text tool in the Toolbox. When you select the Text tool, the pointer turns into a text cursor of the sort that should be familiar to you from word processing programs. After you've worked with some text for a while, you'll notice that the cursor actually comes in two different forms. It's a short vertical bar when it's hovering over a blank part of the artboard or over a graphic. It gains two brackets on either side when it's hovering over text (see Figure 10.1). When the brackets are present, you can select or type text or apply formatting. When the brackets are not present, clicking in the artboard will create a new text block.

Each block of text is a graphic image in its own right that can be assigned colors and formatted, as described later in this chapter. Each text element can be selected as text with one of the two cursors so you can backspace, delete, or type. Scroll across text to highlight it. You can then start formatting using the controls in the Properties panel.

Basic Formatting

When you choose the Text tool, the Text section automatically opens up in the Properties panel. That doesn't mean you see the Text section's options, however. Click on the divider bar just beneath the Appearance tab and drag down so that

Figure 10.1 Brackets appear around the text cursor when you can edit or format text.

Figure 10.2 Use the Text section to adjust text properties.

the Layers panel "rolls down" like a curtain. The large version of the Text section, which appears when you fully roll down the Layers panel, appears in Figure 10.2.

In case the full version of the Text section doesn't appear, click the Show/Hide Advanced Properties triangle to display it. This triangle lets you toggle between the large version and short version; the short version is shown in Figure 10.3.

Figure 10.3 The short version contains the basic text formatting controls.

Tip: All of the sections of the Properties panel have a Show/Hide Advanced Properties triangle beneath them. You can also show and hide the Text section (or any other section of the Properties panel) by clicking the down arrow next to the section's name.

The Text section gives you access to the controls for basic formatting, which are described in the sections that follow.

Choosing Text Styles

The four controls in the shorter version of the Text section let you perform the basic formatting tasks that you're probably familiar with from any graphics or word processing program. Click the down arrow next to the font family list to choose a font for your text. The font list that appears (see Figure 10.4) is divided into three sections: Favorites (the ones that tend to be chosen most often), Most Recent (the fonts you chose most recently), and Typefaces, which displays font names in the font themselves so you can see what they look like.

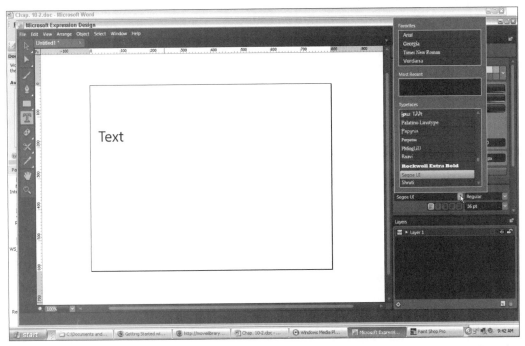

Figure 10.4 The font family list displays fonts in WYSIWYG format so you can choose them by their styles.

Tip: You can move fonts from the Typefaces list to the Favorites box by clicking, holding down the mouse button, and dragging them from one section to another.

The Font Decoration section lets you add common emphases to selected text. (Make sure you select a character, word, or block of text before you select a style.) Choose Bold, Italic, or Bold Italic to add visual emphasis to text; choose Regular to return to the regular type style.

To align selected blocks of text, choose one of the five alignment options: Align Left, Align Center, Align Right, Justify, and Justify All. Justify makes text fill out the right and left margins of the block. Justify All, which is also known as "force justified," forces text to be justified even if the number of characters in a line wouldn't normally permit it. It often results in words that look excessively "spaced out," though the margins on either side are straight or even. An example of justified text that isn't spaced out evenly is shown in Figure 10.5.

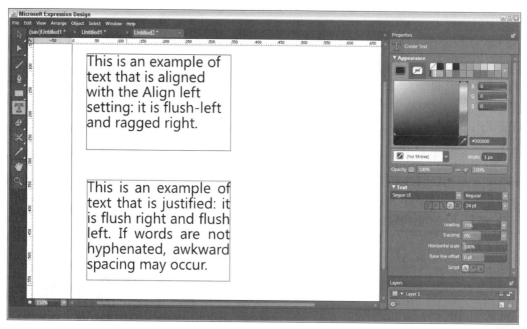

Figure 10.5 Justified text aligns with a surrounding frame, but words can be spaced unevenly.

You can increase the size of text by either clicking the point size down arrow and choosing a size option or hovering over the size menu and clicking and dragging. If you drag up and to the right, the size is increased. If you drag down and to the left, the size decreases. At the same time, the pointer turns into a set of four arrows. As the size decreases, the text accordingly grows smaller as is displayed in the artboard. It's a quick way of adjusting the size of text with great precision; as the size changes point by point, you see the effect interactively and can choose the size you want without having to choose one option after another from the drop-down list.

Placing Text Inside an Area

When you first click the Text tool and start typing on the artboard, you might find that your text just heads off to the right edge of the artboard and then keeps going. You can always press Enter to make a paragraph break. But you can also place text within a container called an *area* in order to contain text. That way, it can be aligned left, centered, or justified. Any shape you draw with Design can be considered a frame. The most obvious text frames are rectangles of the sort depicted in Figure 10.5. But any shape can function as a frame. When you draw a frame, in order to add text to it, you first select the Text tool. Then pass the cursor over the frame's outline while holding down the Shift key. When the cursor assumes the shape shown in Figure 10.6, click once. You can then type inside the area. The resulting text is called *area text*. But be aware that if the frame is too small to accommodate the text you have typed, the extra text will overflow the frame.

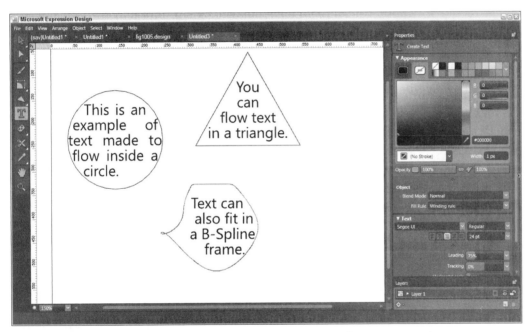

Figure 10.6   Any shape you draw with Design can serve as a frame to contain text.

If you use the Direct selection tool to select the path around the area, then click the Stroke button in the Appearance section of the Properties panel and click None, the area will seem to disappear, and the text will appear to be floating on the artboard.

Fancy Formatting

Click the arrow at the bottom of the Text area to open the Advanced Properties section. This section contains some formatting options that go a step beyond the basics. They should be familiar to you if you have worked with text editors before. If not, the following sections give a quick rundown.

Adjusting Line Spacing

Leading is the space added to lines of text to make them more readable. If a line of text uses 12 point type, the standard practice is to add two points of space to the lines, or in this case, 14 points of leading. The white space makes text easier to read because the letters aren't jumbled together.

Design's Leading control specifies leading in a different way, however. The first option, Auto, creates leading that has the same spacing as the text itself: 12/12, or 12-pt. type with 12-pt. leading. Other options describe leading as a percentage of the font size you are using. Suppose you are using 20-pt. type. Leading of 100% would be 20 points, while 75% leading would be 15 points, 80% would be 16 points, and 120% would be 24 pts. of leading. These options are shown in Figure 10.7.

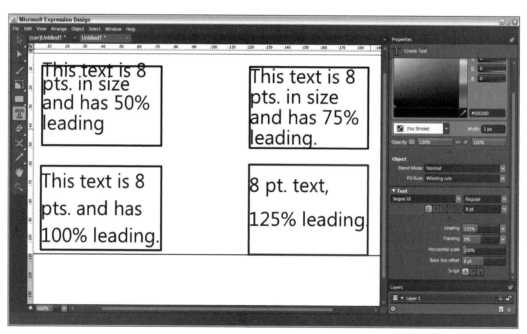

Figure 10.7 Expression Design expresses leading as a percentage of font size.

You don't have to stick with the percentages if you don't want to. You can specify your own setting by single-clicking within the Leading box and typing your own value and pressing Enter. However, the value is always expressed as a percentage. Even if you type 14 pt., for instance, when you type 14 pt. and press Enter, the value changes to 14%. In theory, you can also assign different leading values to different characters, but the results will probably be difficult to read; I suggest applying leading to an entire paragraph or block of text all at once rather than trying to get overly complicated.

Note: Before you apply leading, you need to select the text you want to format. Hover over the text and, when the cursor has the two brackets on either side, scroll across the text to highlight it. The term *leading* originates in old-fashioned printing, when lead was used to set type so it could be printed.

Adjusting Tracking

Tracking, in terms of typography, has nothing to do with running a race or hunting a wild animal. The term refers to letterspacing—the blank space between characters. Type that has "loose" tracking has lots of space. Type that has "tight" tracking has characters that are close together. You adjust the spacing by choosing a value from the Tracking drop-down menu in the Text section, in Advanced Properties.

Values are given in terms of percentages of "normal" letterspacing, just the same way leading is used to adjust line spacing. Zero percent is a normal setting. Percentages above zero (5%, 10%, 25%, and so on) add progressively more space, while those below zero (–5%, –10%, –25%, and so on) remove progressively more space. Some examples are shown in Figure 10.8.

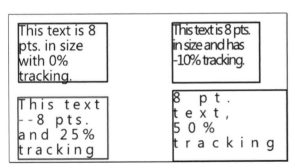

Figure 10.8 Tracking can help fill out a "loose" line of type.

What's the purpose of tracking? When you're working with a small amount of space, such as a rectangle you have drawn and that you're using as a container, it can be difficult to fill out the space so all the characters in a given line of type fit easily. By tightening up the spacing, you can fit more characters in the line. If you have a word or line that doesn't fit the given space, you can make the tracking looser so the letters will fill out the space more evenly. Adjusting tracking is especially useful if you want to make a block of type justified and you don't have any characters that will fill out the line. By making the tracking looser, you use the space more efficiently. Tracking is especially useful when you're trying to make a thin character "squeeze in" so it is closer to another one—when you're trying to fit the number 1 next to a 3 or 4, for instance.

Caution: Tracking is easily misused. You can easily end up with text that looks strange and is hard to read. In most cases, you can stick with flush-left, ragged right text, and default tracking. Only when you want to justify text or make it fit around a shape do you need to adjust the tracking significantly.

Scaling Text

Scaling, or changing the width of individual characters, isn't something you'll find in your typical text editor. It's one of those adjustments that only a graphics program like Design can give you. By adjusting the Horizontal scaling setting, you change the width of each character. A value of 100% is "normal" width. Move below 100%, and you make each character narrower and taller. Move above 100%, and characters become shorter and correspondingly "fatter." Some values are shown in Figure 10.9.

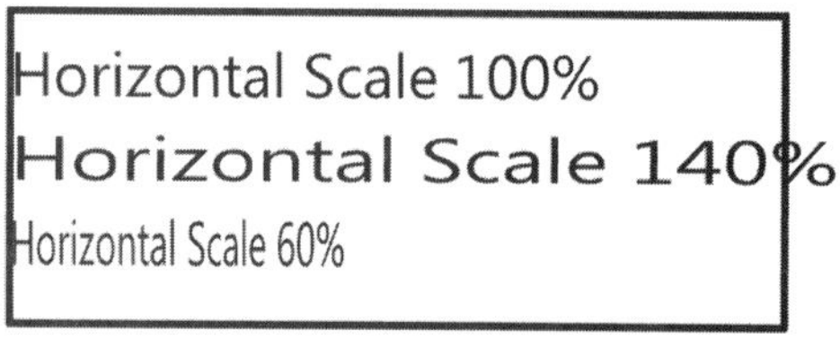

Horizontal Scale 100%
Horizontal Scale 140%
Horizontal Scale 60%

Figure 10.9 Change the horizontal scaling when you want to change size as well as letterspacing.

When you change the width of characters, you change the space between them accordingly. Values greater than 100% give you progressively more letterspacing, while those under 100% bring the letters closer together.

Tweaking Vertical Alignment

The Base Line Offset setting in Advanced Settings lets you change the height of selected characters. First, select the individual letter or word you want to move up or down. Then click the Base Line Offset box and enter a value. The 0 value means the text is on the baseline—the bottom of the x-height of letters that don't have ascenders or descenders. Entering a value greater than zero raises the selected text by the appropriate number of points; a negative value lowers it beneath the baseline. Two examples are shown in Figure 10.10.

The Base Line Offset setting is similar to superscript or subscript, two of the three buttons in the Script section of Text Advanced Settings. But Base Line Offset gives

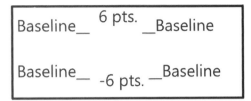

Figure 10.10   Changing Base Line Offset lets you raise or lower individual characters or words.

you a finer-grained level of control. You can even raise or lower alternate letters for a playful effect.

Applying Fills and Strokes

Text in Design isn't like text you create and edit with a word processor. In fact, text you create with Design can be formatted with strokes and fills like any other graphic object. When you begin to think of the text you create with Design as a closed path, you realize that you can treat it graphically. Each character can have its own fill and stroke attributes. Try it: Type the word Design in 72-pt. bold type. Select one of the characters individually with the Text tool. Choose a fill and stroke pattern for each character in turn. You can end up with different patterns for each letter, like the word "Design" shown in Figure 10.11.

Figure 10.11   Each character can have its own stroke and fill attributes.

Tip: You can format characters individually using other attributes. You can make each character a different size, assign different horizontal scaling, and so on.

Converting Text to Paths

In Chapter 9, you learned about manipulating shapes that are made up of paths. By adding or removing nodes or moving the nodes or their respective control handles, you can exercise a great deal of control over an object's shape. You can convert type into a path in a snap by following these steps:

1.   Select the text you want to convert.

2.   Choose Object > Convert Object to Path or press Ctrl+Shift+O. The text is no longer highlighted, but the characters are converted to paths, with nodes all around their outlines (see Figure 10.12).

Figure 10.12 Conventional text (top) converted to vector paths (bottom).

Once you convert text to paths, the Text options disappear from the Properties panel. You can still change the stroke or fill, however. All the characters you have converted are grouped together as a single entity. You can ungroup them by choosing Arrange > Ungroup. Then you can select and edit each character separately using the Selection, Pen, or other path-related tool.

Caution: Once you convert text to a series of paths, you can no longer edit it as text or select it with the Text tool. Make sure you've spelled everything correctly and that the type is the size and font you want before you convert.

Applying Live Effects to Text

"Live effects" are special effects that are applied to vector objects by means of filters. The names of some of these effects—Gaussian blur, Unsharp Mask—are familiar to anyone who has worked with professional graphics applications. The effects are called "live effects" because you can apply and edit the effects, and they don't change the original objects. Rather, they are applied atop the outlines of the original objects. You can remove the effect entirely, and the original object will remain. You can also apply more than one effect to an object.

Live effects can be applied to text just as they are to paths or other vector objects. When you apply an effect, the object is converted from a vector to a bitmapped object. A bitmap, because it is composed of pixels, doesn't have nodes that you can use to edit or alter the shape of the text. But if you remove the effect, the text is returned to vector format.

To add a live effect to text, follow these steps:

1. Select the text by scrolling across it with the text tool.

2. Click the Selection tool to switch back to it.

3. Click the Add Effect drop-down list in the Properties panel, in the Effects section. The drop-down list is marked *fx*.

You can then choose one of the available effects from the list:

Gaussian Blur: This effect blurs objects so their edges are softened; objects blend into other objects, and their edges seem out of focus.

Drop Shadow: This effect makes an object look as though it has an offset background, which appears as a shadow cast behind the object.

Bevel: A three-dimensional appearance is given to an object through the addition of sides and a bottom.

Unsharp Mask: This takes a blurry image (one that is unsharp) and sharpens it by applying a mask to its edges.

Outer Glow: This effect adds a subtle, glowing halo around an object.

All of these are raster effects: They rasterize a vector image, which turns it into a bitmap. Live effects give great depth and polish to text, just as they do to other objects. The best way to learn how live effects can change the look and feel of text is to play with the different options and see how they work. Some suggestions for how to get started follow:

1. Open a new document, if necessary, and type a large (96 pt.) bold word in all caps, such as DESIGN. (Making the word bold and all caps helps you see the live effects more easily.)

2. Select the text you typed with the Selection tool. When you do so, the Effects section appears in the Properties panel.

3. Click the Fill button in the Appearance section and give the text a fill color other than black.

4. Click the Stroke button and give the text a stroke and color. The text should have a bright iridescent appearance (see Figure 10.13).

Figure 10.13   Begin with text that has an easily visible stroke and fill color.

5. Click the *fx* drop-down list at the bottom of the Effects section, choose Effects, and then choose Bevel. The text has a three-dimensional, carved appearance (see Figure 10.14).

Figure 10.14   A Bevel live effect applied to text.

6. Click the *fx* icon again, choose Effects, and then choose Drop Shadow. The text gets a shadow behind it (see Figure 10.15). Notice how the effects are listed in the Effects section.

Figure 10.15   A Drop Shadow effect added to the Bevel effect.

7. Click the eye icon next to the Drop Shadow and Bevel effects listed in the Effects section. Clicking the eye icon, in each case, hides the effects.

8. Choose another effect by choosing *fx*, clicking Paint, and choosing an option such as Water Paper. See the effect this has on text.

9. When you have applied the effect, its name should be highlighted in the Effects section. Delete the effect by clicking the Trash icon at the bottom of the Effects section.

You can now experiment with different live effects and how they change text. So many effects are available under the Adjust Colors, Paint, Sketch, and Surface submenus that you simply have to try them out yourself to see which one(s) you want to use. Design enables you to mix and match effects freely with other attributes. You can apply an Emboss effect, change the stroke and fill levels, add a Paint effect, and so on. You can keep track of the effects that have been applied by tracking the list in the Effects section.

It's important to note that each of the live effects has its own specific controls that let you fine-tune how they affect the text you are formatting. The controls are found at the bottom of the Effects section. If you cannot see the controls, you may need to roll down the section beneath the Effects section; the controls for the live effects might be hidden beneath the other panel. The controls vary, depending on the effect you are using. For instance, if you apply the Emboss effect, you can adjust the Relief setting and the Light position setting to give more specific effects (see Figure 10.16).

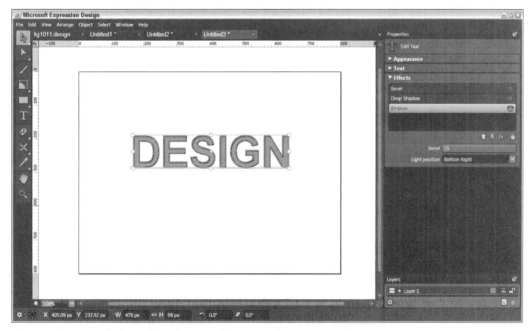

Figure 10.16   Each live effect has specific controls you can adjust.

Tip: When you have applied multiple live effects to text, you can also experiment by selecting an effect and then clicking the up or down arrow at the bottom of the Effects section so that individual effects take precedence over others.

Forming Type to Paths

One of the most effective and frequently used approaches to typography is the arrangement of type along a path. Making type go in a circle or follow a wavy line gives pages additional graphic interest. Expression Design makes it easy to place text along any path, around the outer edge of a shape, or inside a shape.

Making Text Follow a Path

To run text along a path, follow these steps:

1. Choose File > New to create a new document.

2. Click the B-Spline tool.

3. Draw a wavy path from left to right in the document window.

4. To eliminate the fill, click the Fill button in the Appearance section of the Properties panel and then click None.

5. Select the Text tool.

6. Hover the cursor over your path until the curved horizontal line appears with the cursor to indicate you can add text to the path. Click the mouse button.

7. Start typing. A phrase is shown in Figure 10.17.

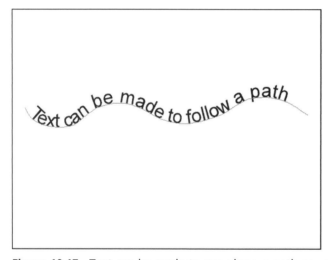

Figure 10.17 Text can be made to run along a path as you type.

You can edit and select text on a path just as you can any other path. You can scroll across text with the Text tool to highlight it. You can also move the entire block of text at once by using either the Selection or Direct selection tool. When you pass the cursor over the first letter of text, it turns into a vertical bar with arrows on either side (see Figure 10.18).

When you see the cursor take this form, click to select the block of text. You can now drag it to the left or right to position it along the path. This clicking and dragging works not only with wavy lines but with circles, polygons, and other shapes

Figure 10.18   Use this version of the cursor with two arrows to select text.

Figure 10.19   You can flip text to the other side of a path by clicking before the first character and dragging the mouse.

that have text running along their paths. If you drag down with the mouse, the text flips to go underneath the path (see Figure 10.19).

Once you have made text flow along a path, you can still edit the path. Select the path by clicking it with the Direct selection tool. You can then click and drag any of the nodes to reposition the path. The text reflows accordingly. If you want to hide the path so that only the text appears—a common graphic format used in many ads and other publications (see Figure 10.20)—select the path, choose Stroke in the Appearance section of the Properties panel, and select none. You can always make

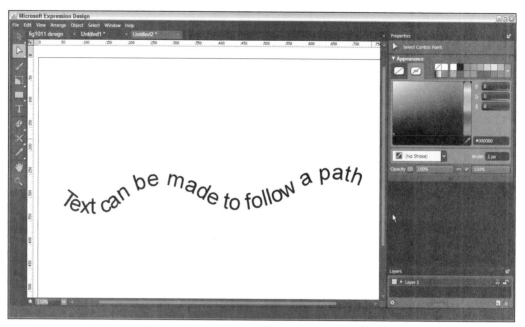

Figure 10.20 If you hide the path, text appears to be floating.

the path visible at least temporarily, so you can edit it, by clicking it with the Direct selection tool.

If you ever want to release text from a path, you need to select it by clicking anywhere in the text with the Selection tool. This tool selects both the text and the path together and draws a selection box around both. Once the text is selected, choose Object > Text on Path > Release Text. The text is separated from the path and now appears in a straight-line format rather than having the shape of the path.

Tip: The Release Text command also works with text you have placed inside an area (see the section "Placing Text Inside an Area," earlier in this chapter). Select the text and the area that surrounds it and choose Object > Text in Path > Release Text. The text immediately jumps outside the area in a separate block.

Attaching Text

Typing text directly onto a path you have already created is only one way to join the two objects. You can also attach existing text (text you have typed previously to any path) so that it assumes the shape of the path. With the Selection tool, select both the text and the path: click on the text, and then choose Object > Text in Path > Attach Text. The text "jumps" onto the path. You can now edit either the text or the path as you did in the preceding section.

The attaching procedure also works with an area such as a rectangle, circle, ellipse, or polygon. Select both the area and text that you want to attach to it. Choose Object > Text in Path > Attach Area Text, and the text jumps inside the area.

Combining Type and Images

One common and practical application for text is creating photo captions. No matter what photo you want to work with, you can create a "label" or caption for it that will be sure to stand out from the background of the image. First, import the image by choosing File > Import, locating the image file you want to work with, and click Open. The image file opens on the artboard.

Once the image is open, you can click the Text tool in front of the image and begin typing your caption. Make sure the size and font you are using will show up within the image. You may have to change the Fill and Stroke attributes so that the caption shows up; white rather than black type shows up best against a dark background, as shown in Figure 10.21.

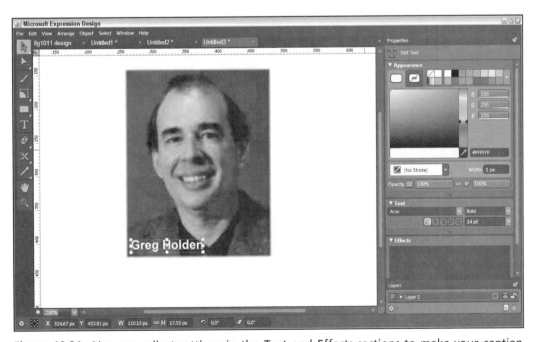

Figure 10.21 You can adjust settings in the Text and Effects sections to make your caption show up atop a photo.

11 Gradients, Transformations, and Live Effects

You learned about transformations and live effects in preceding chapters. But these are among Design's most powerful effects, and there are so many options that exploring them all requires a more lengthy examination. In this chapter you'll actually roll up your sleeves and start working with the program so you can learn about everything you can do with transformations and live effects.

Working with Gradients

As you learned in Chapter 10, Expression Design gives you the ability to apply gradients to closed path shapes such as rectangles and ellipses. You can also apply gradient fills to compound paths and text, as well as individual strokes.

The place to start is the Gradient color swatch in the Appearance section of the Properties panel. By default, the gradient you add moves from black to white; in between you find shades of gray.

To adjust the rate at which the gradient changes color, you move the color stops beneath the Gradient box. The Gradient box is located beneath the Color Picker. In order to move the color stop, you first need to select it. When you have selected a color stop, its pointed tip is filled in. In addition, the color just above the color stop appears in the Color Picker, as shown in Figure 11.1.

The midpoint control just above the Gradient box controls the midpoint of the gradient—the spot where the 50% gradient appears. Click and slide it to the left or right to move the 50% point.

Once you set the midpoint of the gradient, you can pick a color for it by clicking in the Color Picker box. When you click a color, it appears in the Gradient box. You can also pick a color by entering values in the R, G, and B boxes.

Color Stop

Color Stop is Selected

Midpoint Control

Figure 11.1 Gradient color stops control how the color changes.

Specifying Multicolor Gradients

The color stops beneath the Gradient box let you choose different colors to go at the left and right sides of the gradient. Click the color stop on the left and choose a color. Then, click the color stop on the right and choose a different color. The gradient divides into two different colors (see Figure 11.2). You can then move the midpoint control to determine how much of each color appears in the gradient. As you move the midpoint, the fill color you have displayed in the artboard changes to give you an instant view of the effect.

You aren't limited to two color stops. By clicking anywhere in the gradient box, you create a new color stop. You can then assign a different color to the new color stop. This allows the gradient to transition through three separate colors. You can add more color stops as well to create an even more complex multicolor gradient.

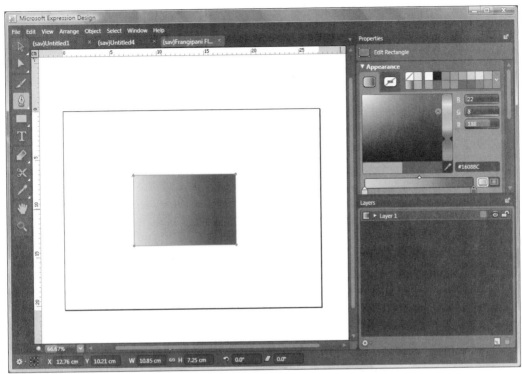

Figure 11.2 Moving the gradient midpoint can add more of one color or another.

Tip: Alt+click on a swatch, and the swatch's color is applied to the color in the gradient that is associated with the currently selected color stop. Be sure to hold down the Alt key when you apply a gradient color; if you simply click a gradient and click a color swatch, that color will be applied to the whole fill. In other words, the fill will become a solid color rather than a gradient.

Changing Opacity

The Stop Alpha box beneath the gradient box gives you another way to adjust the appearance of a gradient. Select one of the color stops and then click inside the Stop Alpha box. Change the value in the box and you adjust the opacity of the color specified by that stop. The checkerboard pattern that appears in the gradient bar indicates that you are at less than 100% of opacity (see Figure 11.3).

Figure 11.3 Adjust opacity of a gradient color by changing the Stop Alpha value.

An opacity rating of zero means that the gradient is transitioning from a color to a transparent area. If you change one color to zero opacity and then place the gradient above another object, you can see the other object through the gradient.

Note: If you don't see the Stop Alpha box, remember to roll down the section beneath the Appearance section. The lower section may be covering up the Stop Alpha box.

Two controls that appear at the bottom of the Appearance section control the overall opacity of the gradient. The Stop Alpha setting displays only the opacity of the color associated with a color stop. The Opacity boxes (Fill Opacity and Stroke Opacity) let you change the opacity of the entire gradient. By default, the two settings are joined together so that when you change a value in one box, the same value is applied to the other box. Click the symbol between the two boxes and the values can be changed separately.

Changing a Gradient's Direction

By default, gradients have color transitions that move from left to right, horizontally. You can change the direction of the color progression by creating a gradient and then clicking the Radial Gradient button. The gradient changes to one that appears to be radiating out from the center in a circular pattern. Linear and radial gradients are compared in Figure 11.4. You can change the opacity, stop colors, and midpoint of a radial gradient the same as a linear one.

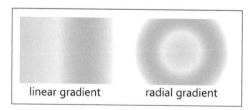

Figure 11.4 Radial gradients provide an alternative to the default linear pattern.

Radial gradients are probably useful only in special situations. Another option for a gradient is probably more common: skewing the direction of the gradient. You can skew the direction and fine-tune other aspects by clicking the button to the right of the Stop Alpha box, which is labeled with the following tool tip: "Move, scale, rotate, or skew the fill of the object." When you click this button, the drop-down

Figure 11.5 Fine-tune a gradient's direction and size using these controls.

menu shown in Figure 11.5 appears. The menu presents you with the following options:

> **X:** This changes the horizontal center point, or pivot point, of the gradient. By default, the X and Y measurements are both expressed in terms of centimeters. A small change (for instance, from 0 to 1) will move a radial gradient's center point from the left to the right in a dramatic way; keep changes small or the gradient will seem to disappear from the shape it is filling.
>
> **Y:** This changes the vertical center point of the gradient. On a conventional gradient that appears to shift from left to right, the gradient will not appear to move when you change the Y value.
>
> **W:** This adjusts the width of the gradient.
>
> **H:** This adjusts the height of the gradient.
>
> **Rotation angle:** This setting (which only appears for a radial gradient) rotates the gradient on an axis.

An additional control, the backward S symbol to the right of the width and height, determines whether or not the width and height are joined to one another. By default, when you change a value in one of these boxes, the same value is automatically applied to the other box. Click the backward S symbol, and the width and height can then be changed separately.

By adjusting the Rotation angle box so that it registers something other than the default zero setting, you change the direction of the gradient. By changing the Rotation angle to 90, for instance, the gradient moves 90 degrees so that, instead of moving from left to right, it moves from bottom to top.

Applying Live Effects

The discussion on live effects in Chapter 10 focused almost exclusively on production effects such as drop shadows, beveling, and the unsharp mask. Design includes a wide range of artistic and other effects, but it isn't easy to know which one to choose. You'll find out more about the general categories of live effects and get some visual examples in the sections that follow.

Note: As you learned in Chapter 10, when Design applies a live effect to an object it is turned into a bitmap. The resolution of the bitmap is listed in the Document Size dialog box. Choose File > Document Size or press Ctrl+Alt+P to open this dialog box. The resolution you want depends on the final output of the image. If the image is intended for a Web page, a resolution of 72 dpi or 96 dpi is adequate. If the image is intended for print publication, an image of 300 dpi or higher is suitable.

Working with Panel Widgets

Panel widgets are the controls near the bottom of the Effects section that let you edit and control the look of live effects you apply. The exact configuration of the widgets depends on the live effect you are applying. Many of the examples in the sections that follow contain descriptions of how the various widgets affect the image you're working with. For example, consider the image shown in Figure 11.6. The image is shown

Figure 11.6 Each live effect has its own set of controls, called widgets, at the bottom of the Effects section.

in its original format; in subsequent sections various effects will be applied to it. The image shows the drop shadow effect, one of the effects described in Chapter 10 and not covered here.

Softness. This changes the softness of the edge of the drop shadow. The default is 1. A setting of zero makes the edge hard; higher settings make the edge softer and the drop shadow less visible.

Offset. This controls the size of the shadow. The default is 5. Larger values make the shadow extend farther out from the image.

Opacity. This changes how transparent the shadow is. The default is 0.6. Higher settings make the shadow less transparent.

Shadow Color. You can change the shadow color to anything you want.

Light Angle. This setting changes the angle at which the shadow extends out from the drop shadow.

Noise. By default, the shadow is smooth in appearance. By increasing this setting, you can make it appear more grainy and textured.

For comparison, you'll notice that the same image shown in Figure 11.7 has softness of 0, offset of 10, opacity of 0.8, and noise of 8. Other sections that follow will show how other widgets and effects change this image.

Figure 11.7 Widgets can dramatically change live effects.

Applying Paint Effects

If you're a painter or artist by nature, you'll be drawn naturally to Design's Paint effects. You'll find them in the Paint submenu of the Live Effects drop-down list at

Figure 11.8　Paint effects let you achieve brushstroke and other artistic effects.

the bottom of the Effects section (see Figure 11.8). If you're not an artist, you'll find that these controls enable you to "fake" brushstroke and other artistic effects. Many of the Paint effects aren't made to work with vector images that have sharp edges. They can work, as you can see below. But some of the examples shown in this section use a bitmap photo of flowers as an example.

Accented Edges: This effect adds dark accents to the tips of the stars in the sample image (see Figure 11.9). The widget's Edge Width, Edge Brightness, and Smoothness change how visible the effect is. If you change the Edge Brightness, the accent is much more visible. In the image below, the sample on the left has the default settings; the one on the right has Edge Width of 2, Edge Brightness of 50, and Smoothness of 15.

Dark Strokes: This makes it look like the image has been painted with dark and light paint strokes. It doesn't always work with photos or images with flat colors, however. Widget controls are Balance, Black Intensity, and White Intensity.

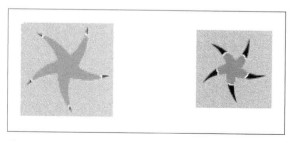

Figure 11.9　Accented edges adds highlights to the tips of sharp objects.

Original   With Fresco Live Effect

Figure 11.10   Fresco can effectively turn a photo into a painting.

Dry Brush: This gives the appearance of painting with a dry brush full of paint. Widget settings include Brush Size, Brush Detail, and Texture.

Fresco: This effect makes it look like the image has been painted onto a stone or plaster surface; the effect on a photo can be very dramatic. Figure 11.10 shows an original photo on the left and the Fresco effect on the right. Widgets are Brush Size, Brush Detail, and Texture.

Paint Daubs: This effect makes it look like paint has been daubed onto the canvas rather than applied with brushstrokes. Widget controls are Brush Size, Brush Type, and Sharpness.

Palette Knife: This effect is especially dramatic; it looks as though paint has been spread on the canvas with a heavy knife (see Figure 11.11). Widget controls are Stroke size, Stroke Detail, and Softness.

Original   With Palette Knife Live Effect

Figure 11.11   Palette knife makes sharp and fine details look bold and broadly applied.

Original   With Sprayed Strokes Live Effect

Figure 11.12 Sprayed strokes makes edges look like they have been sprayed, but in a series of lines.

> **Spatter:** This makes it look like paint has been dropped or spattered onto a canvas. Widgets are Spray Radius and Smoothness.
>
> **Sponge:** This looks like the paint has been daubed on with a sponge; widgets are Brush Size, Definition, and Smoothness.
>
> **Sprayed Strokes:** This gives the effected of spray paint having been applied to paper (see Figure 11.12). Widget controls are Stroke Length, Stroke Direction, and Spray Radius.
>
> **Sumi-e:** This dramatic effect appears like thick black and colored ink strokes on white paper. Widget settings are Stroke Width, Stroke Pressure, and Contrast.
>
> **Watercolor:** This appears as though watercolors have been applied to paper. Widget controls are Brush Detail, Shadow Intensity, and Texture.
>
> **Water Paper:** This looks strongly blurred and textured, as though the image has been drawn on heavily textured paper and water has been applied over it. Controls are Fiber Length, Brightness, and Contrast.

Applying Sketch Effects

Sketch effects are a good choice if you want to make an image look like you just drew it quickly with a pencil or with charcoal. Options are shown in Figure 11.13.

For the most part, sketch effects work best with bitmaps, though patterned fills in vector images can use sketch effects well. Options are these:

> **Angled Strokes:** This simulates a drawing with sharp paint strokes. Widgets are Direction Balance, Stroke Length, and Sharpness.

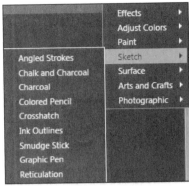

Figure 11.13 Sketch effects give an informal, quickly rendered appearance.

Original   With Chalk and Charcoal Live Effect

Figure 11.14 Chalk and Charcoal gives a quickly sketched, roughly drawn effect.

Chalk and Charcoal: This effect, shown in Figure 11.14, looks like a rough sketch done with chalk and charcoal sticks. Controls are Charcoal Area, Chalk Area, Stroke Pressure, Charcoal Color, and Chalk Color.

Charcoal: This looks as though the image was drawn using a broad charcoal stick and gives only an impression of the original image. Widgets are Charcoal Thickness, Detail, Light/Dark Balance, Charcoal Color, and Paper Color.

Colored Pencil: This makes the object appear as if it were drawn with colored pencils. Controls include Pencil Width, Stroke Pressure, Paper Brightness, and Paper Color.

Crosshatch: This effect makes the image look like it was drawn with diagonal lines that intersect one another. Widgets are Stroke Length, Sharpness, and Strength.

Ink Outlines: This outlines the edges of the image with dark lines like those created with ink pens. Controls are Stroke Length, Dark Intensity, and Light Smudge Stick. This simulates sketching the object's outlines with pastels and then smudging the lines to make them look purposely crude. Widgets: Stroke Length, Highlight Area, and Highlight Intensity.

Graphic Pen: This effect causes short black-and-white pen lines to be drawn across the image. Controls are Stroke Length, Stroke Direction, Light/Dark Balance, Ink Color, and Paper Color.

Reticulation: Reticulation gives an image an antique, abstract look by adding a substantial amount of black-and white "noise" (see Figure 11.15). Widgets are Density, Black Level, White Level, Foreground Color, and Background Color.

Figure 11.15 Reticulation adds black-and-white "noise" throughout an image.

Applying Surface Effects

Surface effects work by changing the background on which an image is drawn. Instead of a smooth, solid color, you can have a three-dimensional surface with many striking features. The nine surface effects available are shown in Figure 11.16.

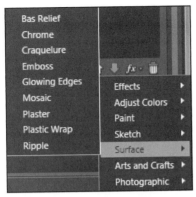

Figure 11.16 Surface effects work well with vector images.

Original

With Bas Relief Live Effect

Figure 11.17 Bas Relief makes an image appear sleek and three-dimensional.

Surface effects generally work better with vector images than the Sketch and Paint effects described earlier. Options are these:

- Bas Relief turns an image into a shiny, three-dimensional surface with a subtle gradient (see Figure 11.17). Controls include Detail, Light Position, Smoothness, Foreground Color, and Background Color.

- Chrome does something very complex to the image. The background surface is made dull gray. The foreground looks ultra-shiny, as though made of molten metal. Two widgets are available: Detail and Smoothness.

- Craquelure, shown in Figure 11.18, creates a fine network of cracks and blemishes on the surface. The effect is similar to but more subtle than Mosaic. Settings are Crack Spacing, Crack Depth, and Crack Brightness.

- Emboss makes the object appear three-dimensional and raised up from the surface. Two settings are available: Relief and Light Position.

Figure 11.18 Craquelure creates a network of cracks on the surface of the object.

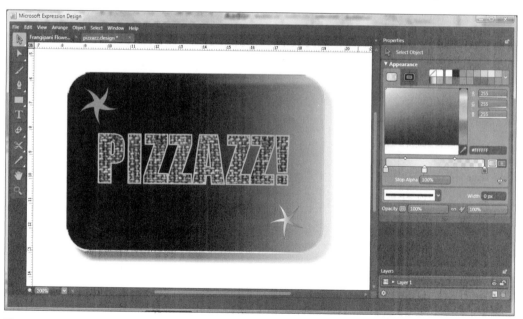

Figure 11.19 Glowing Edges makes an image especially high contrast.

- Glowing Edges turns the surface to black with edges that are lighter and appear to glow (see Figure 11.19). Three widgets are available: Edge Width, Edge Brightness, and Smoothness.

Craquelure   Mosaic

Figure 11.20   Mosaic creates a set of tiles on the surface of the object.

- Mosaic creates a network of tiles on the surface of the object. The effect, shown on the right in Figure 11.20, is compared to Craquelure on the left. Three widgets control the appearance of the tiles that make up the effect: Tile size, Grout width, and Lighten Grout.

- Plaster simulates the look of thick, wet plaster on the surface of the object. Five controls are available: Image Balance, Light Position, Smoothness, Foreground Color, and Background Color.

- Plastic Wrap makes the image look like it has been wrapped in clear plastic wrap. Three widgets are available: Highlight Strength, Detail, and Smoothness.

- Ripple makes the object look like it is being viewed through the ripples in a body of water. Two settings are Ripple Size and Ripple Magnitude.

Applying Arts and Crafts Effects

Arts and Crafts effects simulate printing different effects. The options are shown in Figure 11.21.

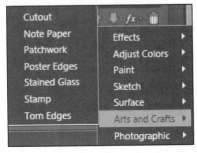

Figure 11.21   Arts and Crafts live effects.

Arts and Crafts effects make the image appear to be printed in different ways. Options are:

- Cutout looks as though the image is made of cut-out pieces of paper that have been roughly shaped together. Widgets include Number of Levels, Edge Simplicity, and Edge Fidelity.

- Note Paper makes it look as though the image has been printed on roughly textured note paper. Settings include Image Balance, Graininess, Relief, Paper Color, and Emboss Color (see Figure 11.22).

- Patchwork makes the object look like it's printed on a heavily ridged surface similar to a patchwork quilt (see Figure 11.23). Two widgets are available: Square size and Relief.

- Poster Edges makes the image look like a poster with a few vivid colors and high contrast. Widgets are Edge Thickness, Edge Intensity, and Posterization.

- Stained Glass can be clearly seen in Figure 11.24. The image is divided into irregularly shaped segments like a stained glass window. Settings enable you to change the stained glass pieces: Cell Size, Border Thickness, Light Intensity, and Border Color.

Figure 11.22 This effect simulates printing on roughly textured note paper.

Figure 11.23 Patchwork makes the image look like it's been quilted.

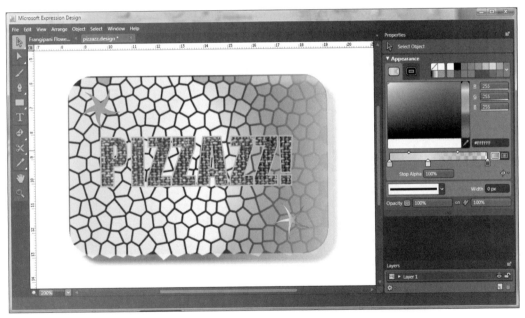

Figure 11.24 Stained glass live effect.

- Stamp looks like a black rubber stamp pressed into white paper. Widgets are Light/Dark Balance, Smoothness, Foreground Color, and Background Color.

- The Torn Edges live effect is best seen with a bitmap image such as the one depicted in Figure 11.25.

Original   With Torn Edges Live Effect

Figure 11.25   Torn Edges live effect.

Applying Photographic Effects

Photographic effects don't necessarily have to be used with photographic images. Rather, their names sound like the sorts of special effects that are sometimes added to photos to give them more character. Six photographic effects are available, and they are shown in Figure 11.26.

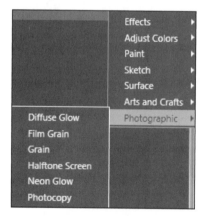

Figure 11.26   Photographic live effects.

The photographic options are described in the sections that follow. Photographic effects, as the name implies, work best with photos, so a photo is shown in the examples below:

> **Diffuse Glow:** This fascinating effect spreads around (or diffuses) the light in the image so that it appears to glow. Any light areas in an image will gain the glow effect; you see an example in Figure 11.27. The four widgets are Graininess, Glow Amount, Clear Amount, and Glow Color.

Original   With Diffuse Glow Live Effect

Figure 11.27   Diffuse glow makes light areas in an image seem to glow.

Film Grain: This effect adds a grainy pattern to images. The three widgets are Grain, Highlight Area, and Highlight Intensity.

Grain: This effect also adds a grainy pattern, but it's generally more pronounced than Film Grain, which appears "filmy" by comparison. The widgets are Graininess, Graintype, Contrast, Foreground Color, and Background Color. Graintype has several variations within it.

Halftone Screen: You can't see the effect in a black-and-white book like this, so apply it to one of your color photos; it turns the photo to a black-and-white image and makes it a halftone—an image that has been processed with a halftone screen to create the little dots used to print images. The widget Size affects the size of the dots and makes the screen either finer or coarser. Screen Type changes the dot shape to line, dot, or circle. Other widgets are Contrast, Foreground Color, and Background Color. Two variations are shown in Figure 11.28.

Size: 5 Type: Dot   Size: 3, Type: Line

Figure 11.28   Halftone screens can use dots, lines, or circles.

Neon Glow: This effect makes a photo turn dark and seem to glow as though created by neon light. Controls are Glow Size, Glow Brightness, Foreground Color, Background Color, and Glow Color.

Photocopy: This effect makes the image look like it was run through an old and poor-quality photocopier (see Figure 11.29). Settings are Detail, Darkness, Foreground Color, and Background Color.

Original   With Photocopy Live Effect

Figure 11.29 Photocopy duplicates the image crudely in black and white.

Hiding or Removing Live Effects

The name of each effect you apply is listed in the Effects section. It's often useful to hide a live effect because hiding lets you see the object you're working on without the effect; still, you don't have to delete the effect altogether. Clicking the eye icon to the right of an effect lets you toggle between making it visible or invisible. When you have hidden an effect, the eye icon becomes a circle. Click the circle and the icon becomes an eye again, and the effect is visible once more.

To remove a live effect, you select its name in the list in the Effects panel. Then click the Delete Effect button, which looks like a trash can and is located at the bottom of the Effects section. The up and down arrows next to the Trash and fx buttons in the Effects section enable you to change the order of effects. By changing which effect appears on top, you can dramatically change the appearance of an image. For instance, Figure 11.30 shows two effects applied to a photo. The image looks quite different, depending on which effect is on top—the one on top takes precedence and is more visible than the one beneath it.

Transforming Objects

Transformation is a fancy way of saying that a change has been made to an image or an object that alters its original appearance. The change can be as simple as moving its position. It can also involve rotating, scaling, or skewing the item in question.

Diffuse Glow atop
Colored Pencil

Colored Pencil atop
Diffuse Glow

Figure 11.30 You can change the appearance of an image by changing the "stacking order" of live effects.

As you might expect, Design provides you with several different ways to transform objects. You can always select an item or multiple items and drag to reposition them. You can scale bitmaps, vectors, text, or custom images. But to exercise more control over transformations, you have two options: the Transform submenu and the Action Bar.

Using the Selection Box

When you select an object using the Selection tool, a selection box is drawn around it. The handles around the selection box give you an easy way to rotate, scale, or skew images. When you pass the cursor over one of the four corner handles, the normal mouse arrow turns into a curved arrow (see Figure 11.31). Click and drag one of the corner handles while the arrow is visible, and you can rotate the object freely. If you hold down the Shift key, you constrain the rotation to 45 degree angles.

Scaling and Skewing

If you click, hold down, and drag on any of the handles when the curved arrow symbol is not visible, you gain the capability to drag the image. Stretch or skew it at will, as shown in Figure 11.32; if the results seem unacceptable, simply press Ctrl+Z or chose Edit > Undo to return to the previous shape. Holding down the Shift key while you drag keeps the original proportions intact; you only scale the image, without distorting it.

On the other hand, you can constrain the skewing by positioning the mouse arrow not directly over a selection handle on the selection box but right next to the handle. Near the handle, the arrow turns into a two-headed arrow with a slanted line between the two arrows. Click and drag while this symbol is visible, and you constrain the skew in the direction you drag—you skew either straight up and down or straight left and right.

Click and Hold Down
to Rotate Image

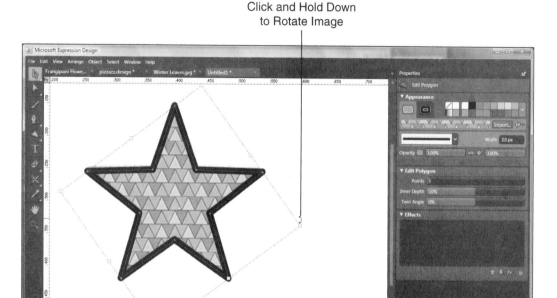

Click and Drag Handles
to Stretch or Scale Image

Figure 11.31 The selection box lets you rotate and scale interactively using your mouse or touchpad.

Tip: You can configure Expression Design so that when you click and drag on an object's selection handles, the object's stroke scales in proportion. The stroke gets bigger as the image is scaled up, in other words. Choose Edit > Options > Stroke. When the Options dialog box opens, check the box next to Scale Stroke Width and then click OK.

Changing the Center Point

When you click on an object with the Selection tool, a small circle appears at (or near) what appears to be its center. This is its center point. When you hover over its corner handles, click, and drag to rotate the object, the object rotates around this center point.

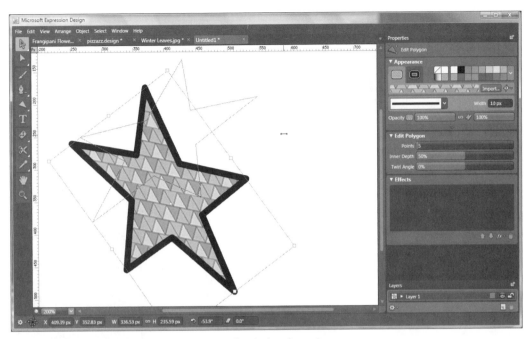

Figure 11.32 You can stretch an image freely by dragging.

The center point isn't a fixed object, however. Click and drag it; you can move it outside the selection box elsewhere on the artboard. Now rotate the image. It still rotates around the center point. But when the center point is moved outside the image, the image rotates around that point in the same way a planet rotates around the sun (see Figure 11.33).

The Registration point icon, which is second from the left in the Action Bar, lets you pick one of the selection box handles as the rotation point. You'll find out more about the Action Bar later in this chapter.

When you skew an image, you skew relative to the center point, which is in the center of the image by default. You can control the skew by moving the center point, in the same way you control the rotation by moving the center point.

Using the Transform Submenu

If you want to rotate objects by a fixed percentage, and you don't feel the need to experiment with positioning and editing, the Transform submenu of the Arrange menu is a good choice. When you choose Arrange > Transform, you access a submenu (shown in Figure 11.34) that lets you perform a number of functions:

> **Rotate:** The first section of the Transform submenu lets you rotate objects by 90 or 180 degrees.

Default Center
Point Position

Center Point Moved
Outside Object

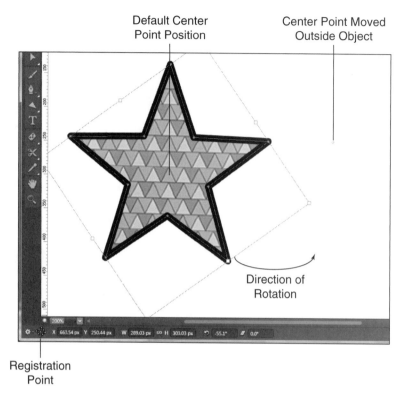

Direction of
Rotation

Registration
Point

Figure 11.33 An object's center point can be moved outside of its own boundaries.

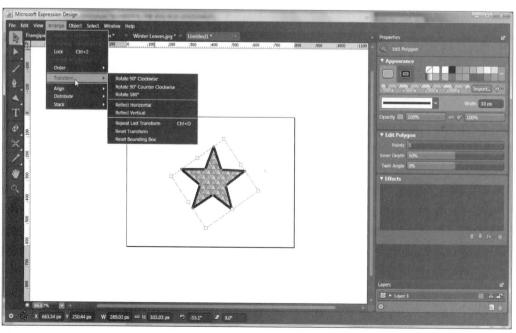

Figure 11.34 The Transform submenu lets you quickly repeat, rotate, or reset transformations.

Reflect: The middle section lets you reflect transformations: If you skew an object up vertically by a centimeter, choose Reflect, and the opposite action will be performed on the object. This command applies not only to the image you just transformed but to any image you have open on the artboard.

Repeat: The Transform submenu also lets you repeat transformations quickly. Suppose you skew an object by precisely 5.5cm vertically. If you want to repeat the skew, you don't have to type the value in the Skew box in the Action Bar. Just choose Arrange > Transform > Repeat Last Transform or press Ctrl+D. The object will be skewed again in the same way. This command applies not only to the image you just transformed but to any image you have open on the artboard.

Reset: Choose Reset Transform if you want the object to return to its original appearance, without any transformations. Choose Reset Bounding Box if you want the object's current appearance to be the starting point, rather than how it looked before the transformation.

Note: Normally, when you scale an image, the fill is not scaled along with it. You can scale the fill as well as the stroke by choosing Edit > Options > General and checking the box next to Transform Image Fill. You won't end up with moiré-style patterns in the fill when it is scaled.

Manipulating with the Action Bar

The Action Bar is the set of controls that appears just beneath the Design artboard, beneath the zoom percentage and the horizontal scrollbar. The Action Bar's controls are visible only when you have selected one or more objects. Otherwise, the space beneath the artboard appears blank. The advantage of using the Action Bar is great precision: You can enter an exact numeric value in order to reposition or scale the object just the way you want.

The x and y coordinates on the left side of the Action Bar control the horizontal and vertical positions of the object (see Figure 11.35). The W and H boxes control the width and height. By default, the width and height are joined to one another, as

Figure 11.35 The Action Bar gives you precise control over positioning.

indicated by the sideways S symbol between them. When you change one of the dimensions (height or width), the other changes accordingly to maintain the proportions. Click on the sideways S symbol, and you separate the W and H values so they can be changed separately.

Note: As with other parts of the Design interface, you can change values in the X, Y, W, and H boxes by either clicking in them and typing a value or scrubbing a value. Then press Enter. When you first pass the mouse pointer over one of these boxes, it appears as a four-pointed arrow. Clicking and dragging up or down increases or decreases the number in the box, respectively.

The box to the right of the width and height boxes, which has a curved arrow, lets you rotate a selected object at a precise angle. So does the box on the far right, which enables you to skew the selected object(s). The values in the boxes can get as precise as one-thousandth of an inch.

It's especially important to note that the Action Bar works interactively with the other tools described in this section. If you rotate an object by clicking and dragging on one of its corner handles, for instance, you see the rotation value change. If you reposition it elsewhere on the artboard, the X and Y values change accordingly.

12 Optimizing Images for Publication

Once you have drawn images, divided them into layers, applied Live Effects, and saved your work, you're ready to do something with the graphics. You're ready to publish them in some format, and I'm using the term "publication" loosely. This chapter will discuss publishing your images on the Web or in print and outputting them to XAML so you can work with them in Blend or other applications.

Locking Images

If you have been working with complex designs, chances are you have multiple objects on the artboard, each consisting of multiple layers of objects. If you are working with a team of designers and editors, it's likely that your images will be used by others when they prepare Web presentations or output files for print publications. In either case, you probably don't want unauthorized users fiddling with the designs you've worked long and hard to get just the way you want.

Locking images enables you to fix them in place with your last set of revisions applied. That way, other editors can't accidentally make changes if they click on a path or shape and move things around in a way you don't want. You, too, might inadvertently select or move something when you're working on a design. To lock, follow these steps:

1. Select the object or objects you want to lock with any of the selection tools (Lasso, Selection, and so on).

2. Choose Arrange > Lock or press Ctrl+2.

3. Try to select the same object; you cannot select it because it has been locked.

If you want to unlock the object that has just been locked, select it again and choose Arrange > Unlock All or press Ctrl+Shift+2.

> **Note:** Unlock All unlocks not only the object you currently have selected, but also all objects that have been previously been locked. The Arrange menu does not have an option called Unlock that simply unlocks a single object. To unlock a single object, use the Layers menu as described below.

You can also lock or unlock objects by using the Layers section of the Properties panel. In an image with multiple objects such as the one shown in Figure 12.1, the Layers section shows all of the objects in that particular layer. Each object has a lock icon next to it. Click the icon to lock it; click the lock icon later if you want to unlock it.

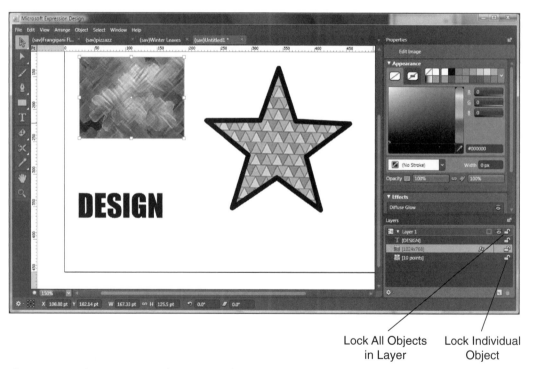

Lock All Objects in Layer   Lock Individual Object

Figure 12.1 The Layers panel gives you fine-grained control over locking and unlocking.

Distributing Objects

Before you output your design, you may well want to arrange objects on the artboard so they are evenly distributed. The Arrange menu's Distribute command enables you to distribute multiple objects evenly so they aren't stacked atop one another. You also might want to even out objects that are close to one another so there is an equal amount of distance between them.

To distribute items, you first have to select three or more of them. Then you can tell Design to distribute them. Consider the pentagons shown on the Design artboard in Figure 12.2. They are unevenly spaced.

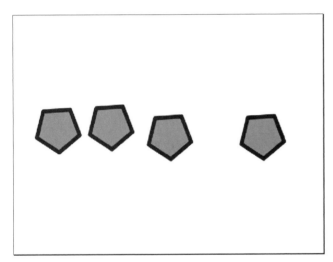

Figure 12.2   Unevenly spaced pentagons.

You can show the ruler and grid and arrange the items evenly if you wish. But you'll save time and trouble by selecting all four and then choosing Distribute. You'll find the option under the Arrange menu, at Arrange > Distribute, or at the right side of the Action Bar near the bottom of the Design window. Choose Left Edges, and the pentagons are evenly spaced (see Figure 12.3).

You can also distribute multiple objects by other attributes: top or bottom edges or vertical or horizontal centers, for instance. It's best to select the objects you want and experiment with the Distribute options to see which ones work best for you.

If you have objects that aren't the same size, things work differently. You can select the objects and choose a Distribute option, and the objects will be distributed as you wish. But they might not look evenly spaced. The objects shown in Figure 12.4 are very different in shape and content, for instance. If you choose Distribute > Left Edges, the objects are arranged so their left edges are spaced equally from one another. But because they are different sizes and shapes, they still look jumbled.

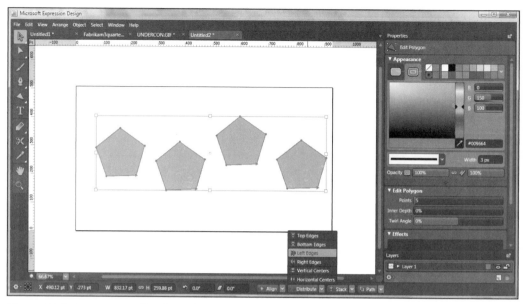

Figure 12.3 Pentagons distributed by left edges.

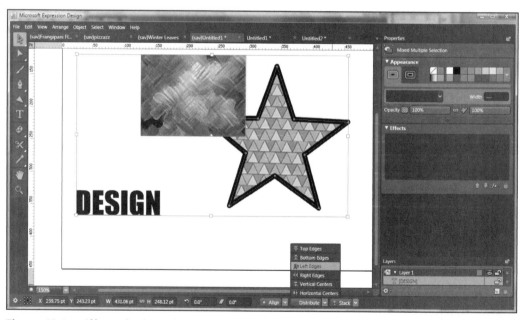

Figure 12.4 Differently shaped objects can also be spaced evenly.

Distributing, in other words, is different than aligning objects. If you want objects to line up, choose Align and choose Left Edges, Right Edges, or any of the other options (which are the same as the Distribute options). If you want to space items precisely, choose Distribute instead.

Adding Crop Marks

Many of the graphics that you scan or draw are, at least initially, too big to fit on a relatively small Web page. It's important to crop the images in order to delete the parts you don't want and to keep the image small, both in file size and physical dimensions (height and width). Cropping is an essential step in preparing images for publication, whether online or off. It's also important to crop before you export your image so it can be used by other programs, because cropping makes files smaller and more portable.

Cropping in Expression Design is the same as in other graphics programs. You draw an outline around the region of the image you want to keep, and then Design deletes the rest. Follow these steps:

1. Choose File > Crop Marks > Set. A set of vertical and horizontal crop marks appears on your image. The crosshatch mark shown in Figure 12.5 marks the upper left corner of the cropping region—the area that will be drawn around the image to preserve it while deleting unnecessary content.

2. Draw a box around the parts of the image you want to preserve.

3. Click and hold when the crosshatch is positioned at the upper left corner of the part of the image you want to save. Then drag down and to the right

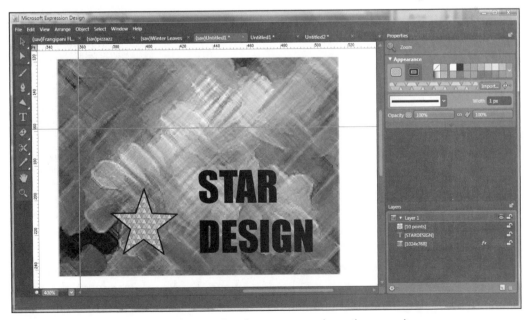

Figure 12.5 Click to position the crosshatch so you can draw the cropping area.

to draw the box. When the crosshatch reaches the lower right corner of the cropping box, release the mouse button. The box is drawn, and crop marks are positioned at the corners (see Figure 12.6).

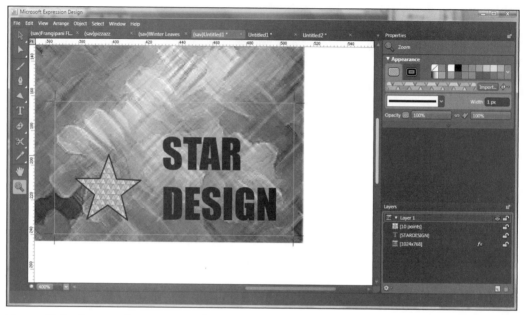

Figure 12.6 Crop marks appear at the corners after you define the cropping area.

Note: You are the only one who will be able to see the crop marks on your image. When you print or export the image, the crop marks aren't visible.

You can always adjust the cropping box by clicking and dragging its sides or corners. Once you have set crop marks, you can remove them by choosing File > Crop Marks > Remove. If you don't want to draw the cropping area by hand, you have the option of letting Design do it for you. Choose File > Crop Marks > Set and click at the upper-left corner of the cropping area. The dialog box shown in Figure 12.7 appears. This dialog box lets you enter the exact positions of the crop marks if you already know where they should appear. The x and y coordinates under From are those that you set when you clicked in your image. By default, the x and y coordinates under To are the same. You must enter different values in the To boxes, or crop marks won't appear at all.

Figure 12.7 This dialog box lets you specify exact crop mark positions.

There's a third way to set a cropping area, and it's one that makes sense if you have a tidy and regular object such as a rectangle, circle, or ellipse. You can create a bounding box around the object by selecting it using the Selection tool. Click the object and, when the bounding box appears, choose File > Crop Marks > From Bounding Box (see Figure 12.8).

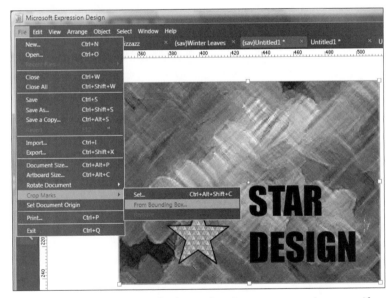

Figure 12.8 You can use the bounding box as a cropping area if you wish.

When the Set Crop Marks dialog box appears, you have the opportunity to either use the bounding box as the cropping area or create space between the box and the cropping area. It's often a good idea to create some empty space between the box and the cropping area so the image doesn't look too tightly compressed. Click OK, and the box is drawn. The one shown in Figure 12.9 has had 10 points of space added between the bounding box and the cropping box.

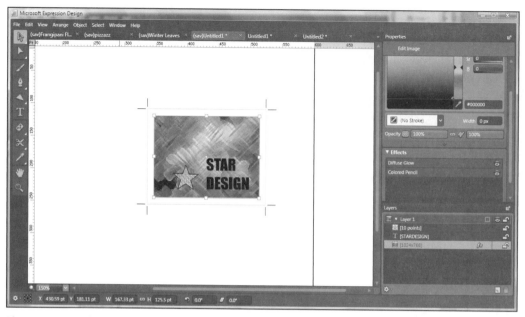

Figure 12.9 Add some empty space between your image's outline and the cropping area.

Observing Best Practices

Whether you plan to output images on the Web, to Expression Blend, to Photoshop, or in print, a few best practices always apply. Keep your file sizes as small as possible, and crop your images judiciously to minimize unnecessary content or white space. In cropping an image, you reduce the image to the correct size in a graphics program yourself before you put it on the page.

You can also reduce file size by adjusting the number of colors in the image as described in "Exporting to Bitmap Format," later in this chapter. The goal is to reduce the file size as much as possible without compromising the communication effectiveness of your graphics.

Outputting Images

Expression Design is typically not the last application you'll use in a project. Rather, it's a program you use to create images that can then be processed by other applications. The most obvious examples are Expression Web and Expression Blend. But you can also print images or export them to files so applications such as Photoshop can process them further. This section examines output options available through Design and how to control the output so images come out looking the way you want.

Printing Images

Once you have cropped your files as described earlier in this chapter, you're ready to print them if needed. Before you choose the Print command, however, it's a good idea to check the size of the document that Design is going to print to by choosing File > Document Size or pressing Ctrl+Alt+P. The Document Size dialog box shown in Figure 12.10 opens.

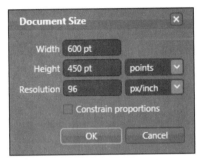

Figure 12.10   Check the output size and resolution in this dialog box.

The height and width need to match the size of the output media. As stated earlier, the Resolution size is also critical and needs to match the output format of your design.

The quality and speed of your printed output depend on a variety of print options. You control the options by choosing Edit > Options > Print and Export. The controls on this page of the Options dialog box are as follows:

Refit curves to output paths. Complex B-spline curves and vector paths can take a long time to print. By default, this option is on; it tells Design to simplify the complex paths so they print more quickly. It doesn't change the quality of your artwork, however.

Split long paths. Turning this option on tells Design to split up complex, long paths so they print more quickly.

Path quality. The three settings in this drop-down list, Normal, Draft, and Best, directly affect how long it takes your file to print and how fine the quality is. The higher the quality, the longer it takes to print.

Information vectorization levels. Levels range from 1 to 16. The higher the level, the more information is contained in the image's vector paths—and the longer the document takes to print. The default setting is 9.

When you're done setting options, click OK. You can now print the file by choosing File > Print or pressing Ctrl+P. The standard Print dialog box opens. Click

Properties and then click Page Setup (or Layout, if your printer uses it) if you want to change the orientation (portrait or landscape) or other settings as listed in Figure 12.11. The exact arrangement of this dialog box depends on the printer you are using.

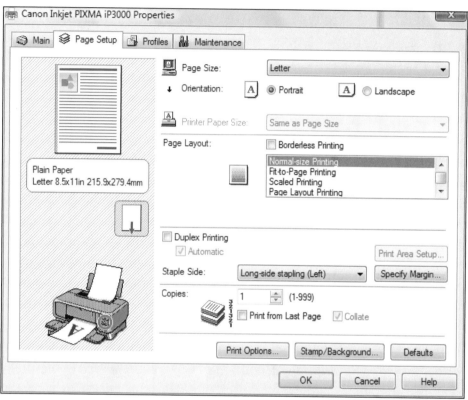

Figure 12.11   Change print orientation in this dialog box.

When you're done, click OK to close Properties and OK to close the Print dialog box. At this point, a second dialog box called Print Rasterization Settings appears. This dialog box, shown in Figure 12.12, gives you another chance to set the print resolution of the image. Click the drop-down menu list next to dpi, and you are presented with a range of quality options for the image. The one labeled Printer Settings corresponds to your printer's capacity. The higher the resolution, the higher the print quality. When you have crop marks included in your file, a second option appears: Print Cropmark Region causes the crop marks to be included in the print-out. The preview to the left of the drop-down list indicates the cropping for the image. Center on Page centers the image both vertically and horizontally on the printed page. When you're done, click OK, and the file is sent to the printer.

Figure 12.12 This dialog box lets you set the print resolution of your image file.

Exporting to XAML

It's important to be able to export images you prepare in Design so they can be used by other programs within the Expression Studio suite. One of the best options for exporting is XAML (pronounced "zammel"), or eXtensible Application Markup Language.

To export, open the file in the Design window or, if it is already open, save it if necessary. Then follow these steps:

1. Choose File > Export or press Ctrl+Shift+X.

2. When the Export dialog box opens, choose the location where you want to save the file by clicking Save In, choosing a location, and double-clicking folders as needed.

3. In the Save as Type dialog box, choose XAML if it's not already selected.

4. Click Save. The Export XAML dialog box shown in Figure 12.13 opens.

Click the arrows next to Document Format and Effects to view the options in these two sections:

> **Canvas.** Choose this option if you want to work with the image in Expression Blend. Two further options are available: Export Editable TextBlocks and Export Flattened Paths. Both provide different ways of exporting text, if your image has them.
>
> **Silverlight.** Choose this option if you plan to present the image using Microsoft's Silverlight technology.
>
> **Resource Dictionary.** If you plan to export the content as assets you can reuse in different situations, choose this option. When you do so, several new options appear that let you specify how you want to group the contents of the image. You can group by document, layers, or objects. Choosing

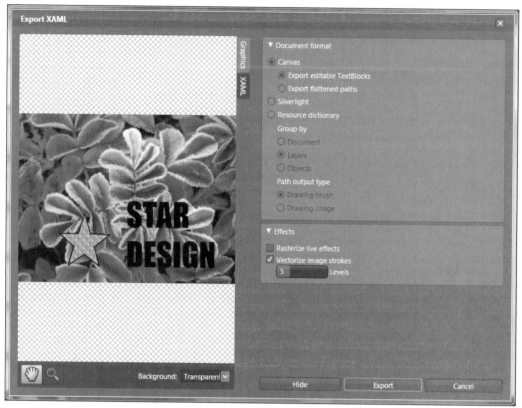

Figure 12.13 Specify XAML settings before you export a Design file.

Document lets you save the contents as a single file. You also choose whether you want the paths in the image to be output in the form of a drawing brush or a drawing image. If you choose to output the image as layers, the layers in the image will be grouped separately, as illustrated at the bottom of the dialog box (see Figure 12.14).

In the Effects section, you have two options. Check the top box if you want Design to rasterize any live effects you have applied. Checking the box lets you see a preview in the box on the left, so you can decide if this option will make your image look the way you want. The Vectorize Image Strokes box turns any bitmapped strokes into vector paths. The higher the vectorization levels, the more detail the image strokes will have when they are exported, and the longer they will take to print.

Once you have made your changes, click Preview to preview the image as it will be exported. If you want to see the XAML code that will be created when your object is exported, click the XAML Code tab on the right side of the Preview area. When you are ready, click Export to export the file.

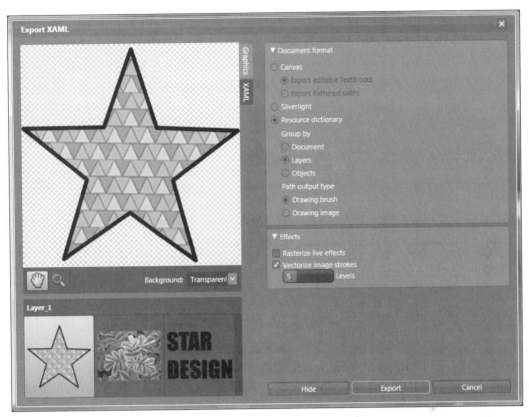

Figure 12.14 You can export an image's contents as separate layers.

Note: If your image consists of separate objects, those objects will be exported to the same folder as the XAML file. They will be grouped in their own folder within the file that contains the XAML file.

Another way to move a file from Design to Expression Blend is not to use the Export XAML window at all, but rather, to simply copy the image and paste it into the Blend window. The image will automatically be converted to XAML format, though you won't be able to exercise as much control over how the exporting is actually done.

Exporting to Bitmap Format

Expression Design can also export images to a variety of bitmap formats. Depending on the format you choose, you can add the images to Web pages or work with them in other graphics programs such as Adobe Photoshop. In fact, one of the formats you can save to is the Photoshop native format, PSD. If you export to TIFF, BMP, or WDP, you can open the file in Windows Photo Gallery or another application.

If you export to one of the Web-friendly image formats—GIF, JPEG, or PNG—you can open them in a layout program such as Expression Web so you can add them to Web pages. No matter what bitmap format you choose, when you export, Design converts your vector objects into pixels.

The first step in exporting to a bitmap format is the same as for exporting to XAML: Choose File > Export. When the Export dialog box appears, choose the file format you want from the Save as Type drop-down menu at the bottom. Give the file a name, and choose the location where you want to save it. When you click Save, the Export dialog box shown in Figure 12.15 appears.

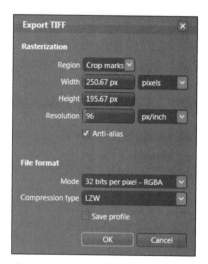

Figure 12.15 Set bitmap export settings using this dialog box.

Note: The Export Image Settings dialog box changes its name according to the file format you choose from the Save as Type list. The options in the dialog box also depend on the bitmap format you choose.

Although the options differ according to the file format, the choices in the Rasterization section are more or less the same from one format to another. Rasterizing is the process of converting digital information to bitmap format, and the general options are the same:

Region. Click the down arrow to make one of two choices: Canvas or Crop Marks. Canvas lets you export the entire artboard, including the crop marks. Crop Marks causes only the area inside the crop marks to be exported.

Width and Height. These boxes let you specify the amount of information in the final bitmap image. Choose an option from the drop-down list to the right of Width to specify a unit of measurement: You can choose pixels, inches, millimeters, centimeters, picas, or points.

Resolution. This setting is related to Width and Height: The Resolution setting determines how big the pixels will be.

Anti-aliasing. This is the process of smoothing the jagged edges caused by bitmap images. Check this box if you want the bitmap to be anti-aliased.

Note: Although anti-aliased graphics look sharper when seen up close, anti-aliasing adds shades of gray or color and increases the file size of a graphic. Sometimes graphics should not be anti-aliased in order to ensure that they appear more quickly in a Web browser. Designers should not automatically anti-alias a bitmap, but instead should save different versions and test them to see how they appear and how big the file sizes are.

The File Format options in the bottom half of the Export TIFF dialog box refer to the file format. The TIFF Format dialog box shown in the preceding image lets you choose one of the compression methods that apply to TIFF, such as the LZW format.

Note: LZW uses a mathematical formula called an algorithm to compress files. LZW was developed by Jacob Ziv and Abraham Lempel in 1978, and it was later modified by Terry Welch to its present format. LZW works by creating shorthand code to stand for repeated segments of binary data in a graphic. If, for example, the color data 10110101 10101 comes up repeatedly, LZW creates a shorthand version of this code, such as 1011. The essential data is preserved, and file size is reduced.

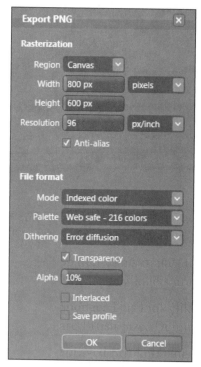

Figure 12.16   The PNG version of the Export dialog box.

The JPEG version of the dialog box has a simple File Format section with only one option, a numeric quality setting. The PNG version shown in Figure 12.16 contains a more extensive set of options, including these:

Mode. Use this list to choose a color palette for the PNG image. The Indexed Color option is suitable for the Web because it limits the number of colors in the image to 256. For a more complex image, choose 24-bit RGB.

Palette. Choose the color palette you want to use for the image here. The "Web safe" 216-color palette used to be important because it assured accurate color reproduction. Newer browsers are able to display colors accurately, and the 216-color palette is no longer considered critical. This option only appears if you choose Indexed Color in the Export dialog box.

Transparency. PNG, like GIF, has the ability to make one color transparent. Check this box to exercise that option. This option only appears if you choose Indexed Color in the Export dialog box.

Interlaced. Interlaced images appear in stages. At the very beginning of the process such images appear very "bumpy" or pixellated. Then the focus gradually becomes increasingly sharper. The advantage is that the initial "bumpy" view of the graphic appears quicker than it would if the browser had to process all the file data before loading the complete image in its entirety. The viewer can get a quick sense of what the image contains. This feature was helpful when most Internet users had slow dial-up connections because it caused an image to be displayed gradually. It's not as important now that so many users have high-speed connections, but check this box if you want to use the Interlacing feature.

Save profile. If you check this box, Design will save the current color profile along with the image.

Click OK and the image is exported to your selected location. If your image is particularly complex, the rasterization process can take time, and a progress bar will appear to help you keep track. If the process is taking too long, you can press Escape to stop it. You may want to try a smaller resolution setting or other settings so the process is not so complex.

Note: If you reduce the number of colors in the image, you may want to specify dithering, which appears as an option in some versions of the Export dialog box. Dithering is a way of simulating any colors that aren't available in the palette you're using.

Reducing File Size

The Palette drop-down list under File Format gives you the capability to select how many colors are in your image, a feature known as *color depth*. If you have an image whose file size is large in terms of the Web (perhaps more than 50K) and are willing to risk losing some color, you can reduce the number of colors. You can also change it to black and white or just two colors.

While it's true that 8-bit, 256-color graphics saved in GIF format are well suited to the Web, sometimes even 8-bit graphics can take up more space than they need to. Some GIFs require a palette of only 64, 32, or 16 colors, for instance. On top of that, the number of colors that a Web browser has available to display a graphic image is also limited. Some of the 256 colors on a computer are already taken up by the operating system, and other colors are used by the browser itself. Browsers might have only about 50 colors that can be used to display images on a Web page.

Table 12.1 Color Palettes

Bits	Colors
1-bit	2 colors
2-bit	4 colors
3-bit	8 colors
4-bit	16 colors
5-bit	32 colors
6-bit	64 colors
7-bit	128 colors
8-bit	256 colors
16-bit	65,500 colors
24-bit	16.7+ million colors

Table 12.1 shows how many colors are available in each type of palette. In 8-bit graphics, each pixel in the image can be one of 256 possible colors. In 4-bit graphics, only 16 colors are available. However, some GIF images are simple enough that they require only a few colors. Reducing the image's color palette might not result in a great decrease in color quality. Another practical way to reduce file sizes even further is to change the image to a 4-bit color palette. The color quality of 4-bit or 5-bit images is by no means as rich or subtle as 8-bit or above; however, on occasion, a slight decrease in color quality can result in a big savings in memory.

Creating User Experiences with Expression Blend

13 Introducing Expression Blend

Most Web sites are relatively simple. You review text and images, you click on some links, you explore information. But Expression Blend isn't made for most Web sites. It's there to help you create sites that present visitors with full-fledged interactive experiences. Professionally created commercial Web sites that promote a company and its brand, and that exist to sell products and services, need to engage visitors who are increasingly sophisticated and who expect high-quality content.

You'll see all around the Web that Expression Blend helps content providers create "rich user experiences." What does that mean, exactly? It means that content responds to mouse hovers and mouse clicks with animation. It means graphics and type are presented in high quality resolution. It means the entire Web site presents a unified and compelling experience for the user, one that is dynamic and invites interaction rather than static. Creating such experiences by writing code from scratch is a difficult challenge; Blend brings it within the range of non-programmers and coders alike with a user-friendly interface. Blend is intended to give graphic designers a way to work directly with user interfaces to make them attractive while still maintaining the functionality programmers may have originally given to them when writing code. This chapter presents an overview of Blend and explains how it works and how you can use it in a production environment.

What Is Expression Blend?

Blend is a complex and powerful application that carries with it extensive requirements as far as processor capability and memory. You can find the requirements either online or in the User Guide. They include the following specifications:

- Windows XP with Service Pack 2 or Windows Vista. No other operating systems are supported.

- 1.0 GHz processor with MMX or equivalent

- 1GB RAM

- 350 MB of available hard disk space

- A video card that is compatible with Microsoft DirectX 9 technology and with 256 MB or more of RAM

To make sure both Blend and the .NET 3.0 framework work at an optimal level you need to make sure you have a graphics driver installed that is compatible. A driver more recent than November 1, 2004 is recommended. In Windows XP, open the Control panel, double-click Display, click the Settings tab, and make sure Highest (32 bit) is selected. Click Advanced, click the Adapter tab, and click Properties. Check the driver date on the Properties tab to make sure it is later than 11/1/2004. If it is not, you need to upgrade your video drivers. On Windows Vista, the steps are similar but slightly different:

1. Click Start, choose Settings, and then choose Control Panel.

2. When the Control Panel opens, click Adjust screen resolution under the Appearance and Personalization heading.

3. When Display Settings opens, make sure Highest (32 bit) is selected under Colors.

4. Click the Advanced Settings button.

5. When the Properties sheet opens, on the Adapter tab, click Properties. If the User Account Control dialog box appears, click Continue.

6. When the next Properties sheet shown in Figure 13.1 appears, click the date next to Driver Date. If the date is earlier than 11/1/2004, click Update Driver and follow the steps shown on subsequent screens.

Note: Of course, in order to use the User Guide, you need to have installed the software already; if you have problems running Blend—if it runs slowly, for instance—search for the Setting up your computer topic to review the requirements.

Windows Presentation Foundation

Windows Presentation Foundation, or WPF, is the technology that allows you to create user experiences with Blend. WPF is an integral part of the Windows Vista operating system. You can make use of WPF even if you don't have Vista, as long as you download the .NET 3.0 technology from Microsoft's Web site. WPF lets you work with animation and high-quality graphics in Blend.

Figure 13.1   Make sure your graphics driver is up to date.

Tip: Go to the Download Center, http://www.microsoft.com/downloads/Search. aspx?displaylang=en, and search for .NET 3.0. Follow the instructions in subsequent screens to download and install this software framework.

What's Behind the Scenes

You don't have to be a programmer to use Blend—but it helps. Even if you don't know how to use the XML markup language or C# programming language, you'll benefit from at least knowing a little bit about them because you'll hear about them in the documentation. Three technologies work behind the scenes to enable Blend to work:

- XAML. XAML, or eXtensible Application Markup Language, was introduced in the preceding chapter. You can export images from Expression Design as XAML files and open them in Blend so you can add them to your presentations. It's similar to Extensible Markup Language (XML).

- C# or C Sharp. This language is the code behind Blend. Visual Basic can also be used, but some observers believe C# is the more popular one these days.

- .NET 3.0 framework. This technology lets you work with Application Programming Interfaces (APIs) in Blend.

Three applications currently take advantage of Windows Presentation Foundation: Visual Studio 2005, Expression Blend, and Expression Design. You can use Visual Studio 2005 to hand-code the XAML you create with Blend, if you need to make changes by hand.

Note: Third-party tools also exist for working with designs and presentations in WPF. ZAM 3D, created by Electric Rain, lets you create 3-D content for the WPF. Adobe Illustrator by Adobe Systems has a XAML plug-in. Adobe Photoshop also lets you work with XAML. If you don't have Expression Design or are more used to working with Illustrator or Photoshop, you can use the XAML plug-in to generate images or other content for your Blend presentations.

Silverlight

Silverlight is a plug-in application that works with Web browsers on different platforms (Mac and Windows) and that lets browsers display movie content similar to Adobe's Flash player. Silverlight is more than simply a player, however. You can program Silverlight applications—the applications that are played by the Silverlight plug-in—if you know XAML and WPF. Silverlight is being promoted by Microsoft as a tool for providing video content on the Web that can be played by Web browsers.

If you want to use Blend to create content for Silverlight, you need to take into account features that aren't supported in Silverlight that are supported in the WPF, such as 3D. Full support for Silverlight is expected to be included by all Expression suite applications but at the time this book was written, support was limited in Blend. To find out more about Silverlight, go to http://www.microsoft.com/silverlight.

Note: Silverlight was originally called WPF/E or Windows Presentation Foundation/Everywhere. It's only important to know this because you still might see references to WPF/E on the Web or in documentation pertaining to Expression Blend.

You'll find an example of the Silverlight plug-in and how it works on Microsoft's own Web site, on the page explaining Expression Blend. You can download the plug-in quickly and begin browsing features of Blend in an interactive way. When you pass your mouse pointer over one of the tabs shown in Figure 13.2, the tab pops up. When you click on one of the tabs, the content appears to fly by quickly in a fast animation.

Figure 13.2 Silverlight functions as a plug-in that plays animated and interactive content.

Exploring the Blend Workspace

Once you install and open Blend, you'll find the work area at once familiar and at the same time strikingly different. The work environment is divided into several panels, which are grouped around a central work area. This general arrangement closely resembles that of Expression Web, the Web site design tool described in Chapters 3–7. But the look and feel of the Blend window is far darker and slicker than that of other Expression Studio applications.

When you first start up Blend, a Welcome screen appears. The Welcome screen is described in more detail in Chapter 14. For now, click Projects, click New Project, and click OK. In the dialog box that appears, choose WPF application (.exe). A new root project opens in the artboard area in the middle of the Blend workspace.

Although the artboard appears to be blank, in fact it's a root project, a WPF window. Inside of that you have a root layout, which has a grid as its default control. The fact that it's the root layout is indicated by the LayoutRoot designation, which is visible in the Window section of the Objects and Timeline section of the Interaction panel (see Figure 13.3). The grid symbol next to LayoutRoot tells you that it has a grid as its layout control.

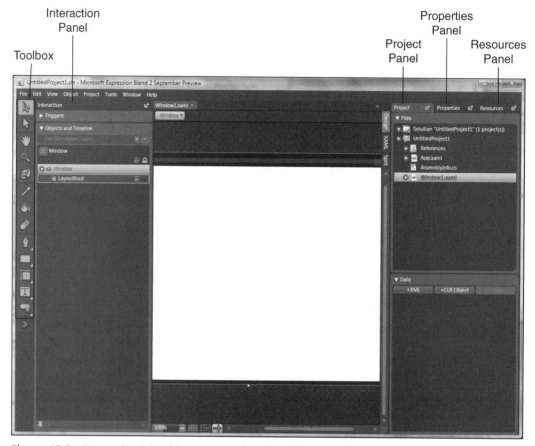

Figure 13.3 Expression Blend has a central artboard surrounded by panels.

Tip: If you don't see the Objects and Timeline section when you first open Blend, don't worry. It might be hidden by the Triggers section of the Interaction panel. Click the arrow next to Triggers to contract the section if necessary. All of the sections of the various panels can be "rolled up" and "rolled down" as they can in Design as well.

As you can see in Figure 13.3, panels can be grouped behind other panels and accessed by means of clickable tabs. The Properties and Resources tabs are grouped behind the Project panel on the right side of the window. Click on a panel's tab, and the panel jumps to the front.

Tip: You can customize the Expression Dark color scheme employed by the Blend workspace so it isn't so dark. Choose Tools > Options. When the Options dialog box opens, Workspace is chosen by Default.

Choose Expression Light from the Theme drop-down list and click OK. The other option in the Workplace section of Options is Zoom. Blend has a unique feature among Studio applications—the ability to zoom in or out of the entire workspace. By default, the zoom level is 100%. Change it to 50% and click OK, and the workspace reduces by half.

Looking Through the Toolbox

The set of tools lined up on the left side of the Blend workspace should be familiar to you from your work with Design as well as other graphics programs. The top half of the Toolbox is shown in Figure 13.4, and descriptions of the various tools are presented below. Each button in the Toolbox has a keyboard shortcut; press that key to access the button immediately:

- Selection (keyboard shortcut V). The Selection tool works like the same tool in Design: Click an object on the artboard and a selection box with handles appears around that object. Use the handles to stretch the object; click inside the box and

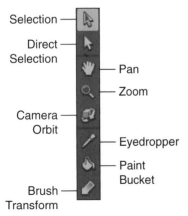

Figure 13.4 The Toolbox contains standard selection, magnification, and brush tools.

drag to move the object; hover over a corner selection handle to rotate; hold down the Shift key to constrain rotation to 45-degree angles, or maintain original proportions while stretching.

- Direct selection (keyboard shortcut A). Use this tool for fine selections—to select objects that are contained inside other objects or individual nodes or paths. (A node, as you learned in the chapters on Design, is a point on a vector path that enables it to change direction.)

- Pan (keyboard shortcut H). Click and drag to move the contents of the artboard around freely as though pushing them with your hand.

- Zoom (keyboard shortcut Z). Click to zoom in on the contents of the artboard; Alt+Click to zoom out.

- Camera orbit (keyboard shortcut C). This tool only works if you have a 3D object on screen. It enables you to "orbit" around the object to view it from different angles.

- Eyedropper (keyboard shortcut I). If you want to copy an entire object, select it and press Ctrl+C. If you want to only copy the color fill, the stroke, or the font (in the case of text), click the object with the eyedropper. Then click another object to move its qualities to the second object.

- Paint bucket (keyboard shortcut K). You might think the paint bucket fills an object with a color, but in the case of Blend, you use it to copy attributes such as colors from one object to another.

- Brush transform (keyboard shortcut B). Once you apply a fill, stroke, gradient, or level of opacity to the image currently displayed on the artboard, you can transform it using the Brush Transform tool. First, you need to choose one of the aforementioned tools. Then, click Brush Transform to change the gradient quality or other properties.

The tools in the bottom half of the Toolbox all have "fly out" sets of supplemental tools. The supplemental tools fly out in a submenu when you click and hold down on the tools. Each set is described below.

Tip: On a laptop, you have to click the topmost tool and hold down the selection button for a second to get the submenu to fly out.

---

within a border layout panel—however, if you place a grid panel within the border panel, you can then work with multiple elements.

- UniformGrid. A uniform grid differs from a grid layout panel in one respect: it always provides an equal amount of space between the contents within it. A grid's rows and columns can be resized freely, but the UniformGrid panel is uniform in its arrangement. An image catalog such as that provided by Expression Media is a good example: contents are arranged uniformly until the grid is filled.

- Viewbox. Contents are arranged in a box that you can zoom in on. You may want to place a canvas or grid panel within it; the viewbox can only contain a single element on its own.

In each case, you make use of these panels by placing elements inside them. The grids and panels within the layout panels act as containers for text, images, animations, forms, and other features. The layouts automatically resize to fit the size of the Web browser window. You can also opt to change a layout panel to a fixed size by changing its width and height to specific values.

Note: This list provides you with a brief overview of the kinds of layout panels you can add to projects. Chapter 15 will discuss working with the different panels in greater detail.

Working with Text Controls

The text button in Blend's toolbar is more advanced than the same button in Design. In Blend, you not only have the option to add text that appears in the body of a Web page but text fields that you might add to a form you are creating. When you click and hold down the Text button, you see the set of buttons shown in Figure 13.11.

Figure 13.11   Blend lets you add both simple and complex text elements.

Most of the time, you'll probably want to add a block of text to a Web page or a presentation. You do so by clicking the TextBlock control and then clicking in the artboard. Click and drag down and to the right to draw the text block. As you enter text, it wraps when it reaches the right-hand boundary of the text block. The downside is that text you enter in the text block isn't editable once you have published it; you need to spell-check it and correct it before it is published.

Font, font size, and emphasis are selected in the text section of the Properties panel, which is similar to the same feature in Design. However, there are features like bulleted paragraphs and line indenting that aren't included in Design. When you click the Show Advanced Properties arrow at the bottom of the Text section, a variety of drop-down lists appear that let you control fine aspects of the type (see Figure 13.12). The FontWeight list, for instance, lets you control just how bold type is supposed to be, for instance.

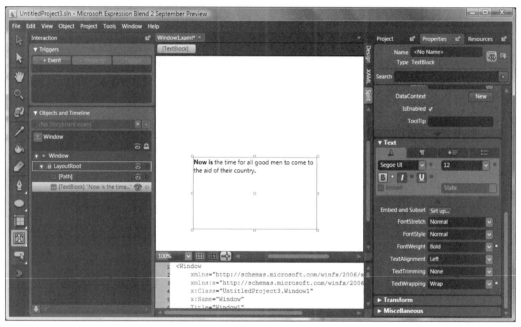

Figure 13.12 You can control stretch, style, weight, and other detailed textual attributes.

Tip: As you type text, Blend automatically spell-checks it for you. Any spellings that its built-in dictionary identifies as mistakes are highlighted with a red wavy line as you type. The feature works in a similar way to the spell-check feature in Microsoft Word. When you click a word that has been highlighted, a dialog box pops up that presents you with suggestions for corrections.

The Label control is intended to let you rate labels that are designed to go next to elements in your application such as images or animations that don't display for some reason. Click the Label button, drag a box inside the artboard and type the text for the label. If a user who is disabled or whose browser isn't adequate cannot see the object, the label lets him or her know what it is.

Other text controls let you create input fields on forms and other interactive Web pages. The TextBox control lets you create a simple text box of the sort you are probably used to entering on Web forms. When you click the TextBox button and drag the border in the artboard, then press F5 to preview the feature, a separate window pops up and you can still type text in it: the text you type in an input box such as this is editable, unlike the text in the label and TextBlock controls, which is fixed and uneditable. You can change the font, color, and other textual attributes in the Text section of the Properties panel, just as you do with simple text controls. However, because the TextBox control has a visible border around it, you can also edit the fill and other attributes (in other words, the Brush) by choosing the Border-Brush control in the Brushes section of the Properties panel.

The Rich Text Box control looks like a regular text box. But this text box lets you customize individual words and many other attributes. You can add an image or a shape to the box, for instance.

A Password Box lets you type in text that appears in the form of dots rather than regular characters. You can customize the password box by changing the foreground color and by choosing an option in the PasswordChar drop-down list, which is one of the Advanced Text Properties, if you want to use something other than the standard dot: you can enter a number, an asterisk, or any character you can type on the keyboard.

The FlowDocumentScrollViewer lets you add the most complex type of text field, one that can have vertical or horizontal scroll bars that the viewer can use to navigate text. Such a text field can also contain images or shapes. It gives the viewer a great deal of control over how to view text, and is thus perfect for showing long documents such as articles that have accompanying images as well as hyperlinks, colors, and other elements.

Tip: You can hide or show the scroll bars and attributes of FlowDocument Scroll-Viewer in the Miscellaneous section of the Properties panel.

The term FlowDocument refers to the ability of this text control to flow text around images. An example is shown in Figure 13.13.

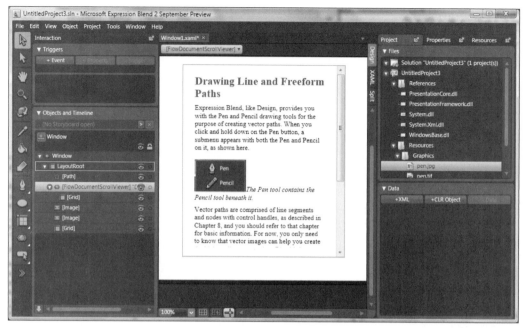

Figure 13.13 A FlowDocument lets you combine text and images in the same layout.

The text control that is included in the Toolbox by default is called FlowDocument-ScrollViewer. As the name implies, it is a viewer that comes with a built-in zoom control so someone who is viewing its contents can zoom in or out at will, or view two or more pages at a time (see Figure 13.14). There are, however, other

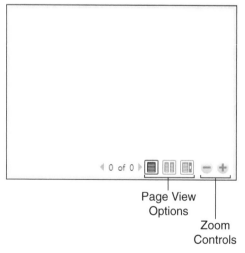

Figure 13.14 FlowDocumentScrollViewer lets viewers control how they navigate text.

FlowDocument controls you can add, such as FlowDocumentReader or Flow-DocumentPageViewer. These are included in Blend's Asset Library, which is described below.

Adding Common Controls

Controls are the basic components of the WPF applications you create with Blend. You have already examined Blend's text controls and layout controls. The Common Controls button, which is just beneath these two buttons near the bottom of the Toolbox, makes it easy to add form elements and other controls commonly used on the Web. The process is simple: when you want to add a radio button to a form, for instance, click and hold down the button that's currently shown at the top of Common Controls. Choose radio button. Click in the artboard and then drag out the space to be set aside for the control, as shown in Figure 13.15.

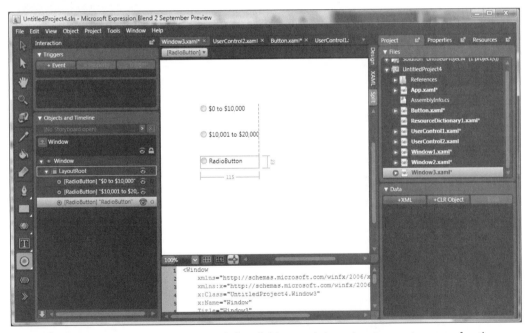

Figure 13.15 You add common controls by clicking and dragging to create space for them.

In the case of a radio button, you need to right-click it and choose Edit Text to change the generic label RadioButton. A text box opens and you can type the new label and press Enter.

Note: Often, you need to line up a series of common controls within a form. Blend helps you do this. After you draw one item, such as a check box or radio button, when you begin to draw a second such item beneath it, guides appear as red dashed lines. The guides help you line one item beneath the previous one so you can make their containers the same size. You see such a line in Figure 13.15.

Accessing the Asset Library

The set of common controls included in the Toolbox is only a small selection of all the controls included within WPF. As the name implies, they're only the most common controls you're likely to use. If you ever need to find a control that's not included under the common controls, take a look in the Asset Library. The Asset Library is accessed from the button at the bottom of the Toolbox, which appears as two greater-than symbols placed close to one another. When you click the Asset Library button, the window shown in Figure 13.16 appears.

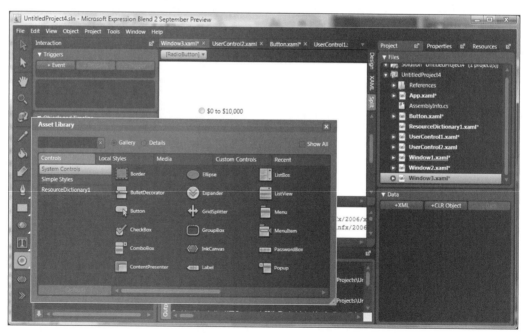

Figure 13.16 The Asset Library contains an extensive set of WPF controls.

When you first open Asset Library, the set of system controls appears. Even this isn't a complete set of controls, however. Check the box next to Show All, and you see all available system controls. An explanation of every one of these controls is beyond the scope of this chapter. However, a few controls are worth noting:

- Canvas. This is a simple container that you can use to assemble a Web page form. You can fill it with a grid or other layout control.

- Control. This generic control is used as a placeholder so you can create your own custom control.

- Document Viewer. This control gives visitors to your Web site a way to view and navigate text documents.

- Frame. This divides the Web page into HTML frames that you can fill with content and make interactive (a link in one frame can make new content appear in an adjacent frame).

- Group Box. This common frame control lets you present a group of menu options in a single box so the viewer can make a choice.

- InkCanvas. This control creates a canvas that you can draw upon in a freeform way.

You don't necessarily have to search through the Help files to find out what each control does. Pass your mouse arrow over a control and a popup message appears that contains a short explanation of its purpose. The custom controls you create are stored in the Custom Controls tab so you can access them more easily later on. When you see a control you want, single-click it, click in the artboard, and drag down and to the right to create a space for it, just as you would any other control.

Switching Workspaces

You have the option of working with not one but two different workspaces in Blend. You can choose the Design Workspace by selecting it from the Window menu or pressing F6. But since you are in the Design workspace by default, you only need to choose this option if you are in the Animation workspace. You access the Animation workspace by choosing it from the Window menu or pressing F7. The Animation workspace is discussed in more detail in Chapter 16.

Tip: If you ever need to return to the default configuration of the current workspace, choose Window > Reset Active Workspace or press Ctrl+Shift+R.

Changing Workspace Magnification

All graphics programs, and many other applications, let you zoom in and out so you get a different perspective of the contents of the artboard. Blend, however, takes zooming to a new level. You change the Workspace Zoom setting in the Options dialog box to zoom in or out of the entire work area. When you choose a Workspace Zoom setting other than 100%, the menus, panels, and other parts of the interface either expand or contract in size.

By zooming out, the workspace becomes smaller; that way, you can fit more content on your computer screen. You can either keep the artboard the same size while making panels smaller, or just the opposite (large panels, small artboard). In Figure 13.17, for instance, a 50% zoom setting shows that the presentation currently on the artboard remains the same size, but the rest of the Blend interface zooms out.

Figure 13.17   Blend lets you focus on the artboard so you get a better view of large layouts.

On the other hand, the 150% zoom setting shown in Figure 13.18 lets you see resources and brushes more clearly while providing less space for the artboard. You might want to use this view if you are keeping track of animations that are especially involved, or if you need to search through an extensive set of images, buttons, or colors stored in your resource dictionary.

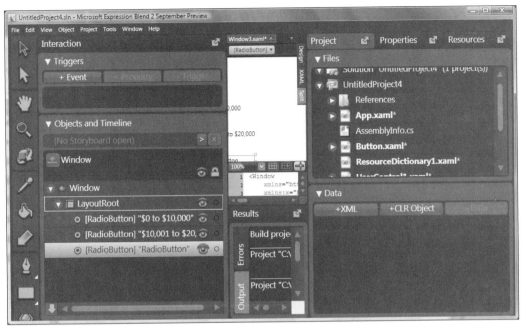

Figure 13.18   Blend lets you focus on the panels so you get a better view of tools you need to work with.

14 Managing Projects

W hen you work with Blend, you gain the capability to create a wide range of content. You can create Web page forms and other layouts, just as you can in Expression Web. You can draw images, just as you can in Design. But you can create animations and interactive presentations—two types of content you can't touch in those other applications. In fact, you can create full-fledged applications—programs that are designed to work within a Web window or play on their own. It helps to think of the overarching designation "project" when you put together many types of content in Expression Blend. In this chapter, you'll explore the components of a Blend project and different ways to manage it.

Building an Expression Blend Project

Many different types of files, folders, and programs comprise a Blend project. You track them, appropriately enough, in the Project panel. No matter whether you have a blank artboard open in the Blend window or a complex presentation, you can always find standard files in this panel. They act as the foundation for any project. Choose File > New Project, and choose one of the three possible project types: WPF Application, Control Library, or Silverlight Application. For learning purposes, it's most practical to choose WPF Application because you can build and test it while you are assembling it with Blend. A control library is used to create a control that can be used in another application. Enter a name such as TestProject or Splash-Page, and click OK. Click the Project tab to bring it to the front (see Figure 14.1).

Under the Files section of the Project panel, you see the following standard files:

- Click the arrow next to Window1.xaml and you see the file that provides the code behind the XAML document. This is literally referred to as the "code behind" document. If you chose the C# (C-Sharp) language when you first created the project, the file will have the filename extension .cs. Otherwise it will end in .vb, which stands for Visual Basic.

- AssemblyInfo.cs or AssemblyInfo.vb, a standard file used by both Blend and Visual Studio.

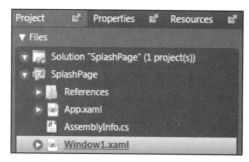

Figure 14.1 These standard files act as the foundation for any project.

- App.xaml. This is a global application file. You can edit this file if you switch to XAML View and make references into any resources or styles you need in your application using this file. Double-click the filename and click the XAML tab to view the code for the file. You can edit the App.xaml file if you need to make references to resources you need to use.

- References folder. This contains a variety of dynamic link library (DLL) files you need to make your application work. They include PresentationCore.dll, System.dll, and other files needed to make a basic Windows Presentation Foundation application work.

- Window1.xaml. This is just a default name for the XAML file you are actually looking at when you first open up a blank artboard. You can rename it MainWindow.xaml or another designation.

What's a Project, and What's a Solution? The moment you click on Blend's File menu, you'll notice that the application actually lets you work with two kinds of files: projects and solutions. Most of this chapter examines projects and how to assemble them. But what are solutions, and how do you work with them?

A *solution file* is a particular type of file that is created with Microsoft Visual Studio. Such files have the filename extension .sln. In Visual Studio, every project you work with is part of a solution, and every solution file has one or more projects associated with it. Solution files can also contain information about HTML and XML files associated with them.

The important thing to know is that Blend can open Visual Studio solution files so you can work with them. Once you have edited them, you can also save them just as you would a project file.

Working with the Project Panel

Once you have an idea of the standard files that come with a Blend project, you can start working with the Project panel to add some folders you'll need to create the assets you're likely to add.

Creating Folders

The project you're working on comes with standard files and a single References folder. But it's a good idea to create containers for the other types of files you'll be working with. Follow these steps:

1. Right-click the name of your project and choose New Folder from the context menu that appears (see Figure 14.2).

2. Right-click the New Folder item that appears in the file tree under the current project name, and then click Rename.

3. Type the name Resources and press Enter. The Resources folder is added beneath the References folder.

4. Right-click the Resources folder name and choose New Folder.

5. Right-click New Folder, choose Rename, type Controls, and press Enter. The Controls folder appears beneath the Resources folder.

6. Repeat Steps 4 and 5 to add the folders Graphics, Styles, and Video.

7. Choose File > Save to save your changes.

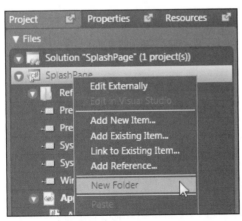

Figure 14.2 Create new folders under your project's file tree.

Four folders should now appear under the Resources folder: Controls, Graphics, Styles, and Video. These are standard folders that will be useful if you create images, controls, styles, and video files you want to add to your project. You can create any other folders you need for your project, depending on the application you're assembling. The same file and folder structure, in fact, is used by Visual Studio applications.

Note: The Styles folder isn't meant to contain Cascading Style Sheet (CSS) files of the sort used by Expression Web to create Web pages. Rather, it will contain XAML resource dictionaries—collections of styles used in a project.

Adding Resources

Once you have created containers for your project's assets—the words, images, video clips, and other contents you'll be assembling—you can add them to your project in one of two ways. You can either copy-and-paste them to the folders you've set aside, or you can link to them.

Note: Assets are different from resources, but you'll see references to both terms in Blend's interface. Assets are contained in the Asset Library; they include form elements and other common controls you can add to forms and other Web pages. Resources are features of WPF that can be used over and over again. They are accessed from the Resources panel. You can save colors, gradients, drawings, or other objects as resources; they are covered in more detail in subsequent sections of this chapter.

Copying Files

If you're used to working with Windows Explorer or the Windows file system, you can use it to locate assets you already have on your file and copy and paste or drag them into your project directly. To copy an image, video clip, or other item into your project, you first need to find the folders you created in your own file system. Since you saved the project with a filename when you first created it, the folders exist on your computer. Follow these steps:

1. Open Windows Explorer, and locate the Expression Blend Projects folder. By default, this is contained in the Expression folder. The Expression folder is located in the default location for documents you create, unless you specified a custom location for it or moved it. On Vista, this is in the Documents folder.

2. Locate the name of the project and click the arrow next to it to open the folders within the project. You should see the Resources folder you created earlier.

3. Click the arrow next to the Resources folder: You should see the folders Controls, Graphics, Styles, and Video (see Figure 14.3).

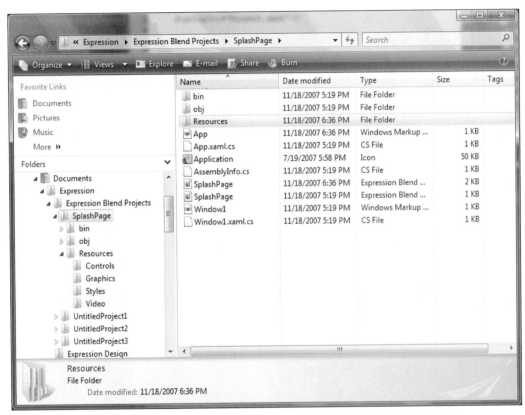

Figure 14.3 Locate your project's folders and files in Windows Explorer.

At this point, moving files into your project is straightforward: You can either select a file, press Ctrl+C to copy it, click the folder, and press Ctrl+V to paste it, or simply drag the file from its current location into your project folder.

As an alternative to Windows Explorer, you can right-click the folder you want to copy to and choose Add Existing Item from the context menu shown in Figure 14.4. (You can also choose Project > Add Existing Item.)

When the Add Existing Item dialog box appears, navigate to the file you want to add. Select the file and click Open. The file appears in the Project panel under the name of the folder to which you added it.

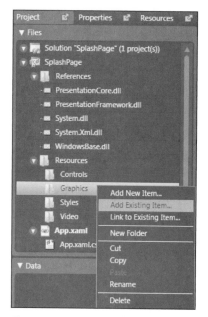

Figure 14.4 You can add an item by right-clicking the destination folder.

When you drag the file, it makes a copy and places it in the folder. But be aware that, if you move the original file from its original location, the link to it will be broken, and your project won't work. For instance, if you move a photo from the Pictures folder into the Graphics folder in your project, it will work as long as the original remains in the Pictures folder. If you move the original out of the Pictures folder, the link to the original won't be found.

Tip: You can make a shortcut to one of these folders on your desktop if you plan to work with it often. Otherwise, you can add images and other files to the appropriate folders in your project's file tree.

Linking to Files

The other way you can add a file to a project is to make a link to it. Right click the destination folder and choose Link to Existing Item from the context menu. When the Link to Existing Item dialog box appears, select the item and click Open. The item quickly appears underneath the folder to which it was added. Files that are linked have an icon with an arrow next to them. Items that have been dragged or copied into the destination folder don't have an arrow next to the icon. In Figure 14.5, the file Oryx Antelope.jpg has been linked to the original.

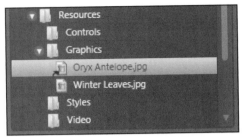

Figure 14.5 Linked files have a special icon next to their name.

Suppose you have made a link to a video clip to the Videos folder. If you then open the Videos folder in Windows Explorer, you won't see the file itself. The advantage of making links is that you can still make changes to files in Design or other applications; since you have made the link, the change will be updated in your Blend application as well.

Adding New Objects

When you right-clicked your project folder as described in both of the preceding sections, you probably noticed an item at the top of the context menu: Add New Item. If you don't have an existing item in your file system that you want to link to or copy, you can create your own item and immediately add it to the appropriate folder. Right-click the destination folder and choose Add New Item. The Add New Item dialog box shown in Figure 14.6 appears.

The choices you see in Add New Item depend on the types of templates you have installed with Blend. Since you have just started working with the application, chances are you don't have any custom templates added as yet. You see four choices: a

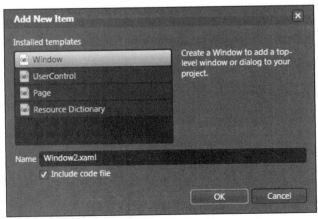

Figure 14.6 Choose the type of new item you want to add to your project.

new window, new user control, new page, or new resource directory. When you're done, click OK. The new item appears under the folder you selected.

Other Objects in the Project Panel

When it comes to managing your projects and the files contained within them, the Project panel is the place to look. You already know that the Project panel contains XAML files, .cs (C-Sharp) code-behind files, and files and folders for images, video, styles, and user controls. A few other files will appear in the Project panel, and it's important to know what they are so you can make use of them:

> **Resource dictionary.** A resource dictionary is a type of XAML file. It can contain many different types of objects, which can be saved as reusable resources. Examples include brush colors, styles, and templates. Resource dictionaries are linked to your project by means of references in the App. xaml file or in another resource dictionary file. You can have more than one resource dictionary in a project.

> **AssemblyInfo.cs.** This is one of the default files in an Expression Blend project. It contains settings for your project that are used when compiling your application, so you should not modify the file.

> **Local item.** An image, audio file, video clip, or other object can be added to a project. When it is added, the item is included in the Files list and is considered a local item.

Once you create a new project, you can configure how Blend will work with it in the future. Choose Tools > Options and click the Project tab. You see three check boxes in this version of the dialog box. The first saves new projects in the Expression Blend Projects folder, which is contained in the Microsoft Expression folder. (Alternately, you can also save projects in other locations by specifying them in the Location box that appears when you open the Create New Project dialog box.) Check the second box if you want Blend to create a temporary project every time you start up the application. The third check box defines the Grid panel as the default layout for every project; it automatically places a Grid layout as the root layout element for the project. Otherwise, the Canvas element will be used as the default element. (See Chapter 13 for brief explanations of these layout controls.)

Working with the Resources Panel

Every Blend project contains colors, patterns, or other attributes you can save and reuse as needed. You do so by designating such objects as resources. Once you have turned something into a resource, you access it through the Resources panel. For instance, suppose you fill a circle with a pattern, and you want to reuse that pattern by designating it a resource. Begin by following these steps:

1. Click File > New Project.

2. Leave WPF Application selected and type a name in the Name box.

3. Click OK.

4. Click and hold down on the Rectangle tool in the Toolbox and choose the Ellipse tool.

5. Hold down the Shift key and click and drag down and to the right to draw a circle.

6. Click Properties to bring the Properties panel to the front.

7. In the vocabulary of Blend, the pattern you apply to the circle is called a Brush. Once you create the pattern you want to reuse, click the button just beneath the Color Picker in the Properties panel. The button, which appears on the right side of the panel, is called Brush and has a plus sign (+) next to it (see Figure 14.7).

Figure 14.7   You can save a pattern as a resource.

8. Click Application to make the resource available throughout all applications you create with Blend. (You could also select the other option, Choose This document, if you want it to be available only in the current application.)

9. Click OK to close Create Brush Resource.

10. Click Resources to move to the Resources panel, and you'll see the resource listed along with any others that are available to you.

You can filter the items in the Resources panel by clicking Filter near the top of the panel and choosing the type of item you want to view (window, page, or resource dictionary). Click an item and then click Properties to change the attributes of the resource if you wish.

Changing Views

You have two distinct ways of looking at Expression Blend's artboard, and they should be familiar to you from your use of Expression Web. The difference is that instead of Code View, you have a view that is specific to the name of the code you'll be working with: XAML View. The other two views are Design View and Split View. You switch between the three by clicking the tabs just to the right of the artboard. In XAML View, you work with the code that is generated by the work you're doing. In either case, you are able to work with your project in real time.

Design View is the view you use to create projects and order sequences of objects. You have an accurate, WYSIWYG representation of your work and get a preview of how it will look. Design View conforms to the Design workspace, which includes the menus, toolbox, artboard, and various panels. You can switch to XAML View either by clicking the XAML tab or by choosing View > XAML.

In Code View, you are able to edit the XAML code for a file and build or run the file to see how it works by pressing the F5 key. When you work with XAML, individual lines of code are color-coded so you can find what you need. You can choose from several options under the Edit menu to jump to particular lines of code:

Find and Find Next. Choose Edit > Find to display the Find dialog box. Enter a command or other term in the Find box and click OK to find the next instance of the item. Choose Find Next to find the next instance, and click OK.

Replace. Choose Edit > Replace to find a term in the code and replace it with another term.

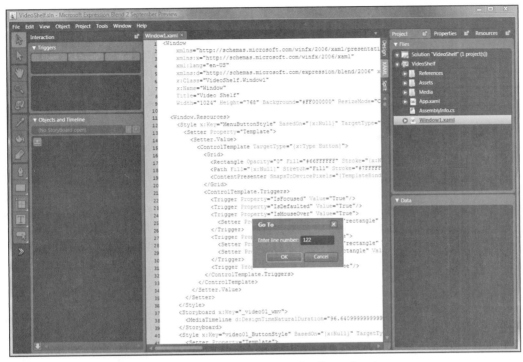

Figure 14.8 Use this dialog box to jump to a particular line of code.

Go To. Choose this option and, when the dialog box shown in Figure 14.8 appears, enter the line number and click OK to jump to that line of code.

Select All. Choose this option to select all lines of code in the file at once.

Once you bring your project into Blend, you can work with it in Visual Studio. The two tools work well together. Visual Studio has Code IntelliSense to help ensure you type the XAML commands correctly. It also has support for code refactoring: a change to code that makes it easier to read and interpret without changing the way the code actually works. Keeping the code clean makes it easier for other developers to read and faster for applications to process.

Tip: Code IntelliSense is a feature that suggests commands you're likely to use based on your initial typing. The feature is intended to ensure that you type everything correctly. Expression Web does the same thing with Web page code; see Chapters 3 through 7 on Expression Web for more information on how it works.

In case you need help working with the XAML code for your project, keep in mind that you can debug it by referring to the Results panel. You don't necessarily have to open the Results panel, though you can display the panel by choosing View > Results. If errors are detected in the XAML file, the Results panel will open automatically and display a list of problems. You see such a list in Figure 14.9.

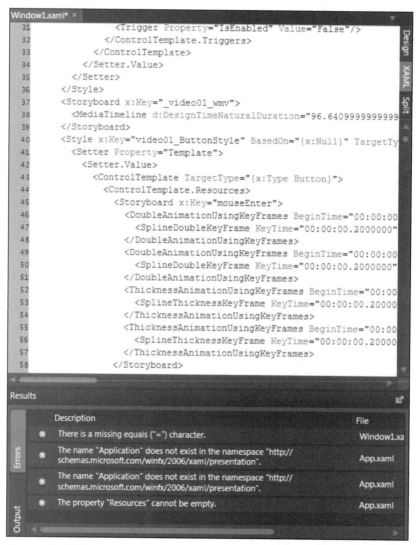

Figure 14.9 The Results panel shows any errors associated with your XAML file.

Understanding Interaction Panel

Once you have created folders to hold your resources and added the necessary files to those folders, the next step is to create a layout for your project. You do this in the Objects and Timeline section of the Interaction panel located in the left side of the Blend workspace. The Interaction panel contains controls for triggers, which are used to identify events that will trigger animations; they are discussed in Chapter 16. So is the Timeline, which is used with Animation View. But the Interaction panel also lets you do layout and manage objects.

Working with the Objects and Timeline Section

The Objects and Timeline section of the Interaction panel contains the all-important LayoutRoot section. This section gives you a visual view of your project's layout. The window positioned above LayoutRoot is the root of the current WPF application. The tiny icon next to the term LayoutRoot indicates what kind of layout control is being used; in Figure 14.10, for instance, the Grid panel is being used. All of the objects on the artboard are contained within the grid.

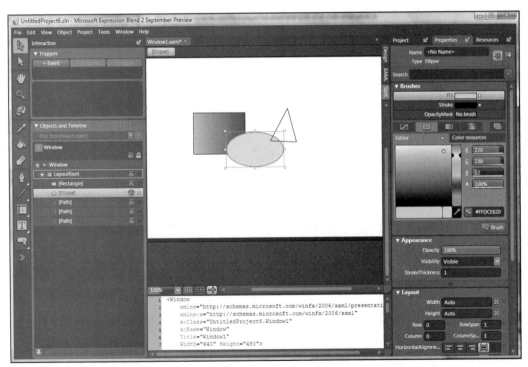

Figure 14.10 LayoutRoot indicates the layout control being used in the current project.

Any objects within the layout are arranged beneath LayoutRoot in tree fashion; click the arrow next to LayoutRoot to view them. The objects beneath LayoutRoot are roughly equivalent to the layers you learned about in Expression Design. In Design, layers let you separate contents so you can edit them individually; the Layers section lists all the layers and lets you hide, view, or rearrange them so you can get different views of your image's contents.

In Blend, the LayoutRoot list functions in much the same way. Each object listed beneath LayoutRoot has an eye icon next to it. The eye icon means that the object is currently visible. You can click the eye icon to hide the object if needed. When you click an object on the artboard to select it, it is highlighted in the tree.

Changing Stacking Order

One potentially confusing thing is that the stacking order is the reverse of what it seems. The topmost element shown on the artboard is actually last in stacking order. You can change the stacking order by clicking and dragging it to a different position. To prevent an object from being moved, you can lock it; pass the mouse arrow over what appears to be an empty area just to the right of the eye icon, and a small circle appears. This is an "unlocked" icon. Click the small circle, and it changes to a closed lock icon, which means the object has been locked in position. If you click the circle next to LayoutRoot, all of the objects in the tree are locked, as shown in Figure 14.11.

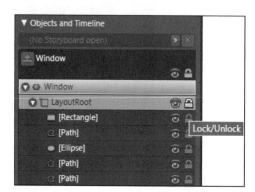

Figure 14.11 Lock an item so that its stacking order cannot be changed.

Specifying Layout Options

The default window size might not be adequate to hold the project you want to assemble. In case you need to change the size of the window, it's helpful to start with some shapes on the artboard, so either open up one of the built-in sample files (see the section "Examples of Blend Presentations," later in this chapter to find the location of the samples) or draw a rectangle or two on the artboard. Click on the window node to select it. Then follow these steps:

1. Click the Properties tab to open the Properties panel.

2. When the Properties panel opens, scroll down to the Layout section.

3. Change the Width to 1200 and press Enter.

4. Change the Height to 800 and press Enter, and see the effect on your artboard contents. As shown in Figure 14.12, they increase in size dramatically as the window grows; however, since the artboard stays the same size, you can no longer see the objects in their entirety.

5. Change all four Margin boxes from 0 to 10 and press Enter each time. Notice how the shapes on the artboard move to accommodate the margins.

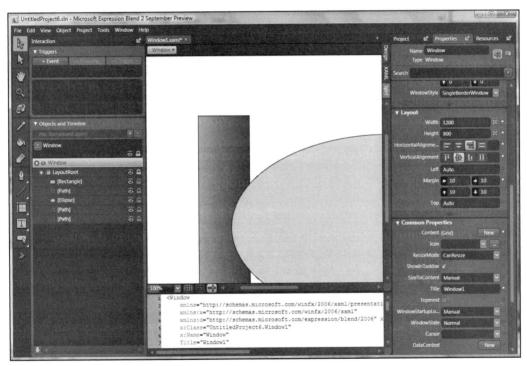

Figure 14.12   Changing the window size does not change the size of the artboard.

In order to view the contents of the project in their entirety, you can click and drag the borders of the panels to make them narrower, so the artboard has more room. You can also reduce the workspace magnification as described earlier in this chapter so the panels take up less room and the artboard has more room.

Styles and Templates

A control is an object you can add to a Web page that enables a user to interact with the page in some way. You can customize controls in many ways, including by creating templates and styles for controls, so you establish a unique and consistent look for your application.

A template defines a control's components, and a style defines the default behavior of the control. You create templates and styles by making copies of the default system styles and templates for a control (because you can't modify system styles and templates). Modifying templates and styles is an easy way to create new controls while staying in Design View and without having to work with XAML code.

Trying Out Your Project

One of Blend's best features is the ease with which you can build applications and test them out. In many cases, you only need to press the F5 key; the application builds and loads in a browser window, and you see it in a matter of seconds.

Debugging must be done through Visual Studio. Errors are reported in the Results panel and fall into three categories:

- Syntax errors

- Compilation errors

- Run-time errors

Note: If Expression Blend is interrupted, or your system crashes while you are working on a project that you haven't saved, the next time you start up Blend you'll be prompted to recover the project. You'll see a dialog box labeled Project Recovery, which gives you the option to recover the file and restore it to the state when it was last saved, discard it, or cancel the decision to restore or discard until the next time you open Blend.

Sharing Projects

Blend is intended to be used in a team environment. On a modern Web site, many different professionals will contribute, each with his own area of expertise. Writers and editors will contribute text, and designers will decide on color and background as well as the general layout. Traditionally, though, making everything work has fallen to the programmers, the people who write the code that creates user interface elements such as buttons, animations, and other features.

Using Blend as a Collaboration Tool

Blend was developed as a tool to improve workflow between designers and programmers. These two groups of professionals speak very different languages and use very different tools. In a traditional work environment, designers come up with the user interface for a Web site. They pass along a document that conveys how they want the design to look but that doesn't make the design actually function. They might create an Adobe Photoshop layout and send it to the programmers, for instance.

Working with Visual Studio

Developers have the advantage of being able to use Blend in conjunction with Visual Studio. They can use Blend to do visual XAML editing, but since Visual Studio 2005 is included with Expression Studio, and it does include a strong XAML visual editor, you can use Visual Studio, instead. For the C# files included in the Project panel, you must use Visual Studio as the editor because you can't open them with Blend at all.

Note: The 2008 version of Visual Studio, which was in beta release at the time this book was written, has an even more fully functional visual XAML editor for WPF than Visual Studio 2005. Chances are it will be released as part of Expression Studio in the future.

You can open a Blend project from within Visual Studio by choosing File > Open Project. You open the project file, which has the filename extension `.csproject` (for *C-Sharp project*). Once it opens, you see the same folder structure that appears in Blend's Project panel. You can then edit a file in either its XAML version or its C-Sharp version, depending on the language with which you are most comfortable. In fact, you can edit the same project with both Visual Studio and Blend at the same time; changes you make in Visual Studio are reflected in the same file in Blend after you save the changes.

Examples of Blend Presentations

What can you do with the Expression Blend projects you put together? The best way to answer that question is to look around the Web at examples of developers who are using the tool already. You don't have to look very far to evaluate some examples of Blend presentations. Blend itself comes with six sample files that show off the different features of the application and that you can use when you're testing out the features. They are located in the Samples folder. Samples, in turn, is located in the Blend folder, which is inside the Microsoft Expression folder. The Microsoft Expression folder is probably located in C:\Program Files, but the exact location depends on where you installed the application.

You can search for the Samples folder using Vista's slick file search feature (click the Start button and enter the term Samples in the box marked Start Search). Otherwise, from within Blend, choose File > Open Project/Solution and navigate through your file system to the Samples folder. The best way to explore the samples is to simply open them up. But here are brief descriptions that should help you find the ones you want:

> **Animation Studio.** This application lets you draw interactively: You grab a pencil and draw colored lines on the central artboard.
>
> **ColorSwatch.** This application lets you choose colors from swatches and assign them to objects in an image.
>
> **GrandPiano.** This application lets you play a virtual piano onscreen.
>
> **PhotoBook.** You can flip through a book of photos.
>
> **VideoShelf.** A series of 3D images unfolds onscreen.
>
> **Viewer3D.** A camera highlights different areas on a motorcycle.

A growing number of Expression Blend presentations are provided on the Web. One set, the Expression Blend Samples and Tutorials Gallery, is posted on the Microsoft Developer Network (http://blogs.msdn.com/expression/articles/543834.aspx) and is particularly good. You'll find others listed in Appendix B of this book.

15 Putting Together Presentations with Blend

Once you know your way around the Blend interface and have a general idea of the tools available to you, you can start putting together presentations that aren't necessarily animations but that combine multiple elements or present graphics in an eye-catching, professional way. It's a step-by-step process that Blend puts well within your reach even if you're not a programmer.

First, you need to assemble the resources you need. These can be images you use frequently for your company Web site. They can be video clips you need to post online, or color schemes you regularly apply to graphics. Then you choose the layouts that fit your needs, and adjust graphics to look the way you want. You then import the content you need to complete your presentation.

Assembling Resources

In the previous chapter, you learned how to select sophisticated layout controls like FlowControl scroll boxes. Inserting the boxes is made easy by Blend's user-friendly interface. But what do you insert into the controls so they contain content that visitors to your Web site will find compelling? You assemble objects you need and store them in as resources that you can apply easily from the Resources panel.

Before you start delving into resources, you might first wonder why you need to create them at all. After all, it would be easier if Blend had an Insert menu and you could simply add resources from your file system. As you learned in Chapter 14, the process of creating resources is similar to inserting your own files. Resources, though, are an integral feature of Windows Presentation Foundation. They enable you to name and save resources in a central location so you can reuse them as needed, much as you would with styles in Expression Web.

Note: The similarities between Web page styles and WPF resources go a step further. It's important to remember that saving an object as a resources means that you only need to update it one time, even if it is deployed in multiple locations. Suppose you have applied an image from the Graphics folder in the Resources panel in six different Web pages. If you need to change a color in the image, you do so in Resources. When the change is saved, the six linked images are updated automatically.

Most designers who work with Blend aren't working from scratch. They have already been given a style sheet or a layout that specifies certain colors and layouts that need to be used when creating pages. Resources enable you to transfer the specs to objects you need and save them so you don't have to create them over and over. Suppose your graphic designer has told you that all buttons on Web pages need to have a two-pixel-thick maroon border and a red gradient fill so they resemble your company's logo. You only need to create a button once. Follow these steps:

1. Select File > New Item or press Ctrl+N.

2. When the Add New Item dialog box appears, choose UserControl from the options shown under Installed Templates.

3. Click OK. A new XAML file, UserControl1.xaml, opens.

4. Click the Rectangle tool in the Toolbox and draw the outline of a rectangular button.

5. Click Properties to open the Properties panel, while leaving the rectangle selected.

6. In the Appearance section, change the RadiusX and RadiusY values to 12 from the default 0. Press Enter after each change. The corners of the rectangle are rounded (see Figure 15.1).

Adding a Solid Color Resource

Once you have the basic shape of your button, you can assign colors to it and save them as resources so you can apply them to other objects. Follow these steps:

1. Scroll up to the Brushes section of the Properties panel and click Stroke.

2. In the Color Picker, click a maroon color of your choice or enter the following values: R: 102, G: 19, B: 19.

3. Turn this color into a resource by clicking the double-arrow symbol next to the Hexadecimal value for this color: #FF661313.

4. When the Create Color Resource dialog box shown in Figure 15.2 appears, enter a name for this color in the Name box: MaroonStroke.

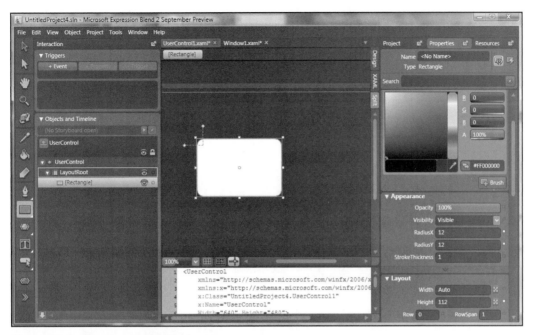

Figure 15.1   Creating a graphic button.

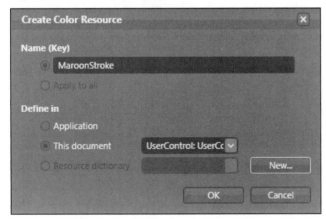

Figure 15.2   You can save a color as a resource so you can reuse it.

5. Make one of three choices from the bottom half of the Create Color Resource dialog box:

> **Application.** This stores the resource in the App.xaml file so you can access it any time you use Blend.

> **Window.** This makes the resource available to you only in the current window.

> **Resource Dictionary.** This adds the resource to a resource dictionary, a set of resources you can use.

For this example, click the New button next to Resource Dictionary. When the Add New Item dialog box shown in Figure 15.3 appears, leave the default name and click OK.

6. You return to Create Color Resource, where the Resource Dictionary option is activated. Click OK. The color MaroonStroke is added to your color resources, as listed in the Properties panel (see Figure 15.4).

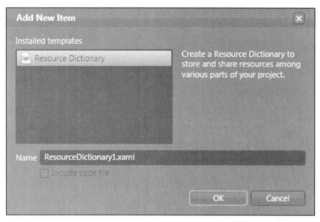

Figure 15.3 Creating a new resource dictionary for frequently used elements.

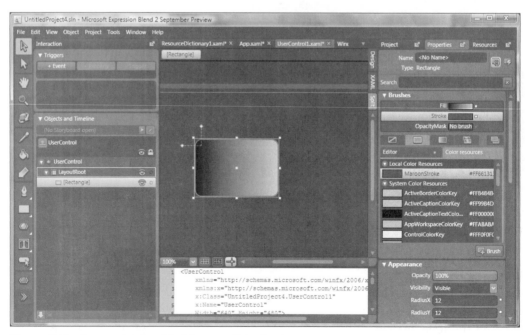

Figure 15.4 Your color is added to your list of color resources.

Adding a Gradient Color Resource

The steps involved in saving a gradient as a color resource are basically the same, but you should save the gradient as a brush color rather than a solid color. Follow these steps:

1. Scroll down to Appearance, enter 2 in the box next to StrokeThickness, and press Enter.

2. In the Brushes section, click Fill and click the Gradient Brush button.

3. Choose a light red gradient by clicking its color in the Color Picker or entering the following values: R: 218, G: 186, B: 186.

4. Turn this color into a brush resource by clicking the brush button with the plus sign next to it.

5. When the Create Brush Resource dialog box appears, enter a name for this color in the Name box: RedGradientFill.

6. Choose Resource Dictionary from the bottom half of the Create Color Resource dialog box and click OK. Since you already created a resource dictionary earlier, you don't need to click New. The color is added to your resource dictionary as a brush resource.

You can find your colors in your resource dictionary by clicking the Resources panel and clicking the arrow next to the resource dictionary ResourceDictionary1.xaml to expand it. The two colors are listed (see Figure 15.5).

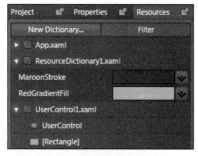

Figure 15.5 Two colors added to your project's resource dictionary.

Once colors have been added to a resource dictionary, they can easily be added to another object you create. The next time you draw a shape, it is automatically filled with the color you worked with most recently. However, you can switch colors by clicking the Resources panel, opening the resource dictionary, and clicking a color you saved earlier. You can also access the colors from the Properties panel by clicking one of brush buttons (see Figure 15.6):

- The solid color brush will let you choose the MaroonStroke color you saved earlier.

- The gradient brush button will let you choose the RedGradientFill color you saved earlier.

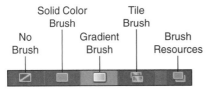

Figure 15.6   Any colors you have saved can be accessed by clicking one of the brush buttons in the Properties panel.

Adding a Drawing Brush

You can also add a drawing to a resource dictionary. Suppose you've drawn a shape that you plan to use frequently as an ornament. The shape shown in Figure 15.7 was created quickly using the Pen tool and then filling with a color.

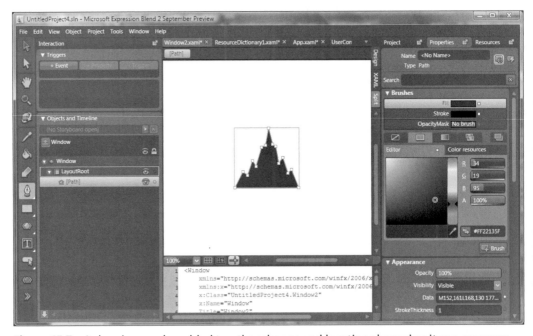

Figure 15.7   A drawing can be added to other shapes and locations by saving it as a resource.

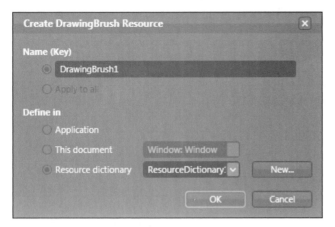

Figure 15.8   Use this dialog box to save a drawing as a brush resource.

By saving this object as a brush, you can apply it to other objects. Follow these steps to turn this drawing into a brush resource:

1. Choose Tools > Make Brush Resource > Make Drawing Brush Resource. The Create DrawingBrush Resource dialog box shown in Figure 15.8 appears.

2. Click Resource Dictionary and click OK. A small preview of the image is added to the resource dictionary.

3. Draw another shape on the artboard, such as a rectangle, and leave it selected. Click Fill and choose No Brush to delete the solid color fill.

4. In the Properties tab, under Brushes, click the small square on the right side of the Fill button. (When you pass your mouse over the rectangle, a tool tip labeled Advanced Property Options appears.)

5. From the context menu that appears, choose Local Resource.

6. Click the drawing brush you just created. The drawing is used as a fill within the new shape (see Figure 15.9).

Once you add resources to a dictionary, you can open the dictionary and inspect it in XAML View. The names of all the resources you added, along with their properties, are listed in the XAML file. You can change the properties there if you wish.

Tip: The button shape you drew earlier in this section can be added as a template. Doing so enables you to add it quickly later on. Click Options > Edit Control Parts (Template) > Edit a Copy. When the Create Style Resource dialog box appears, assign the button a name, click Resource Dictionary, and click OK.

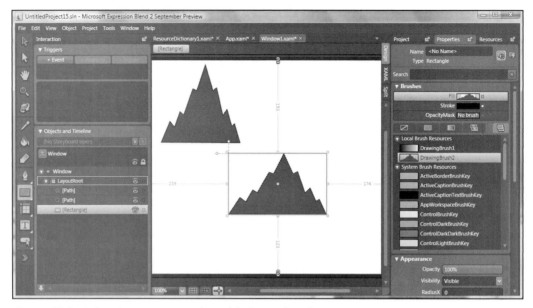

Figure 15.9 A brush resource can be added to other shapes.

Choosing Layout Controls

Chapter 15 introduced you to the various layout controls available in Blend's Toolbox. This section will look at the most popular ones in more detail because they're the ones you are likely to use. You'll learn how to insert each one, how to change its configuration in the Properties panel, and how to incorporate it with other user controls and extra layout panels.

Working with the Grid

The Grid layout control is the one used by default when you create a project, so you don't have to do anything to create the grid; you have it in your artboard already. If you want to start with a new window so you can try out a grid, choose File > New Item. When the Add New Item dialog box appears, leave Window selected, and click OK. When the new blank window opens, close any other panels that might be open in the center of the Blend workspace, such as the Results panel, by deselecting them from the Window menu. Click the Design tab on the right side of the central workspace to switch to Design View. Be sure to scroll up so you see the top of the window. You should be able to see the label Window1 (or Window2, or Window3, depending on how many windows you have open) at the top.

Make sure the selection tool is active in the Toolbox. Hover the mouse pointer over the blue bar behind the label Window1 to produce a gold line with a triangle at the top. Click anywhere in the window to place a blue line there. This is a grid splitter; it divides the window into rows and columns (see Figure 15.10).

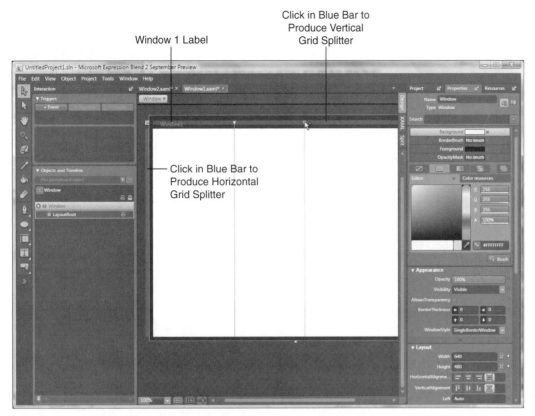

Figure 15.10   Grid splitters are used to define panels within your grid.

Click in the blue bar just to the left of the window to add a vertical grid splitter. Grid splitters can be moved freely around so the grid can be reconfigured. You can, for example, divide a window into two columns by adding two vertical grid splitters and two rows by adding horizontal ones. The result is shown in Figure 15.11.

Resizing and Locking Grid Components

If you want to delete a column, double-click the arrow just above it. Grid splitters can be placed anywhere in a window until you lock them. You lock them in position so they can't be moved accidentally, either by you or someone else in your design team. In order to lock grid splitters, you need to switch views. By default, when you start working on a grid you are in Canvas Layout mode. Blend tells you you're in Canvas Layout mode when you pass your pointer over the tiny grid icon in the upper-left corner of the window, at the point where the two blue bars intersect. Click the icon, and you switch to Grid Layout mode. You know you are in Grid Layout mode because of the lock icons that appear along the top and the left side of the window. When you pass your pointer over the icon, a Tooltip appears that tells you you're in Grid Layout mode as well (see Figure 15.12).

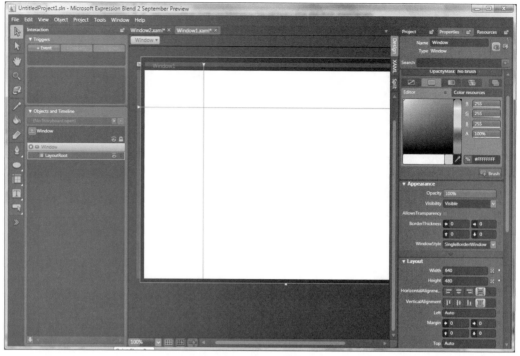

Figure 15.11 Splitters let you arrange content in rows and columns of variable size.

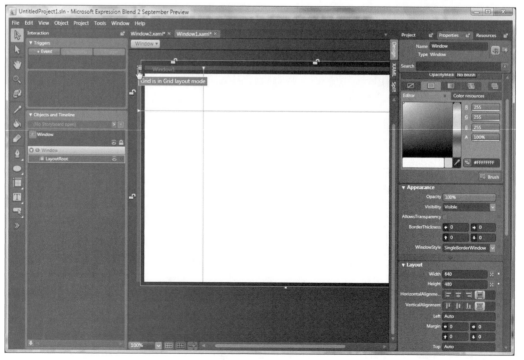

Figure 15.12 Grid Layout mode lets you lock column or row dividers into position.

The lock icon prevents the column or row beneath it from changing in size when the viewer resizes the window in which it appears. When you first switch to Grid mode, however, the lock icons are in the unlocked position, which means they aren't yet preventing rows or columns from changing in size. You can test how locking or unlocking works by following these steps:

1. Draw a single column and single row in the current window.

2. Draw a rectangle in the space created by the intersection of the row and column grid splitters.

3. Press F5 to preview the page.

4. When the application is built and a new window opens, resize the new window.

On an application in which rows and columns are still unlocked, you resize the window and the columns and rows expand in size accordingly. In Figure 15.13, for instance, you see the project with its original configuration in the Blend window,

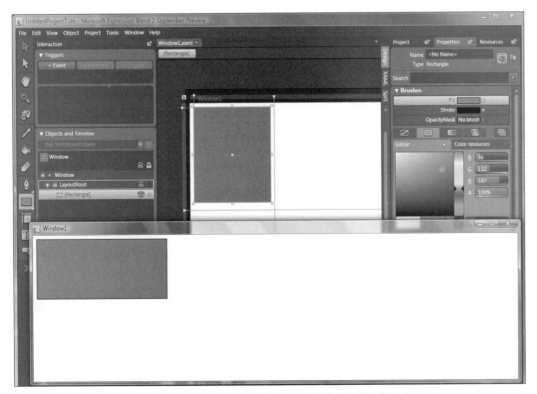

Figure 15.13 Columns that are unlocked can be resized freely by the viewer.

while in front, a preview window appears. The preview window has been elongated and made narrower to show how flexible columns are. The rectangle you drew also becomes narrow and longer.

To see what happens when columns and rows are locked, close the preview window. Then single-click the lock icon in the top border of a window and it changes to locked position. Press F5 to build the application and open the preview window. Then resize the window as you did before. When it's locked, the adjacent column is fixed at the current number of pixels in width. When you lock the column and try to resize it in the preview window, the rectangle doesn't change in width, though it does change in height (see Figure 15.14).

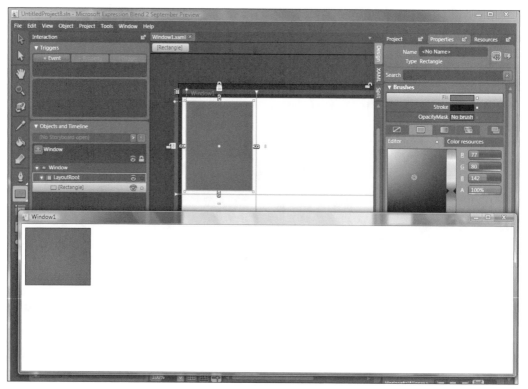

Figure 15.14 Columns that are locked remain at a fixed pixel width.

Similarly, when you lock a row by clicking one of the lock icons on the left side of the window, the adjacent row is fixed in height. Locks have two modes:

> **Star-sized.** The row or column is measured in star-sized proportions.

> **Pixel-sized.** The row or column is a fixed pixel width.

Every time you pass your mouse over the blue bar at the top left side of the window and click when the gold arrow appears, you create a grid splitter, and a lock icon is created as well. The lock controls the size of the row or column you just created.

Tip: At any point, you can press F5 to build your application and display it in a preview window. If you see a message stating that the application cannot be previewed because it is running, wait a few seconds until the process is finished. If that doesn't work, you might have to close and reopen the application so that you can then preview it.

Adjusting Layout

Once you have a grid looking the way you want and the rows and columns fixed, you can add content to it. You can draw within each of the "cells" (the spaces between the splitters) or add content you have saved in the Resources panel. If you draw a rectangle within one cell, you'll find that it won't able to "bleed over" into the adjacent cell; the borders constrain its size.

You can change the size, border, or other properties associated with a grid by single-clicking anywhere within it. When you click, the Properties panel appears. The Layout section lets you change the following general properties of items you add to the grid:

> **Size.** The Height and Width boxes control the overall size of the window that contains the grid.

> **Alignment.** The HorizontalAlignment and VerticalAlignment boxes let you control the alignment of contents within the table cells.

> **Margins.** These let you control the margins between the cell contents and the grid splitters.

For instance, if you draw a rectangle in one of the grid cells and leave that rectangle selected, the margins around it are reflected in the four Margin boxes near the bottom of the Layout section. You can change the margins around the rectangle by entering new values. If you change all of the margins to 0, the rectangle fills the cell completely.

Tip: As an alternative to entering 0 for the Width and Height boxes, you could also type Auto or click the Set to Auto button just to the right of the Width or Height field. Auto causes the width and height to be automatically determined by the size of the browser window in which the current application is displayed.

You can even move the rectangle to a different row or column by entering values in the Row and Column boxes. Suppose you have the grid divided into six cells, and you draw a rectangle in the cell on the top. When you enter 1 in the Row column, the rectangle jumps down one row. When you enter 2 in the column, it jumps over two columns.

Tip: When positioning rows and columns in a grid, remember that the numbering starts at zero. The cell in the upper-left corner of the grid is at row 0, column 0. When you move an object one column to the right, you are at row 0, column 1. This numbering system applies not only to the current grid but to the Uniform Grid layout control, too.

When you click the Show Advanced Properties arrow at the bottom of the Layout section, a new set of options appears:

HorizontalScrollBar. Controls whether the horizontal scrollbar should be displayed or not.

VerticalScrollbar. Controls whether the vertical scrollbar should be displayed or not.

GridIsSharedSizeScope. Check this box if multiple elements should share the same size settings.

MaxHeight. Sets a maximum height for the selected object.

MaxWidth. Sets a maximum width for the selected object.

MinHeight. Sets a minimum height for the selected object.

MinWidth. Sets a minimum width for the selected object.

ScrollViewer. CanContentScroll. Enables a specialized set of objects (those that support the IScrollInfo interface) to scroll the window.

The Common Properties section lets you control more detailed aspects of the window. (Make sure you do not have an object currently selected, so you can see all of these options.):

Icon. You can identify an image to use as an icon along with the title bar of the window.

ResizeMode. Controls whether the viewer can resize the window or not.

ShowInTaskbar. Check this box if you want the window to have a taskbar button.

SizeToContent. Specify whether or not the window will automatically resize to fit its content.

Title. Lets you specify a title for the window.

Topmost. If you want the window to appear at the top (if you have other windows beneath it), check this box.

WindowStartupLocation. If you wish, you can specify the location of the window when it is first opened.

WindowState. Specifies whether or not a window is normal, minimized, or maximized.

Cursor. Specifies how the cursor appears when it hovers over the selected object. Options include an I-beam, cross, arrow, and many others.

DataContext. If the data within the window is to be associated with another parent element, specify the element here.

IsEnabled. Specifies whether or not the item is enabled in the user interface.

ToolTip. If you want the selected object to have a Tooltip, type it in this box.

The Text section of the Properties panel controls the font, font size, and alignment of the text you add to the grid.

Tip: The options shown in Common Properties are common to all layout controls, not just the Grid.

WrapPanel

Expression Blend uses a grid for LayoutRoot by default. You can change the layout control at any time by right-clicking LayoutRoot and choosing Change Layout Type. To more clearly see the difference between the different layouts, draw a circle and two squares in the artboard, or a series of shapes such as circles. You can then choose one of the controls from the context menu that appears, as shown in Figure 15.15.

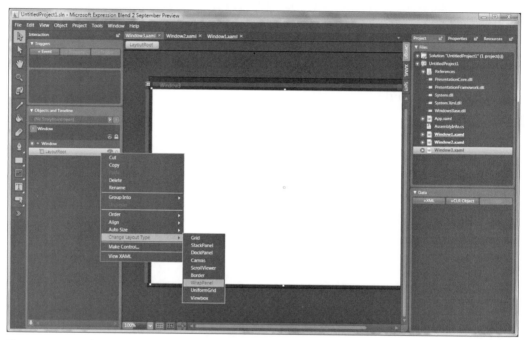

Figure 15.15 Change layout controls using this submenu.

When you choose the WrapPanel layout control, the contents wrap to a new column or row when they reach a boundary. That boundary can be either a column or row divider or the edge of the window. The obvious example is text that reaches the edge of the Wrap panel and then wraps to the next line. Whenever the application is resized by the viewer (by resizing the window in which it is presented), the contents wrap interactively.

Virtually any kind of object can be contained in the WrapPanel, and what's more, the wrap can take place vertically as well as horizontally. In Figure 15.16, a series of ellipses has been stacked vertically; when the stack reaches the bottom of the window, it wraps up to the top again.

Whether the wrap is horizontal or vertical is determined by an option that's specific to WrapPanel but not all other layout controls. Choose either Vertical or Horizontal

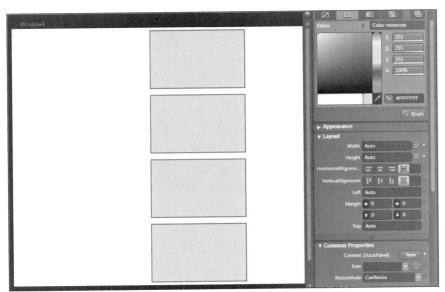

Figure 15.20 Set the window height and width to Auto so the size conforms to the contents.

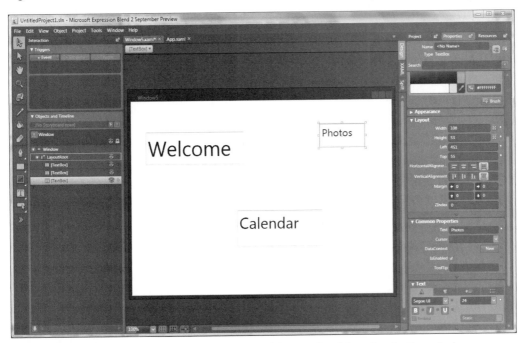

Figure 15.21 Objects on a Canvas can be placed in any fixed location in the window.

each time you draw a shape, its size and location are automatically displayed in the Layout section of the Properties panel. As shown in Figure 15.21, the Width and Height boxes display the size, and the Left and Top boxes indicate the position.

The Left box corresponds to the X setting of the object; if you change the value in the box, the object will move to the right or left. If you change the value in the Top box, the object will move up or down because this box corresponds to the Y setting.

Tip: Rather than typing a number in the Left or Top box and then pressing Enter to change the location of the object, simply "wipe" across the box by clicking and dragging your mouse pointer to the left or right. When you move to the right, the value increases, and the object moves either right or up. When you move to the left, the value decreases (it will actually go into a negative value), and the object moves to the left or down. It's a quick and interactive way to change the object's position in the window.

Because the objects on a Canvas layout are absolutely positioned, when you press F5 and resize the preview window, they'll stay in one place. You can also click and drag containers around on the window; as the boundaries of one object pass by another, red snaplines appear when the objects are aligned (that is, as long as you have the Snap to Snaplines option checked in the Artboard section of the Options dialog box). If you release the object while one of the red lines is visible, it will be in alignment with adjacent containers. You can also choose Tools > Options, click Artboard, and check the boxes next to Show Snap Grid and Turn on Snaping to Gridlines (see Figure 15.22). You can also align objects by choosing options from the Align submenu of the Object menu.

It's important to remember, in other words, that although you can move around objects on a canvas freely, when the application is actually built and the layout is displayed in a browser window, the objects won't be able to be moved around because they are fixed in the most recent X and Y positions you set.

UniformGrid

In a UniformGrid layout, the objects are spaced out uniformly in the window. The objects all have the same amount of space, so together they create a uniform grid. Perhaps the best way to learn how the UniformGrid layout works is to right-click LayoutRoot and choose it from the Change Layout Type submenu. Then follow these steps:

1. Click the Rectangle button in the Toolbox and draw a rectangle anywhere in the window—perhaps near a corner of the window. As you can see, the first rectangle appears in the center, not in the corner where you clicked.

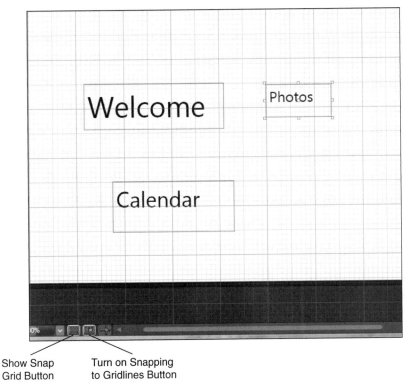

Show Snap   Turn on Snapping
Grid Button   to Gridlines Button

Figure 15.22 Use the grid to help you align objects on the canvas or another layout.

2. Draw a second rectangle in another corner; the first rectangle jumps up so the two rectangles are aligned horizontally.

3. Keep drawing rectangles and notice the pattern that develops: No matter what size you make the rectangles, they are arranged in the form of a grid and spaced uniformly, in accordance with the name of the UniformGrid layout (see Figure 15.23).

The grid in the UniformGrid layout isn't fixed, however. You can move any one of the objects around by clicking and dragging it or by changing the settings in the Margins boxes, just as you can in the Canvas layout. The grid gives you a general guideline for how objects can be arranged in a uniform way. When you move one of the objects in the grid individually, others aren't affected (unless you select them at the same time).

While the Grid panel arranges items in the form of rows and columns, you have to adjust the space between its objects manually. In a UniformGrid panel, everything is

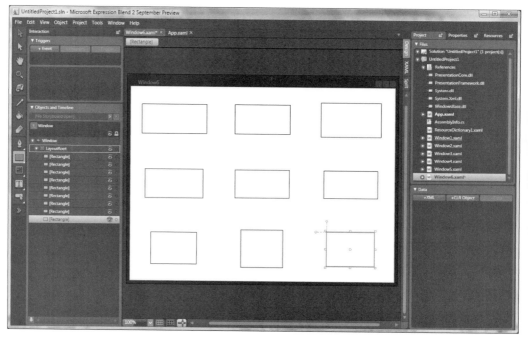

Figure 15.23   Objects you add to this layout are automatically arranged in grid format.

spaced out uniformly to begin with, which saves you time. The Common Properties section of the Properties panel contains options that apply to the UniformGrid (see Figure 15.24). You can change the number of rows and columns if you wish.

Figure 15.24   You can adjust the number of rows and columns in the grid and move items around freely.

Tip: Make sure you select the LayoutRoot option if you want to adjust the number of rows and columns. The Rows, Columns, and FirstColumn items don't appear in Common Properties when you have an object selected in the Uniform-Grid layout or even when the Window item is selected. When Window is selected, a different set of options appears in CommonProperties.

ScrollViewer

When you were trying out the StackPanel layout control earlier in this chapter, you may well have asked yourself a question like this: What if I have 30 items stacked all in a line that takes up 10 inches or more of space? How can all of that content fit in a single browser window? Unless the viewer has a large monitor, all of that content can't fit in one space, of course.

The solution is to place the StackPanel layout within another layout control called ScrollViewer. ScrollViewer accepts only a single element within it, so it makes sense to add another layout panel such as a Canvas, Grid, or StackPanel. The ScrollViewer will let viewers scroll through content (see Figure 15.25).

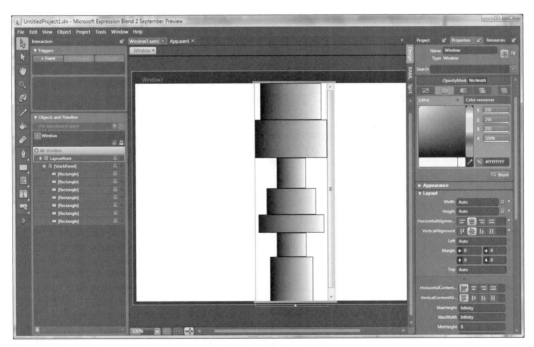

Figure 15.25   Insert a layout panel within the ScrollViewer so contents can be viewed by scrolling.

Once you have created the ScrollViewer by right-clicking Layout Root and choosing it from the Change Layout Type submenu, a scrollbar appears along the right edge of the window. To add another layout control inside the ScrollViewer, select it from the Toolbox. Then click and drag inside the ScrollViewer window to create the outlines of the new layout panel. Once you release the mouse button, you can resize the layout panel by clicking and dragging its handles. The name of the new layout panel (for instance, StackPanel), should appear inside the ScrollViewer window. You can then add content to the new layout panel as described earlier in this chapter.

Note: A ScrollViewer can have horizontal as well as vertical scrollbars. You can control which scrollbars appear, and under what circumstances they appear, by clicking LayoutRoot and then clicking Show Advanced Properties at the bottom of the Layout section in the Properties panel. The HorizontalScrollBarVisibility and VerticalScrollBarVisibility drop-down menus each have four options: Disabled means the scrollbar is never visible; Auto means the scrollbar's visibility depends on the content; Hidden means the scrollbar is never visible; and Visible means it is always visible, whether the content needs a scrollbar or not.

Adding a Border

If you want to enclose an entire layout panel and its contents in a border whose color, thickness, and other visual attributes you can configure, use the Border layout. When you right-click LayoutRoot and choose Border from the Change Layout Type submenu, the Border layout is added. You can then insert another layout panel, such as Canvas, inside of the Border layout.

You gain the ability to configure the size, color, and type of the border when you choose Window in the Objects and Timeline section of the Interaction panel. Expand the Appearance section, and you can change a number of border settings:

Opacity. This controls how solid the border is.

Visibility. You can enable or disable the border's visibility for test purposes if you want to.

BorderThickness. Change the values to change the border thickness in pixels.

CornerRadius. You can specify how rounded the corners of the border are going to be. The default, 0,0,0,0, means none of the four corners is rounded.

the layout control into which the objects were grouped previously disappears from beneath LayoutRoot.

Note: When you group objects into a layout control that forces a change in the relative positions of those objects, such as a StackPanel, the process of ungrouping the objects works differently. When you group three widely spaced objects into a StackPanel layout control, the objects fall into a single column or row. When you ungroup them, they don't jump back to their original positions. They remain stacked, and you have to place them back in their original positions manually—though you can also choose Edit > Undo several times to revert to the previous positioning.

Moving Objects Between Panels

The layout panels described are not mutually exclusive, totally separate entities. You have already learned that you can place one layout control inside another one for greater functionality. You can also move objects from one layout to another for additional flexibility. A single WPF application can have multiple layout panels within it, and often, panels are positioned within panels—a Viewbox within a Grid, a StackPanel within a Canvas, for instance.

Suppose you have a Canvas control inside a Grid, and within the Canvas, you have two objects, a CheckBox control and a square. Also in the Grid, you have a single button control that you have dragged in from the Asset Library. However, the button is not yet part of the Canvas. If you click and drag the button over the Canvas, you'll see a red dotted line appear around the Canvas. If you go a step further and try to drag the button atop the CheckBox control, the helpful note shown in Figure 15.32 appears just above the Canvas, telling you that you need to hold down the Alt key in order to drag the button into it.

When you drag one object into a layout panel such as the Canvas, you can always check to make sure that the move was made successfully by double-clicking the Canvas (or other layout panel) under LayoutRoot. When the Canvas contracts, all the objects that are now within it should disappear from the list.

When you need to move the button out of the Canvas back onto the Grid layout panel, click and hold down on the button. Then drag to move it out of the Canvas.

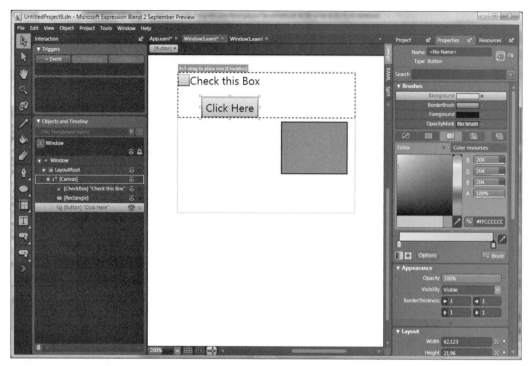

Figure 15.32   Hold down Alt and drag a control from one layout panel to another.

Note: User controls such as the SimpleSlider control mentioned earlier in this chapter give you great functionality and flexibility. The number of controls listed in the Asset Library is far more extensive than can be covered in this chapter. See Chapter 16 for more detailed descriptions of each of the controls and why you might use them.

Transformations

Once you place an object inside a layout panel, the object is hardly fixed. You can still make visual changes to it, and these are called *transformations*. This is a big word to describe something as simple as rotating an object or making it bigger or smaller. If you don't have a window open already and an object open on it, open a window now and draw a rectangle or ellipse. Then select the object. With the object selected, click the Properties tab to display the Properties panel if needed.

Click the arrow next to Transform to expand this section of the Properties panel. Then click the Show Advanced Properties arrow. The Transform panel divides into two sections, which correspond to the two types of transformations you can make:

> **RenderTransform.** These are transformations you make after the objects are positioned on the layout.

> **LayoutTransform.** These are transformations you make before the objects are positioned on the layout.

Most of the time you'll be doing RenderTransform transformations, so for now, you can click the Show Advanced Properties arrow to contract the Transformation section again. The RenderTransform section is divided into six separate sections, marked by six tabs. The tab with the plus sign (+) appears in front by default. This is the Translate section, which enables you to change an object's position by moving it along the x or y axis.

Note: The Z axis box is included in the Translate section in case you need to change the position of a 3D object. Such objects have x, y, and z axes.

Translating Position

All you need to do to change position is to change the numbers in the X and Y settings. These change the vertical or horizontal position of the object. Try it yourself: Increase or decrease the numbers for an object you have selected. Keep in mind that the numbers can go into the negative if needed.

Once you have changed the figures in the RenderTransform section, switch to XAML View by clicking the XAML tab. You'll see that a new section has been added to the XAML code for the current project. The code includes the Render-Transform settings you have just specified:

```
<Rectangle.RenderTransform>
<TransformGroup>
<ScaleTransform ScaleX="1" ScaleY="1"/>
<SkewTransform AngleX="0" AngleY="0"/>
<RotateTransform Angle="0"/>
<TranslateTransform X="-26" Y="21"/>
</TransformGroup>
</Rectangle.RenderTransform>
```

Notice that all the possible different transformations (skew, scale, rotate, translate) are listed, even though you have only performed a TranslateTransform change.

By default, any changes that you make to an object, whether they are translations are not, are made from the center of the object. The square with nine square points just to the left of the X and Z boxes in RenderTransform lets you choose an alternate point—a corner or a side. You choose the point by clicking on one of the nine small boxes. The one that is highlighted in black is the point from which the changes are made. In Figure 15.33, the point on the left side has been selected.

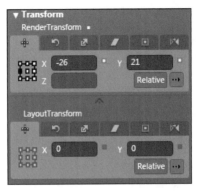

Figure 15.33 You can choose an alternate point other than the center from which to make transformations.

Rotating Objects

The second tab in RenderTransform, rotate, lets you rotate an object you have positioned. The origin point for the rotation is the center of the object, as indicated by the circle at the left of the section. You can change the origin point in one of two ways:

- Move the center point of the object on the artboard. The center point is the small circle at the center of the object.

- Switch to the translate tab and click one of the nine points on the rectangle on the left side of the tab.

One way to rotate the object is to click the visual icon at the left of the rotate tab. Click and drag the line around that points out from the center of the icon. You can also enter a numeric angle if you wish in the angle box—the box immediately to the right of the label Angle.

Scaling Objects

Scaling is the process of making an object larger or smaller. You make these changes by clicking on the scale tab, the third tab in RenderTransform. By default, the X and Y values are both 1. You might think of this as being the same as 100 percent. The value of 1 means the width and height as shown in the Layout tab are maintained as the actual size of the object. Changing either value to 2 means the scale has been changed to 200 percent and the object's size has been doubled.

You can also click and drag on an object's corner handles to scale it. When you do so, the figures in the scale tab change accordingly. Once again, you can change the center point, which determines where your scale transformations are originating.

Skewing Objects

Skewing an object means you are able to achieve some effects that make an object look like it is 3D. By clicking the skew tab (the fourth tab in RenderTransform) and changing the X and Y values, you can watch the object be skewed on either axis. This makes it look like it has been positioned in 3D space. The values can go into the negative if needed. Once again, you can click and drag the corner handles of the object and see the X and Y values change accordingly in the skew tab. If you switch to Split view, you see the following line of code:

```
<SkewTransform AngleX="0" AngleY="0"/>
```

Flipping Objects

In the Flip tab (the fifth tab in the RenderTransform panel) you can flip an object around on either the x or y axis (or, if it's a 3D object, the z axis). Click the Flip X axis box (the first box on the Flip tab) to flip the object horizontally, and click the Flip Y axis box (the second box on the tab) to flip it vertically. The Flip Z axis box is useful only if the object is 3D. Click either the x or y axis again to flip the object back to its original position. This effect is useful if you need to achieve a "reflected" effect in an application.

```
<TranslateTransform X="-26" Y="21"/>
</Rectangle.RenderTransform>
```

16 Adding User Controls and Other Content

In the previous chapter, you learned how Blend's layout controls help you arrange presentations on Web pages in a visually pleasing way. You also learned how to transform the objects you put on those pages. The capability to arrange presentations is only part of Blend's strength as a user interface design tool, however. User controls give your visitors objects with which they can interact and that make your Web sites truly compelling.

It's like rehabbing and designing the layout of a new home: Once the walls are up and the rooms finished, you need to decorate it with furniture. In this chapter, you'll explore the extensive options for furnishing your presentations with Blend. They're called *user controls*, and you'll learn how to locate, choose, insert, and customize them to make your projects truly substantive.

Working with User Controls

A user control is an object that comprises part of the interface an individual encounters when visiting a Web page or interacting with an application. You've probably used such controls dozens of times yourself while surfing the Web: You've entered a username and password, clicked a button labeled Submit, checked off a check box, or slid the volume control up and down on your computer. Controls are the fundamental components of the Windows Presentation Foundation applications you create with Blend, and the sections that follow describe the most common ones you'll want to use.

Accessing Built-In Controls

User controls are found in several places in the Blend interface. Some are found in the Toolbox; the Text tool is a control, for instance. So are shapes you draw, and so are layout panels. The Button controls found just beneath the Text controls in the Toolbox are common objects like scrollbars, sliders, and list boxes. But all of the controls are included in the Asset Library. If Blend isn't currently open, start up the program and open a new project. Then click the Asset Library button at the bottom of the Toolbox to open them. You can add a control to the artboard in one of several ways:

- Double-click the control's icon in the Toolbox (if you see it in the Toolbox).

- Click the icon and then drag it into the artboard, from either the Toolbox or the Asset Library.

- Whether the control is a shape you can draw or a button or other user interface object, you can click it and then draw its shape on the artboard.

- Double-click the control's icon in the Asset Library.

When you perform the last action in the list, the control is added to the current active element on the artboard. It's also added at the default size for the control. You can then scale, rotate, skew, or move it using the tools in the Transform section of the Properties panel.

Parents and Children Create Good Applications When you're browsing through the Blend documentation or talking to any developers you hire to create your applications, you'll hear references to "parent" and "child" elements. These terms are commonly used in programming and application development. A *parent* element is one that contains other elements. Those contained in the parent are *child* elements. Child elements inherit attributes from parents: When you draw a rectangle into a UniformGrid parent element, for example, the rectangle inherits the attribute that causes it to be arranged uniformly in the form of a grid and evenly spaced out from elements.

Try out the different options for inserting controls yourself:

1. Choose File > New Item.

2. Select Window when the Add New Item dialog box appears.

3. Click OK.

4. When the new blank window opens, double-click the Button button in the Toolbox.

A button control is added to your window at the default size determined by Blend (see Figure 16.1). The button is also docked at the upper left corner of the artboard. The corner handles can be dragged out to resize the button if needed.

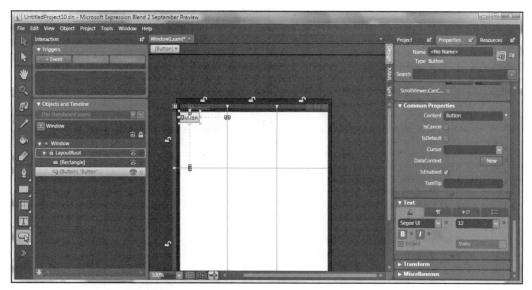

Figure 16.1   Double-click to insert a button at the default size.

Next, click the Button item in the Asset Library, hold down the mouse button, and drag it into the artboard. When the cursor passes over the artboard, it turns into an arrow to indicate that you can drop the object. When you release the mouse, the button is added at the default size. The difference between this and the double-click method is that the button you drag is not docked. It floats in the middle of the artboard or in the grid cell in which you have placed it. The difference is a subtle one, but you might find that dragging and dropping gives you more freedom over the placement of such controls.

Tip: When you click a control in the Asset Library, it is added to the Toolbox just above the Asset Library button. This enables you to add the button quickly in the future.

Browsing Controls

When you first open the Asset Library, you see a set of common WPF controls. As shown in Figure 16.2, controls are divided into several categories, which are listed under the general heading Controls. The sections that follow describe each of the categories.

When you first open up the Asset Library, you see small thumbnails of each one. When you pass your mouse pointer over a control, a Tooltip appears that tells you a little more about it (see Figure 16.3).

Search for a Control
by Keyword

Click Here for a More
Complete View of
Available Controls

Figure 16.2 Controls in the Asset Library are divided into categories so you can find them easily.

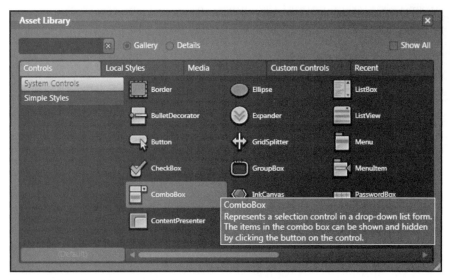

Figure 16.3 Tooltips provide both you and your visitors with more information about each control.

Viewing Details

If you want to find out more about each control without having to have your mouse positioned in a particular place, you can switch to Details View. It's one of two views listed near the top of the Asset Library. By default, you start out in Gallery View. In your haste to browse through controls in Gallery View, you might well skip over the Details View option. Click the button next to this option to view more information about each control without having to wait for a Tooltip to appear.

As you can see in Figure 16.4, the information contained in Details View is somewhat specialized: You get the location for each control in the Location column. In the case of controls that are built into Blend, the location will always be Presentation Framework. When you start creating your own custom controls, however, the Location column becomes more valuable, as it points to a location on your file system. If you ever need to make a reference to the location in a program or a XAML document, you can find it here. Similarly, the Type column gives the name of the control if you need to make a reference to it.

Figure 16.4   Details View provides you with the location of each control.

Tip: When you first choose Details View, the default size of the Asset Library prevents you from seeing all of the information in its entirety. You can't enlarge the Asset Library by clicking and dragging its sides as you can with other windows. You can click the drag bar at the lower right corner of the window to resize it, however. That way you don't have to scroll to see the contents.

Viewing by Type

The contents of the Asset Library are extensive, especially if you check the Show All box in the upper right corner of the window. When you check this box, the full selection of assets is presented. Without the box selected, you get a subset of controls that are more commonly used.

The tabs along the top of the Asset Library help group the contents into their type so you can find them more easily:

> **Local Styles.** These are any styles you have created for the current file or application. You'll learn about styles later in this chapter.
>
> **Media.** This tab contains any audio, video, or other multimedia files you have added to the current project. You'll learn about adding such files later in this chapter.
>
> **Custom Controls.** Any controls you created for the current project are located in this tab.
>
> **Recent.** Any controls you have chosen and added recently are located in this tab. If you added a button to a window as described in the preceding section, and the project is still open on your computer screen, you will see the button listed in the Recent tab of the Asset Library.

Simple Styles Controls

The most obvious controls you can work with are those that let the user submit information to you. The Simple Styles controls, which are found in the Asset Library, let you add such objects. But the objects don't come by themselves. They have the advantage of coming with extensive resource libraries that you can access for greater functionality.

For instance, if you double-click the SimpleButton object in Simple Styles in the Asset Library, the button appears in your window. But the Resources tab is filled with different brushes you can use to style the button (see Figure 16.5). You access them by clicking the arrow next to `Simple Styles.xaml`.

Beneath the brushes, you find a lengthy list of styles you can use, both for the SimpleButton control and for other controls. Simple Styles get their name because it's easy to change their colors and other visual features, using such styles and the brushes that accompany them.

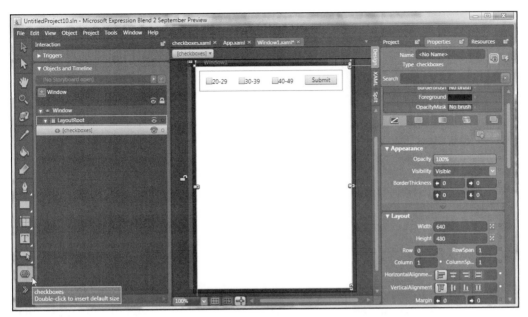

Figure 16.11   You can group frequently used elements into a UserControl.

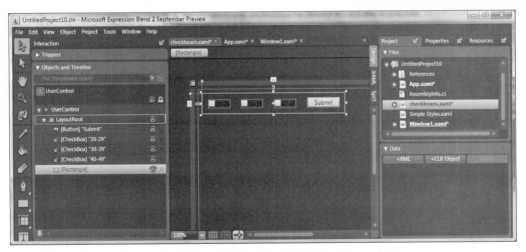

Figure 16.12   Paste the grouped items in the UserControl editing window.

6. Click OK. The UserControl name you assigned appears under your project name in the Project panel. This isn't the actual UserControl, however. You need to paste the items you copied earlier.

7. Click LayoutRoot under UserControl in the Objects and Timeline panel and press Ctrl+V to paste your grouped objects in the editing window for the UserControl as shown in Figure 16.12.

8. Press Ctrl+S to save your changes.

9. Click Window1.xaml, or the name of the window in which you created the checkboxes, and delete your original objects.

10. Press F5 to build your application so you can preview it. When the blank preview window appears, close it.

11. Click the Asset Library button.

12. When the Asset Library opens, click the Custom Controls tab. Your User-Control should be listed in the tab.

13. Double-click your UserControl to add it to the Toolbox.

14. Double-click the UserControl's name to add it to your current page. Press F5 to preview it.

Importing Multimedia Content

You learned in previous chapters that adding files to your presentations is a matter of right-clicking your project's name, choosing Add Existing Item, and adding it to your file. Blend supports a wide variety of audio files:

- AIF and AIFC

- AIFF and AU, two formats often used in Macintosh systems

- ASF

- MID and MIDI

- MP2 and MP3, the two most popular files for online audio clips

- MPA and MPE

- RMI

- WAV, WMA, and WMD, all common Windows audio file formats

As far as video files, Blend can work with formats such as:

- ASF

- AVI

- DVR-MS

- IFO

- MPEG and MPG

- VOB

- WM and WMV

If you want to work with audio or video file types other than these, you can still do so. Open the Asset Library and double-click the MediaElement control to place it in the Toolbox. You can then double-click the Toolbox button to add it to your current application. (You need to choose Show All to view MediaElement.) This control acts as a container for media files. You then make the Source property point to the media file you want to add, as described in the section "Adding Video Content," later in this chapter.

Tip: In order to preview audio or video files by playing them, you must have Windows Media Player 10 or later installed. (At the time this was written, version 11 was the latest release.) You can download the latest version of Windows Media Player at http://www.microsoft.com/windows/windowsmedia/download.

Working with Audio Files

It's just as easy to add audio or video files into your presentations as it is images. But some aspects are different. When you insert an audio or video clip by right-clicking your project and adding an existing item to the file list for that project, the Objects and Timeline section opens up a new Timeline. The Timeline lets you play the sound clip. Also, in the Triggers section, you see the Window.Loaded item under Event. This means that when the window is loaded by the viewer, this event will act as a trigger that causes the file to play. The file itself is listed in the drop-down list at the top of the Objects and Timeline section (see Figure 16.13).

In fact, if you press F5 to launch a preview window, when that window loads, the audio file will play.

Tip: If your file does not play and you see the message Timeline Recording Is Off in a gray bar at the top of the current window, click the radio button at the left of the gray bar to turn on the recording.

If you need to delete an audio or video file, you need to do several things:

1. First, right-click the file where it appears beneath LayoutRoot and choose Delete from the context menu.

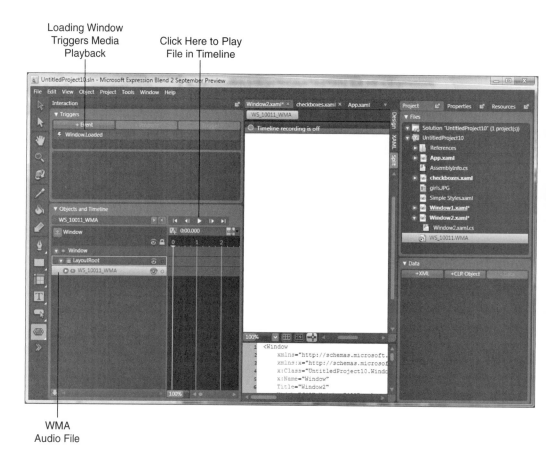

Loading Window
Triggers Media
Playback

Click Here to Play
File in Timeline

WMA
Audio File

Figure 16.13 A Timeline is created to play an audio or video file.

2. Then click the Close Storyboard button (which is marked with an X) in Objects and Timeline to close the Timeline.

3. Then click the Delete Trigger button, which is marked with a minus sign (−) in the Triggers section, to delete the Window.Loaded trigger.

You can adjust the speed and other aspects of the audio playback by expanding the Media section of the Properties panel. The SpeedRatio box controls the speed of playback. The normal playback speed is 1. If you enter 2 as the value in SpeedRatio, you double the playback speed. If you enter 0.5, the file plays at half speed.

Adding Video Content

The process of adding a video file to a presentation is similar to that for audio clips. You can right-click your project's name in the Project panel and choose Add Existing

File. But if you have a file that's not directly supported by Blend, such as the QuickTime MOV files produced by my own digital camera, you need to use the MediaElement control by accessing it from the Asset Library. Follow these steps:

1. Copy the video file to your file system.

2. Click the Asset Library button and double-click MediaElement to add it to the Toolbox.

3. Double-click the MediaElement button to add it to the current window. The MediaElement is added, with a miniature movie camera icon (see Figure 16.14).

4. Drag the lower right corner of the MediaElement icon to expand it so your video display will be bigger and easier to see.

5. Click the Choose an Image button next to Source in the Media section of the Properties panel.

6. When the Add Existing Item dialog box appears, locate the media file you want to add and then click Open. In a few seconds, the file should appear in the window (see Figure 16.15).

7. Press F5 to build the application and play the file in a separate window.

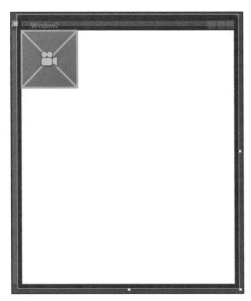

Figure 16.14   MediaElement lets you import nonsupported audio or video files.

Figure 16.15 A video clip might take up only a small part of your available artboard space.

Note: Make sure the MediaElement container is selected before you try to click Source. The Media section appears in the Properties panel only when a media file or a relevant media control is selected.

The video clip described here plays only when the preview window loads because it has been set to play in the Media section of the Properties panel. If you expand the Media section by clicking Show Advanced Properties, you'll see that the LoadedBehavior box is set to Play. This means that when the window is loaded, the file will start playing immediately. You can change this behavior by clicking the down arrow next to LoadedBehavior and choosing another option. The other options are Manual, Close, Pause, and Stop. You can also change the speed of playback by entering another value in the SpeedRatio box. The Volume control lets you turn up the volume when the file is played back.

Importing Graphics and Other Images

Blend lets you import images from Photoshop and other graphics applications easily. As long as you have the image file available on your file system, you can access it by following these steps:

1. Right-click the name of your project in the Project panel.

2. Choose Add Existing Item from the context menu.

3. When the Add Existing Item dialog box appears, locate the file you want to add and click Open. The name of the item appears in the list of files under the name of your project.

4. Double-click the filename to add the image to your current window (see Figure 16.16).

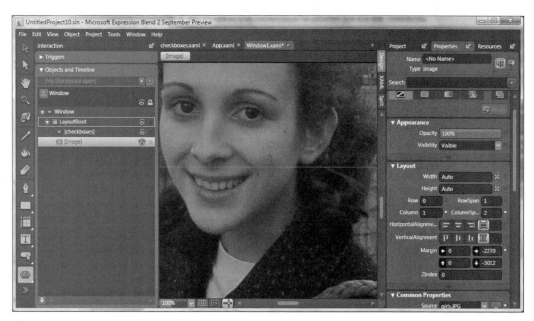

Figure 16.16   You can add any existing image to your project.

In case the image extends beyond the boundaries of the current window, check the Margin boxes in Layout. As you can see from the previous image, there are some huge negative numbers in the boxes. Change the numbers to zero, and the image will fit within the frame (see Figure 16.17).

Tip: You can also add images to a project through the Asset Library by double-clicking the Image control under System Controls. This adds a blank Image container to the window. Under Common Properties in the Properties panel, click the Choose an Image button to the right of the Source box. Locate the image you want to add and click Open. This method doesn't distort the image.

Figure 16.17   Delete negative margins to fit your photo inside the window.

Making Your Presentation Interactive

One of Blend's most popular features is its ability to make animated presentations. To make a presentation interactive, whether through animation or adding controls that the user can employ to control the presentation, you need to create a Timeline and use other critical features such as keyframes and triggers.

Creating Timelines

Rather than actually animating, the first step in creating an animation is to create a Timeline. You might find it easier to create and work with Timelines and animations by switching from the Design workspace to the Animation workspace. The Animation workspace places the Interaction panel and any Timelines within it at the bottom of the Blend window, which is a logical place to track events. To switch, choose Window > Animation Workspace or press F7.

To create a Timeline, click the arrow immediately beneath and to the right of the Objects and Timeline section heading. Then click the plus sign (+) in the dialog box that appears (it has the Tooltip Create New Timeline). When you do so, the Create Storyboard Resource dialog box shown in Figure 16.18 appears.

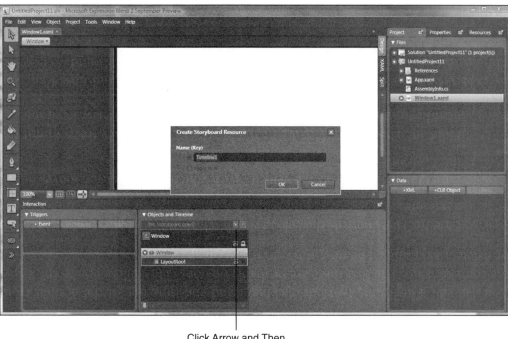

Click Arrow and Then
Plus Sign to Create
a New Storyboard

Figure 16.18   You need to create a Timeline before you create an animation.

Note: The terms "Timeline" and "storyboard" are almost interchangeable in Blend. Both describe a series of events or animations that can be saved as a single resource. The resource can then be added to a Web layout just as you would an image, a user control, or other content.

Leave the default Timeline1 name entered in the Name box and click OK. (Notice, though, that the word Key appears along with Name; the term is used in the XAML code for your project and will be important in the following section on keyframes.) The Timeline1 item is added to the Objects and Timeline section, and your work will now be contained in that Timeline. The message Timeline Recording Is On appears at the top of the window, which means that any formatting or other work you perform in the window will be recorded as part of the Timeline/story-board and then turned into an animation resource.

If you click the Triggers section of the Interaction panel to expand it, you'll see that the Window.Loaded event is listed. Click Window.Loaded to select it, and the action associated with the trigger appears beneath it: When the window is loaded, the Timeline will begin.

Tip: If you ever want to do some formatting in the window that you don't want to be part of the current Timeline, click the red radio button next to Timeline Recording Is On. The message changes accordingly and you can work "off-Timeline." Click the radio button again to turn Timeline recording back on.

The Timeline itself is broken into sections marked by vertical dividers. Each divider marks a second of time. You drag the gold divider with the arrow on top to the right or left to move along the Timeline or use the scrollbar beneath it. You can also click the Zoom box to zoom in or out of the Timeline so you can see the contents in finer detail that reaches to fractions of a second. The button in the upper right corner of the Timeline, shown in Figure 16.19, lets you activate the Snapping feature, which causes the gold bar to snap to increments of time or to dividers.

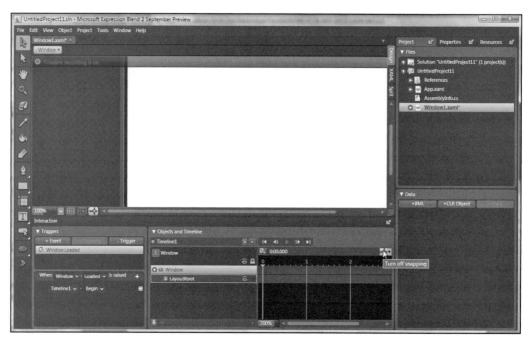

Figure 16.19 You can zoom in on the Timeline and use the Snapping feature.

Using Keyframes

Once you have created a Timeline and set it up the way you want, you can go about the task of animating by means of keyframes. A keyframe is an object on a Timeline that tells you when a change in a property has occurred to one of the objects in the window. Four kinds of keyframes can be used with Timelines:

- Object-level keyframes, which apply to an entire object, such as an entire circle.

- Compound keyframes, which means that a property that is the child of another property is being animated, such as a change in speed in an audio file.

- Simple keyframes, which refer to a single property change at a single point in time.

- Implicit keyframes, which occur when one animation is interrupted by another one.

You might be surprised to discover that keyframes can help you create animations without having to be a cartoonist. You only have to draw a simple shape; you can transform it and capture the repeated transformations in the form of keyframes, which are recorded in the Timeline you have already created. For test purposes, click the Ellipse tool in the Toolbox and draw an ellipse on the artboard. Click Properties and fill the ellipse with a color. Make sure the red line encloses the artboard and the message Timeline Recording Is On is visible.

Notice that, in the Timeline, the gold marker line has a keyframe on it; it appears as a white oval-like shape in the middle of the line. Move the gold line out to the one-second mark, which is marked by the number 1. You'll see that the keyframe does not move with it. On the artboard, move the ellipse to another spot. Another keyframe is created.

For extra visual interest, expand the Transform section in the Properties panel. Click the rotate tab and rotate the ellipse slightly. Move the gold slider to the 1.5 seconds position; move the ellipse and rotate it slightly. Keep performing this series of steps, and a series of keyframes is marked along the Timeline (see Figure 16.20). In addition, a trail of dots is left on the artboard to trace the path of the ellipse. At any time, you can preview the animation by pressing the Play button immediately above the Timeline.

Tip: You can also preview the animation by moving the gold slider back and forth in the Timeline. This enables you to test the animation in reverse as well as forward.

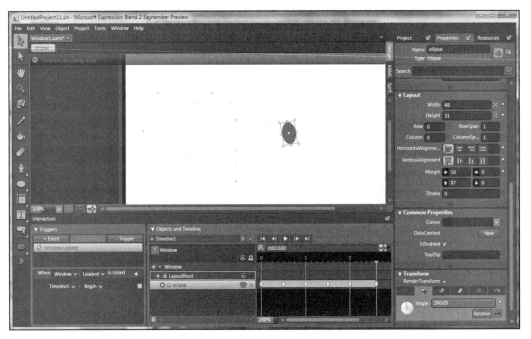

Figure 16.20 Keyframes mark the stages of an animation.

The capability to preview animations isn't just for fun. If you want to edit the animation, you can click the Record Keyframe button (the button with the green plus sign just above and to the left of the Timeline). Position the gold slider at the spot where you want the new keyframe and click Record Keyframe to add it.

You can edit a keyframe by right-clicking it and choosing one of the options from the context menu. The first three are probably obvious. They allow you to cut, copy, or delete a keyframe. The next three aren't so obvious:

> **Ease In.** This controls the velocity with which the animation moves into the keyframe.

> **Ease Out.** This controls the velocity with which the animation moves out of the keyframe.

> **Hold In.** This inserts a pause at the keyframe. The object freezes until the next keyframe is reached, at which point it jumps to the new keyframe.

By experimenting with the percentages associated with Ease In and Ease Out, you can create a more realistic sense of motion as the object moves around.

When you are done working with the storyboard, you can close it. Click the arrow next to the storyboard's name (for instance, Timeline1). Click the Close Storyboard button at the bottom of the dialog box that pops up. The Timeline clears, and you are left with the shape you began with: an ellipse with no fill.

Creating Triggers

A trigger is an event that causes another event to happen. On Web pages, it's common for an event to happen when the page is first loaded. Otherwise, when you pass your mouse arrow over an object, it might change color. When you click an object, a pop-up window might appear. You can use Blend to trigger animations of all sorts.

By default, animations such as the one you created in the preceding section are triggered when the page on which they appear launches. If you highlight the Window.Loaded trigger in the Triggers section and then click the Delete Trigger button, you'll delete the trigger for your animation. (You may need to expand the Triggers panel to see it.) Then when you load the animation in a preview window, it won't be triggered at all, and the object you drew won't move. You can give viewers a way to trigger the animation themselves by clicking a button. Follow these steps:

1. Click Window in Objects and Timeline to highlight it.

2. Click the Button button in the Toolbox and draw a button on the window.

3. With the button selected, under Common Properties, in the Content box, type an alternate label for the button, such as `Animate!`

4. Select the button again if needed and, in the Triggers panel, click the add event trigger button, which is labeled +Event.

5. In the Triggers panel, you see the following trigger and event:
    `When Window Loaded is raised`

6. Click the Button object in the visual tree in Objects and Timeline to highlight it.

7. Click the down arrow next to Window and choose Button.

8. Click the down arrow next to Loaded and choose Click. The trigger and event should now read:
    `When Button Click is raised`

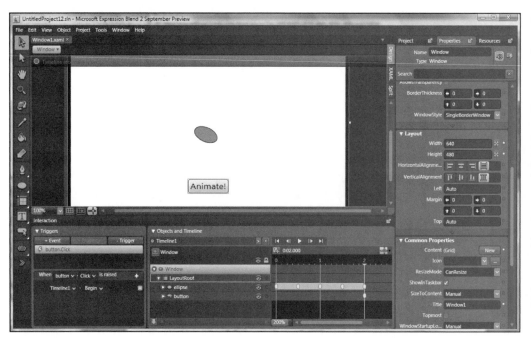

Figure 16.21 Configuring a Timeline to trigger when a button is clicked.

9.   Click the add new action plus sign (+) on the right side of the Triggers panel. The words Timeline1 Begin appear, which means that Timeline1 will begin when the trigger occurs (see Figure 16.21).

10. Press F5 to build the application and open it in a preview window. Click the button you created; the animation should run.

Motion Paths

You can draw your own paths by moving objects from one keyframe to another, but you can also make objects travel along a path as well. These motion paths are usually more graceful than the ones you draw yourself. Keep the ellipse you drew earlier, and this time, draw a circle on the artboard that is considerably larger than the ellipse. Since the circle will be your motion path, you need to select it and then choose Object > Path > Convert to Motion Path. The Choose Target for Motion Path dialog box shown in Figure 16.22 appears.

For this example, choose Ellipse and click OK. The ellipse jumps onto the circle, and a Timeline opens up (see Figure 16.23). If you kept the Timeline with the rotation

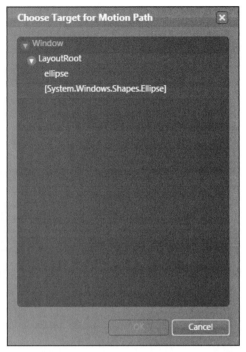

Figure 16.22   Choose the object you want to move along your motion path.

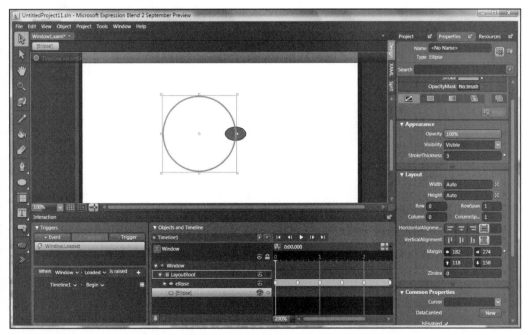

Figure 16.23   You can preview how your object moves along your chosen path.

you created in the previous section, the ellipse will move along the Timeline, past the same keyframes as before, and it will use the same rotation you built into those keyframes. If you are starting from scratch, the ellipse will move around the circle conventionally, without rotation.

Working with Data

Applications gain their real power and immediacy when you bind real-time data to them. One of the most common sources of data on the Web today is an XML data feed of a content source such as a blog. The Really Simple Syndication (RSS) format is a common way of distributing the contents of a blog to those who subscribe to it. You might want to include such a blog feed or a news feed on one of your Web pages.

The first step in using Blend to work with data is to identify an RSS feed as a data source. You do that by opening a page with an RSS feed and copying the URL of the RSS feed. At the bottom of my own blog (www.gregholden.com), there is a link enabling people to subscribe to it. This is the link:

```
http://www.gregholden.com/babylon/atom.xml
```

You can copy such links from news sources and other data sources on the Web as well. To add this link to Blend as a data source, switch to the Project tab, open the Data panel, and click the add new XML data source button, which is labeled +XML. The Add XML Data Source dialog box shown in Figure 16.24 appears.

Figure 16.24 You can identify a data source from the Web that uses XML.

In the box next to URL for XML Data, paste the URL. Then click OK. The feed is added to the Data panel. If you click the arrow next to the name of the feed (in this case, a:feed), you see the names of the data fields in the file, such as Link, Title, Tagline, and Info. You can drag any one of these bits of information

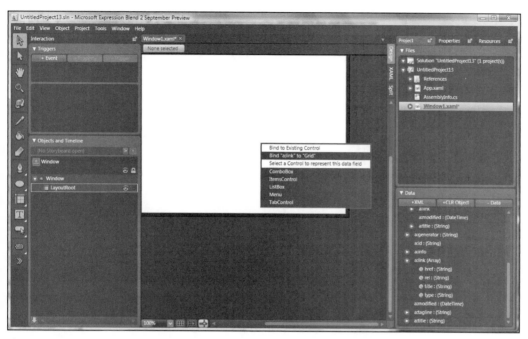

Figure 16.25   Use this window to bind data to a control or other object.

into the window, but the one labeled Array contains the most useful data. Drag it into the window, and the pop-up window shown in Figure 16.25 appears.

The two items at the top of the pop-up window, Bind to Existing Control and Bind "*Item*" to "Grid," enable you to bind data to a user interface element to a data source. Choose ListBox from the list presented in the pop-up window. The Create Data Binding dialog box appears, asking you to identify the field to which you want to bind the data. Leave the default option, ItemsSource, selected and click OK.

The next dialog box, Create Data Template, prompts you to identify the data fields you want to show in your chosen user interface element—in this case, a list box. In the Preview box, you see a preview of the data that will be displayed based on the currently selected fields—and by default, all fields are selected. Uncheck any boxes that you don't want to appear. You might only want the title to appear, for instance. By default, the items are placed in a StackPanel control, though you

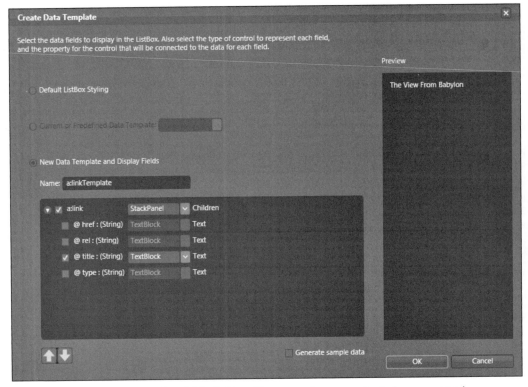

Figure 16.26 You can decide which fields will appear in your selected user control.

can change this by choosing a different option from the drop-down list next to a: link (see Figure 16.26). You could also choose a different option than the default TextBlock to present the title.

Click OK, and in a few seconds (provided you are connected to the Web) the text box appears in your window with the feed presented in it.

Managing Your Image Files with Expression Media

17 Organizing Your Image Files

I f you're like me, chances are your computer is quickly taking the place of your stack of photo albums, as well as shelves full of CDs and LPs. Not only that, but many of my family movies exist only as computer files. Home and business computers alike are becoming filled with media files in many formats. Depending on when the media files were created or downloaded, they can exist throughout your file system and be hard to locate and organize.

That's where Expression Media comes in. Media is a tool for managing your images, movies, and song files. With Media's help, you'll never lose track of a file again, and you can be better organized with your photos and other multimedia assets than ever before. This chapter presents an overview of Media and explains how Microsoft Expression Media can help small businesses and individuals organize, manipulate, and track their digital assets, such as video, graphics, and photo files.

Tip: Digital asset management (DAM) refers to the unique process of managing image and other media files. It involves a wide variety of tasks such as rating, grouping, archiving, and optimizing files so as to better streamline their integration into related projects. DAM has become an important tool for businesses wishing to reduce the cost and time expenditure required in producing media-rich services and marketing.

What Is Expression Media?

Microsoft Expression Media is a program whose primary function is cataloging digital assets as part of digital asset management. It is available for Microsoft Windows and Mac OS X operating systems and is the successor to iView MediaPro, acquired by Microsoft in June 2006. Expression Media is available as a standalone program or as part of the Expression Studio package and is slated for inclusion in the upcoming Office 2008 for Mac (iView MediaPro was originally developed for Mac, and

Expression Media, despite now being owned by Microsoft, is widely supported by users of the Mac platform).

Expression Media is a professional-level program and can support DAM for a wide variety of file formats. In addition to common file types such as JPEG and GIF, it can handle video, music, Adobe PDF and Flash, Photoshop files, and RAW image formats. Expression Media organizes and categorizes files within the program itself, so files don't all have to be in the same location on your hard drive. In fact, Expression Media can even organize files from offline discs. Expression Media will also allow you to produce various types of output, including Web galleries, prints, slideshows, and conversion between types of file formats.

Tip: Although Expression Media is slated for inclusion in the 2008 version of Office for Mac, the Expression Media Encoder, which allows video formats to be batch encoded for use on the Web, on various media player devices, and in various Windows applications, is not available for the Mac version of the product.

Getting Organized with the Organizer

Before you can start using this exciting and versatile media organization tool, you have to get organized in terms of its interface. This section will get you started with the basic features so you can use them to import and manage your media.

When you first open Expression Media, you'll notice three tabs across the top of the window. They give you three ways to view the media files you want to manage: List View, Thumbnail View, and Media View.

List View

This view presents you with a detailed list of files, along with information about their file types and when they were created. The more information you have, the better you are able to organize them. As you can see in Figure 17.1, Media gives you extensive information about each item, including:

- File Size
- File type
- Width and Height
- Duration (for audio or video files)
- Path Name

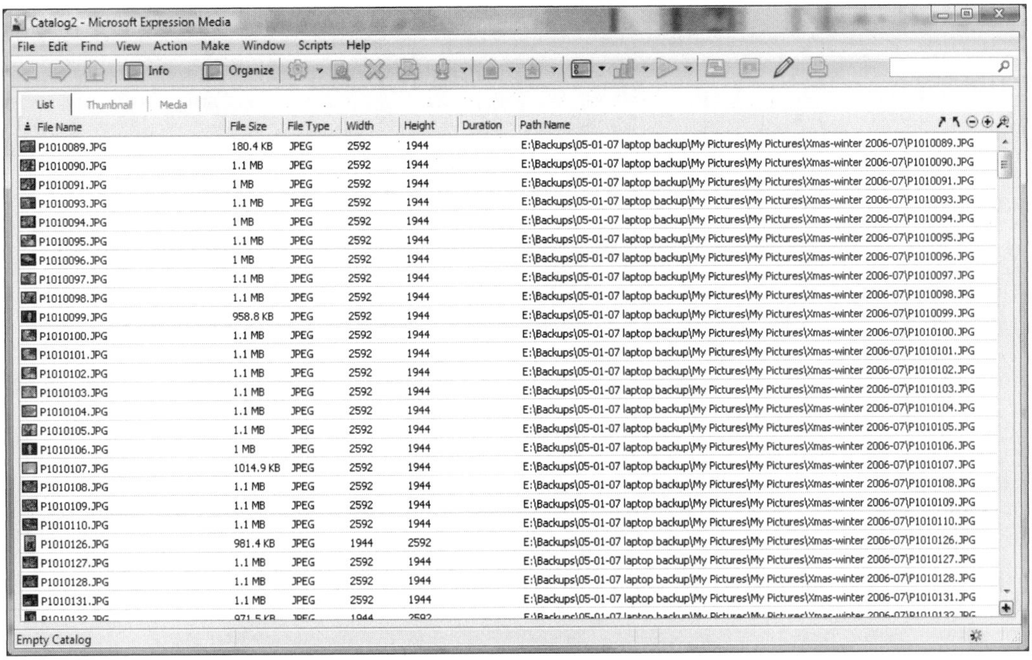

Figure 17.1   List View lets you organize by type, size, or filename.

Note: Figure 17.1 has had the Catalog Fields and Catalog Folders tabs closed for clarity. Normally these two tabs appear by default.

Thumbnail View

Sometimes a quick view of the image is needed so you know what the file contains—after all, the generic numbers created by digital cameras aren't much help in telling you what a photo actually is about. Media's thumbnails are large and clear—you might even find them to be easier to view and work with than those shown by Windows Explorer.

Click the check box beneath an image's thumbnail, and you are able to assign a color to its filename so you can organize images by color if you wish. Choose Thumbnail to view larger groups of images if you want to identify them primarily by sight (see Figure 17.2).

Media View

Media View gives you a close-up view of image files you are organizing (see Figure 17.3). Choose Media if you want to edit image files in detail. Detailed information about the size and location of each file appears in the bar immediately

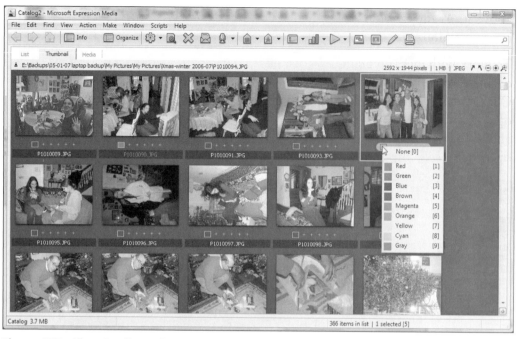

Figure 17.2   Thumbnails can be assigned color-coded labels.

Rotate   Zoom
Image   Controls

Figure 17.3   Media View lets you zoom in or rotate image files.

above it. At the far right of this bar, you see controls that enable you to rotate the image, minimize it, or zoom in or out.

To work with media, you need to open the Catalog Fields and Catalog Folders panes or open a pane that presents detailed information about a file you are working with. Click Organize in the toolbar, and the Catalog Fields and Catalog Folders panes open together (see Figure 17.4). These panes let you tag and enter information about files as described in subsequent sections. To toggle between having them open or closed, click Organize in the Media toolbar.

Figure 17.4   Catalog Fields and Catalog Folders let you enter detailed information that helps Media organize files.

If you select an image currently displayed in the main Media window and then click Info in the toolbar, the Info pane opens with detailed information about the item. You can also enter a caption in the Caption pane (see Figure 17.5). But before you can work with Media's panes and other controls, you need to import some images from your file system.

Importing Image Files

Windows Expression Media offers many ways to import photos. It can be as easy as dragging and dropping from whichever folder you choose. Expression Media differs from simple file viewing interfaces in that it can organize and tag photos once

Figure 17.5 Enter a descriptive label or phrase in the Caption pane.

imported, so you don't have to worry about importing in any particular order. That can be done later.

Tip: When first importing photos from a memory card or camera, it's a good idea to start naming right away. You might even loosely organize your photos immediately as well. It's always better to get this type of task out of the way so you can move on to other things and not have to worry about it (or forgetting about it!) later.

Understanding Catalogs

When you import files into Media, you create a catalog for them. A catalog gives you a window into a selected set of files that's different than your usual file organizers, such as Windows Explorer or My Computer. The catalogs created in Media can't be opened in My Computer or Windows Explorer, in other words. Catalogs can contain up to 128,000 assets within them. Each catalog contains lots of information you can see in the three views mentioned in the preceding section. They also contain a substantial amount of metadata that you don't see: color profiles, annotations, voice annotations, and label information.

Just because you can store 128,000 items in a catalog doesn't mean you should gather that many, of course. The actual capacity of a catalog is determined by the available space in your computer hard disks and the size of the media files. It's generally easier to work with multiple small catalog files than a large one because smaller quantities are easier to organize and label. But the number of catalogs you create and the number of items within each are completely up to you. Smaller catalogs can be gathered into larger ones for better organization as well.

Importing Images

Expression Media can import photos from the following sources:

- Files/Folders

- Digital Camera/Memory Card. You can grab images from a camera directly.

- Catalog File. You can import items from an already existing catalog file.

- URL

Media gives you a variety of ways to import files. When you first start, the dialog box shown in Figure 17.6 appears even before the Media window itself opens. It

Figure 17.6 This dialog box lets you import items when Media first starts up.

gives you the option to import files immediately so you have something to work with immediately.

If you decide not to use this dialog box and open up Media without importing, or even if you have already imported a catalog, you can always import more files by choosing File > Import Items (see Figure 17.7).

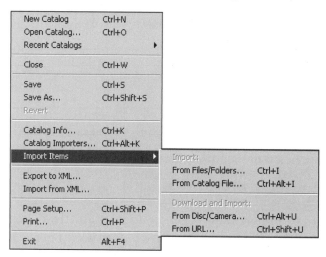

Figure 17.7   You can import files from your file system, from a disc or camera, or a URL.

Once the photos are imported, you can view them in List, Thumbnail, or Media View as described earlier. I personally find the Thumbnail View most useful in selecting large numbers of files to be moved around, dragged, or dropped. When you select an item, click the Info toolbar button and then scroll down. You will notice that there is an empty list of annotations beneath the EXIF information about the item (see Figure 17.8). This section will concern the user-generated elements of your digital asset management, which constitutes one of the primary functions of Expression Media.

Annotating as You Import

Once you create a catalog with Expression Media, you gain many options for annotating items. But you can also annotate while you are still importing. This can save you lots of time later on and keep you from mixing up the files you import from those that are already contained in a catalog and that might have similar filenames.

Suppose you want to import a group of images directly from your digital camera. You connect your camera to your computer through the USB port and make sure the camera is switched on. Open Media, and choose File > Import Items > From Disk/Camera. The Download from Disc-Camera dialog box shown in Figure 17.9 appears.

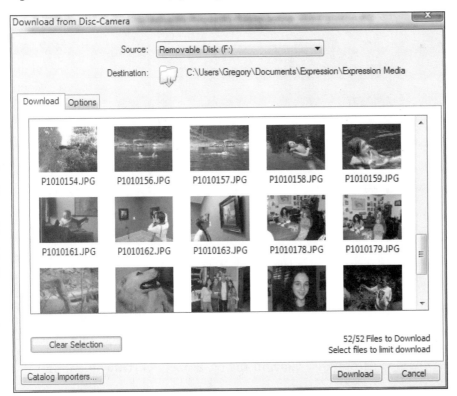

P1010012.JPG

◢ Photo EXIF	
EXIF Version	2.2
Capture Date	0000:00:00 00:00:00
Aperture	f4.8
Shutter Speed	1/125 sec
Exposure Bias	+0.0
Exposure Program	Program
Focal Length	22.9 mm
Light Source	Auto
Flash	ON - Auto mode
Metering	Pattern
ISO Speed	162
◢ **Annotations**	
⌀ Label	■ None
⌀ Rating	None
⌀ Title	-
⌀ Product	-
⌀ Genre	-
⌀ Intellectual Genre	-
⌀ Event	-
⌀ Event Date	-

Figure 17.8   Annotations help you organize items based on criteria you specify.

Download from Disc-Camera

Source: Removable Disk (F:)

Destination: C:\Users\Gregory\Documents\Expression\Expression Media

Download | Options

| P1010154.JPG | P1010156.JPG | P1010157.JPG | P1010158.JPG | P1010159.JPG |
| P1010161.JPG | P1010162.JPG | P1010163.JPG | P1010178.JPG | P1010179.JPG |

Clear Selection

52/52 Files to Download
Select files to limit download

Catalog Importers...   Download   Cancel

Figure 17.9   Use this dialog box to import items directly from a camera or a disk.

Click the Options tab, and you see an extensive set of settings that let you control exactly how to download the files and where to store them:

- You can choose the destination folder for the images or change the file creation date.

- Click the Do Not Annotate drop-down list and choose Create Metadata Template. When the Create Metadata Template dialog box opens (see Figure 17.10), you can click the box to the right of any of the categories shown.

- Click a second time, and a box opens that lets you enter text. You can then enter a title for your images, a rating, a description of the event being depicted, and other helpful information.

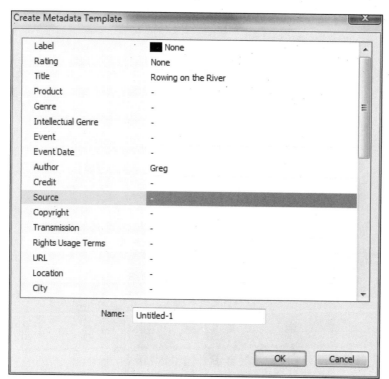

Figure 17.10 Enter metadata before you import your files.

You'll find more about the keyword fields described in this dialog box in the section that follows.

When you're done, click OK to close the Create Metadata Template dialog box. You return to the Download from Disc-Camera dialog box. Click Download, and the files are copied to your computer with the specified metadata information already entered and attached in the background to each of your images.

Assigning Keywords

Once your photos have been imported into Expression Media (or even before, if you use the steps described in the preceding section), you begin the important task of deciding how you wish to organize your digital assets. This part will be highly subjective, and each person will have his own style. Notice, however, that Expression Media gives you some guidance by defining possible annotations. Choices include such categories as these:

- Label
- Rating
- Title
- Product
- Genre
- Intellectual Genre
- Event
- Event Date
- Author
- Credit
- Source
- Copyright
- License

Note: It's especially important to add copyright and license information to your images. If someone copies them without permission and uses them, you can retrieve them based on the information you enter. You can actually Google for a phrase such as "Copyright 2008 Greg Holden" and find any images you have annotated. You can then see whether someone is using the images without your authorization. A warning in the License field, such as "No use without permission," can help you if you find that someone actually has used an image without permission.

Essentially, you are able to assign as many of these keywords as you wish to each image. This in turn allows you to quickly and easily select images from a particular theme later on. Say, for example, I wanted to choose only images of California from my list of pictures. I could assign all pictures taken in California with their Location. If I also assigned the term *sunshine* to the Genre field for those to which it applied, I could then select some pictures from California along with others from Chicago if all fell into the same Genre category. It is easy to select and assign annotation for large batches of photos in Expression Media.

Let's start with this image of a beach in Southern California. If you look at the image in Media View and scroll down the left sidebar shown in Figure 17.11, you see that there is no information regarding the author of the photo. This is a good place to start, especially if you are planning to use your digital media assets for commercial purposes.

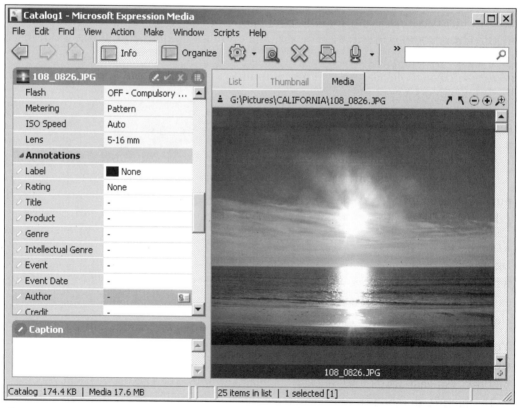

Figure 17.11   Enter metadata information about individual files in the Annotations section.

Clicking on the identification card icon in the Author field brings up a window containing a list of vital information you may wish to attach for contact or copyright

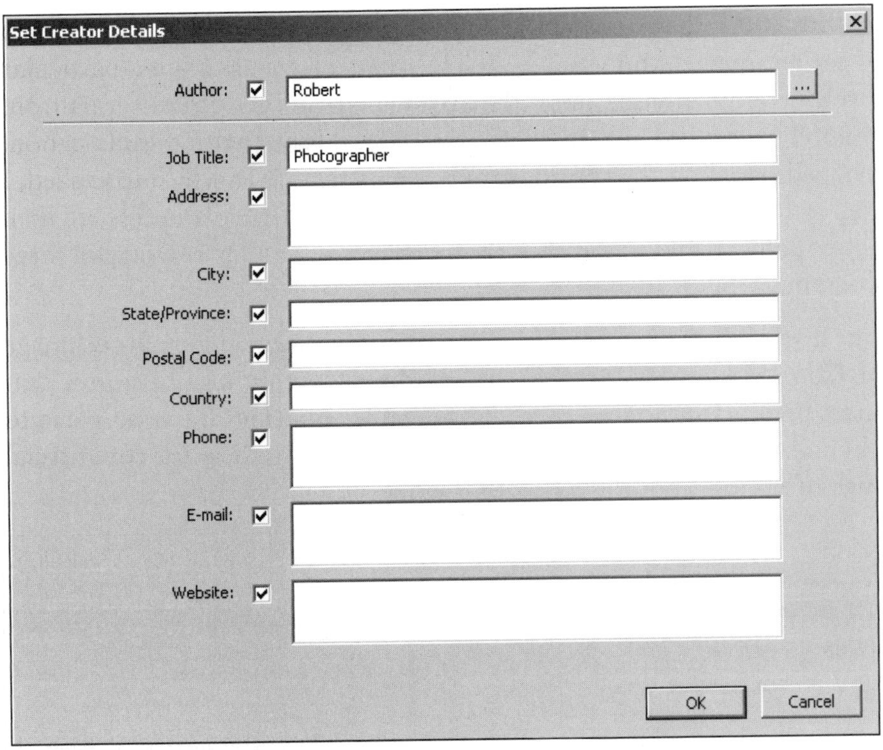

Figure 17.12   Enter detailed data about your authorship here.

purposes (see Figure 17.12). Here, I am only filling in the name and job title for the sake of this tutorial.

You can now select the annotate icon (which resembles a pen set to paper) to the right of the filename in the Info bar and set a metadata template. Call the template whatever you want. Now you can modify this template to apply selected changes easily to multiple files at once. This is one of the truly convenient and useful elements of Expression Media.

You are ready to start organizing! To select multiple items in Expression Media, simply click on the first picture you wish to select, hold Shift, and click on additional pictures. An easy way to select large numbers of files is to click on a picture, then go to the picture diagonally opposite, including all images you wish to keep. Another useful tool is the Inverse Selection option, which can be found under the Edit drop-down menu. This way, you can choose the pictures you *don't* want to include in a larger selection.

Storing Your Image Files

As mentioned earlier, images you work with in Expression Media are stored as catalogs, which you determine based upon the attribute(s) you want represented in a particular group. Think of Media as an enormous database that determines how images are grouped based on the specifications you assign. Catalogs function independent of source folders, so you have to allow Expression Media access to your folders, as it essentially creates a snapshot of the images as you have arranged them within the program.

Now let's make a small but very useful HTML gallery with some of the graphics in our collection. Go to Make > HTML Gallery. The dialog box shown in Figure 17.13 opens; it includes presets for the type of Web page table you want to create and how big each thumbnail should be. Choose some name and size options for the gallery. There is a range of options, but the basics will work very nicely for your purposes.

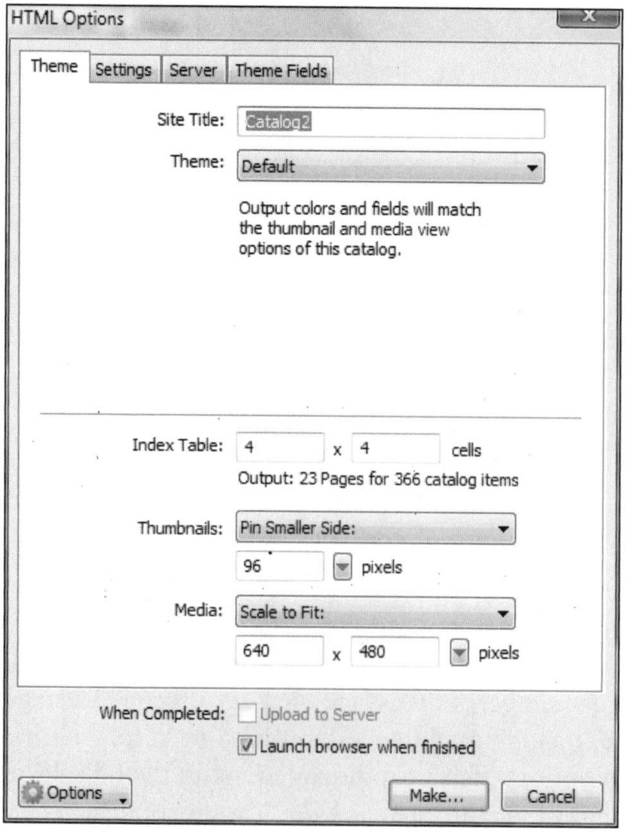

Figure 17.13 Create a Web page that displays your images in the form of a gallery.

Click the Make button to designate a folder to hold your HTML gallery. I will use the default theme, and we'll place that on the desktop. I'll make a new folder. Be careful of the naming; this is the folder that will sit on the Web server after upload, so the name should not be too long or use spaces or capitals. Once the gallery has been created (this can take a while, depending on the number of media files you have in a given catalog), you can open it in a Web browser to see how it looks (see Figure 17.14 for an example).

Figure 17.14   You can create an HTML gallery that can be posted on the Web.

Finding Your Image Files

Finding your files is easy once you have imported them into Media because you have assigned keywords in advance to keep everything organized. Media employs a search engine that functions very much like an online search engine such as Google. If you click down through the levels in the Date Finder, you can see creation dates for the different assets. If you click on the white circle to the right of the date, it turns green and isolates all the assets created on that date. If you want to rank or rate files, there are two different ways to do this. You can go up to the menu and assign labels or rate a file with stars. This all becomes more powerful when you create subsets.

Working Offline

With Microsoft Expression Media, you are able to manipulate files, add information, and organize your files even when they are offline. This means that you could import photo files from a hard drive or DVD, remove the original source of the files, and continue to work on the images without requiring direct access to the originals.

The ability to work offline with Media means that you can import images not only from the computer at which you are sitting but from machines that are located elsewhere on your network. Normally, when you access shared files on networked computers, you can view them only when you are actually on the network—on the Internet or on your local network. Media frees you from the need to be online. When it creates a catalog of images, either from your computer or a network share, it creates a thumbnail of each item that is contained in the catalog. The catalog is on your computer, so you can always look at the media items and work with them even though they're not actually in your local file system.

Tip: Because you can access catalogs offline, this means you can also send the catalog to clients for approval without having to send the assets themselves. If your media files are several megabytes in size, they can be difficult to distribute online—you probably have to save them on a CD and mail them. By assembling them into a catalog, you can send them quickly to clients.

Batch Conversions

Batch conversion is essentially the process of altering metadata for multiple files at once. Choose Action > Batch Rename, for instance, to display the Batch Rename dialog box. You can enter text to add to all selected files or perform a search and replace operation (see Figure 17.15) if you want to search for a particular keyword and rename it throughout a catalog.

What's nice about Expression Media is that this metadata can range anywhere from keywords to file formats. Expression Media is very effective in converting between a wide variety of formats. Stick with the workflow that works for you, and Expression Media will help you streamline it. Support for RAW formats from the most popular cameras and industry-standard metadata formats means that you can depend on Expression Media to read and write metadata in the safest way. Keep keywords consistent with custom dictionaries—just drag and drop to quickly tag thousands of files. Rename an entire folder of files or change their format easily with batch

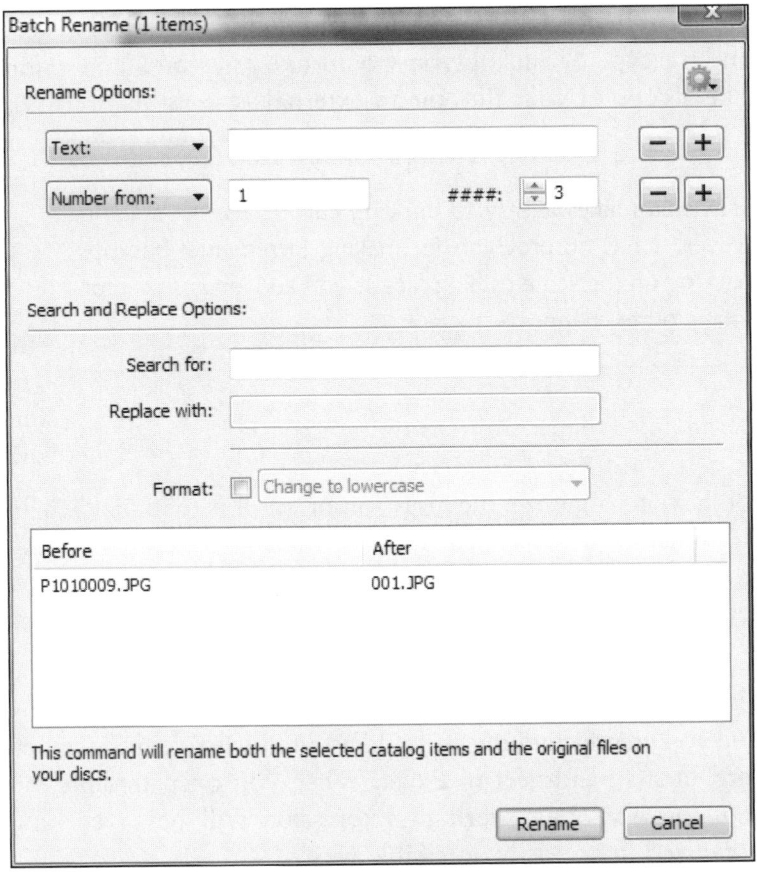

Figure 17.15 You can search and replace annotation text if needed.

conversion, or use flexible scripting tools to get tedious tasks out of your way. Make sure all your valuable digital assets are protected with built-in archiving and backup features.

Making Backups

Maintaining an up-to-date media catalog doesn't do you much good if your hard drive goes down and takes your photos with it. You should always have multiple backup copies of your photos or other image files. The number of backups and the sophistication of the backup routine will vary according to your needs, but one helpful rule of thumb is to have all your photos in at least two or three locations, preferably on different types of media.

You might consider creating a CD or DVD of an important photo session immediately after importing the photos to your hard drive. It is easy and convenient to create backup DVDs by selecting Make from the drop-down menu, choosing Backup To, and choosing the type of backup you would like to create. You might also want simply to make a copy of your files on an external hard drive.

Caution: Expression Media makes it easy to back up catalog files to a CD or external drive. However, it has no provision for making incremental backups. You need to keep backing up the same catalog files as you add images or information to them or make other changes.

Archives

The more media files you have to organize, the more important it is to manage them with Expression Media. When you are called upon to manage several thousand media assets, you'll probably need to archive them—to file away the items you don't need or that aren't current so you can more easily manage the "A list" items.

Creating archives is a simple and efficient task with Expression Media. Once you have organized your files the way you would like them to be, choose File > New Catalog. The new catalog you create can now be saved as an independent file, much like a document in Word or a spreadsheet in Excel. When you open this file, no matter what application you use, your work in Expression will be saved, and your pictures will be organized in an easily accessible way.

When you create an archive, it's essential to use keywords as described earlier in this chapter. That way the people who access your files long after they have been archived will have information about what they're working with. It's important to keep in mind that the keywords you create in other applications, such as Word, are displayed in the Keyword palette within Media. You open the catalog, click Organize, and expand the Keyword option to see all the keywords in the catalog (see Figure 17.16).

You can search for all images that have a particular keyword by clicking in the white circle to the right of any keyword. Because Media is only searching through its catalog and not your file system or network, such a search is performed far faster than in Windows.

It can be difficult to stay organized when manually adding photos to your image library catalog. But Media's Auto-Update feature can save you lots of tedious time and data entry. When Auto-Update is enabled, Expression Media automatically

Figure 17.16 Keywords created in other applications can be opened in Media.

searches the contents of designated folders and imports any images that aren't already in the catalog. Auto-Update is particularly useful when you have a dedicated hard drive or set of folders to store your image library. To enable Auto-Update, follow these steps:

1. Open a catalog, if necessary, from the folder whose contents you want to update automatically.

2. Configure folder watching for the folder by clicking the Configure Folder Watching icon. This icon is located just to the right of the Catalog Folders heading. It looks like a miniature lightning bolt.

3. Choose an option from the menu that pops down when you click on the Configure Folder Watching icon, such as Every 5 Minutes.

4. Right-click the name of the folder that you want to watch. The name appears in the list under Catalog Folders. It might be the standard folder My Pictures, for instance.

5. Choose Switch Auto-Update on from the context menu (see Figure 17.17).

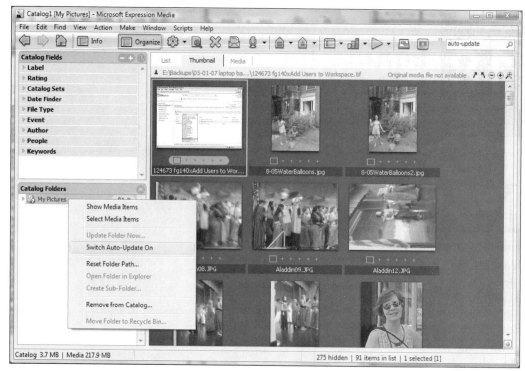

Figure 17.17 You can tell Media to automatically update folders or selected images.

Media will then import photos from your shoots and corrected versions of photos edited in Photoshop. This means your image library catalog is always up to date and complete.

18 Editing Images with Expression Media

Media is much more than an organizational tool. Once you have used Media to gather all your images in one place and located them in different catalogs, you can open and edit them. You can even go a step further and use Media to share your photos with others. Media's editing and presentation features alleviate the need for you to use third-party software to undertake this sort of review and comparison process. Instead, you can stay within Expression Media's environment for all your reviewing and editing needs.

Because Expression Media allows you to quickly and efficiently load and organize photos, the robust and versatile editing program proves to be a powerful tool, allowing you to quickly sort through images, comparing them with one another and choosing the best ones. In addition to the three views previously discussed—List, Thumbnail, and Media—Expression Media can display photos in a format called Light Table. This feature allows close and careful examination of photo edits and can be very helpful if you want to do side by side comparisons. It is useful to keep in mind that Expression Media is not, after all, a media editing program at the level of, say, Adobe Photoshop. It is helpful to employ Photoshop in conjunction with Expression Media by using the relatively robust applications of Expression Media when possible and switching to a program like Photoshop for more sophisticated changes. This chapter explains basic editing options and tools for creating presentations.

Touring Media's Editing Tools

The simplest edits can be done using the tools in the upper right corner of the Media window. They allow you to rotate photos easily and quickly and change the view of the images, adjusting such things as the aspect ratio, the thumbnail borders, and so on. You also get basic information about the currently selected image, such as its size (see Figure 18.1).

The zoom tools were mentioned in Chapter 17, but the one on the far right is worth focusing on in detail. When you click it, you gain access to a variety of common

451

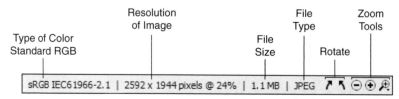

Type of Color
Standard RGB

Resolution
of Image

File
Size

File
Type

Rotate

Zoom
Tools

sRGB IEC61966-2.1 | 2592 x 1944 pixels @ 24% | 1.1 MB | JPEG

Figure 18.1   Media gives you basic file size, format, and other image information.

Actual Size
Scale to Fit

Fit Width
Fit Height
✓ Pin Smaller Side
Pin Larger Side
Tile

25%
50%
100%
200%
400%
800%
1600%

Figure 18.2   Choose from a variety of zoom options.

zoom settings, as shown in Figure 18.2. Some of the settings are obvious, but others are not. These include:

Fit Width. The full width of the image is made to fit inside the current display area.

Fit Height. The full height of the image is made to fit inside the current display area.

Pin Smaller Side. The smaller dimension (width or height) is made to align with one side of the current display area.

Pin Larger Side. The larger dimension (width or height) is made to align with one side of the current display area.

Tile. A small portion of the image is highly magnified so it can be used as a background if needed.

The preceding zoom options appear only if you are in Media view. If you are in List view, the only two zoom options are Large Icons and Small Icons. If you are in

Thumbnail view, you get several options that control how the thumbnails appear:

- **Thumbnail size.** You can zoom so the thumbnails are different sizes, such as 640 pixels × 480 pixels, 480 × 360, and so on. The smaller the size, the larger the number of thumbnails you can fit on a page.

- **Thumbnail ratio.** This controls the ratio of the height to the width of the thumbnail. Normal means the proportions are the same as the original image: 1:1. You can also choose a 4:3 Landscape orientation or a 3:4 Portrait orientation.

- **Thumbnail margin.** This section gives you four choices for the type of margin around each thumbnail: None, Blank, Shadow, and Frame.

Once edits are done, it can be helpful to view them in the Light Table to examine them more closely and decide whether you are satisfied with the results. You can also view several images at once to compare and contrast image quality. View images in the Light Table by selecting your image or images and clicking on the Light Table icon in the toolbar (see Figure 18.3). (The Light Table is described in more detail later in this chapter.)

View in
Light Table

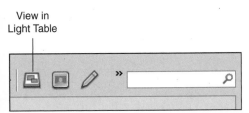

Figure 18.3   Click here to switch to Light Table view.

Working with the Image Editor

More complex editing will entail the use of the Image Editor. To view the Image Editor, choose Window > Image Editor or press Ctrl+Alt+J. The Image Editor pops up in its own window, which you can move freely around your screen (see Figure 18.4).

As you can see, a wide variety of editing tools is offered in Expression Media. You'll notice that, at the bottom of the menu, you are given the option to create a Versions folder. This can be very helpful if you are not sure that the edits you have performed will be approved by your co-workers or if for any other reason you wish to save multiple versions of an image.

I recommend just opening up this menu and spending a few minutes with each of the tools to familiarize yourself with what they do. Many are relatively self-explanatory, but I've included some information on a few key edits to help you along.

Figure 18.4 Media lets you perform simple image editing tasks conveniently.

Tip: Media gives you rudimentary tools for image editing, but other programs give you more options. On the other hand, if you don't have access to Photoshop or one of the more powerful image editing tools, you can use Windows Photo Gallery, a photo editing application that comes bundled with Windows Vista.

Rotating Images

Rotated images are often used in pamphlets, presentations, and other marketing-related formats, not to mention a host of other purposes. If you're in a hurry, click one of the rotate arrows in the set of tools just above the thumbnail of the image you want to edit. Clicking one of these buttons rotates the image in 90-degree increments (see Figure 18.5).

If you want complete control over the degree of rotation, open the image you want in Media View or select the image in Thumbnail View. Open the Image Editor and click Rotate. The Rotate dialog box shown in Figure 18.6 appears.

Figure 18.5 The rotate buttons let you rotate either clockwise or counterclockwise in 90-degree increments.

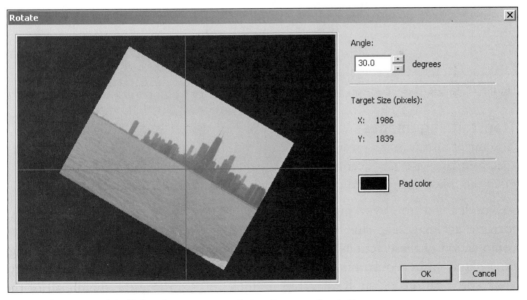

Figure 18.6 Use this dialog box to control the degree of rotation.

The Rotate dialog box allows you to intuitively rotate photos by physically dragging them to your preferred angle, in addition to being able to enter the number of degrees in the Angle field. Pass your mouse arrow over one of the corners of the image, and it turns into a curved arrow. (It's the same kind of curved arrow used by Expression Design to rotate objects on its artboard.) Click and drag to interactively rotate the image.

If you are working with JPEG images, keep in mind that there is an option especially for rotating them. Select the image you want to edit and then choose Action > JPEG Rotate. The options that appear in the dialog box shown in Figure 18.7 let you rotate it in 90-degree increments.

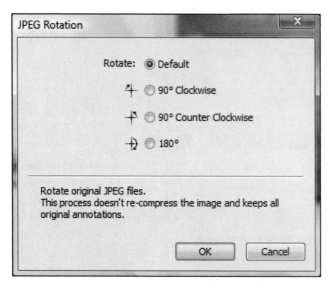

Figure 18.7 Use these controls to rotate JPEG images.

Transforming Images

You might also want to present a photo at a different angle or from a different perspective. This is easily accomplished using the Transform tool. Select the image, open the Image Editor, and click Transform to open the Transform dialog box.

As you learned from working with Expression Design in previous chapters, transforming an image can involve rotating, resizing, skewing, or stretching—or any combination of these actions. Choose the type of constraint you would like to put on a photo in the Constrain field, and then simply click and drag on the image to your specifications. You have three options for Constraining transformations: Perspective, Skew, and Free. It's hard to describe what each does, but a picture illustrates it best. Try each option yourself and press Reset after each edit. The Free transformation is shown in Figure 18.8.

The Perspective option changes the image in a more structured way, as shown in Figure 18.9.

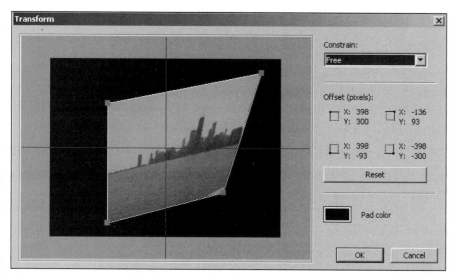

Figure 18.8   Free transformation changes the image in many different ways.

Figure 18.9   Perspective transformation.

Resizing a Single Image

Sometimes the destination format for an image has different dimensions from that of the original photo. Not only does Expression Media make it easy to change the dimensions of a photo, but you can also very easily "fill in the gaps" to make an image conform to its new target dimensions. Media isn't as intuitive as Expression Design when it comes to rotating images. You don't click on an image and get a set of selection handles you can drag at will. But when you select an image and click

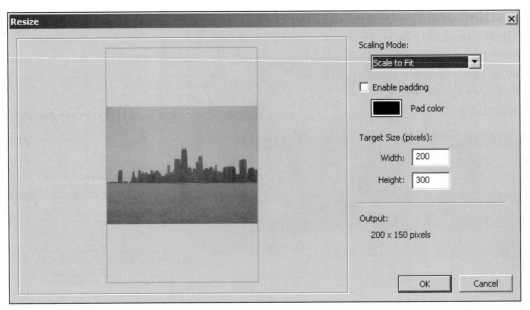

Figure 18.10 This dialog box gives you a preview image and controls to control resizing.

Resize in the Image Editor, the Resize dialog box shown in Figure 18.10 appears, and it gives you a good deal of control over resizing.

I have chosen Fit Height, and voila, the picture is resized (see Figure 18.11).

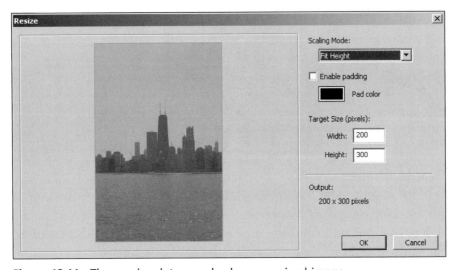

Figure 18.11 The preview lets you check your resized image.

Resizing and Revising Multiple Images

The Resize dialog box lets you resize a single image in your catalog. But suppose you have 50 to 100 images in the catalog, and you want to resize all of the files at the same time. If that's the case, choose Action > Convert Image Files. The dialog box that appears (shown in Figure 18.12) not only lets you resize images in bulk but lets you add other information to the image files as well.

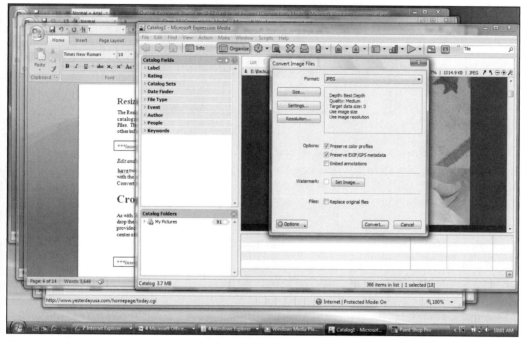

Figure 18.12   Edit and resize multiple images using these controls.

Click Size to resize all the image at once, and enter the height and width you want. Then click OK. Before you close the Convert Image Files dialog box, however, try using the other controls:

- Click Settings, and you access a Quality slider control that lets you control the compression level, and therefore the image quality, of the image.

- Resolution lets you specify the resolution of each of the images in dots per inch (dpi).

- Watermark lets you impose an image on each image. Choose this if you want to protect your images when they appear online. It's common to place a copyright notice atop an image that's published on the Web to discourage (though not prevent) unauthorized users from copying them without your permission. The

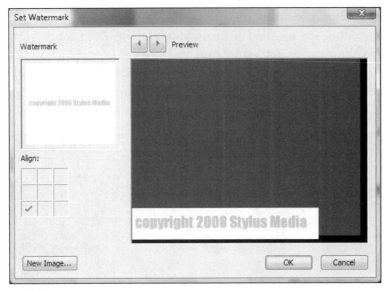

Figure 18.13   Add a watermark file using this dialog box.

Set Watermark dialog box shown in Figure 18.13, which opens when you click Set Image, not only lets you choose the file you want to use but lets you choose its position in the image.

Click New Image to locate the watermark file you want to use. You can create a simple watermark message in Design, for instance, export it as a GIF or JPEG file, and add it to a catalog full of files in Media. By clicking one of the nine boxes under the Align heading, you choose whether the watermark image will appear in the upper left, upper right, center, or other regions in the image. Choose the location carefully so the watermark doesn't obscure the images themselves. Then click OK to add it to the images.

Cropping Images

As with resizing, transforming, and rotating, cropping images can be done either by using the mouse to drag and drop the cropping window to your desired specifications or by manually entering the dimensions in the fields provided. Select the image you want to edit and then choose Crop from the Image Editor. When the Crop dialog box shown in Figure 18.14 appears, drag a cropping box around the image. You can also choose to constrain the aspect ratio or specify the position of the cropping box using the controls on the right.

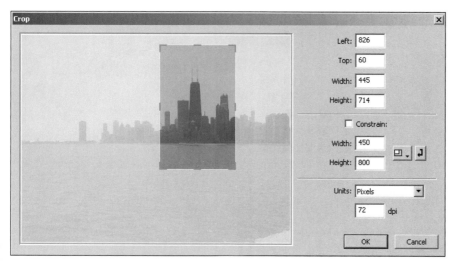

Figure 18.14 Use these controls to crop an image.

Adjusting Colors

The Image Editor gives you a variety of ways to adjust color in Expression Media, and they are described in the sections that follow.

Convert to Duotone

A duotone is an image that has only two tones in it rather than the multiple colors contained in a color image. The Duotone option in Expression Media can give your pictures a sepia tone reminiscent of an old photograph or black-and-white movie, for example. The two colors don't need to be black and white, however. Because you can choose your colors from a color palette, there is an unlimited number of options. You set your light color and dark color separately, giving you a lot of creative control for many artistic possibilities. When you click either the Light Color or Dark Color box in the Convert to Duotone dialog box shown in Figure 18.15, you can choose from a standard Color Picker.

Adjust Saturation

The Adjust Saturation tool lets you adjust both color saturation and color lightness for a wide range of editing capabilities. You work with the colors that are already in the image rather than changing them. By moving sliders to the left or right, you are able to adjust the intensity of the colors currently in the image.

Adjust Color Balance

This tool is similar to the Convert to Duotone tool. It allows you to adjust three individual color bars: Cyan/Red, Magenta/Green, and Yellow/Blue. The primary

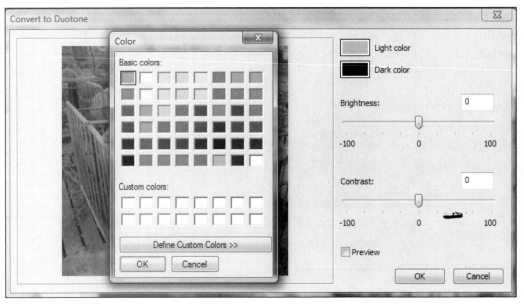

Figure 18.15   You can choose the light and dark colors to create a custom duotone.

difference between the two tools is that in the Adjust Color Balance tool, you are applying a uniform color to your image.

Adjust Color Levels

This tool displays a histogram depicting color levels in the currently selected image (see Figure 18.16). There is a bar beneath the histogram with three markers, whose

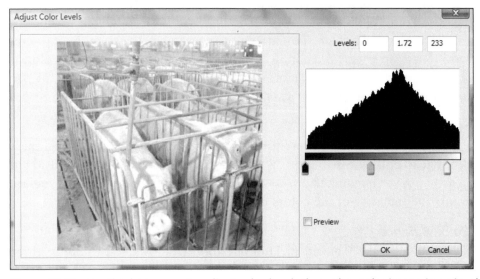

Figure 18.16   Use this histogram to adjust color levels throughout the image in a visual way.

manipulation creates endless possibilities for creative expression. If you are used to working with histograms from Photoshop or other graphics programs, this tool will be familiar to you. But if you have never worked with a histogram before, you might find it confusing and the results difficult to predict.

Improving Sharpness

The Sharpen Edges option in the Image Editor not only lets you adjust the sharpness on a scale from low to high, but it also lets you alter the edge detection on a scale from coarse to sharp. When you select Sharpen Edges in the Image Editor, the Sharpen Edges dialog box appears. The two sliders let you control the degree of sharpening (by Low to High, or by a numeric value you enter) and edge detection. You can also preview the result before choosing to apply the changes by checking the Preview box.

Tip: When sharpening an image, it is always important to be conscious of the effect that the edit will have on your final product. If the photo was taken using a camera with a lower megapixel count, for example, increasing the sharpness may make the picture crisper and clearer, but it will also make it grainier. Play around with the sharpness tools until you find a good balance for each individual picture.

Optimizing Contrast and Brightness

When you select an image, open Image Editor, and click Adjust Brightness & Contrast, the Adjust Brightness & Contrast dialog box appears. This tool has two bars with markers that can be dragged in either direction. In this tool, the bars, not surprisingly, adjust brightness and contrast. When using this tool you may find the results somewhat more subtle than the changes occurring with, say, the color adjustment tools, but changing contrast and brightness can go a long way toward changing the feel of a picture. You can make a picture look crisp and sunny or dark and dramatic without significantly altering the nature of the picture itself.

Getting the Red Out

Red eye is one of the most common problems with color images of people who are told to look straight into the lens of the camera. This Red Eye tool in Image Editor provides precise control of where and how much red eye should be affected. Select the image, choose Remove Red Eye, and move the zoom slider to zoom in on the area you want to correct in the Remove Red Eye dialog box shown in Figure 18.17. The zoom slider is not labeled, but it is at the bottom of the dialog box at the left side.

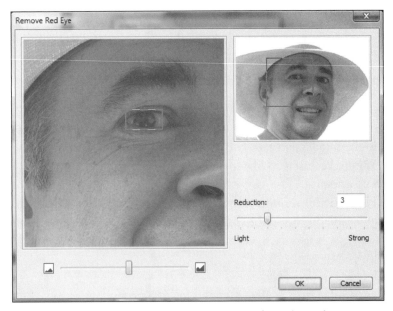

Figure 18.17 Use these settings to correct red eye in an image.

Usually the area you want to correct is someone's eye. Once you zoom in on the eye, move the red rectangular selection area and position it around the eye. Then choose a level of color correct and click OK.

Auto Enhancing Images

If you don't relish opening one editing tool after another to correct an image, consider skipping directly to the Auto Enhancement or Preset Enhancement options and letting Expression Media do the work. With Media's image enhancement tools, the quality of media image files can be quickly and professionally improved without having to use an alternate application.

Preset enhancement is intended to let you make corrections with a single mouse click. This applies preset levels of change to the following common visual aspects:

Color Cast. Images can have a yellowish or bluish cast, depending on the type of light used.

Contrast/Brightness. A special Backlight enhancement helps instantly if the image was lit too much from the back and appears dark in front. Another setting, Under and Over Exposure, changes the range of tones to compensate for photos that were exposed improperly.

Subject. This setting adjusts the skin tone of people in your photo.

Levels (Macintosh only). You can adjust the levels of any filter applied to your image by using this setting.

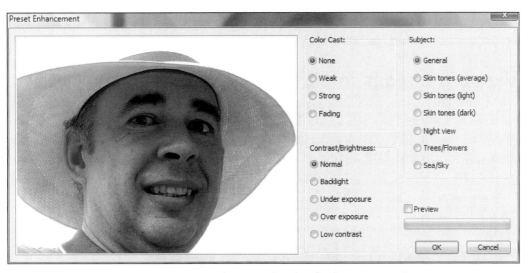

Figure 18.18   Use these settings to apply preset levels of adjustment to images.

Preset enhancements in Windows are shown in Figure 18.18.

The Auto Enhancement feature has advantages that are available the moment you select an image and then select this option from the Image Editor. You immediately see a before and after version of an image (see Figure 18.19). The enhancements are applied without your having to think about them. And as you can see from the following example, the improvements can be dramatic. The lighting on my face was weak and lacking in contrast in the before version; the after version increased

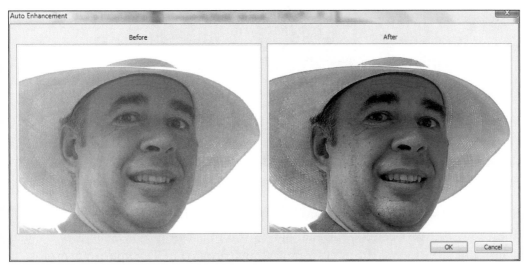

Figure 18.19   Auto Enhancement gives you instant before and after versions of an image.

contrast and clarity to a surprising degree. I didn't know the photo was so bad until I saw the after version, in fact.

Viewing Images in Light Table

Once you have performed the edits you want, switch to the light table to more closely examine the results. Light Table gives you the most accurate editing view in Media because images are presented in a far larger and more detailed format than List, Thumbnail, or Media View. Another good thing about the Light Table is that you can view several images at once by selecting the images you want and then clicking the View in Light Table button in the Media toolbar. When you first click View in Light Table, the box shown in Figure 18.20 appears. Make note of the keyboard shortcuts listed, particularly the ones for adding and removing panels.

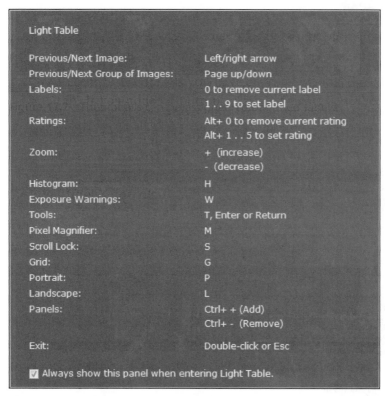

Light Table	
Previous/Next Image:	Left/right arrow
Previous/Next Group of Images:	Page up/down
Labels:	0 to remove current label
	1 . . 9 to set label
Ratings:	Alt+ 0 to remove current rating
	Alt+ 1 . . 5 to set rating
Zoom:	+ (increase)
	- (decrease)
Histogram:	H
Exposure Warnings:	W
Tools:	T, Enter or Return
Pixel Magnifier:	M
Scroll Lock:	S
Grid:	G
Portrait:	P
Landscape:	L
Panels:	Ctrl+ + (Add)
	Ctrl+ - (Remove)
Exit:	Double-click or Esc

☑ Always show this panel when entering Light Table.

Figure 18.20   These settings control the layout of the Light Table feature.

You can also modify the display from within Light Table. By right-clicking on your chosen image, you open a menu that allows you to perform such tasks as displaying a histogram onscreen, sizing your image, and displaying an exposure warning. It also lets you perform some of the organizational edits that are available in the normal layout from within the Light Table, such as rating your pictures, resizing, and rotating.

Tip: You can edit images in the List, Thumbnail, and Media Views using the tools above and to the right of the image display. An efficient workflow solution is to edit in Media View and switch to Light Table View for close examination of the edits you have done. A shortcut for switching to Light Table is to select the image or images you want and press Alt+Enter.

Light Table View enables you to use the Magnifier (press the keyboard shortcut M) to look at your photo at 100 percent magnification to check sharpness and detail. What's more, you can add multiple images to the Light Table to compare sharpness and detail to find the best image in a series. Select between one and four images to compare and contrast side-by-side in full screen view, without any desktop clutter. In other words, this view functions much like a digital version of a photographer's light table, but it is far easier and more intuitive. Press ++ (Ctrl and the plus key two times) to add panels to the Light Table. In Figure 18.21, four panels are visible.

Figure 18.21 Zoom and scroll to the same point on multiple images simultaneously or individually.

Tip: If you use the Light Table View on a regular basis, you may want to customize Media to jump into Light Table View every time you double-click on an image. Choose Edit > Preferences to open the Preferences dialog box. Click General. From the drop-down list next to Double-Click, select View in Light Table. Then click OK.

Labeling and Highlighting Images   Labeling and highlighting aren't editing tasks, technically. You don't actually change the appearance of an image when you label or highlight it. However, labeling and highlighting do change the image's filename. When you're looking through a large group of photos and want to mark the best ones, you can do so quickly by assigning them a color so they pop out quickly in List View.

If you're in List View, right click the image, choose Label, and choose a color from the submenu to the right, as shown in Figure 18.22. You can also press the shortcut key next to the color—press 1 for a red label, for instance.

Like many other workflow programs, Expression Media uses both star ratings and labels that can be selected with a single keystroke. I find the labels invaluable for culling the best photos from the shoot during the editing process.

You may want to choose one color to denote images you aren't happy with and want to throw out and another for images you like and want to keep, for instance. Both List View and the Light Table also have the option of assigning a star rating to files. Light Table's version is shown in Figure 18.23.

Right-click the image, choose Rating from the context menu, and select the number of stars you want to assign to the image from the submenu that appears on the left.

Changing Video Compression and Format

Media supports a wide variety of video formats, including QuickTime movies (which have the filename extension .mov) and MPEG videos. To change a video's compression, you follow the same general procedure as with an image file. Just go to the Action drop-down menu, but this time select Convert Movie Files. You now have the option to convert to a wide range of file types, including QuickTime and MP4. Once again, you can either save over the old file or create a new one.

19 Creating Presentations with Expression Media

Wʜat good does it do to perfect the lighting in a photo or organize a great photo album if there's no way to share it? Expression Media provides many ways to share the work you've done. Your presentation method of choice will vary depending on the purpose of a given set of media assets.

Expression Media provides much more than the standard slideshow that you might use to show pictures from your vacation at a family reunion (although it does this very well). Because Media also allows you to export information about the media assets as a text file or XML data file, a business client could easily look through a catalog of assets, and know the format, the size, the resolution, etc., giving him or her vital information necessary to make an informed decision quickly and efficiently. Media can also export a series of photos as a Contact Sheet, which is ideal for quick presentation of your media assets. Most of the related functions can be found under the Make dropdown menu (see Figure 19.1).

This chapter will describe the options available to you for sharing images, whether you're showing them to family and friends or presenting them to potential employers in the hope of landing a big job or finalizing a project you've already done.

Presenting Your Images

This section will deal specifically with the many ways in which images can be presented. Remember that, because your images are digital assets, their vital information can be expressed as metadata. Presenting images can also refer to the exporting of vital information as metadata, which can give your client a quick and easy solution for viewing, selecting, and understanding the files you are presenting. Expression Media makes it easy to generate reports with information essential to Web presentation or format compatibility.

Showing a Contact Sheet

One of the most important—and obvious—ways of sharing a list of digital assets such as photos is in the form of a list or set of images. In "old fashioned" (in other

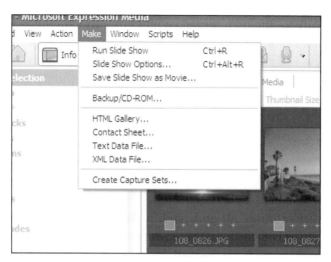

Figure 19.1   Most of Media's presentation options are found under this menu.

words, non-digital) photography, a contact sheet is a single photographic print made from strips of negatives placed close together. Printing the negatives gives the photographer and other interested parties, such as editors, the ability to view a group of images quickly in small format so they can choose which ones to print.

Media's version of a contact sheet is essentially a digital photo album, and is perfectly suited to this task. There are many reasons why you might want to create a contact sheet for personal or business reasons. You may wish, for example, to create a catalog of particular products or present your digital asset modifications with your clients. Expression Media makes creating a contact sheet much easier than the old fashioned method of cutting a roll of negatives into strips and attaching them to a sheet of photographic paper so they can be exposed in chemicals.

Just open the Catalog that you would like to convert into a Contact Sheet. Go to the Make dropdown menu and select Contact Sheet. You will be presented with the window seen in Figure 19.2, which gives a number of settings to choose from, plus a preview of what your contact sheet will look like.

You can now choose between a Thumbnail or List layout, and add a header or footer if you like. You can set the dimensions of your contact sheet in pixels, inches, or centimeters, and choose the appropriate resolution for your images. Because you can set the dimensions freely to whatever size you need, it is easy to get all your assets on one page (depending on how many you have, of course!). For this example, I'm fitting everything on a 8 1/2 × 11-inch sheet for easy output from a laser printer. Setting the dpi at 90 gets all of the images on the page nicely, and while it's not particularly high, it will be sufficient for viewing by a client for review. Moreover, I'm going to click on the Settings button, and set the quality to High.

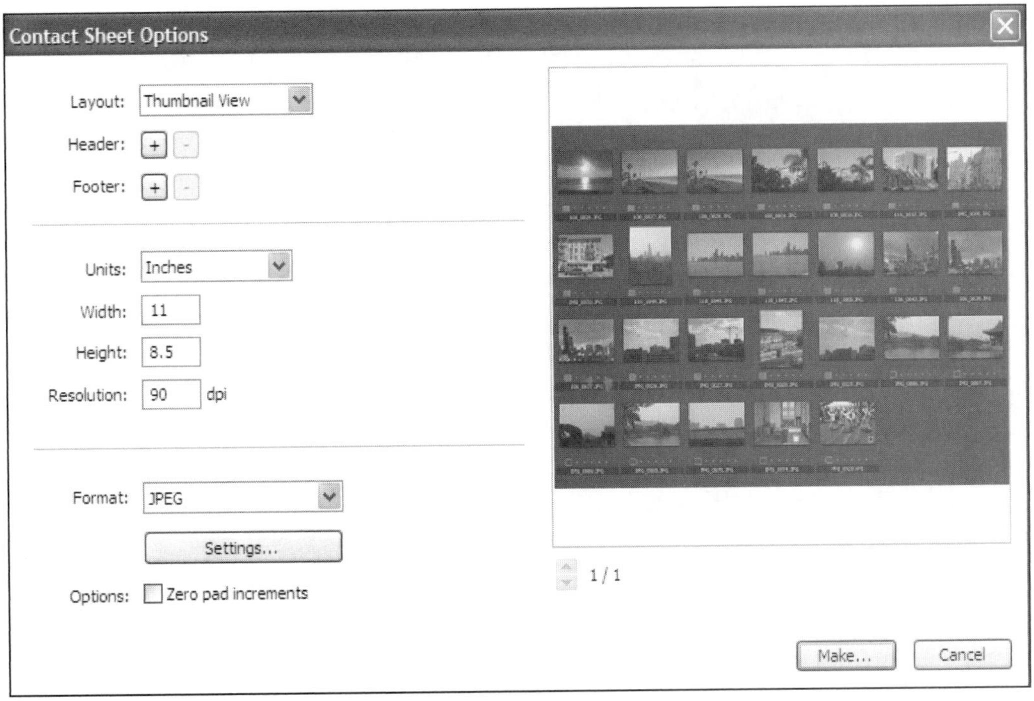

Figure 19.2   Configure your contact sheet options and get a preview using these controls.

I'm going to save my contact sheet file as a JPEG, although you may choose a different file format such as Photoshop, BMP, QuickTime, TIFF, etc., depending on what you want to do with it. When you have chosen a size and file format, click Make. The Save poster as dialog box opens. Enter a file name for your contact sheet in the file name box, and select the location on your file system where you want to save it. Then click Save to save your file. I'm going to be saving it to the folder I've been working from. I'm going to call it Contact Sheet 1. Now I can preview the JPEG, zoom in or out, and verify that it is satisfactory. Notice in Figure 19.3 also that the image filenames are included, which will help your client to reference the images when referring to them later. It can now be emailed or transferred by whatever method you prefer.

Saving a Catalog as a Text File

Sometimes, an image isn't enough, and your client may need more specific information regarding the digital asset. This type of information can be essential, for example, if for no other reason, than for all parties involved in a project to know what name is designated each picture. Knowing the file type is important in the event that the images will be used in a multimedia project. Expression Media allows you to

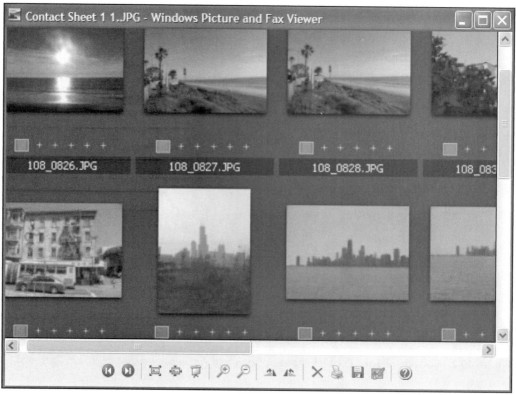

Figure 19.3 Contact sheet images include their original catalog file names.

export your images' metadata as text files to allow for streamlined workflow and maximum efficiency throughout a project.

First, select the photos whose metadata you would like to export. Each one of the photos you include will have a line containing its information in the text file. Then select Make > Text Data File. You will be presented with various options in the Text Table Options window shown in Figure 19.4.

To choose the field you would like to include in your text file, just click on it with the mouse, and then click the arrow icon to copy it from the Available Fields window to the Fields Included menu. You can only select one field at a time, but you do have the option of selecting all fields at once by clicking the double arrow icon. Conversely, if you wish to remove a field, just click the reverse arrow icon.

For this demonstration, I am going to choose only the most basic pieces of information. Information such as the file name, disk name, and path name is relatively essential when sending files back and forth so that everyone knows how to easily find and refer to the files. The text file shown in Figure 19.5 also includes such fields as Frame Rate, Audio Channels, Audio Rate, etc., which are applicable to video files.

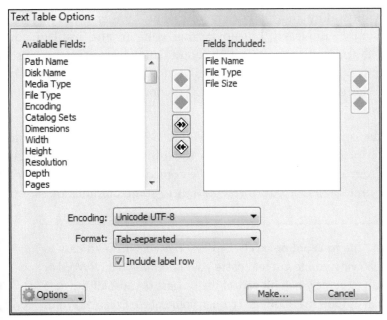

Figure 19.4   Move the data you want to include in your text file from the left to the right side.

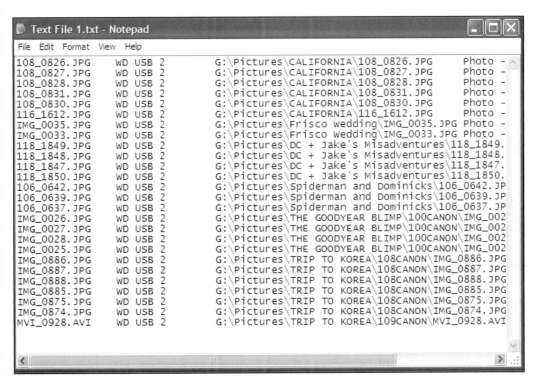

Figure 19.5   You can add video and audio information to your text file.

You can now choose the Encoding and the Format you want. I am going to go with Plain Text, because it is more universal, but notice that you can also use Unicode UTF-8, which is helpful for coding between different languages. You are also presented with the option of saving the settings you've used for future exports by clicking on Options and choosing Save, if this is a set of options you will continuously be using.

When you've selected the options you want, click Make. You now have a text file that can be emailed, or copied in order to share your file information with others or simply to serve as a reference file. The text can also be copied and pasted into Word or Excel, which can be preferable for data presentation in some circumstances.

You can export a text file to Word or Excel: Expression Media makes it easy to share metadata by allowing you to cut and paste your information into Word or Excel. Excel can be an extremely helpful part of the process because of the data organization and analysis tools that it offers. To open your data in Excel (or Word) simply copy all text in the text file and paste it into a spreadsheet. In Excel, the information will automatically be arranged into individual cells.

Creating an XML File

One of Expression Media's most powerful and convenient features is its ability to create an XML file from your digital assets' metadata. This is essential if you want to create multimedia projects with interactive elements. Because XML data files can be opened by a wide range of programs, including Expression Blend and Expression Web, a carefully configured importing system can directly use this data for many different purposes.

For this example, I am going to actually create a new Catalog because, in this case, I only want to send a data file with pictures from California. I'm going create a new Catalog, called Catalog 2, and then select the images I would like to be included. Now, because I want to remove all the pictures *not* selected, I will go to Edit, and Invert Selection. Now I can simply delete (removing the images only from this Catalog without affecting the actual data files). Now I have the Catalog I want, containing only pictures of California.

To make the XML file, you simply choose Make > XML Data File. As you can see in Figure 19.6, the XML Data File Options dialog box presents you with several choices. You can decide which additional information sections to include, what kind of annotation to include, and whether you want to have EXIF data. You can

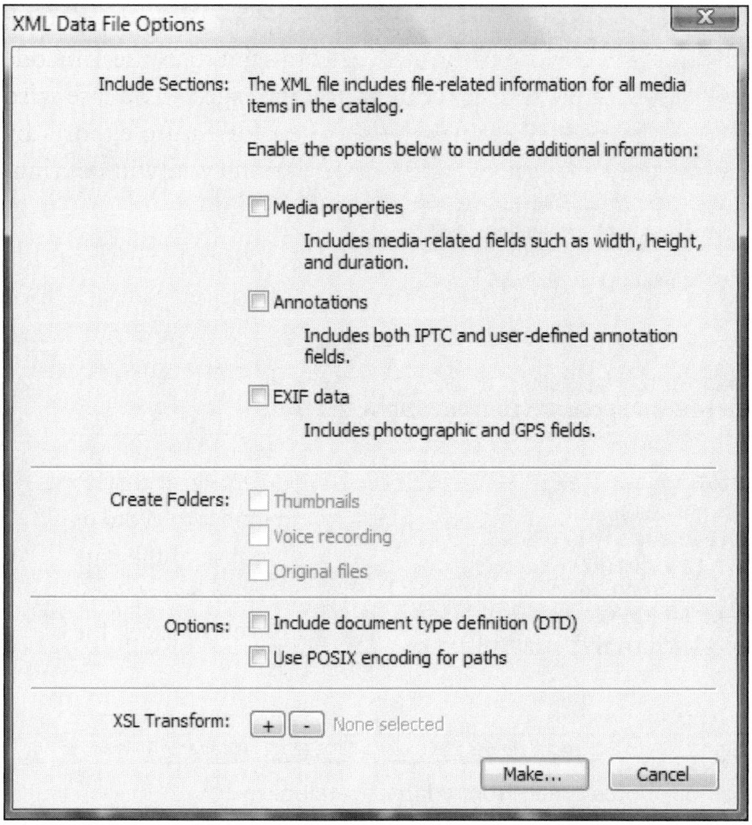

Figure 19.6 Media will export an XML file that includes the data you specify here.

also choose to make individual folders, if you like, which can be useful if you have both audio and video.

For the file shown in Figure 19.7, the options chosen were Media properties, Annotations, and EXIF data, which is particularly relevant to photos.

Now, just go to Make, and you will create an XML data file. You can now view your XML data file using WordPad or any of the other many programs—including Expression Blend and Expression Web—that are able to open it. You will see such useful information as pixel width, pixel height, resolution, color space, compression, not to mention the filename and file path, and so on.

Creating Slide Shows

The PowerPoint presentation has become the constant companion of students and professionals alike, achieving the status of cultural fixture to the point where you have more likely than not heard it as the punch line of a joke or two. Needless to say,

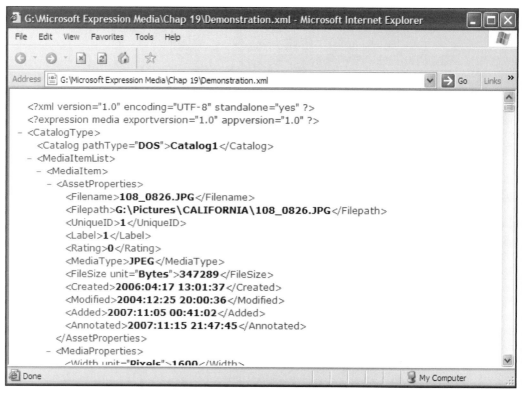

Figure 19.7   An XML version of photos culled from a larger catalog.

the slide show is an integral part of any image presentation, and can assist in presenting any information more generally. Expression Media gives you the ability to create slide shows in a user-friendly and intuitive environment. You can make a slide show interactive, add audio, and configure your images using a wide range of options that will give you the precise slide show that you are looking for.

Running Slide Shows

Because Expression Media makes creating slide shows so simple, the easiest way to get started is to simply run a slide show to see how everything works. You can run a slide show whenever you want by simply going to the Make dropdown menu. Select Run Slide Show and your slide show will automatically begin. A floating slide show controller will automatically appear (see Figure 19.8), presenting you with a wide selection of features.

While your slide show will run automatically, you can make adjustments to such elements as image size, background color, slide transitions, etc., on the fly. By Options (the icon shaped like a gear), you can make your slide show interactive

Figure 19.8 This floating slide show controller lets you adjust your show as needed.

using the controls explained in the section that follows. This allows you to remain on a slide if the image presented needs further explanation during a presentation, or if you wish to change the image layout to display multiple slides at once for comparison.

Expression Media offers the following slide show features:

- **Audio:** Audio attached to image files can be turned on or off. If you want to have a soundtrack playing continuously, simply place that audio file at the beginning of the presentation, and it will play throughout.

- **Video:** Video can be displayed up to 16 channels. The number of channels in which media is displayed will depend on your grid selections.

- **Grids:** This feature lets you choose how many images are displayed at once (up to 16), but it can also be used to determine the number of video channels being used. You should probably play around with this to determine what works best for your needs.

- **Timing:** You can control how long an image is displayed. Video files will play for their entire duration. If you want to add a soundtrack as a separate file, it will be important to adjust the timing of slides in synch with your recording.

- **Transitions:** There are a variety of transition types available to you in Expression Media including Cross Fade, Radial Wipe, Blinds Vertical, etc. Check out the options yourself, and decide what works best for your specific presentation.

- **Size of Media:** To use this feature, go to the Scale menu on the slide show controller. You can zoom in or out, creating changes that will apply globally to your images.

You can also add text by checking the box next to different types of image information. Expression Media gives you a wide variety of fonts and font sizes to choose from for displaying your text.

Specifying Slide Show Options

You can also preset the options for your slide show by choosing Make > Slide Show Options, setting the options accordingly, and clicking OK. (See Figure 19.9)

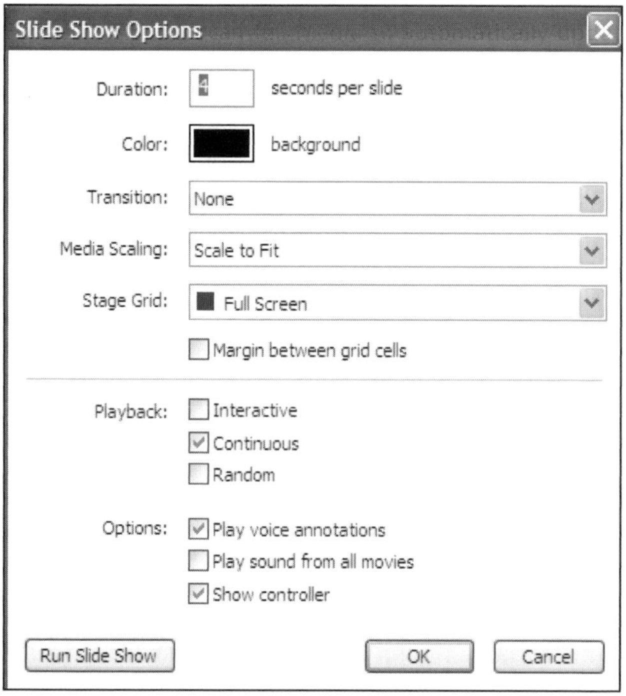

Figure 19.9 Make your slide show more interactive by adjusting presentation options.

Expression Media allows you to assign settings to the following aspects before playing your slideshow:

- **Duration:** Preset the amount of time during which a slide is displayed.

- **Color:** The default background color is black, but you can adjust this to whatever you choose.

- **Media Scaling:** You can zoom into your images for closer examination if desired. This setting will affect all media assets except video, which will be displayed at whatever resolution you choose.

- **Stage Grid:** This lets you choose whether or not to have multiple slides displayed onscreen at once.

- **Playback Options:** You can set playback as either Interactive, which allows you to control it during the presentation, or Continuous, which automates playback, and will progress according to the settings you choose.

- **Margin between grid cells:** If you have chosen to have multiple assets displayed at once, this feature allows you to insert pixels of background color between images for easier viewing.

- **Play voice annotation:** This will automatically play any voice annotation you have added.

- **Play sound from all movies:** You can choose not to play sound from movie files if you wish.

- **Show controller:** This determines whether the controller is automatically displayed when you start the slide show. To hide the controller during the show, simply hit ESC or RETURN.

Note: Two features only available in the Macintosh version are Fade In, which allows you to fade into the start and the end of slide show presentations, and Custom Grid, which allows you design your own grid template.

Turning Your Slide Show into a Movie

To convert your slide show to a movie, just go to the Make dropdown menu, and this time, select Save Slide Show as Movie. You are presented with the dialog box shown in Figure 19.10, which lets you choose from a number of industry-standard sizes. Before you convert your slide show into a movie, you might want to verify the settings in the Slide Show Options to make sure everything is as you want it to be.

Figure 19.10 Convert your slide show to a movie using this set of controls.

You also have the option to switch on the Auto-Start and Full Screen Mode options. This will cause your movie to automatically play in full-screen mode when you select it from your saved location in the future. You can also choose to Include chapter track, which will display the file name in a menu below the movie.

Creating Web Galleries

Expression Media makes it easy to turn your photo sets into HTML galleries that you can upload to the Internet. This can be very helpful if you want to share something online with a client, or if you are at the stage where something is ready to be published online as a catalog, for example. It is also ideal for creating an online portfolio. Ultimately, your web gallery is going to closely resemble an Expression Media gallery, with the primary difference being that it is available online as a web page. Expression Media also makes it easy to upload your html galleries by allowing you to input your FTP login information right into the dialogue box. However, because Expression Media does not encrypt your information, it is important to check with your FTP application provider to be sure that the necessary security technology is in place.

To create a web gallery, go to the Make dropdown menu, and choose HTML Gallery. The dialog box shown in Figure 19.11 presents you with many ways to customize your site. The first tab available is the Theme tab, which determines the look of

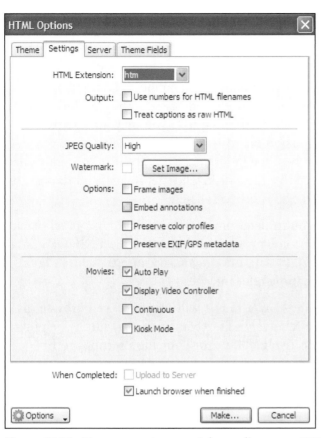

Figure 19.11   You can post your catalog online as an HTML Gallery.

your site. This offers the features that are fundamental to successfully expressing your creative vision, and will be discussed in more detail in the following section. The next tab is the Settings tab, which allows you to customize the following features:

- **HTML Extension:** You can choose to define your file extensions as something other than an HTML file name. Options include .htm, .shtml, .php, etc. This can be important if you are using particular database languages for creating your web page. I am simply going to use .html.

- **Output:** You can choose to express your HTML file names using numerical increments.

- **Treat captions as raw HTML:** You can use HTML code to refer to your images in the Description annotation field.

- **JPEG Quality:** You can adjust the JPEG quality automatically, or choose Custom to set the number of pixels yourself. I am going to stick with quality level High.

- **Watermark:** A watermark, as you may already know, is a visual protection against the unauthorized usage of your image files online. It consists of a translucent image overlaid on your photo or media asset. This can be anything from a copyright mark to any mark identifying it as you or your company's property, or simply that it originated on your website. You must have a watermark already created—this can be done in an image modification program such as Adobe Photoshop—and saved to a local disk. Click Set Image, and Expression Media allows you to place and size it on your asset.

- **Options:** This feature allows you to determine whether to add a 1-pixel black frame, preserve annotations or color profiles, and preserve the EXIF/GPS data. I'm choosing to preserve EXIF/GIS data once again, because these are digital photos, to which this type of data is relevant.

- **Movies:** These settings determine how a movie will play in a web browser as a QuickTime file. While they are relatively self-explanatory, it might be helpful to point out that Kiosk Mode effectively allows for your file's settings to be changed from within a browser window.

As with the slide show, you can choose to save these settings if you plan to export HTML galleries in a similar fashion later on.

The Server tab gives you access to a very handy feature in Expression Media, which is the ability to export your web gallery without actually logging in to a third-party FTP application. You can do it directly from within Expression Media. If you have already uploaded your images, and are just uploading a gallery, you can select Skip existing image files to upload only the HTML.

Finally, if the theme you have chosen allows you to fill in customizable fields—client name, job number, assignment details—you simply fill these in under the Theme Fields tab. I do not have any theme fields, so I am leaving this blank.

Using Presentation Templates

Unless you are experienced in HTML coding, you are going to use the visual themes provided by Expression Media. In fact, even if you do have experience coding in HTML, you may find it easier to pick a theme and modify it. This can be in any HTML editor, including Microsoft Expression Web.

Custom HTML Galleries: If you have good working knowledge of coding in HTML, Expression Media will allow you to create your own HTML template, or, to make things easier, modify an existing one to better represent your creative expression.

Start by choosing Make > Make HTML Gallery. Then choose a title for your site and enter it in the Site Title field shown in Figure 19.12. I am just going to call this Catalog 2, which includes only pictures from California. If you simply go with the Default theme, your web gallery is going to look exactly the way it does in the Expression Media viewer. This can be perfectly acceptable, especially if your goal is merely to present your assets to a client, for example.

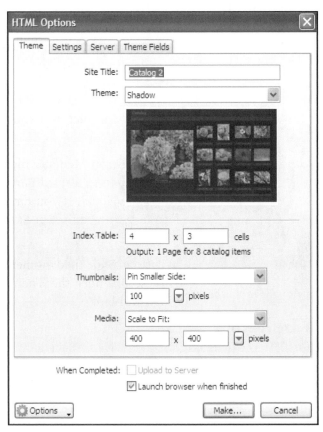

Figure 19.12   You can add a visual theme to make your Web gallery more compelling.

I am going to use the Shadow theme, because I find it to have a clean, dramatic, and professional quality to it. You can now choose the dimensions of your index table, how you want your thumbnails to be presented, and how large you want them to be. Remember that larger images take up more space and take longer to load, so you'll want to find a good balance between quality and size. You can also set the dimensions of your media files.

Finally, choose whether to Launch Browser or Upload to Server when finished (although this will only be available if you have filled in the fields under the Server tab). The results, shown in Figure 19.13, are sure to add visual interest to any Web presentation.

Figure 19.13 Your gallery automatically opens in a Web browser so you can preview it.

Creating Custom Web Galleries

As indicated in the previous section, if you have a good working knowledge of HTML, you can create custom galleries using proprietary HTML tags provided by Expression Media. HTML code can be modified in any HTML editor, including Expression Web. Expression Media offers some perfectly fine prefabricated templates, but it is always preferable to add your own personal touch, and create something that is custom tailored to your specific project. While it is beyond the scope of this book to teach HTML coding, we will go through the fundamental tools provided by Expression Media that make creating your own web gallery simple and accessible.

Once again, it is probably a good idea to start with a preset template, and edit the portions of code to your specifications. Templates in Expression Media are made up of a theme containing HTML tags. Once you create a custom HTML gallery, it will appear in the Theme menu along with the preset themes upon restarting Expression Media. The Theme folder contains an index, HTML templates, and the Assets folder, which contains HTML graphics and an image, named About.jpg, which is essentially a preview of your web gallery.

Choosing Templates

Templates are really just simple HTML pages that contain Expression Media HTML tags (these tags are stand-ins for the catalog content that will be included in your gallery). There are two types of templates, index templates and media templates. The media template refers to one specific media item, and is contained within the index template, which lists a set of media. Both templates are stored in the same folder.

Using Tags to Control Your Presentation

Tags in Expression Media determine the specifications of your gallery. They control everything from image size and resolution to repurposing of image information. For the most part, you can put Expression Media tags anywhere in the HTML page (the exceptions to this rule are covered in the following section). When the page is generated, the tags will be substituted by the information that it represents.

Tip: A complete list of the Expression Media tags and their functions is included in the Expression Media User Guide, which (at this writing) is not included with the software itself. It can be found online by going to http://www.microsoft .com/downloads/. Enter "Expression Media User Guide" in the search box under the blue bar labeled Download Center and click Go. It is important to make sure that all syntax and spelling are exactly as listed in the table shown in the manual, or your Web gallery won't come out looking the way you want.

Make sure you place the following Expression Media tags inside other HTML tags:

- (iView:Running), (iView:Total). These tags cause the total number of files exported and the number of the files from within the sequence to be shown on the Web page.

- **(iView:Date), (iView:Time).** These tags display the date and time of the gallery's export.

- **(iView:Preview), (index page).** These tags are substituted by JPEG images in a table, as defined by the Index Table settings in the HTML Export dialog box.

- **(iView:Index), (index page).** This tag is also replaced by the Index Table settings in the HTML Export dialog box. It must be placed outside of the table containing (iView:iPreview).

- **(iView:Media).** This tag covers any media files that are displayed in the catalog's Media View.

- **(iView:GoNext), (iView).** This tag displays the hyperlink leading to the subsequent HTML page.

- **(iView:GoIndex).** This tag displays the hyperlink to the index of the referring HTML page.

Controlling Image Size and Other Values

HTML Engine Directives control the values that will display in the particular dialog boxes of particular fields. They also control the sizes of images on index and media pages. To help understand engine directive tags, it might help to know that Theme Fields are a variation on HTML Engine Directive tags. These tags can be very useful because they allow for the creation of user-defined fields for text.

In order to use a variable tag, you must create both the variable name and the default value of the variable. You will see the values you have created in the Theme Fields section of the HTML Gallery dialog box. Now, a user can select this variable and assign a value in the Change section in the lower portion of the dialog box. Once the variable has been chosen, it can be used as a standard iView HTML tag, with the value as whatever the user has entered in the HTML Theme Fields dialog box.

Figure A.2 The Notepad lets you record comments about each image in the catalog you are viewing.

support anything. In case you need to convert files so they can be displayed in Media, or if you are building a presentation for the Web, you can use Expression Encoder.

Encoder is specifically designed for converting video and audio files so that they can be played back in software that supports the Microsoft Silverlight technology (see the section on Silverlight later in this appendix). If you have the Silverlight Streaming plug-in application, you can process video files in Encoder and then use the plug-in to deliver video to a site where you stream content on the Web. Encoder can compress video files in Microsoft's VC-1 video codec format. Files in VC-1 can then be played by Windows Media Player.

The user interface, shown in Figure A.3, is similar to that of the other Expression Studio products: a dark work area with white type, and a workspace divided into a

Figure A.3   Use Encoder to prepare video and audio files for presentation through Microsoft Silverlight.

Media pane, a Settings pane, and an Output pane. The Media pane lets you view and navigate your media file's contents, and the other two panes let you control the parameters.

To begin, you import a video or audio clip either from a live source (a streaming file on the Internet) or a file on your file system. Encoder supports a wide variety of file formats, including QuickTime .MOV movies and the 3GP format used by some cell phones to capture video clips. You can then navigate the file using the slider at the bottom of the Media pane. The Output pane lets you choose a file for output; you can choose a format tailored to the average speed of your viewer's Internet connection, for instance. Options in the Settings pane let you tailor the file for a streaming server on your local network rather than a Web presentation. The same kinds of options are available for audio as well as video files.

You can use Encoder not only to do file processing but also to add graphics and captions to video files. In addition, you can resize video clips and add leading and trailing segments to provide an introduction and an ending. Encoder offers a "live encoding" feature that lets you capture incoming video or audio in real time and immediately deliver the content to other computers that are connected to it by a network.

Tip: Encoder is bundled as an extra application along with the standard set of Expression Studio applications. However, if you need to download a more recent version, you'll be able to do so at http://www.microsoft.com/expression/products/overview.aspx?key=encoder.

Visual Studio

At the time this book was written, Microsoft Visual Studio 2006 Standard Edition was bundled as an "extra" application with Expression Studio. A more recent version, Visual Studio 2008, had just been released in a trial version, however, so it's possible that your version of Expression Studio will contain the more recent version.

Visual Studio is an application that allows computer programmers to develop software. It provides for more than just writing code. Visual Studio provides an environment that includes a compiler for building applications and a debugger. It also has a built-in Web server for testing Web-based applications, as well as the capability to drag and drop components needed to build user interfaces.

Of course, when it comes to creating user interfaces, Expression Blend is a newer and more powerful product. Visual Studio, though, can still play an essential role in developing applications.

Tip: You can download different versions of Visual Studio 2008 by following the links at http://msdn2.microsoft.com/en-us/vstudio/aa700831.aspx. Some versions are intended for developing Web applications, while others are designed for use with programming languages like C#.

Silverlight

Silverlight, originally known as Windows Presentation Foundation (WPF), is intended to compete with Adobe's popular Flash presentation system. On one level, Silverlight is a browser plug-in, an application that installs and works within a browser to present animations. Not just any animations, however—Silverlight is able to present Rich Interactive Applications that enable viewers to interact with them, as well as high-quality video that plays within a browser window. Silverlight runs on Internet Explorer versions 6 and later, Mozilla Firefox versions 1.5 or 2.0 and later, and Safari 2.0 and later.

Tip: You can find out more about Microsoft Silverlight and download the software at http://silverlight.net/GetStarted.

Silverlight Streaming

What do you do with the movies you encode with Microsoft Encoder and the presentations you assemble with Blend? You post them on a Web server, and you make a link to them on one of your Web pages. Visitors to your site can click on the links and view them in their Web browsers (provided their browsers are equipped with the Silverlight plug-in).

The video and other files are likely to be large in size and can be costly to present or "stream" online, depending on the amount your Web host charges you. Silverlight streaming is a service that allows anyone to publish streaming audio or video online. In an effort to promote Silverlight, Microsoft initially made its Silverlight Streaming service free for up to 4GB of storage space. In the future, unlimited streaming is expected to be free as long as developers don't mind displaying ads along with their Silverlight content. (Ad-free content will carry a fee.)

Tip: To obtain a streaming account, go to http://silverlight.live.com/. The Resources link on this site contains links to a variety of informational papers and articles, such as a guide to deploying Silverlight within an organization. There is also a link to a community site devoted to Silverlight, http://silverlight.net/forums/.

Appendix B: Expression Studio Resources on the Web

There are many ways to learn about Expression Studio online. Not only can a good deal of information be gleaned from Microsoft's own Web sites, but there are countless user-generated resources as well. I've found that the best way to take advantage of these resources is to try and work through a particular problem to the best of your ability. Web searches work best when you search for something very specific. For example, instead of looking for a phrase such as "publishing photos in Expression Media," you might familiarize yourself with Microsoft's proprietary language to find that searching for "creating HTML gallery Expression Media" might get you more relevant hits. In this appendix, we will briefly go over some of the best ways to get helpful information.

Microsoft Resources

If you're looking for official software releases or updates, as well as supplementary software you'll need to work with Studio, turn to Microsoft's own Web site. You'll also find tutorials and forums that will help you learn more about specific applications.

Microsoft Expression

(http://www.microsoft.com/expression/): The home page for the entire Expression family contains links to all product trials, including updated versions as they are available.

.NET 3.5

http://msdn2.microsft.com/en-us/netframework/default.aspx: The .NET 3.5 Framework that you need before you install Expression Studio software can be downloaded online; a later version may be available by the time you read this.

Microsoft Expression Blend and Design Blog

(http://blogs.msdn.com/expression/): The design teams of these two Expression Studio components contribute postings to this blog. It's not just a place for musings and miscellaneous news about these two components. Scan the list of previous postings, and you'll find useful and detailed tutorials showing how to perform various essential functions with both Blend and Design. The instructional information on Blend is particularly good.

Microsoft Expression Web Design Blog

(http://blogs.msdn.com/xweb/default.aspx): The Expression Web team provides news on the availability of new software related to the Web, as well as tutorials on how to install new browsers and perform other tasks with this Web design tool.

Wayne Smith's Blog

(http://www.wayne-smith.org/): Smith is the Group Product Manager for the Expression team at Microsoft. His blog isn't terribly detailed, but it occasionally provides news about service packs and other software updates.

Expression Studio FAQs

(http://www.microsoft.com/expression/products/faq.aspx): For the most part, if you have the Studio software installed already and you have access to Help files, you have access to a more complete set of supplementary applications than you can find online. But sometimes the FAQs will give you up-to-the-minute answers on problems users have reported recently, so it pays to check here as well.

Discussion Groups

There are many discussion groups online that can help you achieve your goals in Expression Media. Don't be afraid to dive right into discussion forums! There's no time like the present to get your feet wet. Here are some good places to start:

Google Groups

(http://www.groups.google.com): Google Groups is, for those not already familiar, a powerful online resource. Most questions are answered in a relatively short period of time, and you might find a thread already there that answers your questions for you.

Yahoo! Groups

(http://groups.yahoo.com): Yahoo! has its own set of discussion groups, and they often have hundreds or even thousands of members. Go to the Yahoo! Groups home page and do a search for Microsoft Expression; you'll find at least two groups related to Expression Web.

Microsoft Discussion Groups

(http://www.microsoft.com/communities/newsgroups/list/en-us/default. aspx): This is Microsoft's home page for all of its product-related discussion groups. Scroll down the list on the left side of the home page and click the plus sign (+) next to microsoft.public.expression. You'll find a set of groups devoted to Expression products. Click on any one to view its current postings and scroll through archives.

Expression Blend Discussion Group

(http://www.microsoft.com/communities/newsgroups/en-us/default. aspx?dg=microsoft.public.expression.interactivedesigner&cat=&lang =en&cr=US): This is the official Microsoft-hosted discussion group on Blend. At this writing there were 30 pages of posts on the subject. The search box at the top of the Discussion Group page will help you narrow your focus, because navigating through all of those posts can be a slow process.

Third-Party Blogs and Resources

As you might expect, developers and others who create Web content for a living have latched on to Expression Studio. A few have started their own blogs and Web sites devoted to the suite of applications. A few suggested destinations are listed below.

By-expressions

(http://blog.by-expression.com/): A useful site by Cheryl Wise, a Microsoft MVP. Most of the posts are about Expression Web, and there are some excellent instructional materials about Web. There is a handful of posts about Blend and Design as well.

expressionblend.com

(http://expressionblend.com/): A forum and series of blog posts by X-Coders Limited.

TakeGreatPictures.com

(http://www.takegreatpictures.com/): Because this Web site contains information on producing digital photography, it naturally includes useful information regarding Expression Media. Search for entries by Jay Kinghorn, or search for Expression Media itself.

Tutorials

Once you have gotten started with Expression Studio after reading this book, you can take some online tutorials on more specific subjects.

Microsoft Expression Virtual Labs

(http://msdn2.microsoft.com/en-us/virtuallabs/aa740378.aspx): The name of this site is a bit misleading: There are only four virtual labs, and they are all about Expression Web. However, the four labs are good starting points for working with CSS and ASP.NET 2.0.

Lynda.com

(http://www.lynda.com): Well-known graphic designer Lynda Weinmann helped present Expression Web when the product was first introduced. Her Web site contains a variety of online tutorials on Expression Web, Design, and Blend. There are many programs represented, and this site can be very informative. To fully take advantage of this site, you need to become a paid subscriber.

Microsoft Expression Knowledge Center Tutorials

(http://www.microsoft.com/expression/kc/default.aspx): This is Microsoft's own tutorial page. There is a vast number of resources available here: training videos, tutorials, Webcasts, and guides. All Expression Studio products are included—as well as Expression Encoder, which isn't officially part of the Expression Studio family.

Learn Expression Video Tutorials

(http://www.learnexpressionstudio.com/): Austin Drees, the Marketing and Art Director for LearnVisualStudio.net, has created a series of free video tutorials for Expression Web. The site also hosts community forums devoted to Studio components. One thing that's notable is a tutorial on Microsoft Silverlight. There is also a video on Zam3D, a program for working with 3D programs that can be used with Expression Blend.

LearnExpression

(http://www.learnexpression.com/): This site sounds similar to the preceding one, but it's not. It presents a series of tutorials on CSS, classes, IDs, and formatting Web page content.

Expression Blend and Design

(http://blogs.msdn.com/expression/articles/543834.aspx): This site is formatted like a blog, but it contains more than random comments. Members of the Blend and Design development teams provide tutorials that explain how to perform key functions, such as working with data, implementing templates, and creating interactive buttons.

Index